PROBLEM SOLVING AND STRUCTURED PROGRAMMING IN FORTRAN

ADDISON-WESLEY PUBLISHING COMPANY
Reading, Massachusetts • Menlo Park, California
London • Amsterdam • Don Mills, Ontario • Sydney

PROBLEM
SOLVING
AND STRUCTURED
PROGRAMMING
IN
FORTRAN

FRANK L. FRIEDMAN
ELLIOT B. KOFFMAN
Temple University

This book is in the

Addison-Wesley Series in

Computer Science and Information Processing

Consulting editor

Michael A. Harrison

Third printing, May 1979

ISBN 0-201-01967-1
ABCDEFGHIJ-MA-79

To our families
Martha, Shelley, and Dara Friedman
and
Caryn, Richard, Deborah, and Robin Koffman
who graciously accepted us as part-time
family members during the writing of this book

PREFACE

This book is designed as a text for a one-semester, introductory course in computer programming. No background other than high-school algebra is assumed. The material presented reflects the authors' view that good problem-solving and programming habits should be introduced at a very early stage in the development of a student's programming skills, and that they are best instilled by examples, by frequent practice, and through instructor–student interaction. Therefore we have concentrated on demonstrating problem-solving and programming techniques through the use of approximately two dozen completely solved problems.

Discipline and planning in both problem solving and programming are illustrated in the text from the beginning. We have attempted to integrate a number of relatively new pedagogic ideas into a unique, well-structured format that is uniformly repeated for each problem discussed. Three basic phases of problem solving are emphasized: the analysis of the problem; the stepwise specification of the algorithm (using flow diagrams); and finally, the language implementation of the program.

Our goal is to bridge the gap between textbooks that stress problem-solving approaches divorced from implementation and language considerations and programming manuals that provide the opposite emphasis. Language-independent problem analysis and algorithms are described in the same text as the language features required to implement the problem solution on the computer. For each new problem introduced in the text, the problem analysis and algorithm description are presented along with the complete syntactic and semantic definitions of the new language features convenient for the implementation of the algorithm.

The top-down or stepwise approach to problem solving is illustrated repeatedly

in the solution of each of the problems solved in the text. Three pedagogic tools—
a data definition table, a flow diagram, and a program system chart—are used to
provide a framework through which students may practice the definition and
documentation of program variables in parallel with the stepwise development of
algorithms.

The data definition tables provide a description of the attributes (initial values,
types, sizes, etc.) of each variable appearing in the problem solution. The flow
diagrams that are used to represent the algorithms are similar to the D-Chart of
Dijkstra. Each diagram is a short sequence of individual flow-diagram patterns
representing the subtasks of an algorithm; refinements of the subtasks are
diagrammed separately.

The programming language emphasized in the text is an extended version of
the 1966 American National Standard (ANS) FORTRAN. The extensions used in
the text are summarized in the following chart.

Extended FORTRAN features	Extent to which successful use of the text depends on these features*
1. Format-free input and output	1
2. Character variables (CHARACTER declaration)	4
3. IF–THEN–ELSE (block-IF) decision structure	2
4. WHILE loop structure	3
5. FOR loop structure (generalized indexed-DO)	4
6. Remote block (parameterless subroutine)	4
7. Loop escape and next iteration statements	4

These extensions were chosen because they have gained wide acceptance among
FORTRAN users and because they have been found to greatly enhance FORTRAN
as a language for teaching introductory programming. Four of the extensions
(format-free input/output, the block-IF structure, the CHARACTER declaration,
and the generalized indexed-DO) are included in the new (1977) FORTRAN
standard in forms that are similar to those used in the text. The format-free
input/output described in the text is consistent with that already implemented on
several widely used student-oriented compilers, including WATFIV-S. The
character data type used in the text is consistent with WATFIV-S and the new
FORTRAN Standard. However, the text has been designed for use with or without
the character variable and has, in fact, been used successfully at Temple University
for several semesters with compilers that do not support character variables.

---

* *Key:* 1 absolutely essential;
2 important;
3 nice, but not necessary;
4 optional.

The block-IF is also compatible with WATFIV-S and the new standard; the WHILE-loop structure is compatible with WATFIV-S. The block-IF and WHILE structures are also supported, in very similar if not identical forms, on over 100 FORTRAN preprocessors. A small, highly portable preprocessor supporting the block-IF, WHILE loop, FOR loop (a generalized indexed-DO), and the loop exit and next iteration statements may be obtained from the Addison-Wesley Publishing Company.

The text is organized so that students may begin working with the computer as soon as possible. Chapter 1 contains a short discussion of the basic computer hardware components. This is followed by a description of some basic operations that are common to most computers. These include simple input and output operations; the stop operation; the arithmetic operations of addition, subtraction, multiplication, and division; and conditional and unconditional transfers of control.

Each operation is expressed in terms of basic FORTRAN statements, and the effect of the operation is described. Some simple problems are introduced at this point and their solutions are presented in terms of the basic FORTRAN statements. Students are provided with a glimpse of the FORTRAN language and with sufficient deck-formation and keypunching instructions to enable them to write short programs and run them on the computer. We suggest that this latter material be covered early in the chapter so that students can be running programs and getting firsthand experience that will complement the discussions in the text.

The stepwise approach to programming is introduced in Chapter 2. The data definition table and flow diagram are described, and problems involving decisions and loops are examined and solved. The algorithms are represented using flow-diagram patterns for the IF–THEN–ELSE and WHILE loop structures.

These problems can be implemented using the basic FORTRAN of Chapter 1. Alternatively, the programs can be implemented using the IF–THEN–ELSE and WHILE loop structures introduced in Chapter 3. We believe that these structures should be introduced fairly early, perhaps even in parallel with some of the later material in Chapter 2. Students should be motivated early to select the best control structure to implement each flow-diagram pattern, allowing the translator to handle explicit transfers of control.

The use of the structures should enable both student and instructor to concentrate on describing the tasks to be performed (what must be done) in developing and implementing an algorithm, without concern for the details of where to put transfer instructions and their target labels. (We have not found the brief introduction and use of the basic FORTRAN, including the GOTO, a hindrance at this point. In fact, just a brief glimpse of programming with the GOTO readily convinces most students of the advantages of the block-IF and WHILE loop structures, and the use of the GOTO is then quickly abandoned by most students.)

The concept of the language translator (compiler) is also introduced in Chapter 3, and its role in translating more complicated FORTRAN statements into sequences of basic computer operations (as expressed in terms of the basic FORTRAN statements) is carried throughout the text.

Just enough detail is introduced to present a concise, clear description of how each new language feature is translated in terms of the basic computer operations. We feel that this information is beneficial to all students, particularly those who desire to understand how each feature is processed by the compiler. Yet we have avoided digressing too far from the main theme of the text, which is how to use the new features in solving problems.

In Chapter 4, the four most fundamental data types—real, integer, character, and logical—are formally introduced. Since students have been working with both real and integer data since Chapter 1, much of this material will be review, and they should find it easier to concentrate on the study of logical and character data. The use of integer variables for the storage of character data is described for those who do not have access to the character data type.

The principles of format-free input and output are also summarized in Chapter 4, and the standard FORTRAN indexed-DO is introduced. The rules of evaluation of multiple-operator arithmetic statements are given, and some common library functions are described at the end of the chapter.

Arrays are introduced in Chapter 5, and several different techniques for using arrays are demonstrated in the problems solved in this chapter and in Chapter 6. Additional control features—the multiple-alternative IF (block-IF), a generalized indexed-DO (the FOR loop), loop exit and next iteration statements, and the remote block (parameterless subroutine)—are illustrated in Chapter 6. Except for the block-IF, none of these features is emphasized in the remainder of the text, although there are numerous problems in which they could be used conveniently. They are presented for those who wish to use them and may be omitted by others.

Chapter 7 concerns subprograms; the definition and use of functions and subroutines, argument lists, and common blocks are presented. Module independence is stressed in this chapter, and the program system chart is introduced as a means of representing the interrelationships and data flow among the modules of a program system. The development of two small program systems is described in detail in order to illustrate the techniques of planning for the use of subprograms and for documenting and implementing them.

Format-free read and print are used throughout the first seven chapters in order to simplify input and output and to allow students to concentrate on mastering the concepts of algorithm development, control structure and data representation, and coding and debugging, with a minimum of interference from the details of format specification. However, the rudiments of formats can be introduced conveniently as early as Chapter 4, if the instructor so desires.

Details concerning the use of the basic format descriptors are provided in Chapter 8. The material usually appears less threatening to students who have had a liberal sprinkling of format usage prior to this chapter.

Chapters 9 and 10 contain a number of moderately difficult problems illustrating the use of logical and character data (Chapter 9), and multidimensional arrays

(Chapter 10). In Chapter 9, we have assumed that no special character-manipulation facilities are available to the student. If such features are available (substring features, concatenation, etc.), the Appendix should be studied instead of the character manipulations described in this chapter. Chapter 9 is written so that it can be used either with or without the character data type.

It is the authors' intention to provide in this text sufficient material to accommodate the needs of a wide variety of students in a first-semester computer programming course. The depth of understanding of the basic methods, as well as the proficiency demonstrated in the application of these methods, will vary according to the skill of the student and the expectations of the instructor. For the prospective computer-science major, the introductory material on computers and the discussion of the role of the language processor are highly relevant and will provide a good foundation for future study.

In some cases, descriptions of computers and language processors that are more detailed than those provided in this text may be warranted. However, much of this detail is often provided in subsequent computer-science courses and should be postponed in deference to the immediate goal: the presentation of methods of problem solving, algorithm specification, and computer program implementation. This is at least a one-semester task. The material concerning the computer and the language processor is important insofar as it serves to elucidate this presentation—not to complicate or add to it. At first, some of this material may not be fully appreciated by the student. However, we believe that it provides a necessary foundation for numerous subsequent discussions that will inevitably occur, if only in response to questions from students anxious to understand how and why things work as they do.

Although we are very confident that Structured FORTRAN will be more widely available in the future, students using this text should be able to readily adapt to the standard FORTRAN environment if necessary. In addition, they will have been exposed to problem-solving and programming techniques which should provide a solid preparation for the study and use of other programming languages.

ACKNOWLEDGMENTS

There are many people whose talents and influence are reflected in this text. We are especially indebted to Charles Hughes, Brian Kernighan, Loren Meissner, and Charles Pfleeger, who carefully read and commented on the manuscript in detail and unselfishly gave advice and helpful suggestions during all phases of manuscript preparation. We also wish to thank Dorothy Denning and Rob Pecherer for their valuable comments and criticisms of the final draft.

The errors that remain in the text are, of course, our own responsibility. The fact that they are not more numerous is due to the efforts of those mentioned above and to the efforts of our colleagues and students at Temple who have used the manuscript, particularly Ranan Banerji, Leonard Garrett, and James Korsh, who have class-tested two versions of the manuscript. To Nancy H. Klein, we owe a special note of thanks and gratitude for proofreading earlier versions of the manuscript, providing solutions to the exercises, keypunching and testing most of the programs in the manuscript, writing the preprocessor used in conjunction with the text, and helping in other ways that are far too numerous to count.

Philadelphia   F.L.F.
January 1977   E.B.K.

CONTENTS

1

INTRODUCTION
1

1.1 Computer organization / **2** ▪ 1.2 Programs and programming / **8** ▪ 1.3 Introduction to FORTRAN and the fundamental computer operations / **13** ▪ 1.4 Using the computer / **27** ▪ 1.5 Summary / **34** ▪ Programming problems / **36**

2

PROBLEM SOLVING WITH THE COMPUTER
39

2.1 Problem analysis / **40** ▪ 2.2 Description of the problem solution / **42** ▪ 2.3 Algorithms involving transfers and loops / **47** ▪ 2.4 Implementing a flow diagram in FORTRAN / **59** ▪ 2.5 Debugging a FORTRAN program / **64** ▪ 2.6 Summary and review / **65** ▪ Programming problems / **67**

3

BASIC CONTROL STRUCTURES
69

3.1 Introduction to control structures / **70** ▪ 3.2 Decision structures / **72** ▪ 3.3 The WHILE loop structure / **82** ▪ 3.4 Reminders for algorithm development

xiv Contents

using the WHILE loop / **94** ▪ 3.5 The Widget inventory-control problem / **96** ▪ 3.6 Common programming errors / **100** ▪ 3.7 Summary: Control structures and structure in programs / **101** ▪ Programming problems / **104**

4
DATA TYPES—
THEIR USE AND MANIPULATION
109

4.1 Introduction / **110** ▪ 4.2 Data types, declarations, and constants / **110** ▪ 4.3 Format-free input/output statements / **119** ▪ 4.4 Manipulation of character strings and logical data / **123** ▪ 4.5 Integers and the indexed-DO loop structure / **129** ▪ 4.6 Arithmetic expressions / **137** ▪ 4.7 Library functions / **145** ▪ *4.8 Numerical errors / **151** ▪ 4.9 Common programming errors / **153** ▪ 4.10 Summary / **155** ▪ Programming problems / **156**

5
ARRAYS AND SUBSCRIPTS
161

5.1 Introduction / **162** ▪ 5.2 Declaring arrays / **162** ▪ 5.3 Array subscripts / **164** ▪ 5.4 Manipulating arrays / **166** ▪ *5.5 Role of the translator in processing arrays / **176** ▪ 5.6 Searching an array / **177** ▪ 5.7 Processing selected array elements / **180** ▪ 5.8 Common programming errors / **185** ▪ 5.9 Summary / **186** ▪ Programming problems / **187**

6
ADVANCED CONTROL STRUCTURES
193

6.1 Introduction / **194** ▪ 6.2 The multiple-alternative decision structure / **194** ▪ 6.3 The bowling problem / **200** ▪ 6.4 The indexed-DO and the FOR loop / **204** ▪ 6.5 Using structures: Part I—Structure nesting / **210** ▪ 6.6 Using structures: Part II—Structure entry and transfers / **221** ▪ 6.7 Remote blocks and top-down programming / **224** ▪ 6.8 Common programming errors / **227** ▪ 6.9 Summary / **229** ▪ Programming problems / **230**

7
SUBPROGRAMS
237

7.1 Introduction / **238** ▪ 7.2 The program system charts / **238** ▪ 7.3 Function subprograms / **240** ▪ 7.4 Argument list correspondence / **246** ▪ 7.5 Top-down programming The relationship between main program and subprograms / **248** ▪ 7.6 Subroutine subprograms / **252** ▪ 7.7 Name independence: Subprograms and remote blocks / **258** ▪ 7.8 Common blocks / **261** ▪ 7.9 Additional comments concerning subprograms / **269** ▪ *7.10 The role of the compiler in processing subprograms / **271** ▪ 7.11 Common programming errors / **276** ▪ 7.12 Summary / **277** ▪ Programming problems / **278**

8

FORMATTED
INPUT AND OUTPUT
287

8.1 Limitations of format-free input and output / **288** ▪ 8.2 The format statement: A general discussion / **288** ▪ 8.3 Format descriptors / **290** ▪ 8.4 Common programming errors / **311** ▪ 8.5 Summary / **312** ▪ Programming problems / **313**

9

USING LOGICAL AND
CHARACTER-STRING DATA
321

9.1 Introduction / **322** ▪ 9.2 Logical expressions / **322** ▪ 9.3 Character-string manipulation / **329** ▪ 9.4 Character manipulation—Sample programs / **338** ▪ 9.5 Common programming errors / **352** ▪ 9.6 Summary / **353** ▪ Programming problems / **353**

10

MULTIDIMENSIONAL ARRAYS
363

10.1 Introduction / **364** ▪ 10.2 Declaration of multidimensional arrays / **364** ▪ 10.3 Manipulation of multidimensional arrays / **365** ▪ *10.4 Compiler role for multidimensional arrays / **376** ▪ 10.5 Multidimensional arrays as subprogram arguments / **376** ▪ 10.6 Applications of multidimensional arrays / **378** ▪ 10.7 Common programming errors / **399** ▪ 10.8 Summary / **400** ▪ Programming problems / **400**

APPENDIX

THE MANIPULATION OF
CHARACTER-TYPE DATA
A1

A.1 Introduction / **A1** ▪ A.2 The length of character-string entities / **A2** ▪ A.3 Character substrings / **A2** ▪ A.4 The concatenation operator / **A5** ▪ A.5 Use of character expressions / **A6** ▪ A.6 The character-string length function—LEN / **A11** ▪ A.7 Character manipulation—Sample problems / **A12** ▪ A.8 Common programming errors / **A25** ▪ Programming problems / **A25**

GLOSSARY

FORTRAN STATEMENTS
AND STRUCTURES
A27

ANSWERS
ANS-1

INDEX
I-1

INTRODUCTION

1

1.1 Computer Organization
1.2 Programs and Programming Languages
1.3 Introduction to FORTRAN and the Fundamental Computer Operations
1.4 Using the Computer
1.5 Summary
Programming Problems

1.1 COMPUTER ORGANIZATION

A computer is a tool for representing and manipulating quantities. A large variety of computers is currently available, ranging in size from hand-held calculators to large and complex computing systems filling several rooms or entire buildings. There are minicomputers that fit on a desktop; and some manufacturers have introduced microminiature computers the size of a lump of sugar.

The size and cost of a computer is generally dependent upon the amount of work it can turn out in a given time unit. Larger, expensive computers have the capability of carrying out many operations simultaneously, thus increasing their work capacity. They also have more devices attached to them for performing special functions, all of which increase their capability and cost.

Despite the large variety in the cost, size, and capabilities of modern computers, they are remarkably similar in a number of ways. Basically, a *computer* consists of four components as shown in Fig. 1.1. (The lines connecting the various units represent possible paths of information flow. The arrows show the direction of information flow.)

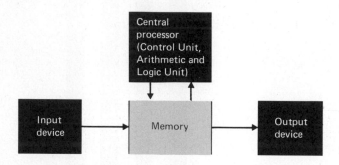

Fig. 1.1 Diagram of the basic components of a computer.

All information that is to be processed by the computer must first be entered into the computer memory via an input device. The information in memory is manipulated by the arithmetic and logic unit, and the results of this manipulation are also stored in the memory of the computer. Information in memory can be displayed through the use of appropriate output devices. All of these operations are coordinated by the control unit. These components and their interaction are described in more detail in the following sections.

1.1.1 The Computer Memory

The memory of a computer may be pictured as an ordered sequence of storage locations called *memory cells*. Each cell has associated with it a distinct *address*,

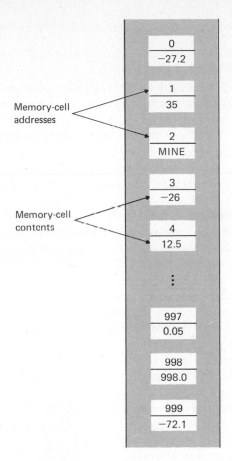

Fig. 1.2 A computer memory with 1000 memory cells.

which indicates its relative position in the sequence. Figure 1.2 depicts a computer memory consisting of 1,000 cells numbered consecutively from 0 to 999. Some large-scale computers have memories consisting of millions of cells.

The memory cells of a computer are used to *represent* information. All types of information—numbers, names, lists, and even pictures—may be represented in the memory of the computer. The information that is contained in a memory cell is called the *contents* of the memory cell. Every memory cell contains some information—no cell is ever empty. Furthermore, no cell can ever contain more than one data item. Whenever a data item is placed into a memory cell, any information already there is destroyed, and cannot be retrieved! In Fig. 1.2, for example, the contents of memory cell 4 is the number 12.5, and the contents of memory cell 998 is the number 998.0.

EXERCISE 1.1 What are the contents of memory cells 0, 2, and 997 shown in Fig. 1.2?

1.1.2 The Central Processor Unit

The information representation capability of the computer would be of little use to us by itself. Indeed, it is the *manipulative* capability of the computer that has enabled mankind to study problems in which the computational requirements would otherwise be beyond the scope of the entire world population. With appropriate directions, modern computers can provide large quantities of new information from old, solving many of these otherwise impossible problems, and providing useful insights into others; and they can do so in exceptionally short periods of time.

The heart of the manipulation capability of the computer is the *central processor unit* (CPU). The CPU can retrieve information from the memory unit. (This information may be either data, or instructions for manipulating data.) It can also store the results of manipulations back into the memory unit for later reference.

The CPU coordinates all activities of the various components of the computer. It determines which operations should be carried out and in what order. The transmission of coordinating control signals and commands is the function of the *control unit* within the central processor.

Also found within the central processor is the *arithmetic–logic unit*. The *arithmetic* portion consists of electronic circuitry wired to perform a variety of arithmetic operations, including addition, subtraction, multiplication, and division. The speed with which it can perform these operations is on the order of a millionth of a second. The *logic* unit consists of electronic circuitry to compare information and to make decisions based upon the results of the comparison. It is this feature, together with its powerful storage and representational facility (the memory), that distinguishes the computer from the simple, hand-held calculators that many of us have used. Most of these calculators can be used only to perform arithmetic operations on numbers; they cannot compare these numbers, make decisions, or store large quantities of numbers.

1.1.3 Input and Output Devices

The manipulative skills of the computer would be of little use to us if we had no means of communicating with the computer. Specifically, we must be able to enter information into the computer memory, and display information (usually the results of a manipulation) in the computer memory in an intelligible form.

The input and output devices enable us to communicate with the computer. These devices are typically *electromechanical,* implying that they have moving parts rather than being purely electronic. Consequently, their speed of operation is considerably slower than that of the arithmetic–logic unit. The input devices are used to *enter* into the computer memory data to be manipulated by the computer. The output devices are used to *display* the results of this manipulation (program output) in a readable, meaningful form.

There are many types of input and output devices. Examples of input devices include card-readers, paper-tape readers, and computer terminals. A common input device is the *card reader*. This device reads pieces of lightweight cardboard called *punch cards*. An example of a typical punch card is shown in Fig. 1.3. The punch card may contain up to 80 columns of information, and each column may contain one character. In the card shown in Fig. 1.3, columns 1 to 26 contain the letter characters A to Z respectively, and columns 36 to 45 contain the decimal digit characters 0 to 9. Additional characters shown here include +, −, ., ,, (,), *, /, $, =, and the blank. Each character is represented by its own unique configuration of holes in a card column. The blank is represented by the absence of any holes.

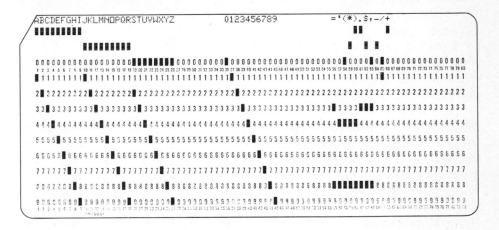

Fig. 1.3 A typical punch card.

Cards to be read into the computer are punched on a standard keypunch, such as the one shown in Fig. 1.4 (top). Most keypunches will also print the punched character at the top of the card. This printed information is solely for our benefit and cannot be read by the card reader. Only the holes in the card are read by the card-reader device.

A common output device is a *line-printer* (Fig. 1.5). This device normally prints 120 to 132 characters across a line at speeds up to 2,000 or more lines per minute. Punched cards may also be produced as output from the computer. A third output medium is a plot or graph of the computed results displayed by a device called a *plotter*. All of the output devices mentioned so far produce a permanent, directly readable record of the results of computation.

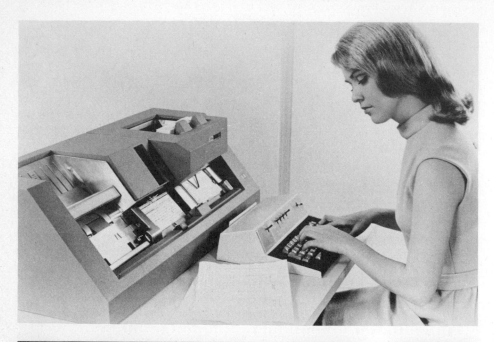

Fig. 1.4 The standard keypunch machine (top); a graphics terminal (bottom).

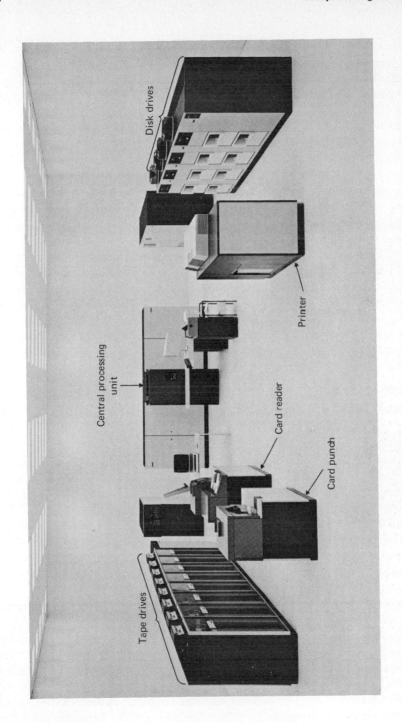

Fig. 1.5 Typical computer system, an IBM System 370 Model 158. (Courtesy of IBM Corp.)

Another type of device that provides both input and output capability is a *computer terminal*. Terminals usually consist of a keyboard on which information required by the computer is typed. The results of a computation may be displayed on a television-like screen normally as *alphanumeric characters* (letters and numbers). Some terminals are equipped with *graphics capabilities*. With such devices the output may be displayed as a two-dimensional graph or picture, and not just as rows of letters and numbers. With some graphics devices, the user can communicate with the computer by pointing at information displayed on the screen with an electronic pointer called a *light pen* (see Fig. 1.4 (bottom)).

Computer terminals are widely used at ticket reservation counters for confirming reservations and printing tickets. They are also used at checkout counters in department stores to assist in keeping track of customer purchases and in inventory control.

A third category of device may be used to serve as either an input or output medium. Included within this category are devices such as *magnetic tapes, disks,* and *drums*, which provide bulk-storage capability. Usually these devices provide a temporary copy of input data or output results. The results of an earlier computation stored on tape or disk may later be the input data for a subsequent computer run. Often a large data file will be processed, the results stored on disk, and printed out at a later time when the hard-working line-printer is not busy.

Examples of some of these devices are shown in Fig. 1.5.

1.2 PROGRAMS AND PROGRAMMING LANGUAGES

1.2.1 Introduction

The computer just described is quite a powerful tool. Information (*input data*) may be stored in its memory and manipulated at exceptionally high speeds to produce a result (*program output*). The problem is that the computer has no will of its own. It cannot do anything without first being told what to do.

We can describe a data manipulation task (often called a *computation*) to the computer by presenting it with a *list of instructions* (called a *program*) that are to be carried out. Once this list has been provided to the computer, it can then assume responsibility and carry out (*execute*) these instructions, in sequence, normally in the order in which they were specified in the list.

The act of making up a list of instructions (writing a program) is called *programming*. Writing a computer program is very similar to describing the rules of a complicated game to people who have never before played the game. In both cases, a language of description understood by all parties involved in the com- munication is required. For example, the rules of the game must be described in some language, and then read and carried out. Both the inventor of the game and those who wish to play must be familiar with the language of description used.

Languages used for communication between man and the computer are called *programming languages*. All instructions presented to a computer must be represented and combined (to form a program) according to the *syntactic rules* (grammar) of the programming language.   There is, however, one significant difference between a programming language and a language such as French, English, or Russian.   The rules of a programming language are very precise, and have no "exceptions" or "ambiguities."   The reason for this is that a computer cannot think!   It can only follow instructions exactly as given.   It cannot interpret these instructions to figure out, for example, what the program writer (*programmer*) meant it to do.   An error in writing an instruction will change the meaning of a program, and cause the computer to perform the wrong action.

1.2.2 The Stored Program

Once a program has been written, we must first have it placed in the memory of the computer before it can be *executed*.   We can then simply tell the computer where the first instruction in the list is located, and the computer will do the rest.

Computers that can execute programs stored in memory are called *stored-program* computers.   Most computers in common use today are of this type. Associated with these computers is a special program, called a *loader*, which, upon request, will take a program and place it in consecutive storage cells of memory, ready for execution.   This process is depicted in Fig. 1.6.

Fig. 1.6 Loading a program for execution by the computer.

As shown in Fig. 1.6, our program is the input data to the loader program. The output from the loader is a copy of our program stored in computer memory. Once execution begins, the control unit examines each program instruction in sequence, starting with the first, and sends out the command signals appropriate for carrying out the instruction. As we shall see later, it is possible to have the control unit skip over some instructions or execute some instructions more than once.

During execution, the program may request that data be entered into the memory of the computer. It may also request that the results of the manipulations performed on this data be displayed. Of course, these things will happen only if the program contains instructions telling the computer to enter or display the appropriate information.

Figure 1.7 shows the relationship between a program for computing a payroll and its input and output, and indicates the *flow of information* through the computer during execution of the program.   The data to be manipulated by the program (employee time cards) must first be entered into the computer memory (Step 1 in

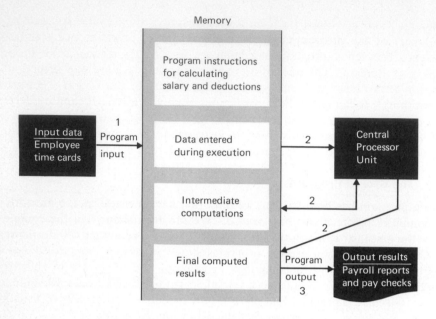

Fig. 1.7 The flow of information through the computer.

Fig. 1.7). As directed by the program instructions, the central processor unit manipulates the data in memory, and places the results of these computations back into memory (Step 2). When the computation process is complete, the results can be output from the memory of the computer (Step 3) in the desired forms (as employee checks and payroll reports).

1.2.3 Machine and Assembly Language

Machine language is the "native tongue" of the computer. It is the only programming language that the computer understands. Unfortunately, it is a language of numbers. If we wish to communicate directly with the computer (by writing a program and having it loaded and executed), we must do it in machine language. To do so, we must provide the computer with a numeric *encoding* of each instruction that it is to carry out. The operation to be performed must have a numeric encoding, and the information to be manipulated must have a numeric representation, which is usually the address of the memory cell containing the information. The exact form of these numeric encodings will differ from computer to computer.

It is rather cumbersome to write a program in machine language since the programmer must remember the numeric code for each instruction and the address in memory of each data item. If for some reason it becomes necessary to move a data item, all instructions that manipulate it must be changed to reflect the new address of the memory cell containing this data item. Consequently, it is difficult to make even minor modifications to machine-language programs.

To alleviate this difficulty somewhat, *assembly language* may be used to write programs. The use of assembly language allows a programmer to refer to each data item by a descriptive name (such as GROSS or TAX) rather than by a numeric address. Furthermore, a descriptive *mnemonic code* is used instead of the numeric operation code.

As an example of the differences between machine and assembly language, we have shown, in Fig. 1.8, both versions of a program written for the Digital Equipment Corporation PDP–11 computer. These programs form the sum of two numbers stored in memory and save the result in a third memory cell. We do not expect you to understand these programs; they are provided solely as an illustration. However, we hope you will agree that the assembly-language program appears more readable.

Machine-language version			Assembly-language version		
013737	000016	000022	GO:	MOV	NMBR1, SUM
063737	000020	000022		ADD	NMBR2, SUM
000000				HALT	
000100			NMBR1:	.WORD	100
000150			NMBR2:	.WORD	150
000000			SUM:	.WORD	0
				.END	GO

Fig. 1.8 Machine- and assembly-language versions of PDP-11 addition program.

Unfortunately, the computer cannot understand assembly language. Therefore, before an assembly language program can be executed, it must first be *translated* into machine language by a special program called an *assembler*. The assembler processes (as its input) the assembly-language program and generates (as its output) the equivalent machine-language program ready for loading, as shown in Fig. 1.9.

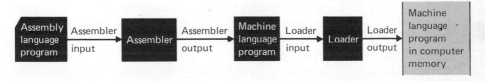

Fig. 1.9 Preparing an assembly-language program for execution.

This process is relatively straightforward since each assembly-language instruction is translated into one machine-language instruction. Programming in assembly language is considerably more convenient because the programmer does not have to keep track of as many details as with machine language. Instead, these details are handled by the assembler when the program is translated, and this makes program construction and subsequent modification easier.

However, there remain many problems associated with the use of assembly language. Assembly language is not very much closer to our natural language than is machine language. In addition, each assembly language is unique to a particular family of computers, so that assembly-language programs written for one computer are not likely to be executable on another. It is for these reasons that higher-level languages were developed.

1.2.4 Higher-Level Languages and Program Translation

It should be clear from the preceding discussion that programming in machine language or assembly language is a time-consuming task requiring almost super-human attention to the *machine-dependent* details of choosing the correct instructions for performing a task, and then specifying the correct encoding for these instructions. The major problem here is in going from a language that we understand to the machine language of the computer. It would clearly be advantageous to be able to communicate to the computer the computations required for the performance of a task in a manner that closely resembles the way in which we might describe these computations to a friend. For example, we might describe the gross-salary and net-pay computations for the payroll problem as follows:

Compute gross salary as the product of hourly wage rate and hours worked.

Find net pay by deducting the tax amount from the gross salary.

While this objective has not been entirely satisfied for all of the various kinds of tasks that can be described for the computer, considerable progress toward achieving this goal has been made. Computer scientists have designed *higher-level programming languages* that permit programmers to write programs containing very little of the *low-level*, machine-dependent details required in machine or assembly language. Instead, these languages allow the programmer to utilize many of the symbols and much of the terminology that are already familiar. It is therefore considerably easier to write programs in higher-level languages than in machine or assembly language. Furthermore, since these programs are relatively free of machine dependencies, they are *portable*. That is, they may be used with little or no alteration on a variety of computers.

There is, however, a price to be paid for all of this luxury, for the symbols and terminology used, while familiar to the programmer, cannot be understood by the computer. As was the case with assembly language, higher-level language programs must be translated into machine language programs, which can then be loaded into the memory of the computer and executed. The translation to machine language of higher-level language programs is performed by a large program called a *compiler*.

A compiler can read programs written in higher-level languages and translate these programs into the machine language of a particular computer. The machine-language translation is in a form ready for loading and subsequent execution by the computer. The compilation process is generally more complex than the assembly process, since one higher-level language statement will often translate to many machine language instructions. The processing of a higher-level language program is shown in Fig. 1.10.

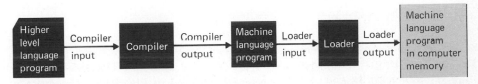

Fig. 1.10 Preparing a higher-level language program for execution.

Examples of higher-level languages include COBOL (*C*ommon *B*usiness-*O*riented *L*anguage), which was designed for business data processing; FORTRAN (*FOR*mula *TRAN*slation), which is well suited for arithmetic manipulation; and SNOBOL (*St*ri*N*g-*O*riented sym*BO*lic *L*anguage), which is useful for manipulating strings of characters, such as textual data including letters, digits, and punctuation marks.

In this book, we shall concentrate on a special version of FORTRAN, but most of the concepts that you will learn will be applicable to other languages as well. This version of FORTRAN contains certain features that are helpful in writing many types of programs for the computer, in addition to arithmetic-manipulation programs. We will discuss a few of the basic fundamental features of the FORTRAN language in the next section. Others will be introduced throughout the remainder of the text.

1.3 INTRODUCTION TO FORTRAN AND THE FUNDAMENTAL COMPUTER OPERATIONS

1.3.1 Use of Symbolic Names in FORTRAN

One of the most important features of FORTRAN is that it permits the use of descriptive symbolic names (called *variable names*, or simply *variables*), rather than numeric addresses, to designate memory cells. This is accomplished through the compiler, which associates the address of a specific memory cell with each variable we use. We need not be concerned with this address. We simply tell the compiler the name of each variable we want to use and let the compiler determine the address of the cell to be associated with that variable.

In the remainder of the text, the phrase "the variable X" will be used instead of "the memory cell associated with the variable name X." Similarly, the phrase, "value of the variable X" or "value of X" will be used instead of "the contents of the memory cell associated with the variable name X."

There are some rules that must be followed in the formation of FORTRAN variable names. These rules are given next.

Variable Names

1. May contain only combinations of letters (A–Z), and the numbers (0–9).
2. Must always begin with a letter (A–Z).
3. May be from 1 to 6 characters in length.

For the payroll problem we might use the variables HOURS (for hours worked), RATE (for hourly rate), TAX (for tax amount), GROSS (for gross salary), and NET (for net pay). These are pictured in Fig. 1.11. The question mark in each box indicates that we have no idea of the current values of these variables (although variables always have values).

HOURS	RATE	TAX	GROSS	NET
?	?	?	?	?

Fig. 1.11 Using meaningful variable names to designate memory cells.

The FORTRAN statement used to inform the compiler that these variable names will designate the memory cells used in a program is:

```
REAL HOURS, RATE, TAX, GROSS, NET
```

This statement is called a *declaration statement*. Note that each variable name is separated from the next one in the list by a comma.

This statement also tells the compiler that these variables will be used for the storage of *real numbers*. In FORTRAN, only those numbers that contain a decimal point are called real numbers (examples of real numbers: 3.14, 0.005, −35., 0.0). Numbers without decimal points are called *integers* (examples of integers: −99, 35, 0, 1). A declaration statement similar in form to the previous one, but beginning with the word INTEGER, indicates to the FORTRAN compiler the names of variables used for the storage of integers. We will use only real numbers in this chapter. The distinction between reals and integers will be discussed in more detail in Chapter 4.

EXERCISE 1.2 Which of the following "strings" of characters can be used as legal variable names in FORTRAN? Indicate the errors in the strings that are illegal.

i) ARK   ii) MICHAEL   iii) ZIP12   iv) 12ZIP
v) ITCH   vi) P3$ vii) GROSS   viii) X123459
ix) NINE + T

1.3.2 Some Basic Computer Operations and Their FORTRAN Descriptions

There are a large number of computers available today, and each has a unique set of *basic operations* that it can perform. These operations generally fall into three categories:

> Input and output operations,
> Data manipulation and comparison,
> Control operations.

Despite the large variety of operations in these categories, there are a few operations in each that are common to most computers. These operations are summarized in Fig. 1.12.

Input/Output Operations

> Read
> Print

Data Manipulation and Comparison

Add	Subtract	Multiply	Divide		
Negate	Copy	Compare	And	Or	Not

Control Operations

> Transfer
> Conditional execution
> Stop

Fig. 1.12 Common basic computer operations.

In the remainder of this chapter we will describe these operations (except for AND, OR, and NOT) in more detail by showing how to use FORTRAN to instruct the computer to perform these operations. We will do this by way of illustration, using the payroll processing problem. (The *Logical Operations* AND, OR, and NOT, will be discussed in Chapter 9.)

PROBLEM 1.1 Compute the gross salary and net pay for an employee of a company, given the employee's hourly rate, the number of hours worked, and the tax deduction amount.

1.3.3 Simple Data Manipulation—Assignment Statements

As shown earlier, we will assume that the variables HOURS and RATE represent the number of hours worked and the hourly wage rate, respectively. GROSS and NET will be used to represent the computed gross and net salary, respectively. The variable named TAX will represent the amount of tax to be withheld from the paycheck. For simplicity, we will assume the withholding amount to be $25.00

regardless of an employee's gross salary. (A more realistic tax schedule would calculate the amount of tax withheld by using a table of varying percentages based on the employee's gross salary.)

Our problem is to perform the two computations described below:

Compute gross salary as the product of hours worked and hourly wage rate;

Find net pay by deducting the tax amount from the gross salary.

We need to learn how to write FORTRAN instructions to tell the computer to perform these computations. This can be done using the FORTRAN *assignment statements*

```
GROSS = HOURS * RATE
NET = GROSS - TAX
```

These statements have the form

$$\text{Result} = \text{Operand}_1 \quad \text{Arithmetic operator} \quad \text{Operand}_2$$

where Operand_1 and Operand_2 are the variables being manipulated, and the arithmetic operator is any of the symbols given in Table 1.1. Result is the name of the variable in which the computation result will be *stored* (placed). The previous value of this variable is destroyed when the new value is stored. However, the values of the operand variables are unaffected by an arithmetic operation.

Table 1.1 FORTRAN arithmetic operators

Arithmetic operator	Meaning
+	Addition
−	Subtraction
*	Multiplication
/	Division

These data manipulation statements are called assignment statements because they specify an assignment of value to a given variable. For example, the statement

$$\text{GROSS} = \text{HOURS} * \text{RATE}$$

specifies that the variable GROSS will be assigned the result of the multiplication of the values of the variables HOURS and RATE. Figure 1.13 illustrates the effect of the two assignment statements used for calculating net salary.

The effect of the first statement is to cause the value of the variable GROSS to be replaced by the *product* of the values of the variables HOURS and RATE, or 135.00. The second statement causes the value of the variable NET to be replaced by the *difference* between the values of the variables GROSS and TAX. We are assuming, of course, that meaningful data items are already present in the variables HOURS, RATE, and TAX. Only the contents of GROSS and NET are changed by this sequence of arithmetic operations.

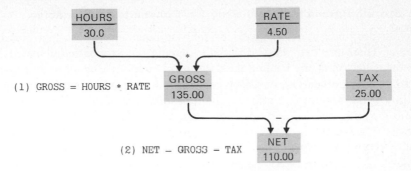

Fig. 1.13 Effect of assignment statements.

In FORTRAN, it is perfectly permissible to write assignment statements of the form

$$SUM = SUM + ITEM$$

where the variable SUM is used on both sides of the equal sign. This is obviously not a mathematical equation, but it illustrates something that is often done in FORTRAN. This statement instructs the computer to add the value of the variable SUM to the value of the variable ITEM and assign the result as the new value of the variable SUM. The previous value of SUM is destroyed in the process.

The statement above will be used in Chapter 2, where it enables us to compute the sum of a large number of data items using only two variables (SUM and ITEM) for data storage. The repeated execution of this statement causes the arithmetic sum of all the data items to be accumulated in the variable SUM.

Assignment statements can also be written with a single operand.

Example 1.1 The statement

$$ABSX = X$$

instructs the computer to *copy* the value of the variable X into ABSX. The statement

$$ABSX = -X$$

instructs the computer to *negate* the value of the variable X and store the result in ABSX. Neither of these statements affects the contents of the variable X. Negating a number is equivalent to multiplying it by -1. Thus, if the variable X contains -3.5, then the statement

$$ABSX = -X$$

will cause 3.5 to be stored in the variable ABSX.

In Chapter 4, we will discuss more complex examples of assignment statements involving the use of multiple operators and more than two operands.

1.3.4 Storing Data in Memory—Program Constants and Variables

No information can be manipulated by the computer unless it is first placed in memory. There are two ways of initially placing data to be manipulated into computer memory: (1) by loading the data into memory along with the program prior to program execution, or (2) by entering the data into memory during the execution of the program. Normally, the first approach is taken for a data item that is a *program constant* and does not change from one use of the program to the next. The second approach is taken for data that is likely to vary. In the payroll problem, the withholding-tax amount is always 25.00 regardless of which employee's net pay is to be computed. This value, therefore, may be loaded into memory prior to the start of program execution. The FORTRAN DATA initialization instruction

DATA TAX /25.00/

is used to instruct the loader to set the value of the variable TAX to 25.00, prior to the start of program execution.

1.3.5 Input and Output Instructions

Since each employee of a company may work a different number of hours per week at his own hourly rate, the variables HOURS and RATE do not represent program constants. Consequently, their values should be entered into memory during program execution. This operation must be done prior to performing the calculations described earlier.

The instruction that tells the computer to enter data into the memory during program execution has the form:

READ, Operand

where Operand is the variable whose value is changed by the READ. The effect of the READ statement is to cause the computer to read a data item punched on an *input data card* into the variable whose name is specified by Operand. The prior value of this variable is lost. Each data item to be entered in this fashion must be punched on a separate input data card. There must be exactly one card for each data item to be read, and the entire collection of input data cards must be placed in sequence in the *data-card section* of the *job-input deck*. The data-card section is separated from the program instructions by a special separator card, as shown in Fig. 1.14.

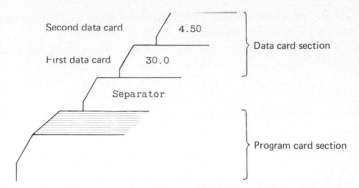

Fig. 1.14 Program and data-card sections of a job-input deck.

The order of the data cards in the data section must correspond to the order in which the READ statements will be executed in the program. Each time the program requests the reading of a data item, the next card in the data-card section of the job-input deck is read. The required READ instructions for the payroll problem are

```
READ, HOURS
READ, RATE
```

For the data-card section of Fig. 1.14, the effect of executing these instructions is indicated in Fig. 1.15. Note that the previous values of the variables **HOURS** and **RATE** are destroyed by the input process.

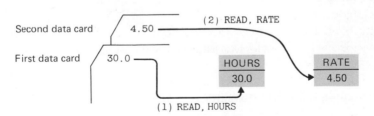

Fig. 1.15 Effect of read statements.

If the order of the two data cards were somehow interchanged during preparation of the card deck, the values read into HOURS and RATE would not be the ones desired. This is a frequent source of error in programming. To minimize the chance of this or other similar input errors going undetected, it is advisable to display or *print out* the value of each variable used for input data. Such a printout also provides a record of the data manipulated by the program. This record is often quite helpful to the programmer and to those who must read and interpret the program output. The statement used to display or print out information in a memory cell is discussed next.

Thus far, we have discussed the FORTRAN instructions required for the input of employee hours and wage rate, and the computation of gross salary and net pay. The computational results have been stored in the variables GROSS and NET, respectively. Yet all of this work done by the computer is of little use to us, since we cannot physically look into a memory cell to see what is there. We therefore must have a way to instruct the computer to display or print out the value of a variable, especially those variables that represent computational results.

The instruction

PRINT, Operand

can be used to cause the value of the variable whose name is specified by Operand to be printed as part of the program output. For example, the instruction

PRINT, NET

would cause the value of the variable NET to be printed as part of the program output (Fig. 1.16). The value of NET is not altered by this operation.

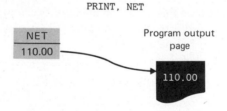

Fig. 1.16   Effect of print statement.

1.3.6 Stopping Computer Execution

Once all desired calculations have been performed and the results displayed, the computer must be instructed to stop execution of the program. The instruction that does this consists of a single word:

STOP

1.3.7 The Payroll Program

We can now collect all of the instructions that have been discussed, and order them to produce a complete FORTRAN program for Problem 1.1 (Fig. 1.17).

```
REAL HOURS, RATE, TAX, GROSS, NET
DATA TAX /25.00/
READ, HOURS
PRINT, HOURS
READ, RATE
PRINT, RATE
GROSS = HOURS * RATE
NET = GROSS - TAX
PRINT, GROSS
PRINT, NET
STOP
END
```

Fig. 1.17   Program for the payroll problem.

Recall that the statement beginning with the word REAL is needed to tell the FORTRAN compiler what variable names will be used to designate memory cells in a program. The DATA statement is used to indicate which variables are to have constants placed in them at load time, prior to the execution of the program.

The REAL, DATA, and END statements are *nonexecutable* statements. They provide information to be used by the compiler in translating a program; they are not translated into machine language and executed. All REAL statements must occur at the beginning of a program, and must be followed by the DATA statements (if any). The END statement must be the very last statement in a program. It serves as a signal to the compiler that there are no more statements to be translated in the current program.

In this example, the PRINT statements have been used to display program results as well as to display or *echo* the values read into the variables HOURS and RATE.

EXERCISE 1.3   Can the order of any of the statements in the program in Fig. 1.17 be changed in any way? Which statements can be moved? Which cannot be moved? Why?

EXERCISE 1.4   What is the difference between the STOP and END statements?

EXERCISE 1.5   If the data-section cards contain

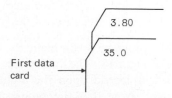

then what values will be printed by the Payroll Program?

EXERCISE 1.6 Let H, R, and T be the symbolic names of memory cells containing the information shown below:

H	R	T
40.0	16.25	0.18

What values will be printed following the execution of the following sequence of instructions?

```
G = H * R        40.0 × 16.25 = G
T = G * T        G × 0.18
N = G - T        G = G -
PRINT, H         40.0
PRINT, R         16.25
PRINT, N
```

1.3.8 Loading and Execution of a Program

Once translated by the compiler, a program in its machine-language form will be loaded into the memory of the computer and executed. In this section, we will illustrate this process, using the payroll program shown in Fig. 1.17.

Recall that the functions of the loader are to place the machine instructions in consecutive cells of memory, and to place constant data in all memory cells, as indicated in the program DATA initialization statements. After this loading has been done, but before execution starts, the payroll program and the memory cells assigned to the variable names of the program would appear as shown on the left side of Fig. 1.18.

The reader should note the following important points concerning this figure.

1. Only the *executable* portion of the original program is loaded in memory. The REAL and END statements are used by the compiler during the translation of the program. The data initialization statement instructs the loader to store the constant 25.00 into the variable TAX during the loading of the program.

2. Specific memory cells have been assigned to each of the 5 variable names used in the program. However, the values of the variables GROSS, NET, HOURS, and RATE are unknown prior to execution of the program.

After the execution of the program is complete, the configuration of memory is as shown on the right side of Fig. 1.18. The final values of the variables HOURS, RATE, GROSS, and NET will depend upon the input values of HOURS and RATE for a given employee. Note that the program remains unchanged by execution.

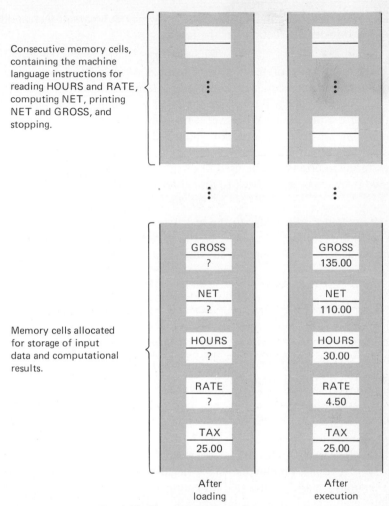

Consecutive memory cells, containing the machine language instructions for reading HOURS and RATE, computing NET, printing NET and GROSS, and stopping.

Memory cells allocated for storage of input data and computational results.

After loading	After execution
GROSS	GROSS
?	135.00
NET	NET
?	110.00
HOURS	HOURS
?	30.00
RATE	RATE
?	4.50
TAX	TAX
25.00	25.00

Fig. 1.18 The payroll program in memory.

1.3.9 Transfer Instructions and Labels

We indicated earlier that the computer executes a list of instructions by starting with the first instruction and continuing to execute all subsequent instructions in the sequence in which they occur. There are times, however, when we wish to have the computer change the order in which instructions are executed. We may wish to have the computer skip a particular sequence of instructions, or make a choice as to which of two or more sequences of instructions is to be executed. The choices that have to be made are usually dependent upon the values of one or more of the program variables.

A *transfer instruction* modifies the order in which subsequent instructions are executed. A transfer instruction has the form:

                    GO TO Label

where Label is a string of from 1 to 5 decimal digits. The label is treated as an identifier of a particular instruction. If a label is written to the left of an instruction, the compiler will associate the label with that instruction during the translation of the program. Whenever a transfer instruction is executed, control immediately passes to the instruction indicated by the transfer, and execution resumes with that instruction.

Transfer instructions can be used to direct the computer to repeat a sequence of statements by transferring back to an earlier one. The instruction

                    GO TO 20

causes the computer to transfer to the instruction with label 20 regardless of the relative position of that instruction in the program. If label 20 precedes the transfer instruction, the statements starting with label 20 will be executed again.

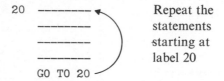

As we will see throughout the text, the ability to repeat a sequence of statements is a powerful tool of programming.

1.3.10 Conditional Statements

The payroll program shown in Fig. 1.17 places a rather unfair tax burden on employees with a small gross salary—especially those whose salary is less than $25.00. It leaves these employees with a negative net pay! We will now try to correct this injustice and ensure that all employees, except those who don't work at all, will receive a positive net pay amount. In order to do this, we will have to modify the payroll program so that no tax will be deducted from the gross pay of employees who earn less than a specified minimum salary, which we will store in the variable MIN. This program modification will require the use of a *conditional statement* of the form

            IF (condition) dependent statement

The conditional statement instructs the computer to first evaluate the condition to see whether it is true or false. The computer then either executes the dependent statement (if the condition is true) or skips it (if the condition is false).

Example 1.2

 a) The conditional statement

            IF (GROSS.GT.MIN) GO TO 20

will cause the computer to transfer control to the statement with label 20 if the value of the variable GROSS is "greater than" the value of the variable MIN.

b) The conditional statement

IF (GROSS.LE.MIN) NET = GROSS

will cause the computer to execute the statement NET = GROSS if GROSS is "less than or equal to" MIN.

The dependent statement may be any of the executable FORTRAN statements discussed so far: read, print, assignment, stop, or transfer statements may all be used. Another conditional statement may not be used as the dependent statement. Nonexecutable statements such as real, data initialization, and end statements may not be used. If a transfer instruction is used as the dependent statement, the conditional statement is called a *conditional transfer instruction*.

The effect of the conditional statement is summarized in Fig. 1.19.

Conditional statement which is not a conditional transfer instruction	*Conditional transfer instruction*
1. Evaluate the condition.	1. Evaluate the condition.
2. If the condition is true, execute the dependent statement; otherwise, skip it.	2. If the condition is true, transfer to the indicated label and continue execution at that point.
3. In any case, continue with the next statement in normal sequence.	3. If the condition is false, continue with the next statement in normal sequence.

Fig. 1.19   Effect of conditional statement.

The form of the condition is

Operand$_1$ Relational operator   Operand$_2$

where the operands may be variables, and the *relational operator* may be any one of the six symbols given in Table 1.2.

Table 1.2 List of relational operators that may be used in FORTRAN

Relational operator	Meaning
.EQ.	Equal
.NE.	Not equal
.GT.	Greater than
.LT.	Less than
.GE.	Greater than or equal
.LE.	Less than or equal

Figure 1.20 shows one way to modify the payroll program using a conditional statement. The conditional transfer instruction is used to transfer control to the assignment statement which deducts a tax (label 20) whenever GROSS exceeds MIN. Otherwise, GROSS is copied into NET and control is transferred to the output statements (label 30).

```
C PAYROLL PROGRAM WITH CONDITIONAL TAX DEDUCTION
C
        REAL HOURS, RATE, TAX, GROSS, NET, MIN
        DATA TAX /25.00/
        DATA MIN /100.00/
C
C READ IN DATA ITEMS
        READ, HOURS
        PRINT, HOURS
        READ, RATE
        PRINT, RATE
C
C COMPUTE GROSS SALARY AND NET PAY
        GROSS = HOURS * RATE
C DETERMINE IF GROSS IS LARGE ENOUGH TO DEDUCT TAX
        IF (GROSS .GT. MIN) GO TO 20
C GROSS TOO SMALL — NO TAX
        NET = GROSS
        GO TO 30
C GROSS EXCEEDS MIN — DEDUCT TAX
     20 NET = GROSS — TAX
C
C OUTPUT RESULTS AND STOP
     30 PRINT, GROSS
        PRINT, NET
        STOP
        END
```

Fig. 1.20 Second version of payroll program.

The statements in Fig. 1.20 that start with a C are descriptive *comments*. They are ignored by the compiler during translation and are *listed* with the program statements to aid the programmer in identifying or *documenting* the purpose of each section of the program. Guidelines for the use of comments will be given in Chapter 2.

EXERCISE 1.7 Write a sequence of statements that computes NET without using any transfer instructions (conditional or otherwise). You should use a conditional statement that has an assignment statement as its dependent statement. Check your program by "executing" it for the following sets of data: HOURS 35.0, RATE 4.0; HOURS 20.0, RATE 3.5; HOURS 25.0, RATE 4.0. Verify that the values of NET computed are correct.

EXERCISE 1.8 The program in Fig. 1.20 is not as useful as it could be, for it forces a rather rigid and unrealistic tax structure upon the company's employees. It might be more appropriate to have the program compute the tax for each employee earning more than the minimum salary by taking a certain percentage (25%) of the amount earned over MIN. How would you change the program to do this?

EXERCISE 1.9

a) Suppose that the variable X has the value 100.00. To which one of the three statement labels (20, 30, or 40) will the following sequence of instructions transfer?

```
IF (X .LT. FIFTY) GO TO 20
IF (X .GT. NINETY) GO TO 30
IF (X .EQ. HUND) GO TO 40
          ⋮
```

Assume that the variables FIFTY, NINETY, and HUND have the values 50.0, 90.0, and 100.0 respectively.

b) Write a sequence of instructions to read a data item into Y, to print the item, and to transfer to statement number 20 if Y is less than 0.0; to statement 30 if Y is equal to 0.0; and to statement 40 otherwise.

c) Write a sequence of instructions to read three data items into A, B, and C, and compute and print:

$$X = B^2 - 4.0\,AC$$

Hint. B^2 may be obtained by multiplying B by itself. Declare and initialize all variables that you will need, including those variables needed to store *partial results*.

EXERCISE 1.10 Given the following data-card section

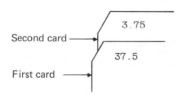

Second card

3.75

37.5

First card

for the revised payroll problem (shown in Fig. 1.20), what will be the values of the variables GROSS, NET, HOURS, and RATE, after execution of the program?

1.4 USING THE COMPUTER

1.4.1 Keypunching a FORTRAN program

Once the writing of a FORTRAN program is finished, the program must be transferred to punched cards so that it may be input to the computer and translated by the compiler. The punched card contains space for a maximum of 80 characters of information (see Fig. 1.3). This space is divided into four subparts called *fields*, as shown in Fig. 1.21.

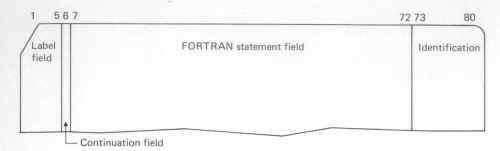

Figure 1.21

Certain rules must be followed in keypunching a FORTRAN statement into a punched card. These rules are summarized below.

Rules for Keypunching FORTRAN Statements

1. All statement labels must be punched in the label field (card columns 1–5).

2. The FORTRAN statement must be punched in the statement field (card columns 7–72 inclusive), and may contain blanks anywhere the programmer desires to improve program readability. Blanks in the statement field have no meaning and may be ignored.

3. If a FORTRAN statement is too long to fit on one card, it may be continued in columns 7–72 of subsequent cards (called *continuation cards*) simply by punching any character except zero in column 6 of each continuation card.

4. Columns 73–80 may be used to sequence and identify the cards in a FORTRAN deck. Normally, they are left blank.

5. If a C is punched in column 1, the card is considered a comment card and rules 1 through 3 do not apply.

Examples of punched FORTRAN statements are shown in Figs. 1.22 and 1.23.

Figure 1.24 shows the original payroll program (listed in Fig. 1.17) keypunched on cards.

You should try to be consistent in the conventions you use for keypunching your FORTRAN statements. We will leave blanks around operators and the equal sign, around conditions, and after commas (see Fig. 1.20).

The above instructions refer to FORTRAN program statements only and not input data cards. In keypunching input data cards, all eighty columns may be used. Each number should be punched in consecutive columns of a card, one number to a card. All real numbers should be punched with a decimal point.

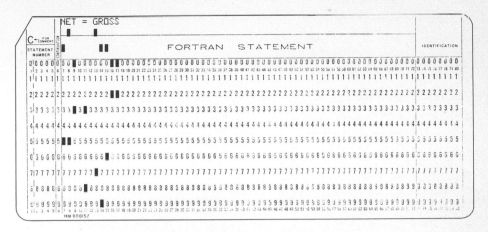

Fig. 1.22 An unlabeled FORTRAN statement.

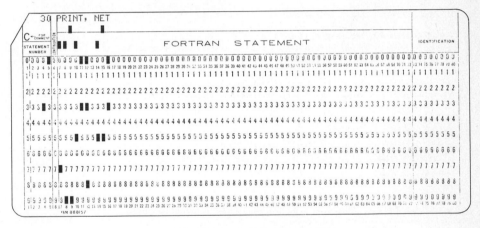

Fig. 1.23 A labeled FORTRAN statement.

Remember to be very careful in keypunching your program cards. The computer cannot guess what you mean. If you misspell a variable name or keypunch an extra character somewhere, your program may not run at all. If it does run, it may produce incorrect results.

1.4.2 Control Cards and the Operating System

Each user program that is keypunched is read into the computer and normally inserted in a large file of user programs. This file is processed by a supervisory program within the computer called the *operating system*. It is the responsibility of the operating system to schedule the resources of the computer in an efficient manner so that as many jobs as possible can be completed.

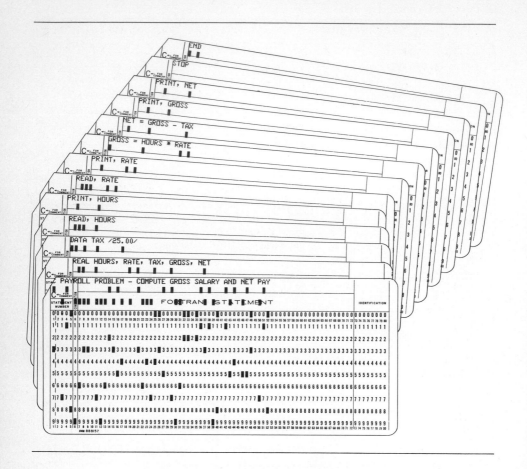

Fig. 1.24 The payroll program in punched cards.

The operating system must know something about your job and its resource needs in order to process it. Some of the necessary information is listed below:

1. Estimated time for completion of job
2. Estimated memory requirements
3. Billing account number
4. Compiler or other processor needed
5. Start of data section for program
6. Physical end of job

We use special cards, called *control cards*, to convey this information to the operating system. The actual form of these cards is very much dependent on your particular computer and installation. Your instructor will provide you with the format for the control cards needed. Figure 1.25 shows the relationship among the control cards, program statements, and data cards of your job-input card deck.

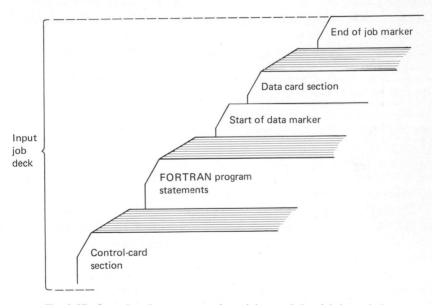

Fig. 1.25   Control cards, program cards, and data cards in a job-input deck.

1.4.3   Possible Errors

There are five general classes of errors that you may encounter when submitting a program to the computer:

  i) Control-card and deck-arrangement errors
 ii) FORTRAN syntax errors
iii) Incorrect use of labels
iv) Inconsistent spelling of variable names
 v) Program logic errors

i) *Control card and deck arrangement errors* are most frustrating because they usually result in a situation where the operating system will not know what it is to do with your program. It may not be able to determine that the FORTRAN compiler will be needed to translate your program. Still worse, it may not even be able to tell that you are the owner of the deck of cards it is processing. Control-card and deck-arrangement errors are easy to avoid. Your instructor will describe to you the control cards and deck arrangement to be used for your computer. If you follow this description to the letter, you will have little difficulty.

ii) *FORTRAN syntax errors* are caused by FORTRAN statements that do not follow the precise rules of formation (*syntax rules*) of FORTRAN. Such statements cannot be translated by the compiler. Often, careless mistakes made in keypunching will cause syntax errors. The compiler will identify these syntax errors by printing error diagnostics for each illegal instruction in your program. It will be up to you to read these diagnostics and review the rules of FORTRAN in order to correct your errors.

At first, the error diagnostics may be difficult to understand. It is worthwhile to try to decipher them yourself rather than to seek help immediately. If you persist, as the course progresses, you will become more proficient at recognizing and correcting your own errors.

An example of a FORTRAN syntax error would be keypunching RESL instead of REAL. A common syntax error is caused by the failure to type the symbol , after the words READ and PRINT in input and output statements. When this error occurs, the compiler is not likely to recognize the statement that has been punched and will tell you so with an appropriate diagnostic. Usually this diagnostic will inform you only that you have punched an *unrecognizable statement*. Some compilers will, however, try to indicate to you what might be wrong with the statement. Whenever you are told of an unrecognizable statement, you should carefully check your punctuation. For example, spelling errors, misuse of slashes in a DATA statement, and incorrect use of the periods or parentheses in a conditional statement are all likely to produce unrecognizable statement diagnostics.

Recall that FORTRAN statements must begin in column 7 or beyond in the punched card. If you accidentally start a statement to the left of column 7, you will cause the compiler much confusion. The compiler might think that you have a continuation card, or that you have punched a label. Since your "label" will not conform to the FORTRAN rules for labels (a string of up to 5 decimal digits), the compiler will indicate that you have used an illegal label.

iii) *Incorrect use of labels associated with transfer instructions* will also cause syntax errors during compilation. Each label referenced in a GO TO instruction must appear in the label field (columns 1–5) of exactly one executable statement in your program. If no statement in the program has that label, the compiler will provide a *missing label* diagnostic. If more than one statement has the same label, the compiler will provide a *duplicate label* diagnostic. In either case, the compiler will be unable to complete the translation of your program, because it will not know where to transfer control when the GO TO statement is executed.

iv) *Inconsistent spelling of variable names* will often go undetected during translation. For example, the statement sequence in Fig. 1.26 will be translated by most compilers with no error indication given.

```
REAL   COUNT, X, TWO
DATA   TWO / 2.0 /
READ, COUNT
X = COUNTR / TWO
PRINT, X
STOP
END
```

Fig. 1.26   A program segment containing a spelling error.

The statement
```
X = COUNTR / TWO
```
will be translated using a new memory cell associated with the variable COUNTR as the dividend, even though the intention was to use the variable COUNT. The error will not become apparent until your program executes and an incorrect value of X is printed.

However, some compilers will try to ensure that all variables have been *defined* —that is, have had data placed in them by the program—before they are to be manipulated or printed. There are three ways of defining a variable:

1. Using a data initialization statement to store a constant before program execution begins;

2. Using a read statement to enter variable information during execution; and

3. Using an assignment statement to perform a computation and store the result.

Obviously, it makes little sense to try to manipulate or print out the value of a variable that has never been defined in one of these ways. Unfortunately, most compilers will not inform a programmer when such a mistake is made. If your compiler does, the diagnostic "attempt to use an undefined variable" would help you find most misspelled variable names.

v) *Program logic errors* are caused by mistakes that have been made in the logical organization of the instructions in your program. Many of these errors can be avoided if a careful, reasoned approach is taken to problem solving and program development. Logic errors that do occur can often be more easily diagnosed if some care and discipline have been applied in the design and coding of the program. It is our intention to provide, through numerous examples, some useful guidelines for problem solving and program writing.

The mistakes described in categories (i) through (iii) will cause errors that are *fatal* to your program because the compiler will not be able to completely translate the program, and the computer will therefore not be able to execute it. The remaining categories of errors are more insidious because the program may be completely translated and executed, but will compute incorrect results.

To verify that your program is indeed producing the correct results, it is useful to add extra print statements to print out intermediate results. These results should be compared against hand calculations for one or more representative sets of data in order to verify that they are correct. The extra print statements can be removed prior to making your final program runs.

EXERCISE 1.11 What will be the value of X printed by the program segment shown in Figure 1.26?

EXERCISE 1.12 Find the syntax errors in the following FORTRAN cards:

```
Card  Columns
No.   1    5 6 7
 1  |          |  REAL NET GROSS HOURS X Y Z
 2  |          |  DATA NET/3/
 3  |          |  DATA GROSS/3,500/
 4  |          |  READ * HOURS
 5  |          |  X + Y = Y + Z
 6  |          |  20 PRINT, X
 7  |          |  IF (X = Y) X = Y + Z
 8  |  PRINT   |  , X * Y
 9  |          |  GO TO THERE
10  |          |  IF (HOURS .GT. ZERO GROSS = HOURS
11  |        * |  RATE
12  |          |  GO TO 3612
```

1.5 SUMMARY

You have been introduced to the basic components of the computer: the memory, the central processor unit, and the input and output units. (Figure 1.27 contains a summary of important facts about computers that you should remember.) You have also seen how to use the FORTRAN programming language to perform some very fundamental operations. You have learned how to instruct the computer to read information into memory, perform some simple computations, and print from memory the results of the computation. All of this has been done using symbols (punctuation marks, variable names, and special operators such as * , – and .GE.) that are familiar, easy to remember, and easy to use. You needed to know virtually nothing about the computer you are using in order to understand and use FORTRAN. In Table 1.3, we have provided a summary of all of the FORTRAN statements introduced in this chapter. An example of the use of each

1. No memory cell is ever empty.
2. The current contents of a memory cell are destroyed whenever new information is placed in that cell (via an assignment, read, or data statement).
3. Programs must first be placed in the memory of the computer before they can be executed.
4. No data may be manipulated by the computer if it is not first stored in memory.
5. The computer cannot think for itself, and must be instructed to perform a task in a precise and unambiguous manner, using a programming language.
6. Programming a computer can be fun—if you are patient, organized, and careful.

Fig. 1.27 A summary of things to remember about the computer.

instruction is also given. You should use these examples as guides to ensure that you are using the correct syntax in the program statements that you write.

The small amount of FORTRAN that you have seen is sufficient to enable you to solve a large variety of complex problems using the computer. However, many of these problems are difficult to solve with just this limited FORTRAN subset. The more you learn about FORTRAN, the easier it will be for you to write programs to solve more complicated problems on the computer.

In the remainder of this text we will introduce you to more of the features of the FORTRAN language, and provide precise descriptions of the rules for using these features. You must remember throughout that, unlike the rules of English,

Table 1.3 Summary of FORTRAN statements

Statement type and use	Examples
DECLARATION: Informs the compiler of the list of variable names to be used in a program and the type of number to be stored in each variable	REAL GROSS, RATE, NET, TAX INTEGER COUNT
DATA INITIALIZATION: Instructs the loader to store program constants in designated variables prior to program execution	DATA TAX/25.00/
ASSIGNMENT: Computes a new value for a variable	GROSS = HOURS*RATE GROSS = NET
INPUT: Enters input data into a variable	READ, HOURS
OUTPUT: Displays the value of a variable	PRINT, NET
TRANSFER: Alters the sequence of statement execution	GO TO 30
CONDITIONAL STATEMENT: Executes dependent statement only if condition is true	IF (GROSS .GT. MIN) GO TO 20 IF (X .EQ. Y) Z = X
STOP: Terminates execution	STOP
END: Informs the compiler that there are no more program statements to be translated	END

the rules of FORTRAN are quite precise, and allow no exceptions. FORTRAN instructions formed in violation of these rules will cause syntax errors in your programs.

You should not find the mastery of the rules of FORTRAN particularly difficult. The rules are precise and relatively few in number, especially compared to English. By far the most challenging aspect of your work will be the formulation of the logic and organization of your programs. For this reason, we will introduce you to a methodology for problem solving with a computer in the next chapter, and continue to emphasize this methodology throughout the remainder of the book.

PROGRAMMING PROBLEMS

1.2 Every Sunday afternoon you take an afternoon drive in your car. Before leaving, you fill your gas tank with lead-free gasoline, which costs 55c a gallon. Write a program that you could use to read in the distance traveled (DIST) each week, the time (TIME) required to make the trip, and the miles-per-gallon estimate (MPG) for your car. Compute and print the average speed traveled, and the estimated cost of your trip.

1.3 Write a program to read in the weight (in pounds) of an object, and compute and print its weight in kilograms and grams. [*Hint.* One pound is equal to 0.453592 kilograms (453.59237 grams).]

1.4 A cyclist coasting on a level road slows from a speed of 10 miles/hr to 2.5 miles/hr in 1 minute. Write a computer program to calculate the cyclist's acceleration, and to determine how long it will take the cyclist to come to rest, given his original speed of 10 miles/hr. [*Hint.* Use the equation

$$a = \frac{v_f - v_i}{t}$$

where a is acceleration, t is time, v_i is initial velocity, and v_f is the final velocity.] How did you get the required input data placed in computer memory? Defend your method.

1.5 Write a program to read three data items into variables X, Y, and Z, and find and print the largest of these items. Keypunch your program and the necessary control cards, and run your program on the computer. [*Hint.* Use an additional variable named LARGE which should always contain the largest of the data items checked so far.

1.6 Write a program to read a single data item into the variable START. Then, divide this data item by 2.0. Continue this division until the result becomes less than 0.01. Then print the result and stop. Declare all variables used (including START). Keypunch and run your program.

1.7 Read in a number and compute and print its absolute value. If the number is positive, the absolute value is the number itself; otherwise, the absolute value is −1.0 times the number.

1.8 Eight track stars entered the mile race at the Penn Relays. Write a program that will read in the race time in minutes (MINUTE) and seconds (SECOND) for any one of these runners, and compute and print the speed in feet per second (FPS) and in meters per second (MPS). [*Hints.* Punch the minutes and seconds for each runner on two separate cards as shown below:

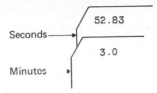

There are 5,280 feet in one mile, and one meter equals 3.282 feet.]

1.9 [Continuation of Problem 1.8.] Modify the program for Problem 1.8 to read in the race time for all eight runners (rather than just one runner) and compute and print the speeds of each. Test your program for the following data:

3.0 minutes 52.83 seconds	3.0 minutes 56.22 seconds	3.0 minutes 59.83 seconds
4.0 minutes 00.03 seconds	4.0 minutes 16.22 seconds	4.0 minutes 19.00 seconds
4.0 minutes 19.89 seconds	4.0 minutes 21.21 seconds	

1.10 Suppose the following distances were correct:

Boston–Hartford	100 miles
Hartford–New York	125 miles
New York–Philadelphia	90 miles

You are planning to rent a car to drive from Boston to Philadelphia. Cost is no consideration, but you want to be certain that you can make the trip on one tankful of gas. Write a program to read in the miles-per-gallon (MPG) and tank size (TNKSZE) in gallons for a particular rent-a-car, and print out the number of cities that could be reached (0, 1, 2, or 3). Test your program for the following data:

MPG	TNKSZE (*gallons*)
10.0	15.0
40.5	20.0
22.5	12.0
10.0	9.0

[*Hint.* You will have to run your program four times, once for each set of test data.]

1.11 [Continuation of Problem 1.10.] Modify your program for Problem 1.10 to process all four data cards in one run of the program.

PROBLEM SOLVING WITH THE COMPUTER

2

2.1 Problem Analysis

2.2 Description of the Problem Solution

2.3 Algorithms Involving Decisions and Loops

2.4 Implementing a Flow Diagram in FORTRAN

2.5 Debugging a FORTRAN Program

2.6 Summary and Review

Programming Problems

2.1 PROBLEM ANALYSIS

2.1.1 Introduction

Now that you have been introduced to the computer—what it is, how it works, and what it can do—it is time to turn our attention to the problem of how to use the computer to solve problems.

Using the computer for problem solving is similar to trying to put a man on the moon in the late 1950's and 1960's. In both instances, there is a problem to be solved, and a final "program" for solving it.

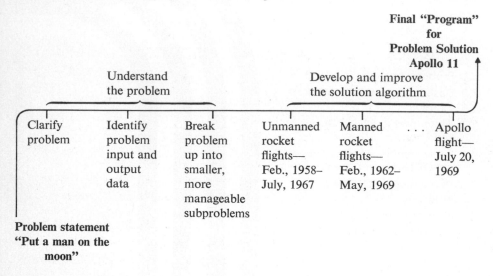

In the moon effort, the final goal was not achieved directly. Rather, it was brought about through the careful planning and organization of subtasks, each of which had to be completed successfully before the Apollo 11 flight could even be attempted.

Writing a computer program also requires careful planning and organization. It is rare, indeed, to see an error-free computer program written directly from the original statement of a problem. Usually, the final program is achieved only after a number of steps have been followed. These steps are the subject of this chapter.

2.1.2 Representation and Manipulation of Data

We stated earlier that the computer is a tool that can be used to represent and to manipulate data. It is therefore not too surprising that the first two steps in solving a problem on the computer require (A) the definition of the data to be represented in the computer memory, and (B) the formulation of an *algorithm*—a list of steps that describe the desired manipulation of this data.

These two steps are not entirely unrelated. Decisions that we make in Step A may be subject to numerous changes throughout the list formulation in Step B.

Nevertheless, it is absolutely essential that we perform Step A in as complete and precise a fashion as possible before embarking upon B. Careless errors, or errors in judgment in deciding what information is to be represented, and what form this information is to take, can result in numerous difficulties in the later stages of solving a problem on the computer. Such mistakes can make the list formulation in Step B extremely difficult, and sometimes even impossible.

Once the definition of the information to be represented in the computer has been made and a precise formulation of the problem statement is available, the algorithm for solving the problem can be formulated.

2.1.3 Understanding the Problem

The definition of the data to be represented in the computer memory requires a clear understanding of the stated problem. First, we must determine what information is to be computed and printed by the computer. Then it is necessary to identify the information that is to be given as input to the computer. Once the input and output data have been identified, we must ask if sufficient information is available to compute the required output from the given input. If the answer to this question is *no*, we must determine what additional information is needed, and how this information can be provided to the program.

When identifying the data items associated with the problem, it is helpful to assign to each item a meaningful variable name that can be used to represent the computer memory cell containing the data item. (Recall from Chapter 1 that we do not have to be concerned with the actual memory cell associated with each variable name. The compiler will assign a unique memory cell to each variable name, and it will handle all bookkeeping details necessary to retain this correspondence.)

To see how this process works, we will apply it to a specific problem.

PROBLEM 2.1 Write a program to compute and print the sum and average of two numbers.

DISCUSSION The first step is to make certain that we understand the problem and to identify the input and output data for the problem. Then we can obtain a more precise formulation of the problem in terms of these input and output items.

All items of information to be used to solve a given problem should be listed in a *data table*, along with a description of relevant properties of these items. The variable used to represent each data item should also be listed in the table. The data table for Problem 2.1 is given on page 42. The entries shown describe the input and output data for the problem.

There are clearly two items of information required as output for this problem. They are the sum and the average of two numbers. In order to compute these values, we must be able to store the data items to be summed and averaged into the memory of the computer. In this example, we will use the variables NBR1ST and NBR2ND to represent these two data items.

Data Table for Problem 2.1

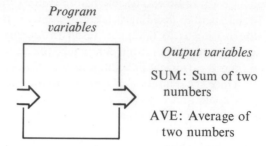

Program variables

Input variables

NBR1ST: First number to be used in computation

NBR2ND: Second number to be used in computation

Output variables

SUM: Sum of two numbers

AVE: Average of two numbers

A more precise formulation of Problem 2.1 is now possible. We must read two data items into the variables NBR1ST and NBR2ND, find the sum and the average of these two items, and print the values of the sum and the average. ∎

2.2 DESCRIPTION OF THE PROBLEM SOLUTION

2.2.1 Developing an Algorithm

At this point we should have a clear understanding of what is required for the solution of Problem 2.1. We can now proceed to organize the problem formulation into a carefully constructed *list of steps* that will describe the sequence of manipulations to be performed in carrying out the problem solution. This list of steps is called an *algorithm*.

Algorithm for Problem 2.1 (Level 1)

STEP 1   Read the data items into the variables NBR1ST and NBR2ND.

STEP 2   Compute the sum of the data items in NBR1ST and NBR2ND and store the result in the variable SUM.

STEP 3   Compute the average of the data items in NBR1ST and NBR2ND and store the result in the variable AVE.

STEP 4   Print the values of the variables SUM and AVE.

STEP 5   Stop.

2.2.2 Algorithm Refinement

Note that this sequence of events closely mirrors the problem formulation given earlier. This is as it should be! If the problem formulation is complete, it should provide us with a general outline of what must be done to solve the problem. The purpose of the algorithm formulation is to provide a detailed and precise description of the individual steps to be carried out by the computer in solving the problem.

The algorithm is essentially a *refinement* of the general outline provided by the original problem formulation. It is often the case that several *levels of refinement* of the general outline are required before the algorithm formulation is complete. This can happen when some steps in the refinement at one level are not sufficiently detailed or precise to indicate in an unambiguous fashion the sequence of actions to be performed by the computer.

The key question in deciding whether or not further refinement of an algorithm step is required is this:

Is it clear precisely what FORTRAN instructions are necessary in order to tell the computer how to carry out the step?

If it is not immediately obvious what the FORTRAN instructions are, then the algorithm should be further refined.

What is obvious to some programmers may not be at all clear to others. The refinement of an algorithm is therefore a personal matter to some extent. As you gain experience in developing algorithms and converting them to FORTRAN programs, you may discover that you are doing less and less algorithm refinement. This may also happen as you become more familiar with the FORTRAN language.

If we examine the Level 1 algorithm for Problem 2.1, we see that only Step 3 requires further refinement. We already know how to write FORTRAN instructions for reading, printing, adding, and stopping. However, we may not know how to use FORTRAN to tell the computer to compute the average of two numbers.

Refinement of Step 3

STEP 3.1　　Divide the value of the variable SUM by the number of items (2.0) used to compute the sum.

Now we have a slight problem, for we have as yet made no provision for the number 2.0 to be placed in the memory of the computer. The computation of the average of two numbers will always require division by the value 2.0—this never changes. Thus, each time our program is executed, it will require the presence of the constant value of 2.0 in the memory of the computer.

Now recall, from Chapter 1, that the decision whether to load a data item or to read the item in as input to the program is based upon the variation in value of the item from one program execution to another. Since the constant 2.0 is needed for all executions of our program, it clearly should be loaded into the computer memory. (On the other hand, the data to be summed and averaged will vary from execution to execution of the program, and should be read into the memory of the computer during execution of the program.)

The data table for Problem 2.1 can now be completed by designating a program variable (TWO) for storage of the constant 2.0.

Program variables

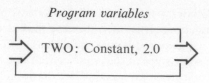

TWO: Constant, 2.0

We now have a complete description of the algorithm and the data table, and can proceed to write the FORTRAN representation for the algorithm (Fig. 2.1). We do this on a step-by-step basis, starting with the necessary declarations as indicated by the data table.

```
C COMPUTE THE SUM AND AVERAGE OF TWO NUMBERS
C
       REAL NBR1ST, NBR2ND, SUM, AVE, TWO
       DATA TWO /2.0/
C
C READ AND PRINT DATA
       READ, NBR1ST
       PRINT, NBR1ST
       READ, NBR2ND
       PRINT, NBR2ND
C
C COMPUTE SUM AND AVERAGE
       SUM = NBR1ST + NBR2ND
       AVE = SUM / TWO
C
C PRINT RESULTS
       PRINT, SUM
       PRINT, AVE
       STOP
       END
```

Fig. 2.1 FORTRAN program for Problem 2.1.

The information on the comment cards indicates which parts of the English version of the algorithm correspond to the FORTRAN version. When properly used, comments can be helpful in identifying the purpose of each logically meaningful segment of a program. A useful guide for using comment cards in a program is to identify the steps in the algorithm from which the program was written. A description of these steps can be obtained from a suitably refined version of the algorithm.

EXERCISE 2.1 Write a data description table and an algorithm to compute the sum and average of four numbers.

2.2.3   Flow-Diagram Representations of Algorithms

As problems become more complex, precise English descriptions of algorithms for solving these problems become more complex and difficult to follow. It is therefore helpful if some kind of descriptive notation can be used to describe an algorithm. We will use one such descriptive notation, called a *flow diagram*, throughout this text.

Not everyone in the computer field believes that flow diagrams are useful, and many experienced programmers do not always use them. However, we believe that flow diagrams are helpful because they provide a graphical, two-dimensional representation of an algorithm. Consistent use of the special flow-diagram symbols and forms shown in the text will make algorithms easy to write, easy to refine, and still easier to follow.

Flow-diagram representations of two levels of the algorithm for Problem 2.1 are shown in Fig. 2.2. They contain a number of symbols that should be noted.

1. Ovals are used to indicate the starting and stopping points of an algorithm.
2. Rectangular boxes are used to indicate manipulation of information in the memory of the computer.
3. A box in the shape of a computer card (with one corner cut off) is used to indicate the reading of information into the computer.
4. A box with a wavy bottom is used to indicate the printing of information stored in the computer memory.
5. Arrows are used to indicate the "flow of control" of an algorithm from one step to another.

You will find it convenient to represent all levels of algorithms with a flow diagram. The first level will often be quite general and imprecise. It will contain a summary, usually written in English, of the basic steps of an algorithm, as shown on the left side of Fig. 2.2. In some cases (usually when the step is very simple), these summaries may be precise and detailed. However, in most cases, one or more levels of refinement will be necessary before a sufficiently detailed and precise diagram is completed. A flow diagram for Problem 2.1, complete with refinements of steps 1, 2, 3, and 4, is shown in Fig. 2.2. The large dotted arrows point to the refinement for each of these steps.

2.2.4   Problem-Solving Principles

Up to now we have presented a few suggestions for solving problems on the computer. These suggestions are summarized in the list of steps given below.

1. Understand what you are being asked to do.
2. Identify all problem input and output data. Make certain there are sufficient input items provided to complete the solution.

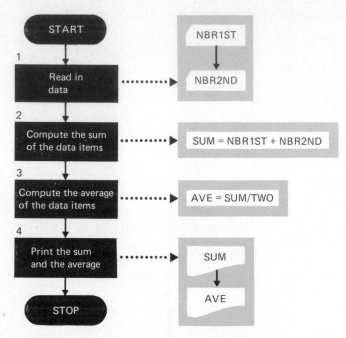

Fig. 2.2 Level 1 flow diagram and refinements for Problem 2.1.

3. Formulate a precise statement of the problem in terms of the input and output data.

4. State clearly the sequence of steps necessary to produce the desired problem output through manipulation of the input data; i.e., develop the algorithm and represent it as a flow diagram.

5. Refine this flow diagram until it can be easily implemented in the programming language to be used.

6. Transform the flow diagram to a program.

Steps 4 and 5 are really the most difficult of the steps listed; they are the only truly creative part of this process. People differ in their degree of capability to formulate solutions to problems. Some find it easy to develop algorithms for the most complex problem, while others must work diligently to produce an algorithm for solving a simple problem.

The ability to solve problems is fundamental to computer programming. The transformation of the refined algorithm to a working program (Step 6) is a highly skilled clerical task, which requires a thorough knowledge of the programming language available. This detailed knowledge can normally be acquired by anyone willing to devote the necessary effort. However, a flow diagram that correctly

represents the necessary problem-solving operations and the
first be developed.

In this book, we will provide many solutions to example
these solutions carefully should enable you to become more adep...
your own solutions, because the techniques used for one problem may freq...
be applied in a slightly different way to solve another. Often, new problems are
simply expansions or modifications of old ones.

The process of refinement can be used to break a complex problem up into
more manageable subproblems which can be solved individually. This technique
will be illustrated in all of the problems solved in the text. We suggest you practice
it in developing your own solutions to the programming problems.

2.3 ALGORITHMS INVOLVING DECISIONS AND LOOPS

2.3.1 Decision Steps and Transfers

Normally, the steps of an algorithm are performed in the order in which they are
listed. In many algorithms, however, the sequence of steps to be performed is
determined by the input data. In such cases, decisions must be made, based upon
the values of certain program variables, as to which sequence of steps is to be
performed. Such decisions are usually based upon the evaluation of a condition
that is expressed in terms of the relevant program variables. The result of the
evaluation determines which algorithm steps will be executed next.

The algorithm step that describes the condition is called a *decision step*. The
simplest kind of decision step involves the evaluation of a logical condition—that
is, a condition that may be either true or false.

Figure 2.3 contains an example of such a decision step. The diagram in this
figure describes the algorithm for the payroll problem shown in Chapter 1. The
decision step shown in step 10 is used to describe a condition (GROSS is greater
than MIN) that is evaluated in order to decide which algorithm step is to be
executed next. If the condition is false, step 15 is performed next. Otherwise,
step 20 is performed next. In either case, step 30 will be carried out following the
completion of the chosen step (15 or 20). The FORTRAN implementation of this
flow diagram is shown in the program in Fig. 1.20.

The decision step just discussed involves a choice between two alternatives—a
sequence of one or more steps to be executed if the condition is true (the true
task), and a sequence to be executed if the condition is false (the false task). Such
an algorithm step is called a *double-alternative decision step*. The general flow-
diagram pattern for this step is shown in Fig. 2.4.

Quite often, a decision step in an algorithm will involve only one alternative:
a sequence of one or more steps that will be carried out if the given condition is
true, but skipped if the condition is false. The flow-diagram pattern for this
single-alternative decision step is shown in Fig. 2.5.

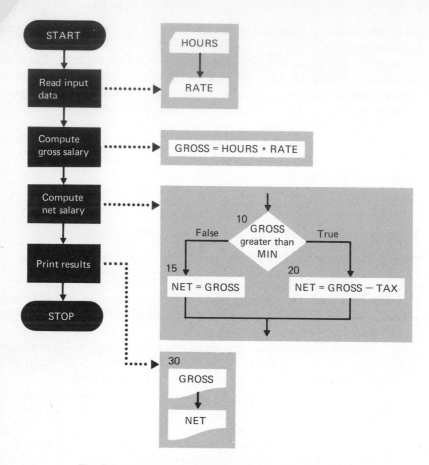

Fig. 2.3 Flow diagrams for payroll program (see Fig. 1.20).

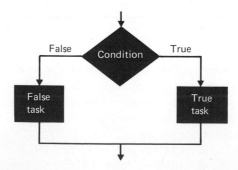

Fig. 2.4 Flow-diagram pattern for the double-alternative decision step.

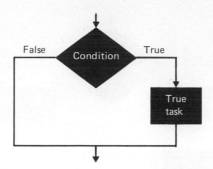

Fig. 2.5 Flow-diagram pattern for the single-alternative decision step.

In the next chapter, we will see how to express decision steps more naturally in FORTRAN. We will see that the flow-diagram-to-program conversion process is relatively easy, even when complicated decision steps are required.

Example 2.1 Draw the flow-diagram patterns for each of the decision steps described below.

a) If BASE exceeds 15,000 dollars, then set BASE equal to 15,000 dollars. Otherwise, skip this step. Then compute the Social Security tax for the base. The translation of the above yields the flow diagram shown next.

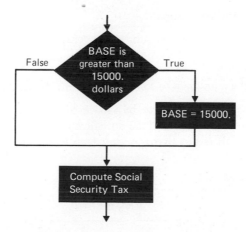

b) If CHECK is less than or equal to BALANC, then recompute balance by subtracting CHECK from BALANC. Otherwise, print an "account overdrawn note" and subtract $1.50 (for penalty) from BALANC.

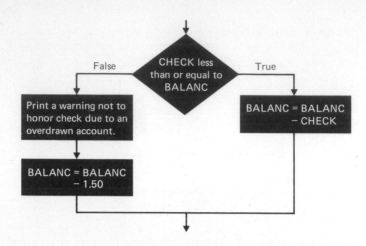

EXERCISE 2.2 Write the flow-diagram pattern to represent the following English descriptions:

a) If ITEM is not equal to ZERO, then multiply PRODCT by ITEM. Otherwise, skip this step. In either case, then print the value of PRODCT.

b) If ITEM exceeds LARGER, store the value of ITEM in LARGER. Otherwise skip this step. In either case, then print the value of ITEM.

c) If X is larger than 0.0, add X to SUMPOS. Otherwise, if X is smaller than 0.0, add X to SUMNEG. Otherwise, if X = 0.0, add one to CNTZRO.

2.3.2 The Motivation for Loops

The flow diagrams for finding the sum and average of two numbers work quite well. Suppose, however, that we are asked to solve a slightly different problem.

PROBLEM 2.2 Write a program to compute and print the sum of 2000 data items.

DISCUSSION The first question to be answered now concerns whether or not the approach previously taken will be satisfactory for this problem too. The answer is clearly *no*! It is not that the approach won't work, but rather that no

Data Table for Problem 2.2

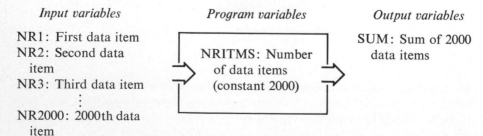

Input variables	Program variables	Output variables
NR1: First data item	NRITMS: Number of data items (constant 2000)	SUM: Sum of 2000 data items
NR2: Second data item		
NR3: Third data item		
⋮		
NR2000: 2000th data item		

reasonable person is likely to have the patience to carry out this solution for 2000 numbers. Our difficulties would begin in attempting to produce a data table listing the differently named variables for each of the 2000 items involved. (See data table at bottom of page 50.)

This in itself is a horrendous task. Then, assuming we could finally name all 2000 variables, we would have quite a boring task in describing the algorithm for solving the problem. Not even little children enjoy drawing pictures that much!

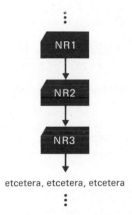

etcetera, etcetera, etcetera

A new approach is needed in order to solve this problem. Regardless of what this new approach involves, it will still be necessary to tell the computer to read in and add together 2000 numbers. The essence of the problem is to find a way to do this without writing separate instructions for the reading and the addition of each of the 2000 data items needed to compute the sum. It would be ideal if we could write one step for reading, one step for accumulating the sum, and then repeat these two steps for each of the 2000 items.

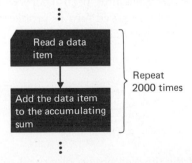

It happens that we can actually achieve this goal quite easily. All that is necessary is to (a) solve the problem of naming each data item, (b) learn how to describe a repeated sequence of steps in a flow diagram, and (c) learn how to specify the repetition of a sequence of steps in FORTRAN.

The solution to the naming problem rests upon the following realization:

Once a data item has been read into the computer memory and added to the sum, it is no longer needed in the computer memory.

Thus, each input data item can be read into the same variable. After each item is entered, the value of this variable can be added to SUM, and the next data item can be read into the same variable. This, of course, destroys the previous data item, but it is no longer needed for the computation.

To see how this works, consider what happens if we try to carry out an algorithm consisting solely of the repetition of the steps

 i) Read a data item into the variable named ITEM.

ii) Add the value of ITEM to the value of SUM and store the result in SUM.

To begin, the memory cells ITEM and SUM appear as shown below.

Let us assume that the first three data items are the numbers $+10.0$, -11.0, and $+6.0$. After steps (i) and (ii) are performed the first time, the variables ITEM and SUM will be defined as follows:

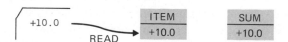

Note that the number 10.0 has now been incorporated into the sum that we are computing, and is no longer required for this problem. We may therefore read the next data item into the variable ITEM. After the second execution of (i) and (ii), we have:

and upon completion of the third execution of (i) and (ii), we obtain:

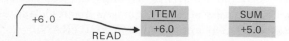

This process continues for all 2000 data items. With each execution of steps (i) and (ii), the data item just read in is used as required by the problem and can be replaced in memory by the next data item.

With this solution to the naming problem, the data table for Problem 2.2 can be rewritten relatively easily. ▌

Revised Data Table for Problem 2.2

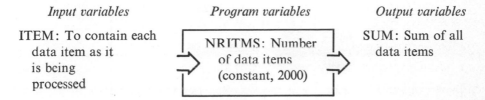

Input variables	*Program variables*	*Output variables*
ITEM: To contain each data item as it is being processed	NRITMS: Number of data items (constant, 2000)	SUM: Sum of all data items

We can also write a Level 1 version of the flow diagram for our algorithm (Fig. 2.6). This diagram reflects the three phases of an algorithm, the *initialization phase*, the *data manipulation phase*, and the *output phase*.

Fig. 2.6   Level-one flow diagram for Problem 2.2.

From this diagram, it is clear what is required in the output phase of the algorithm. However, part of the computation phase (step 20) and the initialization phase (step 10) require further refinement before the program can be written. We will now proceed to further refine step 20. We will see that the initialization phase of the algorithm will necessarily remain unspecified until the refinement of the computation phase has been completed. Only then will we have available enough information to refine the initialization phase.

In order to refine algorithm step 20, we need to have a flow-diagram representation for a sequence of repeated steps. This representation, shown in Fig. 2.7, is called a *loop*.

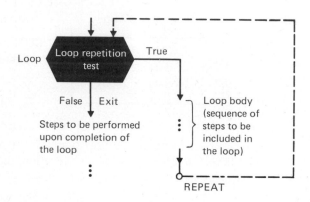

Fig. 2.7 Flow-diagram pattern for a loop.

The *body of the loop* is the sequence of steps that is to be repeated. It is connected to the rest of the flow diagram by an arrow drawn to the right of the diagram. This arrow always points to the first step in the algorithm that is to be repeated in the indicated loop. In Problem 2.2, this is the step to read in a data item. The exit arrow always points to the first step in the algorithm that is to be carried out upon completion of the loop. The dashed line in Fig. 2.7 serves as a reminder that control returns to the loop-repetition test each time the loop body is executed. It is not part of the flow diagram and we shall omit it in later chapters.

How do we know when the loop is complete? More importantly, how can we tell the computer when it has completed the execution of the loop? A human might do it ten or one hundred times and then ask, "Am I done yet?" However, we are developing an algorithm that will eventually take the form of a sequence of steps to be performed by a computer—and, the computer cannot think!! Therefore, if we want to tell it to repeat a sequence of steps, it is not enough to tell it what those steps are. We must also tell the computer when to stop performing these steps. This requires three additional *loop-control steps* in the algorithm:

1. A loop-repetition test;
2. A loop-control initialization step;
3. A loop-control update step.

Normally, each of these steps will involve the manipulation of a *loop-control variable* (LCV), a variable that is used specifically to control loop repetition.

The diagram in Fig. 2.8 shows the relationship among these steps. The loop-repetition condition is always tested prior to each execution of the loop. As long as the condition is true, the loop body and the LCV update will be executed. When the condition becomes false, algorithm execution continues at the point marked exit in the loop pattern. (The LCV update is usually the last step in a loop; however, this is not always the case.)

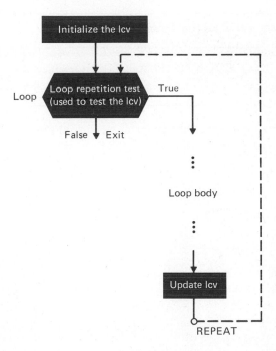

Fig. 2.8 Loop-control steps.

Exactly how the loop-repetition test is constructed depends upon the problem to be solved. For each problem, we must decide how to define the repeat condition to ensure precisely the number of loop executions that we require: no more, and no fewer. For some loops, this is an extremely difficult task; for others it is easy.

Let us examine what is required in defining the loop-control steps in the algorithm for Problem 2.2. Clearly, we want the steps in the loop (the *loop body*) to be executed once for each data item to be input. This means that we must perform the input and summation steps of the loop exactly 2000 times. One way to do this is to use a variable in the program as a *counter* to count the number of data items processed at any point during the execution of the algorithm. This variable will serve as the loop-control variable for the summation loop. The value of the counter will initially be zero, because at the start of the algorithm no cards have been read in. After each data item is read into the computer and processed, the value of the counter will be *incremented* (increased) by one. When this value reaches 2000, we can tell the computer to *exit* from the loop. At this point, 2000 data items will have been read into the computer memory and added to the variable SUM.

To follow this sequence of steps, we should first complete the data table for Problem 2.2. There is an additional program variable entry to be made as shown below.

Additional Program Variables (for Problem 2.2)

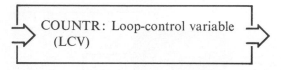

COUNTR: Loop-control variable
(LCV)

Now we can complete the refinement of step 20 in the Level 1 flow diagram of Fig. 2.6. This refinement is shown in Fig. 2.9.

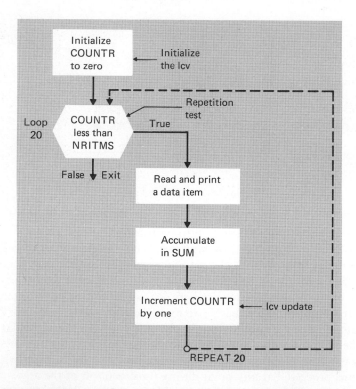

Fig. 2.9   Refinement of step 20 (Fig. 2.6): read data and compute the sum.

COUNTR must be initially set to zero in order to indicate that the loop body has not yet been executed. Otherwise, the loop will not be repeated the correct number of times.

The refinement of step 10 (see Fig. 2.6) is now also clear. SUM must be initially set to zero in order to guarantee that the result in SUM after all cards have been processed is correct. If SUM is not initialized to zero, the result will be incorrect by an amount equal to whatever had been stored in SUM prior to the execution of the program.

The Level 1 flow diagram and refinements for Problem 2.2 are shown in Fig. 2.10. We have numbered those steps requiring refinement and certain other steps for reference purposes.

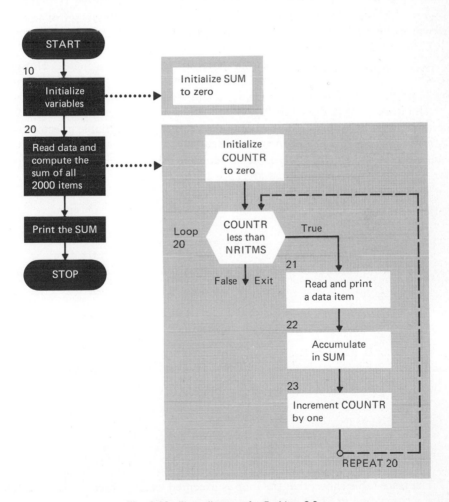

Fig. 2.10 Flow diagrams for Problem 2.2.

2.3.3 Manual Simulation of a Flow Diagram

Once the algorithm and data table for a problem are complete, it is important to verify that the algorithm specifies the sequence of steps required to produce the desired results. This algorithm verification can be carried out by manually *simulating* or *tracing* the sequence of steps indicated by the algorithm. Such traces can often lead to the discovery of a number of logical errors in the flow diagram. The correction of these errors prior to writing the FORTRAN instructions can save considerable effort during the final checkout (or *debugging*) of the FORTRAN program.

Program traces must be done diligently, however, or they are of little use. The flow diagram must be traced carefully, on a step-by-step basis. Changes in variable values must be noted at each step and compared to the expected results of the program. This should be done for at least one carefully chosen set of test data for which the final and intermediate results are determined even before the first-level flow diagram is developed.

It is clear that we cannot trace the program for 2000 data items. However, we will perform the trace assuming NRITMS has the value 3. If the algorithm works properly for this simpler case, it should work for 2000 data items as well.

The trace table is shown in Fig. 2.11. The algorithm step numbers are from the flow diagram in Fig. 2.10. Only the new value of the variable affected by an algorithm step is shown to the right of the step. All other variable values are unchanged. The value of all variables at the start of loop 20 are shown in the first line. The data items being tested are 12.5, 15.0, and -3.5.

Algorithm Step	Variable Affected		
	SUM	COUNTR	ITEM
	0.0	0	unknown
21			12.5
22	12.5		
23		1	
21			15.0
22	27.5		
23		2	
21			—3.5
22	24.0		
23		3	
30	Print the value of SUM, 24.0		

Fig. 2.11 Trace of algorithm in Fig. 2.10.

The trace table shows that the loop is executed exactly three times. The final value accumulated in SUM is 24.0.

EXERCISE 2.3 Carry out a complete trace of the flow diagram shown in Fig. 2.10. Assume NRITMS contains the number 5, and that your data cards are those shown below.

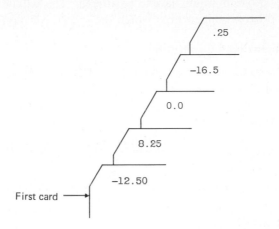

2.4 IMPLEMENTING A FLOW DIAGRAM IN FORTRAN

2.4.1 Integers and In-line Constants for Counting

If we carefully examine the program trace shown in Fig. 2.11, we will see that the numbers read into ITEM are real numbers (containing a decimal point), while the numbers stored in COUNTR are integers. In general, program counters and program constants used in counting operations should be type integer because their values can be represented without a fractional part.

In performing the counting operation, the integer constant one is added to COUNTR each time the loop is repeated. FORTRAN permits us to use constants in-line in executable program statements, as in:

$$COUNTR = COUNTR + 1$$

The use of in-line constants saves us the trouble of having to declare and initialize a memory cell for every constant we wish to use in a program. Instead, the compiler will assume this task for us. When a constant is first encountered by the compiler, it automatically allocates an unused memory cell to hold the value of that constant. The address of this compiler-assigned cell is then used whenever subsequent references to the constant are encountered in the program. Furthermore, the compiler instructs the loader to initialize each memory cell allocated to an in-line constant with the proper value prior to program execution.

We urge you to use some restraint in writing constants in-line to your FORTRAN statements. Constants such as zero and one, which are commonly used in programming for variable initialization and counting, may certainly be written in-line as they are needed. However, it is still better to declare and initialize constants which have special significance in particular problems (NRITMS in

Problem 2.2). Then if it becomes necessary to change the value of such constants because of changes in the problem specification, only the data-initialization statements of the program would have to be altered. This will be much easier than modifying each program statement in which the special constant was used in-line.

2.4.2 Complementing a Condition

To implement the program loop using the basic FORTRAN we have seen so far, we must add a transfer statement immediately after the loop body, which transfers control back to the loop-repetition test. The loop-repetition test must precede the first statement in the loop body.

```
20    (loop-repetition test)
      ---
      ---
      ---            loop body
      ---
      ---
      GO TO 20
```

The loop-repetition test should enable another repetition of the loop body whenever the number of items already processed is less than NRITMS; it should stop loop execution when the number of items processed equals (or exceeds) NRITMS. We can implement this using a conditional transfer statement which causes loop exit by transferring to the first statement after GO TO 20 when the condition (COUNTR .GE. NRITMS) becomes true. With the limited FORTRAN features available to us, it is more convenient to use such a loop-exit condition rather than the loop-repetition condition shown in Fig. 2.10.

The loop-exit condition is the complement of the loop-repetition condition. The *complement* of a condition is defined to be true whenever the condition is false, and vice versa. The complement may be obtained by prefixing the condition with the word "not." Thus, the complement of the condition "X is equal to Y" is "not (X is equal to Y)." This may be restated as "X is not equal to Y." Similarly, the complement of "COUNTR is less than NRITMS" is "not (COUNTR is less than NRITMS)," or "COUNTR is greater than or equal to NRITMS." Table 2.1 shows the complements of the relational operators of FORTRAN.

Table 2.1 Relational operator complements

Relational operator	Complement
Equal .EQ.	Not equal .NE.
Greater than .GT.	Less than or equal .LE.
Less than .LT.	Greater than or equal .GE.
.NE.	.EQ.
.LE.	.GT.
.GE.	.LT.

With these points in mind, we can implement the flow diagrams of Fig. 2.10, as shown in Fig. 2.12.

```
C COMPUTE THE SUM OF 2000 DATA ITEMS
C
      REAL ITEM, SUM
      INTEGER NRITMS, COUNTR
      DATA NRITMS /2000/
C
      SUM = 0.0
C INITIALIZE LOOP CONTROL VARIABLE
      COUNTR = 0
C
C LOOP TO READ DATA AND ACCUMULATE SUM
C LOOP CONTROL VARIABLE TEST
   20 IF (COUNTR .GE. NRITMS) GO TO 30
         READ, ITEM
         PRINT, ITEM
         SUM = SUM + ITEM
C        UPDATE LOOP CONTROL VARIABLE
         COUNTR = COUNTR + 1
         GO TO 20
C
C END OF LOOP - PRINT SUM AND STOP
   30 PRINT, SUM
      STOP
      END
```

Fig. 2.12 Implementation of Fig. 2.10 flow diagram.

The indentation of the statements between labels 20 and 30 aids in identifying the statements that are repeated in the program. This practice will be continued throughout the textbook.

This completes the discussion of Problem 2.2. Note that, in Figs. 2.10 and 2.12 we have both a flow diagram and a FORTRAN program, which contain the description of a repeated sequence of steps, and we only had to write this sequence of steps once. We have therefore achieved the goal described earlier, and we have done so using some very simple flow-diagram structures and the basic FORTRAN statements introduced in Chapter 1. In the next chapter, we will see how to write loops and decisions in FORTRAN in a more natural way, without the use of labels and transfers.

2.4.3 Solving the Most General Case of a Problem

Suppose that you are asked to solve Problem 2.2 for 20,000 data items instead of 2000; or for 1995 items; or for 10 data items. Will the approach just taken work here too? The answer, of course, is *yes*. In fact, the only change that we must make in each case is in the data-initialization statement for the variable NRITMS in the FORTRAN program.

It is often advantageous to be able to develop algorithms and write programs in the fullest possible generality, so that the most general case of a problem can be solved using the program with no alteration whatsoever. In such full generality, the FORTRAN program for Problem 2.2 would compute the sum for an arbitrary, but pre-specified, number of data items. In this case, NRITMS should be treated as a program variable (rather than a constant) to be read in by the program at the beginning of execution. In this way, a collection of data of arbitrary size may be processed by the same program, as long as the first item input to the computer is the *number of items* in this data collection.

To accomplish this, we must insert, as the first card in the data-card section, a card containing the number of data items to be processed (2000 in this case). The statement

DATA NRITMS /2000/

in the program of Fig. 2.12 should be removed, and the pair of statements

READ, NRITMS
PRINT, NRITMS

should be inserted in the initialization section of the program (before SUM = 0.0). The form of the data-card deck for the revised program follows:

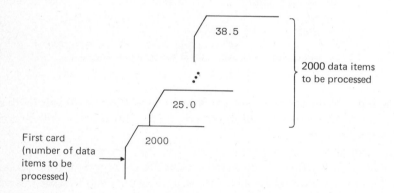

EXERCISE 2.4   Write the flow diagram for a loop to read in a collection of seven data items, and compute the product of all nonzero items in the collection, and print the final product. Check your flow diagram with a hand simulation.

2.4.4   Character-String Constants as Output Identifiers

Often we wish to annotate the output values printed by our program so that we can identify which variable values they represent. This can be accomplished through the use of a character-string constant. We will learn more about character strings in Chapter 4, but for the present it would be useful to know how to use them to clarify our program output.

A *character-string constant* is a sequence of symbols enclosed in apostrophes. In some compilers, we can insert these constants directly into FORTRAN print statements in order to provide descriptive messages or column headers in the program output. The character string will be displayed exactly as it is keypunched (with the apostrophes removed).

Example 2.2 The output for Problem 2.2 consists of a single-column list of each data item read, and the sum and the average of these items. We could use the print statements below to produce annotated output for this problem:

```
      SUM = 0.0
      PRINT, 'LIST OF INPUT DATA'
C INITIALIZE LOOP CONTROL VARIABLE
      COUNTR = 0
C
C LOOP TO READ DATA AND ACCUMULATE SUM
C LOOP CONTROL VARIABLE TEST
   20 IF (COUNTR .GE. NRITMS) GO TO 30
         READ, ITEM
         PRINT, ITEM
         SUM = SUM + ITEM
C UPDATE LOOP CONTROL VARIABLE
         COUNTR = COUNTR + 1
         GO TO 20
C
C END OF LOOP - PRINT SUM AND STOP
   30 PRINT, 'THE SUM OF THE ITEMS IS ', SUM
      STOP
      END
```

The output produced by these print statements is shown in Fig. 2.13, for the data sample used in Exercise 2.3, with NRITMS assumed to be 5.

```
            LIST OF INPUT DATA
               -12.50
                 8.25
                 0.00
               -16.50
                  .25
            THE SUM OF THE ITEMS IS -20.5
```

Fig. 2.13 Problem 2.2 annotated output for data sample of Exercise 2.3.

A close examination of the output for Example 2.2 reveals the following important points:

1. All character strings to be used as messages or column headers must appear in the print statement enclosed in apostrophes.

2. Character strings may appear in a print statement by themselves, or in combination with variable names. The combination of character strings and

variable names together constitute an *output list*. Each element of the list must be separated from the others through the use of a comma. The comma merely serves to separate list items; it is never printed.

Example 2.3 If the variables GROSS and NET have values 135.00 and 110.00 respectively, then the statement

```
PRINT, 'GROSS SALARY = ', GROSS, 'NET PAY = ', NET
```

would produce the annotated output

```
GROSS SALARY =      135.00   NET PAY =      110.00
```

The number of spaces before and after the numbers 135.00 and 110.00 is a function of the particular compiler being used.

2.5 DEBUGGING A FORTRAN PROGRAM

The process of removing errors or "bugs" from a program is called *debugging*. You will find that a substantial portion of the time you spend programming is used for debugging. The debugging time can be reduced if you follow the steps outlined in this chapter faithfully, without taking any shortcuts.

This approach requires a careful analysis of the problem description, the identification of the input and output data for the problem, and the development of a data table and the flow diagrams for the problem solution. The algorithm development should proceed on a step-by-step basis, beginning with an outline of the algorithm in the form of a Level 1 flow diagram. Additional algorithm detail (flow-diagram refinements) should be provided as needed, until enough detail has been added so that writing the program is virtually a mechanical process. The data table should be updated during the refinement process, so that all variables and important constants used in the algorithm are listed and clearly defined in the table.

Once the algorithm and data table are complete, a systematic hand simulation (or trace) of the flow diagrams, using one or two representative sets of data, can help eliminate many bugs before they show up during the execution of your program. When the hand trace is complete, the program may be written, by following the data table and the refined flow diagrams, and then keypunched. Before submitting your program, it is worth devoting an extra few minutes to check that there are no obvious errors in your keypunched program, control, or data cards.

If you have constructed and refined your flow diagrams properly, and carefully and completely traced their operation, there should not be any program logic errors. The only errors you should have to contend with are syntax errors caused by keypunching mistakes or unfamiliarity with the syntax rules of FORTRAN. The error diagnostics generated by the compiler should help you detect and correct these errors.

If your program runs but does not produce the desired results, you may be using an undefined variable in a computation, or perhaps there is an error in logic. If there was not enough output information printed in your first run, it is often worthwhile to make an extra debugging run in which all pertinent variable values are printed at different steps in the execution of your program. This will help in determining what is wrong and in pinpointing the location of an undefined variable or a logic error. (Some compilers have special diagnostic tracing facilities.)

If there is a logic error, go back to your flow diagrams, modify the steps which you believe are in error, and then completely retrace the execution of the modified algorithm. This last step is extremely important and one that is often overlooked. Each algorithm change may have important side effects which are difficult to anticipate. Making what seems to be an obvious correction in one step of the algorithm may cause another step of the algorithm to operate improperly and produce several new errors. The only way to establish that there are no side effects is to systematically retrace the revised flow diagrams.

Once the revised flow diagrams have been checked out, write the new program statements that are needed, and keypunch and rerun your program. There is always a temptation to save time and make your changes directly in the program without first going back to the flow diagrams. If you resist this temptation, you will normally be better off in the long run.

2.6 SUMMARY AND REVIEW

In the first part of this chapter we outlined a method for solving problems on the computer. This method stresses six points:

1. Understand the problem given.
2. Identify the input and output data for the problem as well as other relevant data.
3. Formulate a precise statement of the problem.
4. Develop an algorithm.
5. Refine the algorithm.
6. Implement the algorithm in FORTRAN.

So far, we have not examined any problems of sufficient complexity to warrant a detailed refinement of a portion of an algorithm.

In the remainder of the chapter, we introduced the flow-diagram representation of the various steps in an algorithm. Flow diagrams provide a graphical representation of an algorithm consisting of a number of specially shaped boxes, and arrows, as well as several *patterns* of boxes and arrows used to describe decision steps and loops. These boxes and patterns are summarized in Fig. 2.14.

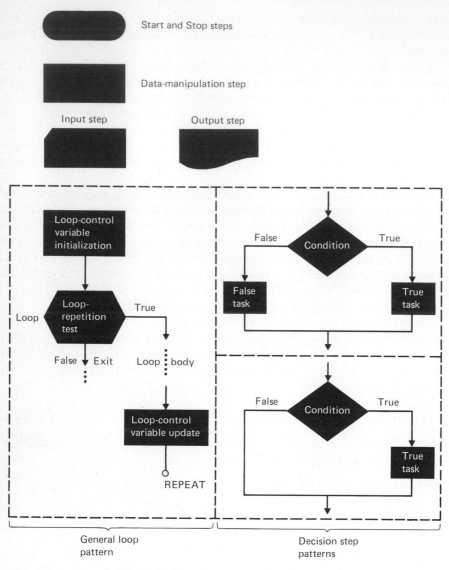

Fig. 2.14 Flow-diagram symbols and patterns.

While algorithms consist of three phases: initialization of variables, data manipulation, and output of results, the data-manipulation phase is most critical. This phase can be started once the input data and desired problem outputs have been clearly defined, and a precise understanding of the problem has been achieved. The initialization of variable values that is required usually depends on the particular method chosen to perform the data manipulation.

Often, additional entries are made to the data table as the data-manipulation phase progresses. For example, in Problem 2.2, the need for the program variable

COUNTR was not readily apparent until the algorithm for manipulating the data was chosen. Furthermore, it was not until this point that the need to initialize SUM and COUNTR to zero became obvious, and could be added to the algorithm.

The flow diagram is quite helpful in this respect. We can first concentrate our efforts on describing the primary data-manipulation algorithm, and then later add whatever initialization is required, without having to rearrange or relabel any of the data-manipulation steps.

Flow diagrams also provide a convenient form of representation of the loop and decision steps of an algorithm. By using these patterns we can maintain a clear separation between the relevant control information in a loop or decision step, and the steps to be carried out subject to this control.

In the next chapter we will provide convenient forms for FORTRAN representation of loop and decision steps based upon the flow-diagram patterns just described. Use of these forms will enable us to translate our flow-diagram representations of algorithms into FORTRAN programs with a minimum of effort. This will enable us to solve some relatively complex problems on the computer, using programs that clearly reflect the careful planning and organization used in our algorithm development.

PROGRAMMING PROBLEMS

2.3 Given the bank balance in your checking account for the past month and all the transactions in your account for the current month, write a program* for an algorithm to compute and print your checking-account balance at the end of the current month. You may assume that the total number of transactions for the current month is known ahead of time. [*Hint.* Your first data card should contain your checking-account balance at the end of last month. The second card should contain the number of transactions for the current month. All subsequent cards should represent the amount of each transaction for the current month.]

2.4 Write a program* for an algorithm to compute the factorial, $N!$, of a single arbitrary integer N. ($N! = N \times (N - 1) \times \cdots 2 \times 1$). Your program should read and print the value of N and print N! when done.

2.5 If N contains an integer, then we can compute X^N for any X, simply by multiplying X by itself $N - 1$ times. Write a program* to read in a value of X and a value of N, and compute X^N via repeated multiplications. Test your program for

$$X = 6.0, \qquad N = 4$$
$$X = 2.5, \qquad N = 6$$
$$X = -8.0, \qquad N = 5$$

2.6 [Continuation of Problem 2.5.]

a) How many multiplications are required in your program for Problem 2.5 in order to compute X^9? Can you figure out a way of computing X^9 in fewer multiplications?

---

* Provide a data table and flow diagram for each problem.

b) Can you generalize your algorithm for computing X^9 to compute X^N for any positive N?

c) Can you use your algorithm in part (b) to compute X^{-N} for any positive N? How?

2.7 Green Thumb brand grass seed costs $3.20 per pound, and one pound will cover 500 square feet. Write a program that will compute and print the number of pounds of seed and total cost to cover areas between 0 and 10,000 square feet, in steps of 250. Your program should read in the cost per pound of the seed and the coverage rate per pound, and then print a table, as shown below.

Area in square feet	Amount of seed (pounds)	Total cost
0	0.00	0.00
250	⋮	—
500	⋮	—
⋮	⋮	⋮
9500	—	—
9750	—	—
10000	—	—

(If you are working in the metric system, use the following figures:

  Seed cost: $7.05 per kilogram

  Area of coverage for one kilogram: 0.2 square meters

Print your table of kilograms of seed and total cost to cover areas of from 0 to 2000 square meters in steps of 50.)

2.8 Your neighbor owns a large drugstore chain in a state which has just raised its sales tax to 5 percent, effective in 3 days. He needs to produce copies of the new tax tables for his sales people and checkers. Write a program to produce a new tax-rate table, as shown below.

Purchase amount	Tax amount
0.00–0.09	0.00
0.10–0.29	0.01
0.30–0.49	0.02
0.50–0.69	0.03
0.70–0.89	0.04
0.90–1.09	0.05
1.10–1.29	0.06
⋮	⋮
9.50–9.69	0.48
9.70–9.89	0.49
9.90–10.09	0.50

BASIC
CONTROL
STRUCTURES

3

3.1 Introduction to Control Structures

3.2 Decision Structures

3.3 The WHILE Loop Structure

3.4 Reminders for Algorithm Development Using the WHILE Loop

3.5 The Widget Inventory-Control Problem

3.6 Common Programming Errors

3.7 Summary

Programming Problems

3.1 INTRODUCTION TO CONTROL STRUCTURES

Translation performed by the FORTRAN compiler eliminates a tremendous amount of highly detailed work that we would otherwise have to do ourselves in writing machine-language programs. We have already seen how the use of meaningful names and symbols, rather than machine-language encodings, can simplify the programming process. In addition, the few FORTRAN programs we have seen are clearly easier to understand because of our familiarity with the names and symbols used in the programs.

Despite these vast improvements, our work is far from complete, for the FORTRAN language has many additional features that can make programming even easier. As you learn more of the features of FORTRAN, you will discover that the programs you write will more closely mirror your English-language descriptions of how to solve a problem. You will also see that the process of translating the flow-diagram representation of an algorithm into a FORTRAN program will become easier because fewer levels of flow-diagram refinement will be required for you to write your programs.

You might conclude from this that the development of correct, precise algorithms is a rather important part of using the computer to solve problems. You are right! Furthermore, the English descriptions of these algorithms are most critical, for if these descriptions are incorrect or imprecise, all further refinements as well as the resulting programs will reflect these maladies. Therefore, as we introduce new features of FORTRAN, we will continue to emphasize algorithm development through the use of the flow diagram.

3.1.1 Standard and Nonstandard FORTRAN

In Chapter 1 we mentioned that programs written in higher-level languages such as FORTRAN are considerably more portable than machine-language programs. That is, they can be moved from one computer to another with relative ease provided the appropriate compiler is available on the new computer.

To help ensure a high degree of portability for FORTRAN programs, a standard has been developed for the FORTRAN language, which defines the syntax rules for a minimal set of FORTRAN features that must be available on all compilers. Unfortunately, the FORTRAN standard which is currently in use was developed in 1966, and does not contain many new features that programmers often find useful. As a result, many compiler designers have added certain *nonstandard features* to facilitate programming in FORTRAN. An example of such nonstandard features are the read and print statements that we have been using. These are called *format-free input and output statements*, and they are described in detail in Chapter 4. Standard FORTRAN requires the use of *formatted input and output statements*, which are discussed in Chapter 8.

While these nonstandard features make it more convenient to program in FORTRAN, they reduce the portability of a program in which they are used.

Since there are no standard syntax rules for these features, they are often implemented in different ways on different compilers. Because of this, we will introduce only those nonstandard features that are generally accepted and widely used. We will clearly indicate any nonstandard features discussed, so that you will be aware of the fact that these features may not correspond to what is available on your compiler.

3.1.2 Review: Loops and Decisions

In the first two chapters we saw how decision steps and loops could be described using flow diagrams and some very basic FORTRAN statements. In the flow diagram, special patterns were used to represent decision steps and loops. In FORTRAN, we used the conditional statement (IF statement) and the transfer (GO TO statement) to implement decisions and loops. In this chapter, we will introduce three new FORTRAN language features, called *control structures*, which also can be used to implement decisions and loops. These structures are not included in Standard FORTRAN, but are part of an extension to the language that has been developed specifically to improve the programming environment provided by FORTRAN. This extension is often referred to as *Structured FORTRAN*. Not all computer installations have translators for Structured FORTRAN, and of those that do, many have differing syntactic rules of formation for their control structures.

For the purpose of illustration we will provide a syntactic prototype for each structure. These prototypes are very similar to the structures found in WATFIV-S (a widely used, student-oriented FORTRAN compiler) and are easily adapted to the particular syntax used at each computer installation. We believe it would be best to flow-diagram your algorithms in terms of the control structures introduced in this chapter, and then implement these structures using whatever syntax is available at your installation. If your computer center does not have a version of Structured FORTRAN, you will have to translate the flow-diagram structures yourself into Standard FORTRAN statements. This is a relatively simple and mechanical process, which we will illustrate in this chapter.

3.1.3 Statement Groups

Prior to examining the new control structures, we shall introduce the concept of a *statement group*. A statement group is a sequence of statements in a program which together define a particular algorithm step or task to be performed by the computer. A program itself is a statement group describing a task to be performed. Within the program, there are usually a number of subtasks to be performed. For example, the body of a loop describes a subtask to be carried out. The sequence of statements to be executed if a condition is true also describes a subtask.

In the example given in Fig. 3.1, there are four statement groups, including the entire list of statements.

```
       ⎧  ① ⎧  SUM = 0.0
       ⎪     ⎩  COUNTR = 0
       ⎪    ⎧ 20 IF (COUNTR .GE. NRITMS) GO TO 30
       ⎪    ⎪      READ, ITEM
    ④ ⎨  ② ⎨      PRINT, ITEM
       ⎪    ⎪      SUM = SUM + ITEM
       ⎪    ⎪      COUNTR = COUNTR + 1
       ⎪    ⎩      GO TO 20
       ⎪  ③ ⎧ 30 PRINT, SUM
       ⎩     ⎩      STOP
```

Fig. 3.1 Statement groups for Problem 2.2 program.

Statement group ① is always executed. On the other hand, statement group ③ is executed only when the condition COUNTR .GE. NRITMS becomes true; otherwise, statement group ② is executed. The statement group ② forms a loop that will be executed as long as COUNTR is less than NRITMS.

Note that every statement in the above list appears in at least one statement group and that statement groups are either separate from one another (①, ③) or *nested* (completely contained one within another) (②, ④). In fact, statement groups ① and ③ are also nested within ④, since every statement in any of these groups is also a statement in group ④.

It is important to be able to identify the individual statement groups within a program and to associate each statement group with a particular task or subtask to be performed by the program. The identification of these tasks is of considerable help in understanding a program, in correlating the program with the flow diagram, and in finding and correcting logical errors that may exist. The FORTRAN features to be discussed in this chapter will not only simplify the job of programming but will also make the logical organization of your program more apparent, making it easier for you to identify the various statement groups in the program.

EXERCISE 3.1 Provide English descriptions of the tasks performed in statement groups ①, ②, ③, and ④ of Fig. 3.1. (One or two sentences for each description should be sufficient. See Problem 2.2 for help, if necessary.)

3.2 DECISION STRUCTURES

3.2.1 Decision Structures with One and Two Alternatives

In this section we will be concerned with the FORTRAN structures used to represent the single- and double-alternative flow-diagram patterns described in Chapter 2.

In the double-alternative decision structure (Fig. 3.2(b)), if the condition is true, the algorithm steps specified by $Task_T$ are carried out; otherwise, the steps specified by $Task_F$ are performed. Exactly one of the paths from the condition

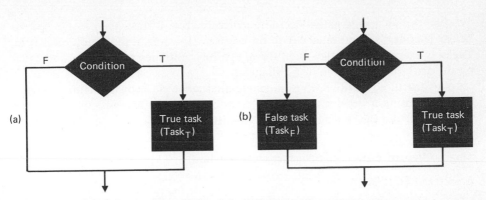

Fig. 3.2 (a) Single- and (b) double-alternative decision-step patterns.

test will be taken. Execution will then continue at the point indicated by the arrow at the bottom of the diagram. $Task_F$ and $Task_T$ may each consist of a number of different boxes and flow-diagram patterns. In general, however, it is a good idea to keep these task descriptions simple, and refine them in a separate diagram if additional details are needed.

The Structured FORTRAN prototype for the double-alternative structure is described in Fig. 3.3.

Double-Alternative Decision Structure (Nonstandard)

Structured FORTRAN Form:

```
IF (condition) THEN
    ___  ___  ⎫
    ___  ___  ⎪  Statement
    ___  ___  ⎬  group S_T
    ___  ___  ⎪
    ___  ___  ⎭
ELSE
    ___  ___  ⎫  Statement
    ___  ___  ⎬  group S_F
    ___  ___  ⎭
ENDIF
```

Interpretation. The condition is evaluated. If the condition is true, then the statement group S_T is executed (and S_F is skipped). Otherwise, S_F is executed (and S_T is skipped).

Note. The statement group S_T corresponds to $Task_T$ in the flow diagram in Fig. 3.2. Similarly, S_F corresponds to $Task_F$.

Fig. 3.3 Double-alternative decision structure.

For the single-alternative decision structure (Fig. 3.2(a)), there is no task to be carried out if the indicated condition is false. However, if the condition is true, $Task_T$ is executed. In either case, the algorithm continues at the point indicated by the arrow at the bottom of the diagram.

In Structured FORTRAN, the single-alternative decision structure is represented by using a degenerate form of the double-alternative structure, with the word ELSE and the statement group S_F omitted (Fig. 3.4).

Single-Alternative Decision Structure (Nonstandard)

Structured FORTRAN Form:

```
IF (condition) THEN
   --- ---  ⎫
   --- ---  ⎬  Statement
   --- ---  ⎪  group S_T
   --- ---  ⎭
ENDIF
```

Interpretation. The condition is evaluated. If the condition is true, then the entire statement group S_T will be executed. If the condition is false, then S_T will be skipped, and execution will continue with the first statement following the ENDIF.

Note. The statement group S_T is the list of FORTRAN statements required to instruct the computer to carry out the steps in $Task_T$ of the flow-diagram pattern in Fig. 3.2.

Fig. 3.4 Single-alternative decision structure.

In both the single- and double-alternative decision structures, the statement IF (condition) THEN is called the *header statement* of the structure. The statement ENDIF is called the *terminator statement*. These statements mark the beginning and the end of the statement group, respectively. For each structure header used in a program, a terminator statement must appear somewhere below the header statement.

We have already seen an example of the use of the double-alternative decision structure in the flow diagram of Fig. 2.3 (computation of NET). This decision step can be implemented in Structured FORTRAN as:

```
IF (GROSS .GT. MIN) THEN
   NET = GROSS - TAX
ELSE
   NET = GROSS
ENDIF
```

The statement groups in this structure have been indented in order to improve readability. Some compilers will automatically perform this indentation when listing a program. If your compiler does not, we suggest that you indent the statement groups inside control structures when keypunching your program.

Another example of the use of the double-alternative decision structure is shown in Problem 3.1.

PROBLEM 3.1 Read two numbers into the variables X and Y and compute and print the quotient QUOT = X/Y.

Data Table for Problem 3.1

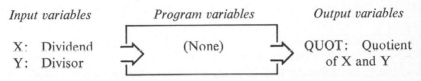

Input variables	Program variables	Output variables
X: Dividend	(None)	QUOT: Quotient
Y: Divisor		of X and Y

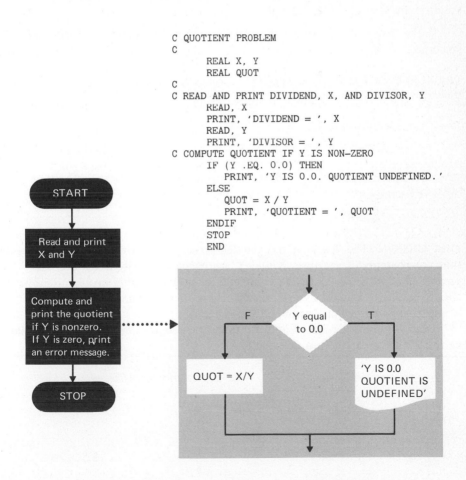

```
C QUOTIENT PROBLEM
C
      REAL X, Y
      REAL QUOT
C
C READ AND PRINT DIVIDEND, X, AND DIVISOR, Y
      READ, X
      PRINT, 'DIVIDEND = ', X
      READ, Y
      PRINT, 'DIVISOR = ', Y
C COMPUTE QUOTIENT IF Y IS NON-ZERO
      IF (Y .EQ. 0.0) THEN
          PRINT, 'Y IS 0.0. QUOTIENT UNDEFINED.'
      ELSE
          QUOT = X / Y
          PRINT, 'QUOTIENT = ', QUOT
      ENDIF
      STOP
      END
```

Fig. 3.5   Flow diagram and FORTRAN program for Problem 3.1.

DISCUSSION This is a problem that looks quite straightforward, but it has the potential for disaster hidden between the lines of the problem statement. In this case, as in many others, the potential trouble spot is due to unanticipated values of input data—values for which one or more of the data manipulations required by the problem are not defined.

In this problem, the quotient X/Y is not defined mathematically if Y equals 0.0. If we instruct the computer to perform the calculation X/Y in this case, it will either produce an unpredictable, meaningless result, or it will not even be able to complete the operation and will prematurely terminate or *abort* our program. Most computers will provide the programmer with a diagnostic message if division by zero is attempted, but some will not. In order to avoid the problem entirely, we will have our program test for a divisor of zero and print a message of its own if this situation should occur. The flow diagram and FORTRAN program for this solution are shown in Fig. 3.5. ▌

In the next problem, we will illustrate the use of the single-alternative decision structure.

PROBLEM 3.2 Read two numbers into variables X and Y and compare them. Place the larger in X and the smaller in Y.

Data Table for Problem 3.2

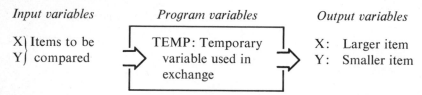

Input variables	Program variables	Output variables
X⎱ Items to be Y⎰ compared	TEMP: Temporary variable used in exchange	X: Larger item Y: Smaller item

DISCUSSION The flow diagram for this program is shown in Fig. 3.6. Note that the contents of variables X and Y are exchanged only if the condition "Y greater than X" is true. In the completed program for this problem (shown in Fig. 3.7), this exchange is implemented using an additional variable, TEMP, in which a copy of the initial value of X is saved.

To verify the need for TEMP, we trace the program execution for the data-card deck shown at the top of page 78.

Program Trace	Variables Affected		
FORTRAN statements	X	Y	TEMP
READ, X	3.5		
READ, Y		7.2	
TEMP = X			3.5
X = Y	7.2		
Y = TEMP		3.5	

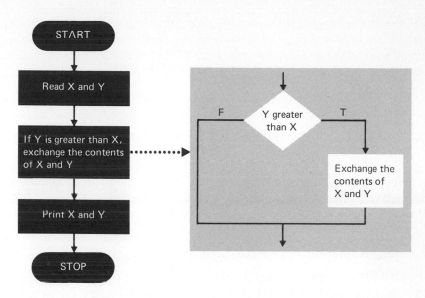

Fig. 3.6 Flow diagram for determining the largest of two numbers (Problem 3.2).

```
C LARGEST OF TWO NUMBERS PROBLEM
C
      REAL X, Y
      REAL TEMP
C
C READ DATA AND PRINT
      READ, X
      PRINT, 'X = ', X
      READ, Y
      PRINT, 'Y = ', Y
C
C TEST AND SWITCH IF NECESSARY
      IF (Y .GT. X) THEN
         TEMP = X
         X = Y
         Y = TEMP
      ENDIF
C
C PRINT RESULTS
      PRINT, 'LARGEST = ', X
      PRINT, 'SMALLEST = ', Y
      STOP
      END
```

Fig. 3.7 Program for Problem 3.2.

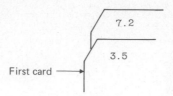

First card

As indicated in the trace, following the execution of the statement

$$X = Y$$

the value 3.5 is no longer available in X.   Previously, copying X into TEMP
prevented this value from being lost.   ▮

3.2.2 Single-Alternative Decision with One Dependent Statement

Very often, the statement group S_T of a single-alternative decision structure will
consist of only one FORTRAN statement.   In such cases, the use of the single-
alternative structure header and terminator becomes a burden; and the FORTRAN
conditional statement introduced in Chapter 1 can be used instead.

Example 3.1 The accompanying flow diagram can be implemented in FORTRAN using
the structure

```
IF (X .GT. LARGE) THEN
    LARGE = X
ENDIF
```

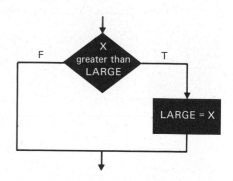

or the conditional statement

```
IF (X .GT. LARGE) LARGE = X
```

EXERCISE 3.2 Flow-diagram the decisions stated below, using either single- or double-
alternative decision structures.

a) Read a number into the variable NMBR.   If this number is positive, add one to the
contents of NPOS.   If the number is not positive, add one to the contents of NNEG.

b) Read a number into NMBR.   If NMBR is zero, add one to the contents of NZERO.

c) (A combination of (a) and (b)) Read a number into NMBR. If NMBR is positive, add one to NPOS; if NMBR is negative, add one to NNEG; and if NMBR is zero, add one to NZERO.

EXERCISE 3.3 The statement group in the decision structure of the program for Problem 3.2 contains three statements and uses an additional variable TEMP. Could we have accomplished the same task performed by this group with either of the statement groups

```
a) X = Y      or    b) TEMP = Y
   Y = X              X = TEMP
                      Y = X
```

What values would be stored in X and Y after these statement groups execute? Modify statement group (b) so that it works properly.

EXERCISE 3.4 Convert the following English descriptions of algorithms to flow diagrams and FORTRAN statement groups, using the single- and double-alternative decision structures or the conditional statement.

i) If the remainder (REM) is equal to zero, then print N.

ii) If the product (PROD) is equal to N, then print the contents of the variable DIV and read a new value into N.

iii) If the number of traffic lights (NBRLTE) exceeds 25.0, then compute the gallons required (GALREQ) as total miles (MILES) divided by 14.0. Otherwise compute GALREQ as MILES divided by 22.5.

EXERCISE 3.5 Let X, Y, Z be three variables containing information produced by earlier computations in a program. Write a flow diagram and FORTRAN program segment for finding and printing the largest of the numbers in X, Y, and Z.

*3.2.3 Compiler Role for Decision Structures

You will note that the single-alternative decision structure contains no explicit transfer instructions, yet the only way the computer can alter the order in which it executes instructions is through the use of a transfer. It is the function of the compiler to translate the single-alternative decision structure into a sequence of machine-language instructions, with the appropriate transfers, that can be carried out by the computer.

To understand the compiler role, we must recall the meaning of the single-alternative decision structure. The structure specifies the conditional execution of a statement group S_T. If the given condition is true, then S_T is executed. Otherwise, S_T is skipped, and execution continues beginning with the first statement following the structure.

To illustrate this sequence of steps, we have written the control structure for Problem 3.2, together with its translation.

---

* This section is optional.

Original Structure	Translation
| ```
IF (Y .GT. X) THEN
    TEMP = X
    X = Y
    Y = TEMP
ENDIF
next statement
``` | ```
       IF (Y .LE. X) GO TO 10000
           TEMP = X
           X = Y
           Y = TEMP
10000  CONTINUE
       next statement
``` |

This shows the compiler translation of the single-alternative decision structure using basic FORTRAN statements. Each FORTRAN statement (except the CONTINUE) used in the translated version represents one of the basic operations of the computer, as discussed in Chapter 1. (The CONTINUE statement does not represent a computer operation; it serves solely as a placeholder statement for attaching the label indicating the end of statement group S_T.) We will employ this technique to demonstrate the compiler translation of all control structures discussed in this book. You should remember, however, that the compiler will not produce basic FORTRAN but will generate the encodings of these basic operations in machine language.

The double-alternative decision structure must also be translated into the basic operations of the computer with the appropriate transfers.

For an example of this translation, we examine the FORTRAN instructions for part of Problem 3.1.

Original structure	Translation
| ```
IF (Y .EQ. 0.0) THEN
    PRINT, 'Y is 0.0...'       } S_T {
ELSE
    QUOT = X/Y
    PRINT, 'QUOTIENT=', QUOT)  } S_F {
ENDIF
STOP
``` | ```
       IF (Y .NE. 0.0) GO TO 10000
           PRINT, 'Y is 0.0...'
           GO TO 10001
10000      QUOT = X/Y
           PRINT, 'QUOTIENT=', QUOT
10001  CONTINUE
       STOP
``` |

The double-alternative decision structure specifies the conditional execution of one of two statement groups, S_T or S_F. As indicated in the translation example, the complement of the structure condition is used in the translation. If the complement is false (the original condition is true), then S_T is executed and S_F is skipped. A labeled CONTINUE statement must be placed after S_F so that control can be transferred here (skipping S_F) after S_T is executed. If the complement condition is true, S_T is skipped (the GO TO 10000 is executed), and S_F is executed.

EXERCISE 3.6 Write equivalent FORTRAN statements for the conditions described below. Also write equivalent FORTRAN statements for the complements of these conditions.

X is less than Y; A is greater than ZERO; ITEM is not equal to SNTVAL; COUNT is less than NRITMS.

*3.2.4 Implementing Decision Structures in Standard FORTRAN

Even if the version of FORTRAN available to you does not have decision structures, you should still continue to develop algorithms using the IF–THEN and IF–THEN–ELSE flow-diagram patterns. You can implement these algorithms by manually carrying out the translation shown in the previous section.   The translation steps are listed below.

1. Choose a statement number sn_1 not used in the program to use for control transfer.
2. Using the complement of the condition in the flow-diagram decision step, write the statement

   ```
   IF (complement of condition) GO TO sn1
   ```
3. Write the statements for statement group S_T (corresponding to the true task).
4. For a single-alternative decision: complete the translation by placing the statement

   ```
   sn1 CONTINUE
   ```

   immediately after the last statement in S_T.

   For a double-alternative decision: choose an unused statement number sn_2 and add the statement

   ```
   GO TO sn2
   ```

   after the last statement in S_T. Then attach the label sn_1 to the first statement in S_F and list the statements in S_F.
5. For a double-alternative decision: add the statement

   ```
   sn2 CONTINUE
   ```

   immediately after the last statement in S_F.

3.2.5 Additional Remarks

The decision structures described earlier provide a more natural way of representing decision steps in FORTRAN. These structures free us from using explicit transfer instructions and labels in order to skip certain groups of statements. Instead, we simply enclose within the decision structure the relevant statement groups that most closely mirror the description of the original algorithm and let the compiler generate the needed transfer instructions.   This simplifies the programming process and provides more readable programs, which are less likely to contain careless errors.

---

* This section is optional.

3.3 THE WHILE LOOP STRUCTURE

3.3.1 Introduction

We will now turn our attention to control structures that are useful for describing loops. There are a number of different loop-control structures, but we will confine our attention to two of the most fundamental of these structures. One of these, the WHILE loop structure, will be the subject of the remainder of this chapter. A brief introduction to a second loop structure, the Indexed–DO, will be given in the next chapter. This structure will be discussed in more detail in Chapter 6.

If you review previous discussions about loops, you will note that all loops consist of two parts: a *loop body*, or sequence of algorithm steps that must be repeated, and a *loop control*. The loop control is used to specify the number of times a loop must be executed or, alternatively, to specify some condition under which the loop is to be repeated or terminated.

For example, in the algorithm for Problem 2.2 (shown again in Fig. 3.8), there are two steps comprising the loop body. The first step reads a data item into the variable ITEM, and the second step adds the contents of ITEM to the variable SUM. The loop control in Fig. 3.8 consists of the steps to initialize COUNTR to zero, increment COUNTR by one, and compare the value of the counter to the number of data items.

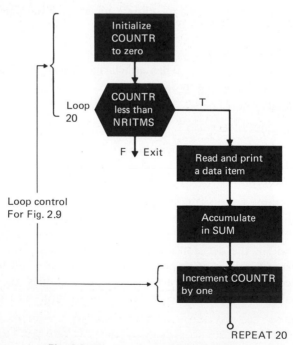

Fig. 3.8 The loop pattern for Problem 2.2.

It is to our advantage to have an effective means for maintaining a clear separation between the body and control portions of a loop. This is true for both the flow diagram and the FORTRAN program. Once the need for a loop is recognized, it is often helpful to first decide precisely what steps of an algorithm must be repeated in the body of the loop, and then worry about defining the appropriate loop control.

The loop structures that will be introduced here and in later chapters will be useful to varying degrees in helping to maintain the appropriate separation between loop body and loop control. Each of these structures provides facilities for specifying some or all of the loop-control information at the head or beginning of the loop. The more elementary loop structures allow, at most, the repeat condition to be specified at the loop head. However, the more powerful loop structures allow the specification in the loop header of all relevant loop-control information.

The loop structures will also make the identification of loops in the program itself easier because they will enable us to identify the entire range of these loops at a glance. We will have little difficulty locating the beginning and ending statements of loops written using the loop structures.

3.3.2 WHILE Loop Flow-Diagram Pattern and Syntax

The first loop-control structure that we will examine is called a WHILE loop. The flow diagram for this structure is shown in Fig. 2.7 and is repeated here for convenience, with the word WHILE added to the loop-repetition test box. (See Fig. 3.9.)

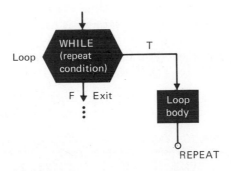

Fig. 3.9 The WHILE loop pattern.

The repeat condition is evaluated prior to the execution of the loop body. As long as (while) the condition is true, the loop body is repeated. Once the condition becomes false, loop execution terminates, and the algorithm continues at the point marked exit. It is important to remember that the loop-repetition test for the WHILE structure is at the beginning of the loop. The loop body will not be executed at all if the repeat condition is false the first time that the repetition test is encountered. The general form of the WHILE loop is shown in Fig. 3.10.

WHILE loop structure (Nonstandard)
Structured FORTRAN form:

```
WHILE (condition) DO
    ___ ___ ⎞ Loop body
    ___ ___ ⎪ statement
    ___ ___ ⎬ group S
    ___ ___ ⎠
ENDWHILE
```

Interpretation. The condition is evaluated first. If the condition is true, then the loop body will be executed. This sequence is repeated as long as the condition evaluates to true. If the condition is false, the loop body will be skipped, and execution will continue with the statement following the ENDWHILE.

Fig. 3.10 The WHILE loop structure.

Normally, when a WHILE control structure is used in a program, a particular variable may be identified as the *loop-control variable*. The loop-control variable is the variable whose value is continually tested in the repeat condition. In order for the repeat condition to correctly determine the number of executions of the loop body, the loop-control variable must be *initialized* prior to the start of the WHILE structure. Also, within the loop body, the value of the loop-control variable should be *updated* (modified) with each loop execution; otherwise, the repeat condition will always produce the same test result, and the loop exit may never occur. The updating of the loop variable is usually the last step within the loop body.

This loop control can be illustrated by rewriting the loop portion of the algorithm for Problem 2.2 (see Fig. 2.12) using a WHILE structure.

```
C INITIALIZE LOOP CONTROL VARIABLE
      COUNTR = 0
C
C LOOP TO READ DATA AND ACCUMULATE SUM
C LOOP CONTROL VARIABLE TEST
      WHILE (COUNTR .LT. NRITMS) DO
         READ, ITEM
         PRINT, ITEM
         SUM = SUM + ITEM
         COUNTR = COUNTR + 1
      ENDWHILE
C
C END OF LOOP. PRINT SUM AND STOP
```

The loop-control variable is COUNTR. It is initialized prior to entry into the loop, and updated in the last statement inside the loop. In this instruction sequence, the range of the loop is clearly marked by the WHILE header statement and the matching ENDWHILE. The repeat condition may be immediately identified because it appears in the header statement of the structure.

EXERCISE 3.7 Use a WHILE loop structure and write the flow diagram and program for a loop that will find the largest cumulative product of the numbers 1, 2, 3, 4, ... that is smaller than 10000. [*Hint.* The idea is to compute $1 * 2 * 3 * 4 * \cdots$ and continue while the resulting product is less than 10000. Then the last product computed that was less than 10000 is the one you want to print. Use an additional program variable to "remember" this value.]

*3.3.3   Compiler Role for the WHILE Loop Structure

The WHILE loop structure permits us to implement program loops without the explicit use of either conditional or unconditional transfer instructions. As was the case with the decision structures introduced earlier, this frees us from concern about how to use transfer statements and where to place them and their associated labels. Instead, we need only enclose the loop body within the WHILE structure and let the compiler insert the appropriate transfer instructions into the sequence of basic operations that it generates.

An example of this translation for the loop in Problem 2.2 is shown below. The translation is described using the basic FORTRAN statements discussed in Chapter 1.

Original structure		*Translation*
		10000 IF (COUNTR .GE. NRITMS)
WHILE (COUNTR .LT. NRITMS) DO		XGO TO 10001
READ, ITEM		READ, ITEM
PRINT, ITEM	Loop	PRINT, ITEM
SUM = SUM + ITEM	body	SUM = SUM + ITEM
COUNTR = COUNTR + 1		COUNTR = COUNTR + 1
ENDWHILE		GO TO 10000
		10001 CONTINUE

Here we see that if the complement of the repeat condition is true, then execution skips over the loop body to the CONTINUE statement with label 10001. Otherwise, the loop body is executed, and control is transferred back to the conditional transfer instruction which controls loop repetition (label 10000).

*3.3.4   Implementing Loops in Standard FORTRAN

Even if the version of FORTRAN available to you does not permit the use of the WHILE structure, you can still program effectively by manually carrying out the translation shown in the previous section. The translation steps are summarized below.

1. Choose two statement numbers sn_1 and sn_2 not used in the program for control transfer.

---

* This section is optional.

2. Using the complement of the condition in the loop-repetition box of the flow diagram, write the statement

```
sn₁ IF (complement of condition) GOTO sn₂
```

3. List the statements to be included in the loop body.

4. Write the statements

```
         GO TO sn₁
     sn₂ CONTINUE
```

immediately following the loop body.

In the translation shown earlier, the label sn_1 was 10000, and sn_2 was 10001.

Although we will continue to use the WHILE structure in all of the FORTRAN examples in this chapter, we will, in certain instances, also show how these examples can be written without the WHILE.

Several compilers provide the IF–THEN decision structure but do not recognize the WHILE loop. For these compilers, the IF–THEN decision structure may be used to implement the WHILE loop as outlined below.

1. Choose a label sn.

2. Use the loop-repetition condition (not its complement) in an IF–THEN header statement.

```
     sn IF (condition) THEN
```

3. List the statements to be included in the loop body.

4. Write the statements

```
         GO TO sn
     ENDIF
```

immediately following the loop body.

The implementation of the loop for Problem 2.2 using the IF–THEN follows.

```
     65 IF (COUNTR .LT. NRITMS) THEN
        READ, ITEM
        PRINT, ITEM
        SUM = SUM + ITEM
        COUNTR = COUNTR + 1
        GO TO 65
     ENDIF
```

3.3.5 Additional Examples Using the WHILE Loop Structure

Controlling Loop Repetition with Computational Results The WHILE loop structure is well suited for use in controlling loop repetition in which the repetition condition involves a test of values that are computed in the loop body. For example, in processing checking-account transactions, we might want to continue processing transactions as long as the account balance is positive or zero, and stop and print a message when the balance becomes negative.

In problems of this sort, the loop variable serves a dual function: It is used for storage of a computational result as well as for controlling loop repetition. Occasionally, more than one computed value will be involved in the repetition test, as illustrated in the following problem.

PROBLEM 3.3 Two cyclists are involved in a race. The first has a headstart because the second cyclist is capable of a faster pace. We will write a program that will print out the distance from the starting line each cyclist has travelled. These distances will be printed for each half-hour of the race, beginning when the second cyclist departs, and continuing as long as the first cyclist is still ahead.

Data Table for Problem 3.3

Input variables	*Program variables*	*Output variables*
SPEED1: Average speed of first cyclist in mph	INTERV: Time interval—half-hour (constant, 0.5)	TIME: Time elapsed from start of second cyclist in hours
SPEED2: Average speed of second cyclist in mph		DIST1: Distance travelled by first cyclist
HEADST: Headstart expressed in hours		DIST2: Distance travelled by second cyclist

DISCUSSION   This problem illustrates the use of the computer to *simulate* what would happen in a real-world situation. We can get an estimate of the progress of the cyclists before the race even begins and perhaps use this information to set up monitoring or aid stations.

The loop-repetition test will involve a comparison of the total distances travelled by each cyclist. We will make use of the formula

$$\text{Distance} = \text{Speed} \times \text{Elapsed time}$$

in the computation of distance travelled. We will have to compute the distance travelled by the first cyclist before the second cyclist departs and the incremental distance travelled by each cyclist during each subsequent half-hour.

The initial flow diagram and first refinement are shown in Fig. 3.11. The initial value of DIST1 is computed as the product of speed (SPEED1) and the duration of the headstart (HEADST). DIST2 is initially zero. The loop-repetition test involves a comparison of the two output variables DIST1 and DIST2, both of which are updated at the end of the loop (step 30).

To refine step 30, we must compute the incremental distance travelled in each time interval and add it to the distance traveled prior to the current time interval. This computation can be described as

$$\text{Distance} = \text{Distance} + \text{Incremental distance}$$

where

$$\text{Incremental Distance} = \text{Speed} \times \text{Time interval}$$

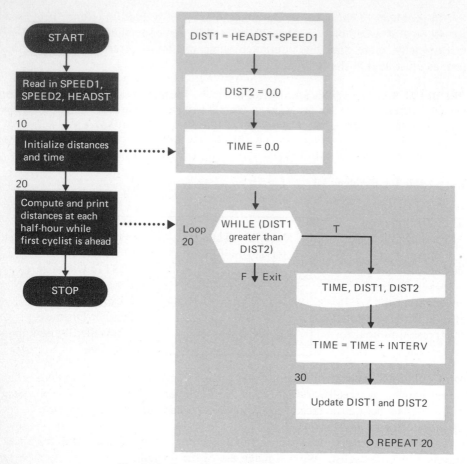

Fig. 3.11 Flow diagrams for cyclist problem (3.3).

To carry out these computations for each cyclist, we must introduce two new program variables INC1 and INC2.

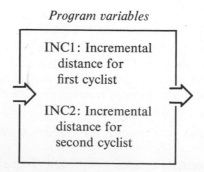

Program variables

INC1: Incremental distance for first cyclist

INC2: Incremental distance for second cyclist

Given these variables, we can refine step 30 as follows:

```
INC1 = SPEED1 * INTERV
DIST1 = DIST1 + INC1
INC2 = SPEED2 * INTERV
DIST2 = DIST2 + INC2
```

At this point we note that the value of INC1 and INC2 will never vary while loop 20 is repeated. They remain the same because SPEED1 and SPEED2 never change and INTERV is a program constant. There is consequently no reason to continually recompute the values of INC1 and INC2 for each execution of loop 20. This pair of computations should be removed from the loop and performed prior to loop entry rather than in step 30.

This change in the algorithm is reflected in the final program for Problem 3.3, shown in Fig. 3.12. (For those who do not have the WHILE loop structure, the

```
C CYCLE RACE PROBLEM
C
      REAL SPEED1, SPEED2, HEADST
      REAL INTERV, INC1, INC2
      REAL DIST1, DIST2, TIME
      DATA INTERV /0.5/
C
C READ DATA ITEMS AND INITIALIZE PROGRAM VARIABLES
      READ, SPEED1
      PRINT, 'FIRST CYCLIST SPEED = ', SPEED 1
      READ, SPEED2
      PRINT, 'SECOND CYCLIST SPEED = ', SPEED2
      READ, HEADST
      PRINT, 'FIRST CYCLIST HEADSTART IN HOURS = ', HEADST
      DIST1 = SPEED1 * HEADST
      DIST2 = 0.0
      TIME = 0.0
C COMPUTE DISTANCE INCREMENTS
      INC1 = SPEED1 * INTERV
      INC2 = SPEED2 * INTERV
      PRINT, '        TIME        DISTANCE 1        DISTANCE 2'
C
C COMPUTE DISTANCES PER HALF HOUR ⎫   100 IF (DIST1 .LE. DIST2) GO TO 101
      WHILE (DIST1 .GT. DIST2) DO ⎪       PRINT, TIME, DIST1, DIST2
        PRINT, TIME, DIST1, DIST2 ⎪       TIME = TIME + INTERV
        TIME = TIME + INTERV      ⎬ ⇒     DIST1 = DIST1 + INC1
        DIST1 = DIST1 + INC1      ⎪       DIST2 = DIST2 + INC2
        DIST2 = DIST2 + INC2      ⎪       GO TO 100
      ENDWHILE                    ⎭   101 CONTINUE
C END OF LOOP
C
      STOP
      END
```

Fig. 3.12 Program for Problem 3.3 (translation of loop is on the right).

program is shown along with the Standard FORTRAN implementation of the WHILE loop.) The computation of INC1 and INC2 immediately follows the initialization of the variable TIME. The technique of removing computations from the body of a loop yields a faster-executing program because the multiplications required to compute INC1 and INC2 are performed only once, instead of many times. In general, any computations producing the same result for each repetition of a loop should be removed from the loop in this manner.

The output from the program shown in Fig. 3.12 would appear as follows:

```
FIRST CYCLIST SPEED = speed1
SECOND CYCLIST SPEED = speed2
FIRST CYCLIST HEADSTART IN HOURS = head start
     TIME          DISTANCE 1      DISTANCE 2
     0.0             ----            ----
     0.5             ----            ----
     1.0             ----            ----
     ----            ----            ----
     ----            ----            ----
     ----            ----            ----
     ----            ----            ----
       .               .               .
       .               .               .
       .               .               .
     ----            ----            ----
```

The statement

            PRINT, TIME, DIST1, DIST2

will cause the display of the values for TIME, DIST1, and DIST2 on a single line (rather than separate lines), allowing us to print the program results in an easy-to-read, tabular form. The spacing between the columns may differ from compiler to compiler; the spaces in the heading output card

    PRINT, '   TIME   DISTANCE 1   DISTANCE 2'

may have to be altered accordingly. ▮

Use of the Sentinel Card   Often, when we need to perform a task such as the one in Problem 2.2 (form the sum of a set of data items), we do not know exactly how many items there are to be processed. We might be handed a stack of data cards and asked to count them exactly in order to determine the value of a variable such as NRITMS (number of items).

One way to avoid this trying task is to insert a *sentinel card* at the end of the stack of data cards. A sentinel card can be used to signal the program that all of the data cards have been read into the computer memory and processed. A sentinel card contains a value that would not occur as a normal data item for the program. When that value has been read as a data item, it can be recognized by the program as an indication that all of the actual data items have been processed.

The concept of a sentinel card can be incorporated in the WHILE loop pattern as shown in Fig. 3.13.

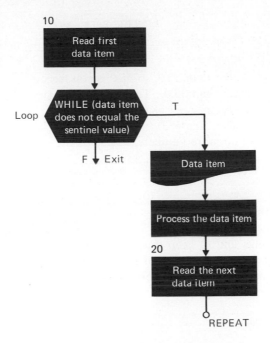

Fig. 3.13 Use of the sentinel card in WHILE loop pattern.

The variable into which each data item is read acts as a loop variable. It must be initialized using a read step (step 10) prior to the first test of the repeat condition, and its value must be updated during each execution of the loop body, using a second read step (20). This is normally the last step in the loop, and is executed after all other processing of the current value has been performed. We illustrate these and other points concerning the use of the sentinel card in the following problem.

PROBLEM 3.4 Write a program that will read all of the scores for a course examination and compute and output the largest of these scores.

DISCUSSION In order to gain some insight into a solution of this problem, we should consider how we would go about finding the largest of a long list of numbers without the computer. Most likely we would read down the list of numbers, one at a time, and remember or "keep track of" the largest number that we had found at each point. If, at some point in the list, we should encounter a number, N, that is larger than the largest number found prior to that point, then we would make N the new largest number, and remember it rather than the previously found number.

An example of how this might proceed is given in the monologue shown in Fig. 3.14.

Test scores	*Effect of each score*
35.0	"Since this is the first number, we will consider it to be the largest number initially.
12.0	"This is smaller than 35.0, so 35.0 is still largest.
68.0	"This is larger than 35.0. Therefore, 35.0 cannot be the largest item. Forget it and remember 68.0.
8.0	"This is smaller than 68.0, so 68.0 is still the largest.
	"There are no more numbers, so 68.0 is the value we seek."

Fig. 3.14 Finding the largest of four numbers (a monologue).

We can use this procedure as a model for constructing an algorithm for solving Problem 3.4 on the computer. We will instruct the computer to process a single score at a time, and to keep track of the largest score it has processed at any given point during the execution of the program. The variable LARGE will be used to store the largest value encountered at any point in the processing of the input data.

Data Table for Problem 3.4

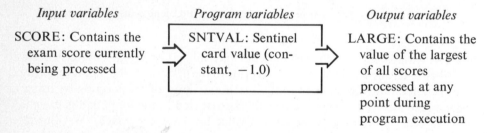

Input variables	*Program variables*	*Output variables*
SCORE: Contains the exam score currently being processed	SNTVAL: Sentinel card value (constant, -1.0)	LARGE: Contains the value of the largest of all scores processed at any point during program execution

Figure 3.15 shows the flow-diagram representation of the algorithm to compare each new score to LARGE and change LARGE if a new largest score is found.

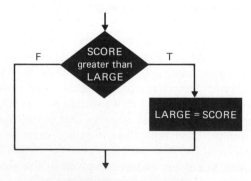

Fig. 3.15 Updating LARGE.

This constitutes the main task to be performed and it will have to be repeated once for each score read in. In order to terminate the loop repetition, we will use a sentinel card containing the number −1.0, which is not within the possible range of scores for the exam. The use of the sentinel value is required since we do not know how many test scores are to be processed.

Figure 3.16 shows the flow diagrams for this problem. Note that LARGE is initialized to the first score read in since, in the beginning, this is the largest (and only) score processed.

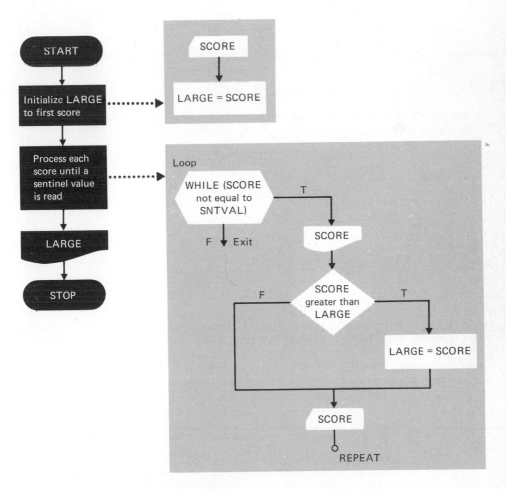

Fig. 3.16 Flow diagram for largest-score problem (3.4).

From the description of the level-one flow diagram, we see that SCORE is the variable to be used for loop control. Each time a score is read in, it must always be compared to the sentinel value in order to determine when loop execution is complete. The repeat condition in this solution is "score not equal to sentinel value." Prior to performing this test for the first time, we must initialize the loop-variable SCORE via a read statement. Finally, at the end of the loop, we must update SCORE (also via a read statement).

The Structured FORTRAN implementation of this algorithm is shown in Fig. 3.17 along with the Standard FORTRAN implementation of the WHILE loop, for those who do not have the WHILE structure.

```
C FIND THE LARGEST OF A COLLECTION OF EXAM SCORES BETWEEN 0.0 AND 100.0
      REAL SCORE, LARGE, SNTVAL
      DATA SNTVAL /-1.0/
C
C INITIALIZE LARGE
      READ, SCORE
      LARGE = SCORE
      PRINT, 'LIST OF SCORES PROCESSED'
C
C READ SCORES. SEE IF NEW SCORE LARGER THAN PREVIOUS ONES
      WHILE (SCORE .NE. SNTVAL) DO           50 IF (SCORE .EQ. SNTVAL) GO TO 60
         PRINT, SCORE                           PRINT, SCORE
         IF (SCORE .GT. LARGE) LARGE = SCORE    IF (SCORE .GT. LARGE)...
         READ, SCORE                    ⇒       READ, SCORE
      ENDWHILE                                   GO TO 50
                                            60 CONTINUE
C
C SCORES PROCESSED. PRINT LARGEST
      PRINT, 'LARGE = ', LARGE
      STOP
      END
```

Fig. 3.17   Program for Problem 3.4 (translation of loop is on the right).

3.4 REMINDERS FOR ALGORITHM DEVELOPMENT USING THE WHILE LOOP

The flow-diagram pattern for the loop in Problem 3.4 is identical to the patterns developed earlier. This pattern may be characterized as shown in Fig. 3.18.

In addition, the steps leading to the construction of all of the loops seen so far are the same. These steps are summarized in the following list.

1. Complete a description of what must be done in the loop (the loop body).

2. Identify the loop-control variable. This variable may already be a part of the loop body (such as SCORE), or it may need to be added (such as COUNTR in Problem 2.2).

3. Set up the loop-control variable test to be performed at the head of the loop body.

4. Initialize the loop-control variable just prior to the test.

5. Update the loop-control variable as the last step of the loop.

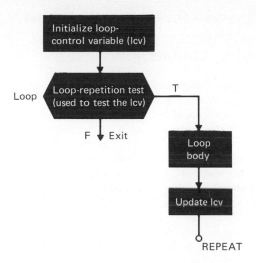

Fig. 3.18 Loop pattern for Problems 2.2 and 3.3.

Not all loops will fit the category just described by the above pattern and loop-construction steps. However, a significant percentage of the loops you will write do fit into this category, so you should familiarize yourself with both the pattern and the construction steps.

EXERCISE 3.8 What would happen in the execution of the program in Fig. 3.17 if we accidentally omitted all data except the sentinel value?

EXERCISE 3.9 Modify the data table, flow diagram, and program for the largest-value problem, to count and print the number of scores processed.

EXERCISE 3.10 In Problem 3.4, we could have initialized LARGE to 0.0 instead of the first exam score. However, if our input data was not restricted to the exam-score range of 0.0 to 100.0, but was allowed to assume any values, initializing LARGE to 0.0 would not always work. Provide a sample set of data for which initializing LARGE to 0.0 would cause the program to produce the wrong answer.

EXERCISE 3.11 Modify the largest-value problem (Fig. 3.16) flow diagrams and data table so that the smallest score (SMALL) and the largest score are found and printed. Also, compute the range of the grades (RANGE = LARGE − SMALL).

EXERCISE 3.12 On January 1, the water-supply tank for the town of Death Valley contained 10,000 gallons of water. The town used 183 gallons of water a week, and it expected no rain in the foreseeable future. Write a loop to compute and print the amount of water remaining in the tank at the end of each week. Your loop should terminate when there is insufficient water to last out a week.

3.5 THE WIDGET INVENTORY-CONTROL PROBLEM

We will now turn our attention to the solution of a problem that illustrates the use of all of the structures introduced in the chapter.

PROBLEM 3.5   The Widget Manufacturing Company needs a simple program to help with the control of the manufacturing and shipping of widgets. Specifically, the program is to process orders for shipments of new widgets and check each order to ensure that an inventory sufficient to fill the order is in stock. If an order cannot be completely filled due to insufficient stock, the program should print the message NOT FILLED next to the shipment request. After all orders have been processed, the program should print out the final value of the inventory and the number of additional widgets that must be manufactured to fill all outstanding orders. Each order shipment size should be punched on a separate card, and the initial widget inventory should be the first data item read by the program.

DISCUSSION   A loop will be needed to process all orders. The loop will be terminated by a sentinel value. As each order is read in, it must be compared to the widget inventory. If the order amount is less than the inventory, it will be filled and the inventory reduced. If an order is too large to be completely filled, the number of widgets needed for unfilled orders will be increased by the amount of this order. Since inventory records and orders involving a piece or fractional part of a widget are impossible, we may treat all data to be processed by this program as type integer. The data table follows; the flow diagrams are shown in Fig. 3.19.

Data Table for Problem 3.5

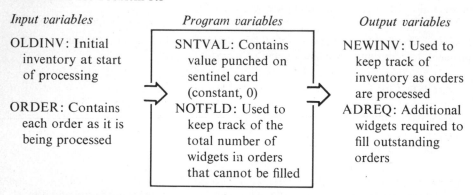

Input variables	*Program variables*	*Output variables*
OLDINV: Initial inventory at start of processing	SNTVAL: Contains value punched on sentinel card (constant, 0)	NEWINV: Used to keep track of inventory as orders are processed
ORDER: Contains each order as it is being processed	NOTFLD: Used to keep track of the total number of widgets in orders that cannot be filled	ADREQ: Additional widgets required to fill outstanding orders

The input information for this problem is the initial inventory (OLDINV) and each shipping order (ORDER). The output information will be the remaining widget inventory (NEWINV) and the total number of additional widgets required to fill the outstanding orders (ADREQ). ADREQ can be computed by accumulating the sum of all widgets in orders that cannot be filled (NOTFLD), and subtracting from this total the number of widgets remaining in the inventory after all orders have been processed.   ∎

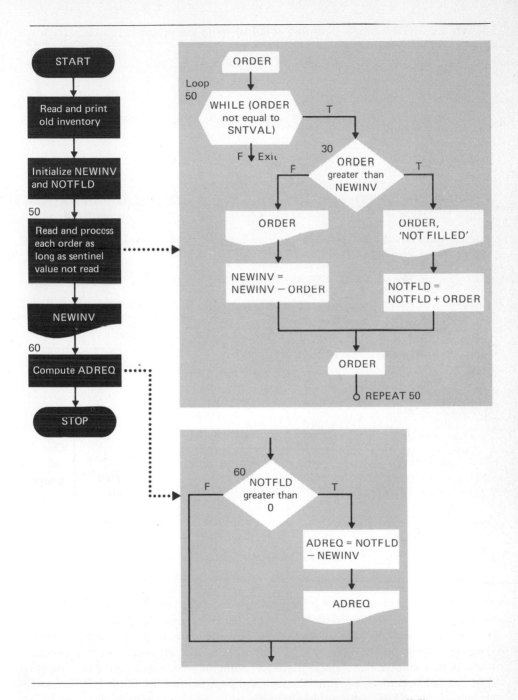

Fig. 3.19 Flow diagrams for the Widget inventory-control problem (3.5).

We now have enough algorithm detail to write the program, which is shown in Fig. 3.20.

```
C WIDGET INVENTORY CONTROL PROBLEM
C
      INTEGER OLDINV, ORDER, SNTVAL, NOTFLD, NEWINV, ADREQ
      DATA SNTVAL /0/
C
C INITIALIZATION                                                     } Initiali-
      READ, OLDINV                                                   } zation
      PRINT, 'INITIAL INVENTORY = ', OLDINV                          } phase
      NEWINV = OLDINV
      NOTFLD = 0
C
C READ AND PROCESS EACH ORDER
      READ, ORDER                                                    } (Step
      WHILE (ORDER .NE. SNTVAL) DO                                   } 50)
C        DECIDE IF ORDER CAN BE FILLED                      } (Step  } Pro-
         IF (ORDER .GT. NEWINV) THEN                        } 30)    } cess-
            PRINT, ORDER, ' NOT FILLED '          } S_T     }        } ing
            NOTFLD = NOTFLD + ORDER               }         }        } phase
         ELSE                                               }        }
            PRINT, ORDER                          } S_F     }        }
            NEWINV = NEWINV - ORDER               }         }        }
         ENDIF                                              }        }
         READ, ORDER                                                 }
      ENDWHILE                                                       }
C END OF LOOP
      PRINT, 'FINAL INVENTORY = ', NEWINV                            } Out-
C                                                                    } put
C COMPUTE AND PRINT ADDITIONAL WIDGETS NEEDED, IF ANY                } phase
      IF (NOTFLD .GT. 0) THEN                               } (Step  }
         ADREQ = NOTFLD - NEWINV                  } S_T     } 60)    }
         PRINT, ADREQ, ' NEW WIDGETS NEEDED '     }         }        }
      ENDIF                                                 }
      STOP
      END
```

Fig. 3.20 Program for Problem 3.5.

In Fig. 3.20, all statement groups are marked by brackets. At the beginning of this chapter, we mentioned that the use of the new control structures would make it easier to associate each subtask in a flow diagram with its corresponding statement group in the program. This program, like all others we will write, consists of a sequence of statement groups, some of which are control structures. The control structures are either distinct entities (60 and 30, 60 and 50) or are completely nested one within the other (30 inside 50).

A version of the Widget program, written without the structures discussed in this chapter, is shown in Fig. 3.21. We encourage all students, especially those who cannot use the structures, to examine this program, and compare it to the one shown in Fig. 3.20.

```
C WIDGET INVENTORY CONTROL PROBLEM (WITHOUT CONTROL STRUCTURES)
C
      INTEGER OLDINV, ORDER, SNTVAL, NOTFLD, NEWINV, ADREQ
      DATA SNTVAL /0/
C
C INITIALIZATION
      READ, OLDINV
      PRINT, 'INITIAL INVENTORY = ', OLDINV
      NEWINV = OLDINV
      NOTFLD = 0
C
C READ AND PROCESS EACH ORDER
      READ, ORDER
   10 IF (ORDER .EQ. SNTVAL) GO TO 50
C         DECIDE IF ORDER CAN BE FILLED
         IF (ORDER .LE. NEWINV) GO TO 20
            PRINT, ORDER, ' NOT FILLED '
            NOTFLD = NOTFLD + ORDER
         GO TO 30
   20    PRINT, ORDER
         NEWINV = NEWINV - ORDER
   30    CONTINUE
         READ, ORDER
         GO TO 10
C END OF LOOP
   50 CONTINUE
      PRINT, ' FINAL INVENTORY = ', NEWINV
C
C COMPUTE AND PRINT ADDITIONAL WIDGETS NEEDED, IF ANY
      IF (NOTFLD .LE. 0) GO TO 60
         ADREQ = NOTFLD - NEWINV
         PRINT, ADREQ, ' NEW WIDGETS NEEDED '
   60 CONTINUE
      STOP
      END
```

Fig. 3.21 Program for Problem 3.5 (without the decision and loop structures).

EXERCISE 3.13 Is it possible for an order for widgets to be filled even if the one before it was not? Hand-trace the execution of this program for the data cards 75, 20, 50, 100, 3, 15, 2, 0.

3.6 COMMON PROGRAMMING ERRORS

In using control structures, there are many opportunities for making syntax errors. The header and terminator statements of each control structure must satisfy the syntax rules. Care should be taken to ensure that header and terminator statements are included for each structure in a flow diagram, and that the header and terminator matches the structure used in the diagram.

Missing terminators can be diagnosed easily by the compiler, which will print a diagnostic indicating that the terminator statement is missing. If the terminator statements for two nested control structures (a decision structure and a loop structure) are interchanged, the compiler will not be able to translate these structures properly and may provide a diagnostic indicating that the structures overlap. An example of overlapping structures is shown in Fig. 3.22. Use of the wrong structure (for example, using a decision structure when a loop is required) will often go undetected until execution of the program. It is advisable to adopt a set convention for translating flow diagrams into Structured FORTRAN and to double-check the translation before key punching the program.

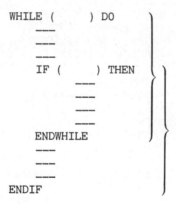

Fig. 3.22 Overlapping structures.

A common error in using loop structures involves the specification of too many or too few loop repetitions. You should check carefully that all loop-repetition counters are being initialized properly and that the loop-repetition condition specifies exactly the number of required loop repetitions.

It is always essential to verify that either your input data or some computation will eventually cause a loop-repetition condition to become false. This is especially important when the condition involves a test for equality or inequality. In Problem 3.4, the loop-repetition condition (SCORE .NE. SNTVAL) will become false only if a sentinel card (containing a score of −1.0) is read in. Otherwise, the loop will never terminate.

Nonterminating loops can cause a great waste of computer paper and time. Eventually, a program with a nonterminating loop will either exceed the amount of computer time allocated to it, or will run out of input data. The latter problem will be indicated by an *execution-time error message* indicating "an insufficient amount of data," or an "attempted read past a data deck terminator card."

3.7 SUMMARY: CONTROL STRUCTURES AND STRUCTURE IN PROGRAMS

In this chapter we have discussed some of the control structures that are available in an extended version of FORTRAN called Structured FORTRAN. Two decision structures and one loop structure were described. The flow-diagram patterns for these structures are shown in Fig. 3.23.

Structured FORTRAN prototypes of each of these structures were also provided. These prototypes are characterized by the lack of explicit transfer instructions. All of the prototypes are quite similar in appearance. They begin with a header statement and end with a special terminator statement.

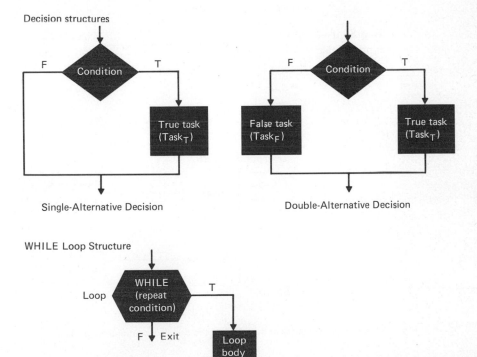

Fig. 3.23 Summary of structure flow-diagram patterns.

The header statement is used to distinguish each structure from the others and to indicate the type of the structure. The IF–THEN header indicates a decision structure; the WHILE–DO header indicates a loop. Each header has its own meaning, and this meaning is defined by the way in which the structure is translated by the compiler into the machine-language encodings of the basic operations.

Terminator statements serve as end markers, indicating to the compiler where the physical end of a structure is in the program. The ENDIF indicates the physical end of a decision structure; the ENDWHILE marks the end of a loop.

In formulating your solution to a programming problem, it is essential that you think in terms of the structures and their functions. The emphasis should be on how the structures affect what is to be done, and not on the various transfers of control that are inserted by the compiler during translation. To emphasize this point further, we urge you to review the interpretation of the IF–THEN, IF–THEN–ELSE, and WHILE structures, as given in the boxes in Figs. 3.3, 3.4, and 3.10, and summarized in Figs. 3.24 and 3.25.

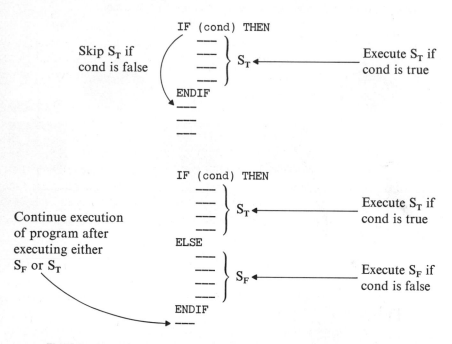

Fig. 3.24 Graphical summary of the effect of the decision-control structures.

One advantage to the use of these structures is that less flow-diagram refinement is necessary in order to complete the translation from problem statement to FORTRAN program. This is primarily due to the fact that these structures closely mirror the problem-solution formulations that we find most natural in

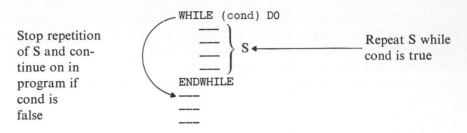

Fig. 3.25   Graphical summary of the effect of the WHILE control structure.

dealing with everyday problems. Such formulations are usually reflected in the first or second levels of the flow diagrams that we construct, and these control structures permit us to go directly from these diagrams to FORTRAN with little or no additional refinement.

A second, and perhaps even more important, advantage results directly from the absence of transfer instructions and associated labels in programs in which these structures are used. The structures allow us to specify decisions and loops without concern for the details of where and how to use transfers. This simplifies the programming task, improves program readability, and removes many of the sources of error found in programs with numerous transfer instructions and labels.

With these new control structures, we can design and implement algorithms in a more organized and systematic fashion, spending less time on flow-diagram refinement and programming details. Instead, a greater percentage of our effort can be directed toward the development of correct and efficient algorithms, which can be converted to programs simply by organizing statement groups into structures and combining the appropriate structures and statement groups to produce a program. Thus we can concentrate on describing the tasks that need to be done, rather than on telling the computer to transfer here and there in order to carry out the proper instruction sequence.

Entire problem solutions can be described in a *modular*, *stepwise* manner, from the design of the algorithm through the program implementation. Individual tasks and subtasks to be performed can be easily identified and programmed as separate groups of statements. The solutions to the smaller subparts of the original problem can then be put together to form the total problem solution. The final program will consist of a linear sequence of steps, many of which will be control structures, which themselves will consist of a linear sequence of algorithm steps.

The importance of all these points cannot be stressed too much. A programmer often spends considerably more time in checking out and debugging a program than in writing it. This is because each additional run to remove the "last error" involves extra time in reading, interpreting, and modifying the program listing, keypunching program corrections, and waiting to enter and receive the completed run.

We recommend the use of the structures introduced in this chapter whenever possible in the formulation and implementation of algorithms. Careful understanding and use of the structures will pay off in programs that are easier to write and have fewer and more easily detected errors. You should also find that correcting errors will be easier when these structures are used.

PROGRAMMING PROBLEMS

(Unless indicated otherwise, a data table and flow diagram should be provided for each problem.)

3.6 Write a program for the following problem: Read in a list of integer data items punched one to a card, and find and print the index of the first card containing the number 12. Use a sentinel value of 0. Your program should print an index value of 0 if the number is not found. (The index is the location of the card containing 12 in the data-card section. For example, if the 11th card read in contains 12, then the index value 11 should be printed.)

3.7 Write a program to read in a collection of exam scores ranging in value from 1 to 100, and count and print the total number of scores, and the number of outstanding scores (90–100), the number of satisfactory scores (60–89), and the number of unsatisfactory scores (1–59). Test your program on the following data:

63	75	72
72	78	67
80	63	75
90	89	43
59	99	82
12	100	

3.8 (Expanded Payroll Problem) Write a program to process weekly employee time cards for all employees of an organization. Each employee will have three cards indicating an identification number (IDN, an integer), the hourly wage rate (RATE), and the number of hours (HOURS) worked during a given week. Each employee is to be paid time-and-a-half for all hours worked over 40.0. A tax amount of 3.625 percent of gross salary (GROSS) will be deducted. The program output should show the employee's number and net pay (NET). An employee number of 0 will serve as the sentinel card.

3.9 Complete the flow diagram, and write the program for Exercise 3.12. Have your program indicate whether or not the town has enough water to last for one year.

3.10 Suppose you own a beer distributorship that sells Piels (ID number 1), Coors (ID2), Bud (ID 3), and Iron City (ID number 4) by the case. Write a program to (a) read in the case inventory for each brand for the start of the week; (b) process all weekly sales and purchase records for each brand; and (c) print out the final inventory. Each case transaction will consist of two cards. The first card will contain the brand identification number (an integer). The second will contain the amount purchased (a positive integer value) or the amount sold (a negative integer value). The weekly inventory for each brand (for the start of the week) will also consist of two cards—the identification and inventory cards—for that brand. For now, you may assume that you always have sufficient foresight to prevent the complete depletion of your inventory for any brand. [*Hint.* Your data-card deck should begin with eight cards representing the case inventory. These should be followed by all the transaction cards, followed by a sentinel card.]

3.11 Write a program for the following problem: Read in a (positive) integer N and compute $SUMSLO = \sum_{i=1}^{N} i = 1 + 2 + 3 + 4 + \cdots + N$ (the sum of all integers from 1 to N, inclusive). Then compute $SUMFST = (N \times (N + 1))/2$ and compare SUMFST and SUMSLO. Your program should print both SUMSLO and SUMFST and indicate whether or not they are equal. (You will need a loop to compute SUMSLO and three arithmetic statements to compute SUMFST. Which computation method is preferable?

To verify your hypothesis of the relationship between SUMSLO and SUMFST, modify your program so that it will process a collection of numbers (use a loop that will terminate when a value of 0 is read).

3.12 Write a program to find the largest value in a collection of N numbers, where the value of N will be the first data card read into the program. If the value of N were unknown, could a sentinel value be used to terminate execution of the main program loop for this problem?

3.13 Write a program to process a collection of checking-account transactions (deposits or withdrawals) for Mr. Shelley's account. Your program should begin by reading in the previous account balance (OLDBAL), and then process each transaction (TRANS), computing the new balance (NEWBAL). Use a 0.00 transaction as your sentinel value. Your output should appear in three columns, with withdrawals on the left, deposits in the middle, and the new balance (after each transaction) on the right. To accomplish this, use the print statement

$$PRINT, ZERO, TRANS, NEWBAL$$

if the transaction is a deposit (a positive number), and

$$PRINT, TRANS, ZERO, NEWBAL$$

if the transaction is a withdrawal (a negative number). The value of the variable ZERO should be 0.0. Test your program with the following data.

$$\text{Old balance} = 325.50$$

Transactions: 25.00, -79.25, -60.00, 16.75,
-259.47, 42.00, -5.50

3.14 (continuation) Modify the data table, flow diagram, and program of Problem 3.13 to compute and print the following additional information:

The number of withdrawals; The number of deposits;
The number of transactions;
The total sum of all withdrawals;
The total sum of all deposits.

3.15 (continuation) Following the processing of the transaction -259.47 in Problem 3.13 (or 3.14), the value of NEWBAL was negative, indicating that Mr. Shelley's account was overdrawn. Modify your data table, flow diagram, and program for Problem 3.13 (or 3.14) so that the resulting new program will test for withdrawal amounts that are not covered. Have your program completely skip processing each such withdrawal, and instead use the following print statement to indicate an overdrawn account:

```
PRINT, TRANS, ' ***WITHDRAWAL NOT COVERED AND NOT PROCESSED,*** '
```

The value of NEWBAL should not be altered by withdrawals that are not covered. Your program should count the number of such withdrawals and print a total at the end of execution. (Note that, in Problem 3.13 (or 3.14), Mr. Shelley's final balance was positive. This indicates that he made a deposit during the current time period to cover the $259.47 withdrawal. What could be done to prevent such a transaction from being considered as overdrawn as long as the final account balance for the current period is positive?)

3.16 Write a program to compute and print the fractional powers of two (1/2, 1/4, 1/8, 1/16, ...) in decimal form. Your program should print two columns of information, as shown below:

Power	Fraction
1	0.5
2	0.25
3	0.125
4	0.0625
.	.
.	.
.	.

The program should terminate when the decimal fraction becomes less than or equal to 0.000001. Draw a flow diagram first.

3.17 (continuation) Modify the program for Problem 3.16 to accumulate and print the sum of the fractions computed *at each step*. Add a third column of output containing the accumulated sum.

Sum
0.5
0.75
0.875
0.9375
.
.

Explain the results in this column. Could this value ever reach 1.0?

3.18 The trustees of a small college are considering voting a pay raise for the 12 full-time faculty members. They want to grant a $5\frac{1}{2}$ percent pay raise. However, before doing so, they want to know how much additional cash this will cost the college. Write a program that will provide this information. Test your program for the following salaries:

$12,500.00	$14,029.50
$16,000.00	$13,250.00
$15,500.00	$12,800.00
$20,000.50	$18,900.00
$13,780.00	$17,300.00
$14,120.25	$14,100.00

3.19 The assessor in the local township has punched, one value per card, the estimated value of all 14 properties in the township. Properties are assessed a flat tax rate of 125 mils per $100.00 of assessed value, and each property is assessed at only 28% of its estimated value. Write a program to compute the total amount of taxes that will be collected on the 14 properties in the township. (A mil is equal to 0.1 of a penny). The estimated values of the properties are:

$50,000.00	$48,000.00
$45,500.00	$67,000.00
$37,600.00	$47,100.00
$65,000.00	$53,350.00
$28,000.00	$58,000.00
$52,250.00	$48,000.00
$56,500.00	$43,700.00

3.20 Write a program that will read in a positive real number and determine and print the number of digits to the left of the decimal point. [*Hint.* Repeatedly divide the number by 10.0 until it becomes less than 1.0.] Test the program with the following data:

4703.62	0.01
0.47	57642.00
10.12	4000.00

DATA TYPES— THEIR USE AND MANIPULATION

4

4.1 Introduction

4.2 Data Types, Declarations and Constants

4.3 Format-Free Input/Output Statements

4.4 Manipulation of Character Strings and Logical Data

4.5 Integers and the Indexed-DO Loop Structure

4.6 Arithmetic Expressions

4.7 Library Functions

*4.8 Numerical Errors

4.9 Common Programming Errors

4.10 Summary

Problems

---

* These sections are optional and may be omitted.

4.1 INTRODUCTION

While writing earlier programs you may have thought about, and perhaps even written, FORTRAN assignment statements containing constants, parentheses, and more than one arithmetic operator. You may have wondered whether or not FORTRAN could be used to instruct the computer to manipulate something other than numbers and, if so, how?

In this chapter, we will see that FORTRAN can be used to manipulate character strings, logical values (true and false), as well as numbers. We will learn how to form FORTRAN assignment statements of greater complexity than those used so far to specify numeric data manipulations, and we will introduce some simple manipulations of character and logical data. (Additional features of character-string and logical data manipulation will be described in Chapter 9.) All of these features will make it still more convenient to program in FORTRAN.

4.2 DATA TYPES, DECLARATIONS AND CONSTANTS

4.2.1 External Representations of Different Data Types

In all our programming so far, we have manipulated only numeric information. This is, in fact, an unnecessary restriction since it is possible to write FORTRAN programs to manipulate a number of different types of data. In this text, we will discuss four *data types*: real, integer, character, and logical.

In order to best understand the differences among the four data types, it is helpful to examine the differences in their external representations. The *external representation* of a data item is the representation that is used in writing constants in FORTRAN programs, and in keypunching information that is to be read by a program. It is also the form in which results of program computations are printed for us to read. The external representations of the four data types are defined in Fig. 4.1.

The apostrophe form of character data is not standard and is not allowed on some FORTRAN compilers. These compilers allow only a very limited use of character data, and require this data to be written in the form:

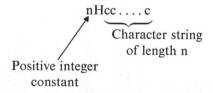

The constant n indicates the number of characters following the letter H. The H is not considered part of the data item; it simply indicates to the compiler that the characters that follow are all to be considered part of a character-string constant. In counting the n characters following the H, the compiler will include all blanks.

External Data Representations in FORTRAN

1. *Integer data:* Type integer data must be represented as a string of decimal digits 0–9, (possibly) prefixed by a plus (+) or minus (−) sign. No other character is permitted in the representation of an integer. (*Examples:* 0, −9, +12, −68, 123456)

2. *Real data:* Type real data may be represented using the digits 0–9 and a decimal point, (possibly) prefixed by a (+) or (−) sign. The decimal point must always be used for type real data. It is the sole means available for the compiler to distinguish between real and integer constants. (*Examples:* 0., 12.0, −6.325, .00625, +7.2)

A FORTRAN *scientific notation* for real data may also be used. A real-data item written in FORTRAN scientific notation consists of a sign followed by a standard real or integer constant, followed by the letter E, another sign, and an integer constant (+ signs may be omitted). (*Examples:* −.000325E6, 325E+5, 13764.25E−10, −110.E02)

The value of any number written in the above form is determined as follows:

Multiply the first constant times 10^n, where n is the integer constant following E. (*Example:* −.000325E6 = −.000325x10^6 = −325)

3. *Logical data:* There are only two type logical data values. They are true and false, and are represented in FORTRAN as .TRUE. and .FALSE..

4. *Character data:* Character-string data items consist of any sequence of legal FORTRAN characters enclosed in apostrophes. (*Examples:*

'A', 'JIMMY', 'HARRIET BEECHER STOWE',
'SOON, I WILL LEAVE', '3*X*2−6+X+4', '*/,+−W)X$'.

A pair of apostrophes is used inside a string to indicate contraction or possession: 'I''M DREAMING', 'JOE''S HAT'. When character-string data is printed, the enclosing apostophes are omitted.

Fig. 4.1 External representations of the four data types in FORTRAN.

We will assume that the apostrophe form of character constant is allowed by your FORTRAN compiler, and use this form throughout the rest of the text.

Example 4.1

a) The following are legal integer constants:

−7	−456789
2463	13
0	+32

The following are illegal integer constants:

−27E3	Use of exponential form is not legal.
32.	Decimal point indicates real.

b) The following are legal real constants:

```
3.14159        0.1E-6
0.0           -22.3E12
-22.0          0.3889E-10
0.000031      57E18
```

The following are illegal real constants:

```
6382                        No decimal point indicates integer.
.TRUE.                      Logical constant.
```

c) The following are legal character-string constants:

```
'THE'          'ITSY, BITSY'
'4*AC'         '679'
5HIT IS        '72.H'
```

The following are illegal character-string constants:

```
'IT'S'                      Extra (or missing) apostrophe inside the string.
'HERMAN                     Missing apostrophe.
3.0'                        Missing apostrophe.
.TRUE.                      Logical constant.
2HTHE                       One extra character.
```

d) The following are legal logical constants:

```
.TRUE.
.FALSE.
```

The following are illegal logical constants:

```
'.TRUE.'                    Character string constant.
1                           Integer constant.
TRUE                        Missing periods.
```

EXERCISE 4.1 Indicate which of these data items are legal FORTRAN constants and identify the type (real, integer, character, or logical).

a) 37.86   f) -18.E-3

b) 219-40-0677   g) 18+4

c) .FLAG.   h) 'WHAT'FOR'

d) 'OOPS'   i) $16.27

e) -64   j) WHYNOT

4.2.2 Internal Representation of Data

Just as each data type has a unique external form, each data type has its own *internal representation format* as well. This is the format which the computer uses when storing data in memory. Although the details of the internal-representation formats of data will vary from computer to computer, there is a substantial degree of commonality in each format that should be understood by all FORTRAN programmers. In this section, we will describe some of the common attributes of the internal-representation formats of the four types of data.

The internal formats of representation of real and integer data items are called *floating point* and *fixed point*, respectively. Floating-point form is analogous to *scientific notation*. Recall that the number 6,850,000,000 can be written very compactly in scientific notation as 6.85×10^9, where multiplying by 10^9 is equivalent to shifting the decimal point nine positions to the right. Similarly, a very small number such as $-.0000000012$ can be written as -1.2×10^{-9}, where multiplication by 10^{-9} implies that the decimal point should be shifted nine positions to the *left*.

The advantages of the use of floating-point as opposed to fixed-point notation are twofold. First, floating-point form enables the representation of numbers with decimal points and fractional parts (real numbers); fixed-point form may be used only to represent numbers without a fractional part (integers). Second, the floating-point form facilitates the representation of numerical quantities of considerably larger magnitudes than is permitted in fixed-point form. For example, the range of positive real numbers that can be represented in floating-point form on the CDC 6000 series computers extends from 10^{-294} to 10^{+322}, approximately. The range of positive integers that can be represented in fixed point extends from 1 to approximately 10^{15}.

The internal, floating-point representation of type real numbers consists of three parts: an exponent, a mantissa, and the sign of the number. The internal, fixed-point representation of an integer, however, consists only of a sign, followed by a representation of the magnitude of the number. These differences are illustrated in Fig. 4.2.

The most important thing to remember from Fig. 4.2 is that the contents of a variable represents one numerical quantity if it is interpreted as being in fixed-point form (integer variable) and a different numerical quantity if it is interpreted as being in floating-point form (real variable). For this reason, it is essential that the internal format of a data item stored in a variable be consistent with the declared type of the variable.

To further complicate matters, the formats of internal representation of *character* and *logical* type data are different from each other, and from the internal representations of integer and real numbers. Recall, however, that internally, even character and logical type data are *numbers*. It is the interpretation given to these numbers by the compiler that distinguishes them.

Most compilers represent and interpret logical data in terms of two integers. For example, .TRUE. might be represented as -1, and .FALSE. as $+1$.

Fig. 4.2 Formats of the internal representation of integer and real data.

The representation of character data, on the other hand, is a bit more complicated. In most computers, the internal representation of a single character is given in terms of a unique two- or three-digit integer called a *character code*. The internal representation of a character string consists of a *concatenation* (joining) of these individual codes to represent the entire string.

Once a variable name is declared to be a certain type, the compiler will always instruct the computer to represent and interpret all data items placed in that variable according to the internal format of the designated type. If the actual internal format of a data item should differ from the format of interpretation, unpredictable (and usually incorrect) results will be obtained.

4.2.3 Type Declarations

When writing FORTRAN programs, it is important to remember the differences in the external representations of the four data types. It is equally important, however, to understand that the internal representation of each of these data types is a number. The computer cannot distinguish among the different data types; it treats all information stored in its memory as numbers. It is therefore the responsibility of the programmer to instruct the computer to *interpret* the data stored in memory in a manner that is consistent with the type of the data. The FORTRAN compiler can provide a considerable amount of help in this matter. If we inform the compiler of the type of information to be stored in each memory cell used in a program, the compiler will then ensure that the data stored in these cells is properly interpreted and manipulated.

We can tell the compiler the type of data to be stored in each memory cell in one of two ways: through the use of explicit *type declarations*, or through the use of the type conventions that are implicit in the FORTRAN language.

We have already seen how to declare the data type of variables used for storage of integer and real numbers. The type declaration for logical variables is similar except that the word LOGICAL is used instead of INTEGER or REAL.

On some compilers (WATFIV-S and SITGO, for example), there is a character type declaration as well. Its form is shown in the box below.

CHARACTER Type Declaration (Nonstandard)

FORTRAN Form:

```
CHARACTER * n list
```

where list is a list of variable names separated by commas and n is an integer constant.

Interpretation. The n denotes the length or *character capacity* of each character variable in the list. Each character variable will be allocated sufficient memory storage space to accommodate a character string of length n (consisting of n characters).

The type declarations used in a program must all precede the executable statements of the program, although the declarations themselves can appear in any order. The compiler allocates a fixed amount of memory storage space called a *storage unit* for each of the variable names appearing in a declaration statement of type REAL, INTEGER, or LOGICAL. The storage units allocated to real variables (*real storage units*) are all the same size. Similarly, *integer storage units* are the same size, as are all *logical storage units*. However, character variables require varying amounts of storage space depending on their length. The compiler determines the size of the *character storage unit* that will be needed for each character variable from its declared length. The maximum possible length of a character variable depends on the compiler.

The character variable is not part of Standard FORTRAN. If your compiler docs not recognize the character declaration, we recommend storing character strings in integer variables. However, the size of an integer storage unit is fixed for each computer. This means that the character capacity of all integer variables is the same, whereas the capacity of a character variable can be defined as required by the programmer when that variable is declared. The character capacity of an integer variable may differ from computer to computer, but it is usually in the range of two to ten. You should find out the character capacity of integer variables on your computer.

Often, the length of a character string does not match exactly the character capacity of the variable in which it is to be stored. The character-string storage convention given below describes how the compiler handles such cases. This convention is followed for all data initialization, read, and assignment operations involving character strings.

Character-String Storage Convention

If the character string is smaller than the capacity of the variable in which it is to be stored, the character string will be extended or padded on the right with blanks until its length exactly matches the character capacity. If the length of a character string to be stored exceeds the character capacity, excess characters on the right will be truncated until the length of the character string remaining exactly matches the character capacity.

The proper typing of all of the variables used in a program is essential if the program is to produce the desired results. It is equally important that each variable be used in a manner that is consistent with its declaration.

Data Storage Rule

Data items should always be stored in variables of the same type. The only exception is that character strings may be stored in integer variables if the character data type is not available.

In most instances, violations of this rule will be recognized by the compiler and corrected. Occasionally, however, a violation will go undetected by the compiler, showing up instead in the printing of incorrect results during the execution of the program.

Some examples of type declarations are:

```
REAL X, ALPHA, LAX, NIMBLE
LOGICAL   FLAG, SWITCH
INTEGER   BETA, LOON, DOPE
CHARACTER * 4 NAME, FLOWER
CHARACTER * 2  N25, N26
CHARACTER * 1  B, C, D
```

EXERCISE 4.2 What type declarations would you use to declare the following variables? Defend your choice.

a) GROSS   Employee gross salary

b) HOURS   Employee hourly wages

c) NOFAIL   Number of failures in a class examination

d) SOLD   Indicates whether or not a house in a multiple real estate listing has been sold

e) COLOR   The color of a car

f) CURSET   The current assets of a corporation

g) ID   A student identification number

h) SSNO   Your Social Security number

i) GPA   Your grade point average

j) TOOBIG   Indicates whether or not your new car will fit into your old garage

4.2.4 Implicit Typing of Variable Names

In addition to the explicit type declaration facility, FORTRAN has an implicit "first-letter" typing convention for all variable names that are not explicitly declared through a type declaration. We recommend that you always explicitly declare the names used in your programs, but you should be aware of the existence of the typing convention and how it works.

Typing of Undeclared Variable Names

Variable names that are not declared in explicit type declarations are typed implicitly by the FORTRAN compiler as follows:

1. If the variable name begins with any one of the letters A through H, or O through Z, it is typed as REAL.

2. If the variable name begins with any one of the letters I through N, it is typed as INTEGER.

3. No variable names are implicitly typed as LOGICAL or CHARACTER.

Any variable name that does not appear in a type declaration is automatically associated with the address of a computer memory cell when it is first encountered in a FORTRAN program. The type of such a name is determined according to the first-letter typing convention described above.

4.2.5 The DATA Statement

The DATA initialization statement may be used to indicate that constants are to be loaded into designated variables by the loader. We have already seen examples of how this can be done for real variables and constants. Some previously seen examples are:

```
DATA TAX /25.00/
DATA SNTVAL /-1.0/
DATA NRITMS /2000/
```

In this section we will describe the general form of the data statement and present some examples of its use.

The DATA Statement

FORTRAN Form:

```
DATA variable list /initial value list/
```

Interpretation. The variable list is a list of names of variables that are to be initialized by the loader at program load time. The initial value list contains the list of constants to be used in this initialization. There must be a one-to-one correspondence between the items in these two lists; each constant in the initial value list must agree in type with the corresponding variable in the variable list and there should be the same number of items in both lists.

Note. If the same constant is to be loaded into a number of successively designated variables, then a *repetition factor* of the form n * c may be specified, where n is the number of variables involved, and c is the constant.

Data statements are not executable statements, and are not translated into machine language. Standard FORTRAN requires that all data statements used in a program must follow the type declarations. The usual practice is to place the data statements immediately after the type declaration statements and before the first executable statement of a program.

Example 4.2 (with the CHARACTER Data Type)

```
REAL  PI
INTEGER I,J
CHARACTER * 2 ART1, ART2
CHARACTER * 3 ART3
DATA PI,I,J,ART1,ART2,ART3 /3.14,2*0,'A','AN','THE'/
```

The data initialization specified by these statements is:

PI	I	J	ART1	ART2	ART3
3.14	0	0	A▢	AN	THE

Since the character string to be stored in ART1 is smaller in length than the character variable, the character string is padded on the right with a blank (indicated by symbol ▢).

Example 4.3 (without the CHARACTER Data Type)

```
REAL  PI
INTEGER I,J
INTEGER ART1,ART2,ART3
DATA  PI,I,J,ART1,ART2,ART3 /3.14,2*0,'A','AN','THE'/
```

Assuming the character capacity of an integer variable is four, the data initialization specified is:

PI	I	J	ART1	ART2	ART3
3.14	0	0	A▢▢▢	AN▢▢	THE▢

Each character string is padded on the right with as many blanks (indicated by symbol ▢) as are needed to satisfy the character-string storage convention.

EXERCISE 4.3 Each of the declaration statement sequences written below contains one or more errors. Identify and correct each error. There may be more than one possible correction for each mistake.

a) REAL X
   INTEGER I
   LOGICAL Y
   CHARACTER * 4 NAME   [or INTEGER NAME]
   DATA X,I,Y,NAME /1.0, −62.5, '.FALSE.', 'AL'/

b) REAL X,Y,Z,W
   INTEGER A
   DATA X,Y,Z,W,A /5*0.0, 347/

c) LOGICAL FLAG
```
   LOGICAL FLAG
   INTEGER SSN01, SSN02, SSN03
   CHARACTER * 4 NAME1, NAME2  [or INTEGER NAME1, NAME2]
   DATA FLAG /1.0/
   DATA SSN01, SSN02 /219, 40, 0677/
   DATA NAME1, NAME2 /'HERB',.TRUE./
```

EXERCISE 4.4 Write the type declaration and DATA statements needed to carry out the loading of cells shown below:

A	B	C	BOOZE1	BOOZE2	BOOZE3	SWITCH
1.0	1.0	1.0	GIN□	RUM□	BEER	.TRUE.

4.3 FORMAT-FREE INPUT/OUTPUT STATEMENTS

4.3.1 Format-Free Input

Just as lists of variable names can be used in declaration statements, they can also be used in input and output statements.

For example, the statement

$$\text{READ, IDN, HR, BA, RBI}$$

will cause four numbers to be read into the variables listed. The statement

$$\text{PRINT, X, Y, Z}$$

will cause three data items to be printed in separate columns on the same line of program output. The items will be separated by blanks.

Statements such as those above and the ones that we have used in earlier programs are called *format-free input and output statements*. This is because these statements provide no information about the *format* or layout of the information to be read or printed.

Since we have been using the more general forms of format-free output throughout the text, we will concentrate on format-free input in this section.

The general forms for format-free input statements are shown in the following display.

Format-free input (Nonstandard)

FORTRAN Form:
$$\text{READ, list}$$
or
$$\text{READ (u,*) list}$$

where u is a number that is used to indicate an input device other than the card reader. (Your instructor can tell you if you need to use the number u, and if so, which number to use.) The list is a list of names of variables to be filled with input data. The names listed must be separated by commas.

Interpretation

1. A new data card is read and examined (*scanned*) from left to right.
2. As each data item is located, it is converted to internal form and placed in the next variable named in the list.
3. If the end of the card is reached before all the variables in the list are filled, then the next card will be processed.
4. If there are more data items on the card being scanned than are needed to satisfy the list of variables, the extra data items are ignored.

There are a number of important things to be remembered when using format-free input.

1. All data items on the same card must be separated from one another by at least one blank or a comma.
2. Except for character strings, no data item may extend from the end of one card to the beginning of another.
3. If the last data item is entered before all the variables in the input list of a read statement have been filled, your program will be terminated immediately due to insufficient data.
4. If any card read contains more data than is required to satisfy the input list being processed, then this excess data will be lost. It is a good practice to punch on each data card the exact number of items needed to satisfy the input list of the read statement that processes this card.
5. The Data Storage Rule and Character-String Storage Convention both apply (see Section 4.2.3).

Example 4.4 Given the data cards shown below,

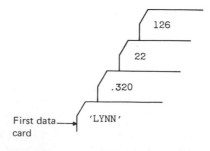

126

22

.320

First data ⟶ 'LYNN'
card

if NAME has a character capacity of 4, BA is real, and HR and RBI are integers, then the read statement

READ, NAME, BA, HR, RBI

will read all four cards, and place the contents of these cards in the named variables as indicated below.

NAME	BA	HR	RBI
LYNN	.320	22	126

Note that this read statement has the same effect as the four statements:

READ, NAME
READ, BA
READ, HR
READ, RBI

The single data card

'LYNN'   .320   22   126

could also be used in conjunction with the read statement

READ, NAME, BA, HR, RBI

However, if this card were used with the four read statements above, only the first data item on this card would be processed. The items stored in BA, HR, and RBI would be read from subsequent data cards (if any); and this would probably result in a proliferation of errors during program execution.

Example 4.5 Given the declarations

INTEGER   SSN01, SSN02, SSN03
REAL GROSS, PAY
CHARACTER*6 LASTNA, FRSTNA

and the data card

219 40   0677   'MONK'   'THEO.'   500.00   417.26

the read statement

          READ, SSNO1, SSNO2, SSNO3, LASTNA, FRSTNA, GROSS, PAY

will process this card and place the data items on the card in the named variables, as shown below.

SSNO1	SSNO2	SSNO3	LASTNA	FRSTNA	GROSS	PAY
219	40	677	MONK□□	THEO.□	500.00	417.26

The print statement

          PRINT, FRSTNA, LSTNA, PAY

would produce an output line of the form:

          THEO. MONK   417.2600

EXERCISE 4.5 Write an appropriate sequence of type declarations and read statements for entering the data shown here. Use meaningful names. The first card contains the ID number, initials, and class abbreviation for a student. The last three cards contain the course ID, credit hours, and a grade for each of three courses taken by the student. These three cards should be processed by a read statement within a program loop.

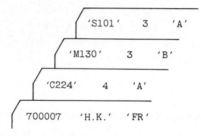

*4.3.2 Compiler Role in Format-Free Input and Output

The format-free input statement simply informs the compiler what variables are to receive values. It provides no information concerning the appearance of the input values on the cards to be read. No information is provided concerning the type of each item, the position of each item on a card, or the number of cards to be read. In format-free input, a special program (called a *format analyzer*) must scan each data card and determine the location and type of each item punched on the card. Then the format analyzer passes this information along to another program, called a *data converter*, which converts the external representation of this data to its equivalent internal representation. This process is depicted in Fig. 4.3.

In format-free output, it is necessary to determine the external form of the data to be printed. In this process, the data converter program first converts to external form the internal representation of the contents of each variable to be

_____

* This section may be omitted.

Fig. 4.3 Format-free input.

printed. The converter interprets the contents of each variable according to the type of the variable. The external form is then printed in the appropriate *print positions* of the current output line. The exact spacing in the output line is determined by the *output format program* according to a set of predefined rules. This process, depicted in Fig. 4.4, is the reverse of the one shown in Fig. 4.3.

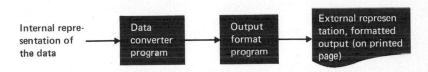

Fig. 4.4 Format-free output.

4.4 MANIPULATION OF CHARACTER STRINGS AND LOGICAL DATA

In this section, we will introduce assignment statements and conditions involving character and logical data. Of the operators we have seen so far, only the assignment operator (=) and the relational operators should be used with character data; only the assignment operator should be used with logical data. (Additional logical operators will be discussed in Chapters 5 and 9.) The arithmetic operators should not be used with character or logical data as operands, since the result of such manipulations would be meaningless. (As an example, what would the sum of two character strings represent?)

Character strings can be stored in variables using simple assignment (copy) statements. If STAR and SYMBOL are type character (or integers used for character string storage), the statement:

SYMBOL = STAR

is a character assignment statement which copies the character string stored in STAR into SYMBOL.

Many compilers permit the use of character string constants in-line in executable statements. For these compilers, the statement

SYMBOL = '*'

would cause the indicated character string to be stored in SYMBOL.

Remember that the character-string storage convention described earlier (Section 4.2.3) applies to all character-string assignment statements.

The statement sequence below contains a pair of logical assignment statements.

```
LOGICAL ERROR, SWITCH
ERROR = .TRUE.
SWITCH = .FALSE.
```

Their effect is to assign the value true to the logical variable ERROR, and assign the value false to the logical variable SWITCH.

Logical variables can also be used to specify a condition in a decision structure (or conditional statement) and a WHILE loop structure.   For example, the statements

```
IF (ERROR) THEN
WHILE (SWITCH) DO
IF (ERROR) PRINT, 'ILLEGAL SYNTAX'
```

are all permitted in FORTRAN (although the first two are nonstandard). In each case, the value of the condition depends entirely upon the value of the logical variable: if the variable has the value true, the condition is true; otherwise the condition is false.

4.4.1 Character-String Comparison

If both operands of a relational operator in a condition are character strings, then a character comparison operation is performed. Recall from the discussion in Section 4.2.2 that a character string is internally represented as a string of numeric character codes. This string of codes is treated by the computer as a single number. Thus, the comparison of two character strings actually involves a comparison of two numbers.

The numeric code for each character is not the same on all computers. Consequently, comparing the same two character strings on different computers will often yield different results. However, on most (if not all) computers, the relative ordering of the numeric codes for the letters corresponds to their alphabetical sequence. Hence, if the character strings being compared contain letters only, the results of a character comparison operation should reflect their lexicographic ordering (dictionary sequence). This means, for example, that all character strings beginning with the letter "A" will be considered less than character strings beginning with any other letter.

In comparing two character strings that contain numbers or special symbols as well as letters, the results often vary from computer to computer. In this case, we suggest you restrict yourself to the relational operators .EQ. (equal) and .NE. (not equal) until you learn more about the numeric character codes on your computer.

The statements listed below will be true on most (if not all) computers.

```
'ABC' is less than 'CBA'
'BETA' is greater than 'ANT'
'ANSI' is less than 'ANTS'
'1234' is not equal to '131'
'*/.' is not equal to ' []*/.'
',/,' is equal to ',/,'
```

4.4.2 Checking Account Transaction Problem

The next problem illustrates the use of all of the data types discussed so far.

PROBLEM 4.1 Write a program to process the checks and deposit slips for a checking account at the close of each month. The date, amount, and type of each transaction should be printed out along with information which summarizes the monthly transactions.

DISCUSSION. Before developing the algorithm, we must first identify the input information that will be available and determine the desired form of the printout. We will design a header card for each account which will indicate the account identification number, the account name, the starting balance, and the month. Each transaction card will contain an account number, the type of transaction ('C' for check, 'D' for deposit), the amount, and the day of the transaction.

The final printout should list all transactions in column form with summary statistics as shown below:

```
DATE        CHECK       DEPOSIT     PENALTY
SEPT  9     79.15
SEPT 11                 3.57
SEPT 12     125.67                  5.00
              .
              .
              .
              .

JOHN SMITH          ACCOUNT NO.  11385
STARTING BALANCE  85.67    ENDING BALANCE  2.45
NO. OF CHECKS PAID    10    NO. OF DEPOSITS  3
NO. OF OVERDRAWN CHECKS   1
TRANSACTION CARD WITH INVALID ACCOUNT NUMBER PRESENT
```

This printout indicates that checks were written on the ninth and twelfth of the month and a deposit was made on the eleventh. Furthermore, the check on September 12 was for more money than the account balance; consequently, it was not paid and a $5.00 penalty was assessed. The last line is printed when one or more transaction cards containing a different account number have been read; all such transaction cards are ignored.

The data table is shown next. Note that we have added the type of each variable to its definition. The flow diagrams are shown in Fig. 4.5(a, b).

Data Table for Problem 4.1

Input variables	Program variables	Output variables
Input variables	*Program variables*	*Output variables*

MONTH: Monthly period covered (character * 4)
NAME: Account name (character * 10)
IDNUM: Account identification number (integer)
STBAL: Starting balance (real)
NUMBER: Account number for each transaction (integer)
TYPE: Type of each transaction (character * 1)
AMOUNT: Amount of each transaction (real)
DATE: Day of each transaction (integer)

CHECK: Contains character string 'C' (character * 1)
PENLTY: Contains penalty amount— $5.00 (real)
INVAL: Indicates whether or not an invalid transaction card was read (logical)
SNTVAL: Sentinel card value, 0 (integer)
SPACE: Used to line transactions up in correct columns of printout; character string, '□□□□□□□□□□' (character * 10)

ENDBAL: Ending balance (real)
NRCHEK: Number of checks (integer)
NRDEP: Number of deposits (integer)
NROVER: Number of rubber checks (integer)

The variable INVAL (type logical) is used as a *program flag*. That is, the value of INVAL is used to signal or indicate the results of some prior data manipulation at a later point in the program. INVAL will be initially set to the logical constant .FALSE.. If an invalid account number appears on a transaction card, the value of INVAL will be redefined to be the logical constant .TRUE. (see Step 31, Fig. 4.5(b)). By testing INVAL at Step 40 (Fig. 4.5(a)), the program can print out a warning message if an invalid account number was encountered at any earlier point in its execution.

The remaining numbered steps (19, 29, and 39) need no explicit refinement. The transaction should be listed under the correct column of the printout, the value of ENDBAL updated, and the appropriate counter (NRCHEK, NRDEP, or NROVER) incremented by one. The program is shown in Fig. 4.6.

We have used the character data type for storage of character strings. If this is not available, you should change those declarations to type integer. Depending on the character capacity of an integer variable on your computer, you may have to abbreviate the month further (4 characters is assumed here) and use initials to represent the account name. The length of SPACE may also have to be adjusted so that the output columns line up properly. ∎

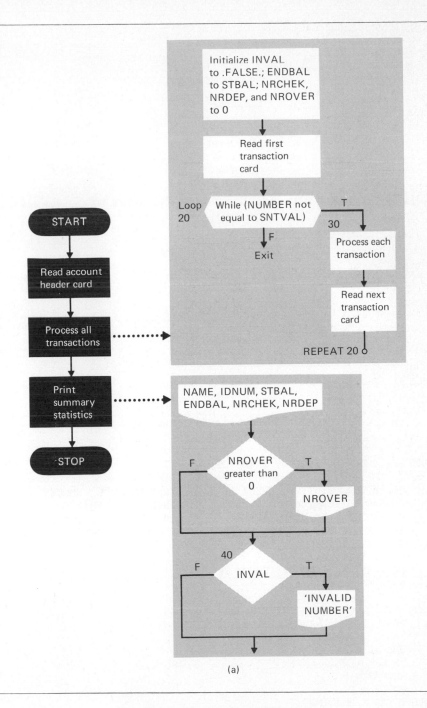

Fig. 4.5(a) Flow diagrams for Problem 4.1.

Refinement of Step 30

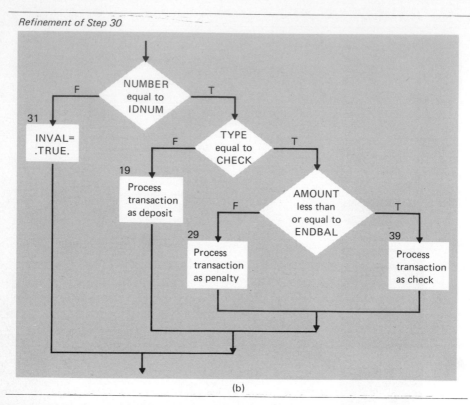

(b)

Fig. 4.5(b)   Refinement of Step 30 from Fig. 4.5(a).

```
C PROCESS CHECKING ACCOUNT TRANSACTIONS
C
      CHARACTER * 1 TYPE, CHECK      [or INTEGER TYPE, CHECK]
      CHARACTER * 4 MONTH            [or INTEGER MONTH]
      CHARACTER * 10 NAME, SPACE     [or INTEGER NAME, SPACE]
      INTEGER IDNUM, NUMBER, NRCHEK, NRDEP, NROVER, DATE, SNTVAL
      REAL STBAL, ENDBAL, AMOUNT, PENLTY
      LOGICAL INVAL
      DATA SNTVAL, PENLTY, CHECK /0, 5.0, 'C'/
      DATA SPACE /'          '/
C
C READ HEADER CARD AND INITIALIZE VARIABLES
      READ, IDNUM, NAME, STBAL, MONTH
      INVAL = .FALSE.
      ENDBAL = STBAL
      NRCHEK = 0
      NROVER = 0
      NRDEP = 0
C PRINT TABLE HEADING
      PRINT, '     DATE      CHECK       DEPOSIT        PENALTY'
C
```

```
C READ AND PROCESS EACH TRANSACTION
      READ, NUMBER, TYPE, AMOUNT, DATE
      WHILE (NUMBER .NE. SNTVAL) DO
C         CHECK FOR INVALID ACCOUNT NUMBER
         IF (NUMBER .EQ. IDNUM) THEN
C            TEST TYPE OF TRANSACTION
            IF (TYPE .EQ. CHECK) THEN
C               TEST FOR RUBBER CHECK
               IF (AMOUNT .LE. ENDBAL) THEN
C                  PROCESS CHECK
                  PRINT, MONTH, DATE, AMOUNT
                  ENDBAL = ENDBAL - AMOUNT
                  NRCHEK = NRCHEK + 1
               ELSE
C                  PROCESS RUBBER CHECK
                  PRINT, MONTH, DATE, AMOUNT, SPACE, PENLTY
                  ENDBAL = ENDBAL - PENLTY
                  NROVER = NROVER + 1
               ENDIF
            ELSE
C               PROCESS DEPOSIT
               PRINT, MONTH, DATE, SPACE, AMOUNT
               ENDBAL = ENDBAL + AMOUNT
               NRDEP = NRDEP + 1
            ENDIF
         ELSE
C            INVALID ACCOUNT NUMBER
            INVAL = .TRUE.
         ENDIF
C         READ NEXT TRANSACTION
         READ, NUMBER, TYPE, AMOUNT, DATE
      ENDWHILE
C
C PRINT SUMMARY STATISTICS
      PRINT, NAME, '   ACCOUNT NO.    ', IDNUM
      PRINT, 'STARTING BALANCE ', STBAL, ' ENDING BALANCE ', ENDBAL
      PRINT, 'NO. OF CHECKS PAID ', NRCHEK, ' NO. OF DEPOSITS ', NRDEP
      IF (NROVER .GT. 0) PRINT, 'NO. OF OVERDRAWN CHECKS ', NROVER
      IF (INVAL) PRINT, 'TRANSACTION CARD WITH INVALID ACCOUNT NUMBER
     Z PRESENT'
      STOP
      END
```

Fig. 4.6 Program for Problem 4.1.

EXERCISE 4.6 Design a sentinel card which could be used with this program.

4.5 INTEGERS AND THE INDEXED-DO LOOP STRUCTURE

Since an integer can always be represented as a real number simply by indicating that its fractional part is zero, the question may be asked: "Why use fixed-point form at all?" One reason is that fixed-point operations are usually considerably simpler and faster than floating-point operations; hence, programs that use integers whenever possible will execute more efficiently.

Another reason for using integers is that they can always be represented exactly in fixed-point form. However, just as there are some numbers that cannot be represented exactly in the decimal number system (for example, $1/3 = .33333...$), there are many real numbers that cannot be represented exactly in a computer in floating-point form. Therefore, although the range of numbers that can be represented in floating-point form is greater than for fixed-point form, the accuracy of representation in fixed-point form is more precise.

As an example of one possible effect of this imprecise representation, consider the loop shown in Fig. 4.7 which utilizes a real counter for loop control. This loop may execute 10 times on some computers and 11 times on others. This is because the floating-point representation of the fraction 0.1 is not exact and is, in fact, numerically less than 0.1. As the internal representation of 0.1 is repeatedly added to FRAC, the difference between the number actually stored in FRAC and what we would expect to be there increases. After ten additions, the value of FRAC should be equal to 1.0; however, the actual number stored in FRAC may be sufficiently less than 1.0 that an extra loop repetition will occur.

```
                 REAL FRAC
                 FRAC = 0.0
                 WHILE (FRAC .LT. 1.0) DO
                         .
                         .
                         .
                     FRAC = FRAC + 0.1
                 ENDWHILE
```

Fig. 4.7 Loop control using a real variable as a counter.

To avoid such difficulties, it is best to use integers as counters to control loop repetition. Counters do not normally require fractional parts. In addition, counting is done in a loop and is usually supplemental to the main activity of the loop. It should therefore be done in the simplest and most efficient manner possible.

4.5.1 The Indexed-DO Loop Structure

The Standard FORTRAN language has a structure called the *indexed-DO loop structure*, which is particularly useful in writing loops whose repetition is controlled by a counter. It enables us to specify, in a single statement, the name of the counter as well as the initial, increment, and end values for the counter. The counter is then automatically treated as the loop-control variable. We need not be concerned with the actual initialization, increment, and repetition involving the counter. The compiler will handle all of this work for us if we provide it with the necessary information in the indexed-DO header statement.

The general form of the standard FORTRAN indexed-DO loop is described below.

Indexed–DO Loop Structure (Standard FORTRAN)

FORTRAN Form:

```
DO label loopvar = initval, endval, increment
   ___
   ___
   ___ } Loop body
   ___
   ___
label CONTINUE
```

Interpretation. Loopvar is the *loop-control variable for the indexed-DO*, and initval, endval, and increment are the *loop parameters.* The loop body is executed once for each value of loopvar beginning with loopvar = initval, and continuing in steps specified by increment until the value of loopvar exceeds endval. The label is used to specify the *range* or physical extent of the loop, and must appear as shown in both the header and terminator statements.

Example 4.6

```
DO 16 LCV = 1, N, 1
   PRINT, 'LCV = ', LCV
16 CONTINUE
```

If N is 9, this loop will be executed 9 times. Each time it will print the next integer between 1 and 9. LCV and N are both integers. Whenever initval and increment are both one, the number of loop-body repetitions in an indexed-DO is equal to endval.

Example 4.7

```
VALUE = 0
DO 978  INDEX = 3, 10, 2
   VALUE = VALUE + INDEX
978 CONTINUE
PRINT, VALUE
```

This loop is executed once for values of INDEX = 3, 5, 7, and 9. VALUE and INDEX are integers. The number printed will be 24.

There are a number of rules that must be followed when using an indexed-DO. These rules are summarized next.

Rules for Using the Indexed-DO Structure

1. The loop variable must be an integer variable name. The parameters initval, endval, and increment must be either integer variable names, or integer constants. The value of endval must be greater than or equal to the value of initval, and all three values must be positive.

2. None of the variables in the indexed-DO header statement may have their values changed within the loop body.

3. If an indexed-DO is executed to normal completion (instead of exited prematurely via a GOTO statement), then the loop variable is considered to be undefined. In this case, the loop variable cannot be used elsewhere without first being redefined. If a transfer out of the loop is taken via a GOTO, then the loop variable is still defined and may be used at later points in the execution of the program.

4. If the increment value is the constant 1, it (and the preceding ",") may be omitted from the header statement.

As long as these rules are followed in writing an indexed-DO loop, the loop will have the equivalent effect of a counting loop written using the WHILE loop structure. This is illustrated in the following example.

Example 4.8 Equivalent loops for computing the SUM of a collection of N data items (COUNT and N are integers; SUM and ITEM are real).

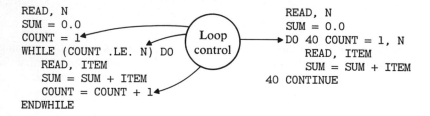

```
    READ, N                                      READ, N
    SUM = 0.0                                    SUM = 0.0
    COUNT = 1                                    DO 40 COUNT = 1, N
    WHILE (COUNT .LE. N) DO                         READ, ITEM
        READ, ITEM                                  SUM = SUM + ITEM
        SUM = SUM + ITEM                      40 CONTINUE
        COUNT = COUNT + 1
    ENDWHILE
```

As illustrated in this example, the indexed-DO header statement can be used to specify all three control functions for a counting loop:

1. loop-control variable initialization: COUNT = 1
2. loop-control variable test: WHILE (COUNT .LE. N) DO
3. loop-control variable increment: COUNT = COUNT + 1

The flow diagram for the indexed-DO is shown on the right in Fig. 4.8. The equivalent WHILE loop pattern is shown on the left of this figure.

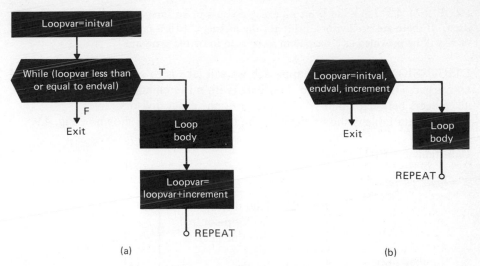

Fig. 4.8 Flow-diagram patterns for indexed-DO.

EXERCISE 4.7 Write an indexed-DO loop which computes the product of all integers less than or equal to N. Modify this loop so that it computes the product of the even integers only.

4.5.2 Integer Division: A Prime Number Problem

Although the actual steps performed by the computer in adding, subtracting, multiplying, and dividing integers are quite different from those used to manipulate reals, the results of most computations are the same. Thus,

3 * 4 = 12   3 + 4 = 7

and   and

3.0 * 4.0 = 12.0   3.0 + 4.0 = 7.0

and so on. The only exception to this is the operation of division, /. Since the result of an arithmetic operation with integers must be an integer as well, there is never any *remainder* associated with integer division. For example:

9.0/5.0 = 1.8   9.0/−5.0 = −1.8

but   but

9/5 = 1   9/−5 = −1

Any remainder in integer division is *truncated*, regardless of its size.

This property of integer division is used to advantage in the following problem.

PROBLEM 4.2   Find and print all exact divisors of an integer N other than 1 and N itself. If there are no divisors, print out the message "N is a prime number." The value of N will be provided as a data item to be read in by the program.

DISCUSSION. The general approach we will take is to see whether we can find an integer, DIV, which divides N evenly (with no remainder). We shall examine all integers between 2 and N − 1 and print any exact divisors.

The data table is shown below. The flow diagrams are shown in Fig. 4.9.

Data table for Problem 4.2

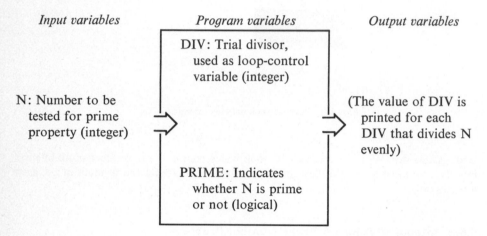

The variable PRIME (type logical) is used as a program flag. The value of PRIME is initially set to the logical constant .TRUE. (step 12). If a divisor of N is found in loop 20, then DIV is printed and the value of PRIME is redefined to be the logical constant .FALSE. (step 29). When step 30 is reached, PRIME is tested to determine whether or not a divisor of N was found. If PRIME is still true, this indicates that no divisor of N was found in loop 20, and that N therefore is prime.

The integer variable LIM should be added to the data table. It is required because the expression N − 1 cannot be used as a loop parameter (step 19).

As shown in the flow diagram, the algorithm proceeds by checking all integers between 2 and N − 1 inclusive as possible divisors of N (loop 20). The actual sequence of steps needed to carry out the divisibility test (refinement of step 25) is shown in Fig. 4.10.

The strategy is to first calculate QUOT, the quotient of N divided by DIV. If there is no remainder (DIV is a divisor of N), then when we multiply QUOT by DIV we should get N back:

$$(N/DIV) * DIV = N$$

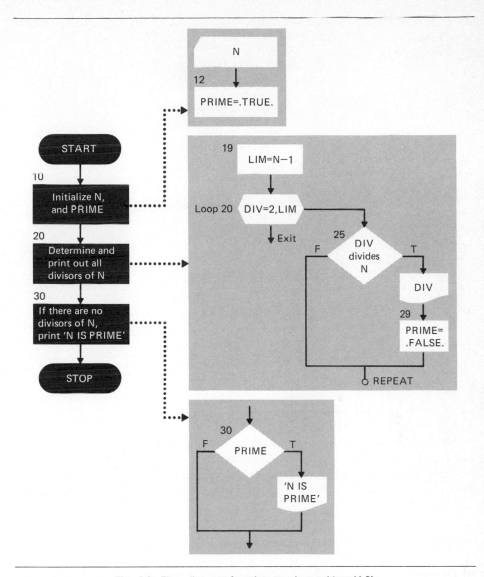

Fig. 4.9 Flow diagrams for prime-number problem (4.2).

However, if DIV does not divide N exactly, the remainder is lost (remember, all of the variables involved in this computation are integers). Consequently, when we multiply QUOT by DIV, the result is less than N and the value of DIV should not be printed. For example, if N is 5, and DIV is 2, then

$$(N/DIV) * DIV = (5/2) \times 2 = (2) \times 2 = 4 \neq 5.$$

Box 25 Refinement:

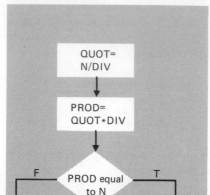

Fig. 4.10 Test for divisibility of N.

The additional program variables needed are shown below.

Program variables

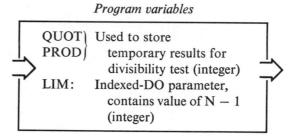

The program for Problem 4.2 is shown in Fig. 4.11. ▌

EXERCISE 4.8 (for the more mathematically inclined) The program shown in Fig. 4.11 tests all integer values between 2 and N − 1 inclusive to see if any of them divide N. This is, in fact, quite inefficient, for we need not test all of these values.   Revise the algorithm shown in Fig. 4.11 to minimize the number of possible divisors of N that must be tested to determine whether or not N is prime.   Make certain that your improved algorithm still works. [*Hints.* If 2 does not divide N, no other even number will divide N. If no integer value between 2 and N/2 + 1 divides N, then no integer value between N/2 + 1 and N − 1 will divide N. (In fact, we can even compute a smaller maximum test value than N/2 + 1. What is it?)]

```
C PRIME NUMBER PROBLEM
C
      INTEGER N, DIV, QUOT, PROD, LIM
      LOGICAL PRIME
C
      READ, N
      PRINT, 'LIST OF DIVISORS OF ', N
      PRIME = .TRUE.
C
C TEST ALL POSSIBLE DIVISORS OF N
      LIM = N - 1
      DO 20 DIV = 2, LIM
         QUOT = N / DIV
         PROD = QUOT * DIV
C        PRINT OUT EACH DIVISOR
         IF (PROD .EQ. N) THEN
            PRINT, DIV
            PRIME = .FALSE.
         ENDIF
   20 CONTINUE
C END OF LOOP
C
C TEST FOR PRIME
      IF (PRIME) PRINT, N, ' IS PRIME.'
      STOP
      END
```

Fig. 4.11 Program for Problem 4.1.

4.6 ARITHMETIC EXPRESSIONS

4.6.1 Introduction

In the remainder of this chapter, we will describe in some detail the Standard FORTRAN features for the manipulation of integer and real data. In Chapter 1 we mentioned that FORTRAN was particularly well suited to the programming of mathematical problems, because it permitted a convenient representation of mathematical formulas. Indeed, FORTRAN was designed with the formulas and functions of basic mathematics in mind. Although the FORTRAN language is often used for solving a wide variety of problems, the formula-specification facility is one of the most important aspects of the language.

Until now, however, we have rather neglected this aspect of FORTRAN, concentrating instead upon some of the fundamental techniques of problem solving and data manipulation with the computer. In this section, we will turn our attention to the use and understanding of formulas in FORTRAN.

In FORTRAN, formulas are expressed primarily in terms of assignment statements. The general form of the FORTRAN assignment statement is shown next.

Assignment statement

FORTRAN form:

```
name = expression
```

Interpretation. This statement is used to assign a particular value (indicated by the expression) to the variable whose name appears on the left side of the assignment operator, "=".

The assignment statement, itself, is quite simple and rather unexciting. In fact, we have used many assignment statements in earlier programs. For example:

```
SUM   = 0.0
GROSS = RATE * HOURS
TOTAL = TOTAL + GRADE
QUOT  = N/DIV
```

It is really the expression part of the assignment statement that is of primary interest. Until now, we have been limited when writing expressions in FORTRAN. However, there is a good deal of variation actually permitted in the expressions that may be used.

An *arithmetic expression* is a grouping of real or integer variables and constants, and the arithmetic operators. In FORTRAN, it is possible to write arithmetic expressions containing more than one operator and nested levels of parentheses. For example, expressions such as

```
HOURS * RATE - TAX
B * B - 4.0 * A * C
(40.0 + 1.5 * (HOURS - 40.0)) * RATE
(N/DIV) * DIV
```

are all legal expressions in FORTRAN.

Since the computer is capable of performing only a single basic operation at a time, however, the compiler must translate each such complex expression into an equivalent sequence of basic operations. We must specify each expression in a precise form or the compiler translation may not conform to our expectations. For example, there must be no confusion in our own minds concerning the meaning of expressions such as $A + B * C$ or $X/Y * Z$. Do we mean $(A + B) * C$ or $A + (B * C)$? Do we intend to compute $(X/Y) * Z$ or $X/(Y * Z)$?

In programming in a language such as FORTRAN, the meaning of all expressions is completely determined by the rules of translation that are followed by the compiler. That is, the meaning is determined by the order in which the compiler specifies that the list of basic operations will be carried out. Figure 4.12 shows an example of how the translation process works for the statement $X = A/(B + C)$. The compiler translates this statement into a sequence of statements, each of which involves one of the basic operations described in

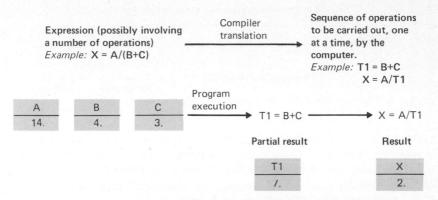

Fig. 4.12 The translation of a simple arithmetic expression.

Chapter 1. In the process, the compiler uses an additional variable, T1, to store some of the partial computational results before obtaining the final result, which is then stored in X.

We must understand the way expressions are evaluated in FORTRAN in order to write expressions that produce the desired results. Unfortunately, the algorithms used by most compilers to analyze an expression and to specify the list of basic operations indicated by the expression are beyond the scope of this text. However, it is possible to formulate a set of *rules of expression evaluation* which, if followed, will produce the same computational results as the rules followed by the compiler. To illustrate the application of the rules for expression evaluation, we will provide diagrams like the one in Fig. 4.13. The numbered circles in these diagrams will be used to represent the expression operators and the order in which they are evaluated. The lines will be used to connect each operator with its operands.

In the expression shown in Fig. 4.13, the order of evaluation of the operators is $+$, $*$, $/$, and finally, $-$. The operands manipulated by these operators are described in Table 4.1.

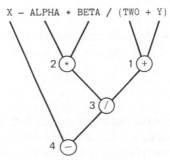

Fig. 4.13 An example of expression evaluation.

Table 4.1 Operand/Operator association for Fig. 4.13

Operator	Left operand	Right operand
+	TWO	Y
*	ALPHA	BETA
/	Result of ALPHA * BETA	Result of TWO + Y
—	X	Result of division operation

EXERCISE 4.9 How would you evaluate the expressions A + B * C and X/Y * Z? Try assigning small values to the 6 variables involved in these operations. Verify for yourself that grouping the operands differently produces different results.

4.6.2 Evaluation of Arithmetic Expressions

The basic arithmetic operations that can be expressed in FORTRAN are the binary operations (+, −, * (multiplication), / (division), and ** (exponentiation)), and the unary minus operation (−). (Exponentiation is not a basic computer operation, but it will be treated as such for the purpose of this discussion.) A *binary operation* is one that involves two operands (such as X * 4.0). A *unary operation* involves only one operand (as in −X). The rules of evaluation of expressions containing these operators (and parentheses) are given next.

Rules of evaluation of arithmetic expressions

a) All parenthesized subexpressions must be evaluated first. Nested parenthesized subexpressions must be evaluated inside-out, with the innermost expressions evaluated first.

b) Operators in the same subexpression are evaluated according to the following hierarchy.
   i) exponentiation, **   Top level
   ii) unary minus, −
   iii) Multiplication and division, *, /
   iv) Addition, subtraction, +, −   Bottom level

c) Operators in the same subexpression and at the same hierarchical level (such as + and −) are evaluated left to right. The only exception to this rule is that consecutive exponentiation operators are evaluated right to left.

The above rules are not the same as the ones followed by most compilers, but they produce the same results. We will now illustrate these rules with a few examples. The order of evaluation and the rule applied at each step are indicated alongside the operator.

Example 4.9:

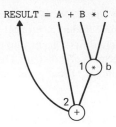

RESULT = A + B * C

Example 4.10:

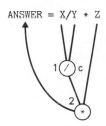

ANSWER = X/Y * Z

Example 4.11:

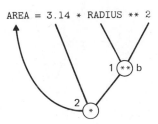

AREA = 3.14 * RADIUS ** 2

Example 4.11 shows the FORTRAN form of the formula for the area of a circle, πr^2, where r is the radius of the circle and multiplication of π (3.14) by r^2 is implied. AREA and RADIUS should both be type real. This expression specifies that RADIUS should be "squared" or raised to the power 2. This operation is done first in the above expression. The result is then multiplied by 3.14.

Example 4.12:

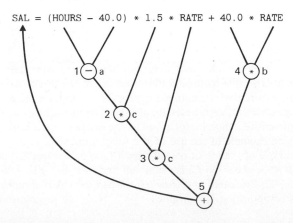

SAL = (HOURS − 40.0) * 1.5 * RATE + 40.0 * RATE

This expression could be used to calculate the salary for an employee who has worked more than 40 hours, and is paid time and a half for all hours worked over 40.0. The sub-expression in parentheses is evaluated first, according to rule (a). All multiplications are performed before the addition because of rule (b). The multiplications are performed in left-to-right order according to rule (c). Finally, the addition operation is performed and the assignment is carried out.

Example 4.13 In this example, one of the roots of a quadratic equation of the form $AX^2 + BX + C = 0$ is calculated. The formula for the root is

$$ROOT1 = \frac{-B + \sqrt{B^2 - 4AC}}{2A}$$

This is written and evaluated in FORTRAN as shown next.

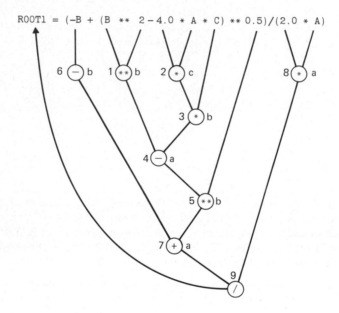

We will learn a better way to take the square root ($\sqrt{\ }$) of a quantity later, but for the time being we can accomplish this by raising that quantity to the power 0.5. Note the use of the parentheses to ensure that the entire quantity ($B^2 - 4AC$) is raised to the power 0.5 and not just the variable C. Parentheses are also used to force the evaluation of the entire numerator and the entire denominator prior to the division operation. The $-B$ part of this expression is an example of the use of the unary minus.

This is an example of the use of nested parenthesized subexpressions. The innermost subexpression (B**2 − 4.0 * A * C) is evaluated first, according to rule (a). Within this subexpression, B**2 is evaluated first (rule (b)). Then 4.0 * A is computed (rule (c)), and the result of this computation is multiplied by C. Now the subtraction is performed to complete the evaluation of the innermost subexpression. The difference is raised to the 0.5 power (rule (b)). Next $-B$ is evaluated (rule (b)), and then the evaluation of the left parenthesized subexpression is completed by evaluating the addition operation (rule (a)). Finally, $2.0 * A$ is computed (rule (a)) and the division is performed.

EXERCISE 4.10 Write the following formula in FORTRAN and draw a diagram indicating its order of evaluation:

$$A = C + \frac{S}{Q} + \frac{H \times Q}{2.0 \times R}$$

4.6.3 Syntax Rules for Arithmetic Expressions

In the last section, we listed some rules of evaluation for arithmetic expressions. We stated that familiarity with these rules is essential if we are to be able to write arithmetic expressions that have the desired meaning. Whenever there is any doubt concerning the rules of evaluation, you should always use parentheses to clarify the order in which you wish to have your specified operations performed.

In this section, we turn our attention to the syntactic rules for forming arithmetic expressions, and for using them in assignment statements. These rules may appear formidable, but they are quite basic and have been used consistently throughout this chapter.

Arithmetic expressions

FORTRAN rule of formation:

An arithmetic expression may consist of a single operand (a variable name or a constant), or a combination of operands formed according to the following rules.

1. No two operands can appear adjacent to one another in an arithmetic expression. Each pair of operands must be separated by an operator.
   Example
   $$4.0 * A * C \text{ is legal} \qquad 4.0 \ AC \text{ is illegal}$$

2. No two operators can appear adjacent (except for $**$ meaning exponentiation). Each pair of operators must be separated by an operand.
   Exception: When the negation operator " $-$ " is adjacent to another operator, both the $-$ and its operand should be enclosed in parentheses.
   Example
   $$A * -B \text{ is not legal}$$
   $$A * (-B) \text{ is legal}$$
   $$A * / BC \text{ is not legal}$$
   $$A * B / C \text{ is legal}$$

3. All operands appearing in an expression should be of the same type. *Exception:* When a number is being raised to a power (p) using the exponentiation operator (**), p may be of type integer even if the number is real. In fact, you are encouraged to use an integer value whenever possible, since this is more efficient and likely to produce more accurate results.

4. Expressions formed according to rules 1 through 3 may be enclosed in parentheses, and combined as operands in still larger expressions.

There are two inherent difficulties in representing a mathematical formula in FORTRAN. Multiplication can often be implied in a mathematical formula simply by writing the two items to be multiplied side by side: e.g., $a = bc$. In FORTRAN, however, the * operator must always be used to indicate multiplication, as in A = B * C.

The other difficulty arises in formulas involving division. These can be written with the numerator and denominator on separate lines:

$$m = \frac{y - b}{x - a}$$

so that the expression is unambiguous. In FORTRAN, however, all assignment statements are written on a single line. Consequently, parentheses are often needed to separate the numerator from the denominator, and to clearly indicate the order of evaluation of the operators in the expression.

Example 4.14 The formula

$$X = \frac{AB}{C^D E} - \frac{F + G}{H - I}$$

can be written in FORTRAN as

$$X = (A * B)/(C ** D * E) - (F + G)/(H - I)$$

EXERCISE 4.11 Let A, B, C, and X be the names of four variables of type real, and I, J, K the names of three type integer variables. Each of the statements below contains a violation of the rules of formation of arithmetic expressions. Rewrite each statement so that it is consistent with these rules.

a) X = 4.0 A * C

b) A = AC

c) I = 2 * −J

d) K = 3(I + J)

e) X = A/BC

f) I = J3

EXERCISE 4.12 Write the FORTRAN equivalents for the following arithmetic expressions. (Each symbolic name consists of a single letter.)

a) $x(y + w)z$

b) $x^2 + y^2$

c) $(xy)^2$

d) $\dfrac{ax + bg}{aw + by}$

e) $3.0(xy + wz) - 12.0$

f) $(3.2 - 7.5y)^2$

g) $3.14 \times 10^6 - .013 \times 10^{-4}(x + y)$

h) $\dfrac{18.0x - 12.5 \times 10^3 x}{x^{(n-3)} + y^{(n-2)}}$

4.7 LIBRARY FUNCTIONS

There are several numerically oriented operations, such as finding the square root or logarithm of a number, or computing trigonometric functions, that many users of FORTRAN need to perform. These operations are not among the basic operations of most computers. However, they are provided as part of a library of FORTRAN-related programs produced by each computer installation or by the manufacturer of each computer that has a FORTRAN compiler. These programs are called *library functions*.

A function may be thought of as an operator that performs a transformation on its input data and produces a single output value. The input data and the resulting output value have a particular relationship that is determined by the *definition* of the function. The input provided to a function is called its *argument(s)*; most functions have only a single argument, but the use of multiple arguments (separated by commas in an argument list) is allowed. A function will not alter the value of the input argument(s) in computing the output value (Fig. 4.14).

Fig. 4.14 Transformation of input to output by a function.

To *reference* or *call* a library function, we need only write its name followed by the argument list (enclosed in parentheses) in an expression. For example,

$$R1 = ABS(X) + 6.0$$

calls the function named ABS to operate on the argument X. ABS is the name of a very simple library function that computes the *absolute value* of a real number. The definition of ABS may be stated as follows:

If the input (X in this case) is negative, compute as output the negation of the input $(-X)$;
If the input is not negative, the output is identical to the input (no computation is necessary in this case).

In the previous example, if the variable X contains −7.5, then ABS(X) will be equal to 7.5, and the value stored in R1 will be 13.5. The value of the argument X is not altered by the function computation.

FORTRAN allows nested function calls in an expression. For example, when executed, the statement

$$S1 = SQRT(ABS(THETA))$$

causes the following sequence of actions.

1. A call to the ABS function to find the absolute value of THETA.

2. A call to the square-root function, to take the square root of the absolute value of THETA.

Similarly, a function call can be part of a complicated expression and may have expressions as well for its arguments:

$$R1 = (-B + SQRT(B ** 2 - 4.0 * A * C))/(2.0 * A)$$

Here the function SQRT would be called after the computation necessary to evaluate its argument B ** 2 − 4.0 * A * C was performed. Then the quantity − B would be added to the result (the square root), and the entire quantity would finally be divided by the product 2.0 * A.

To use a library function in a program, the only information that we need to know about the function is its name, the type of its argument(s), and the type of the result that is returned. The type of the result is determined by the first letter of the name of the function. Thus, the value returned by a function whose name starts with any of the letters I through N will be of type integer. The values returned by all other library functions will be of type real.

A list of some library functions and the types of their input arguments and output values are listed in Table 4.2. (Functions are discussed in more detail in Chapter 7.)

Example 4.15 The library function MOD can be used to test one integer (N) for divisibility by another integer (DIV). The value returned by the function call

$$MOD(N,DIV)$$

is the remainder of the division of N by DIV. For example, if N = 17, and DIV = 3, then the value 2 would be returned. If the value returned is 0, then N is evenly divisible by DIV. The loop to test all possible divisors of N (see the Program for the Prime Number Problem, Fig. 4.11) can be rewritten using the MOD function as shown next.

```
        LIM = N - 1
        DO 20 DIV = 2, LIM
          IF (MOD(N,DIV) .EQ. 0) THEN
             PRINT, DIV
             PRIME = .FALSE.
          ENDIF
     20 CONTINUE
```

Table 4.2 Some commonly used library functions

Function name	Type of argument(s)	Type of result	Example of call
ABS (absolute value-real)	Real	Real	Y=ABS(X)
IABS (absolute value-integer)	Integer	Integer	J=IABS(I)
SQRT (square root)	Real	Real	X=SQRT(Y)
MOD (I modulo J)	Integer	Integer	K=MOD(I,J)
ALOG (base e or natural logarithm: $\log_e$ W)	Real	Real	X=ALOG(W)
ALOG10 (base 10 logarithm: $\log_{10}$ W)	Real	Real	X=ALOG10(W)
AMAX1 (find maximum value of two or more real arguments)	Real	Real	XMAX=AMAX1(X1,X2,X3)
*MAX0 (find maximum value of two or more integer arguments)	Integer	Integer	MAX=MAX0(I1,I2,I3,I4)
AMIN1 (find minimum value of two or more real arguments)	Real	Real	XMIN=AMIN1(X1,X3)
*MIN0 (find minimum value of two or more integer arguments)	Integer	Integer	MIN=MIN0(I1,I2,I3)
SIN (trig sine)	Real (radians)	Real	X=SIN(THETA)
COS (trig cosine)	Real (radians)	Real	X=COS(THETA)
TAN (trig tangent)	Real (radians)	Real	X=TAN(THETA)
IFIX (convert real to integer)	Real	Integer	I=IFIX(Y)
FLOAT (convert integer to real)	Integer	Real	Y=FLOAT(K)
EXP (exponential e^Y)	Real	Real	X=EXP(Y)

* The last character in the function name is a zero.

The next example illustrates the conversion of formulas from physics into FORTRAN statements. You need not be concerned if the formulas are unfamiliar; the main point of the example is to illustrate the implementation of these formulas in a FORTRAN program.

Example 4.16 Prince Valiant is trying to rescue Rapunzel by shooting an arrow with a rope attached through her tower window which is 100 feet off the ground. We will assume that the arrow travels at a constant velocity. Hence, the time it takes to reach the tower is given by the formula

$$T = \frac{X}{V \cos \theta}$$

where X is the distance Prince Valiant is standing from the tower, V is the velocity of the arrow and θ is its angle of elevation.

Our task is to determine whether or not the Prince's arrow goes through the window by computing its distance off the ground when it reaches the tower as given by the formula

$$H = VT \sin \theta - \frac{GT^2}{2}$$

For the arrow to go through the window, H should be between 100 and 110 feet. We will print out an appropriate message to help Prince Valiant correct his aim.

The program is shown below:

```
C PRINCE VALIANT TAKES AIM AT RAPUNZEL
C
      REAL H, T, V, THETA, PI, X, RADIAN, G
      DATA PI, G /3.14159, 32.17/
C READ AND PRINT INPUT DATA
      READ, X, V, THETA
      PRINT, 'DISTANCE FROM TOWER = ', X
      PRINT, 'VELOCITY OF ARROW = ', V
      PRINT, 'ANGLE OF ELEVATION = ', THETA, 'DEGREES'
C
C THE FORTRAN TRIG FUNCTIONS REQUIRE INPUT ANGLES
C IN RADIANS.  CONVERT THETA FROM DEGREES TO RADIANS.
      RADIAN = THETA * (PI / 180.0)
C COMPUTE TRAVEL TIME OF ARROW
      T = X / (V * COS(RADIAN))
C COMPUTE ARROW HEIGHT
      H = V * T * SIN(RADIAN) - G / 2.0 * T ** 2
C PRINT MESSAGE TO CORRECT PRINCE'S AIM
      IF (H .LT. 100.0) THEN
         IF (H .LT. 0.0) THEN
            PRINT, 'ARROW DID NOT REACH THE TOWER'
         ELSE
            PRINT, 'ARROW WAS TOO LOW, HEIGHT WAS ', H
         ENDIF
      ELSE
         IF (H .GT. 110.0) THEN
            PRINT, 'ARROW WAS TOO HIGH, HEIGHT WAS ', H
         ELSE
            PRINT, 'GOOD SHOT PRINCE'
         ENDIF
      ENDIF
      STOP
      END
```

EXERCISE 4.13 Modify this program so that the velocity of the arrow will automatically be increased by 10 feet/sec if the arrow is too low and decreased by 8 feet/sec if the arrow is too high. This repetition should terminate when the arrow enters the window. [*Hint.* Use a program flag as the loop control variable.]

EXERCISE 4.14 Let X = 10.0, START = 3.0, and YNEW = 0.0, as shown in the program below. What will be the value of YNEW, as printed by this program? (Show all intermediate output from your hand simulation. Keep your computations accurate to 4 decimal places. Two repetitions of the loop should be sufficient.) *Hint.* This program computes an approximation to the square root of X.

```
      REAL X, Y, YNEW, START, ERRLIM
      DATA X /10.0/
      DATA ERRLIM /0.001/, START /3.0/
```

```
          Y = START
          YNEW = (Y + X / Y) / 2.0
          WHILE (ABS(YNEW - Y) .GT. ERRLIM) DO
             Y = YNEW
             YNEW = (Y + X / Y) / 2.0
          ENDWHILE
          PRINT, YNEW
          STOP
          END
```

4.7.1   Using FLOAT and IFIX—Avoiding Mixed Type Operations

In rule 3 of the Rules of Formation of Arithmetic Expressions, we indicated that the operands in an expression should all be of the same type. Some compilers will allow the use of mixed type or mixed mode expressions containing both real and integer operands. However, computers cannot carry out mixed type computations directly, so the compiler must eliminate any mixed-mode operations that occur. If one operand involved in an operation is an integer and the other is a real, the compiler will first form a real number which is numerically equivalent to the integer, and then use the real equivalent in the computation. The original integer operand is left undisturbed by this *type conversion*.

Unfortunately, the compilers that allow mixed mode expressions use different criteria for deciding when mixed mode conversions are required. Hence, we suggest that you avoid using mixed mode expressions. This can be done by using the two library functions FLOAT and IFIX. The function FLOAT takes an integer argument (in fixed point form) and provides as output an equivalent real value (in floating point form). The function IFIX takes a real argument; it provides as output an integer value corresponding to the integral part of its argument. Neither IFIX nor FLOAT alters its argument.

Example 4.17 The program below computes and prints a table showing the conversion from degrees Centigrade to degrees Fahrenheit for temperatures ranging from 1°C to 100°C.

```
C COMPUTE AND PRINT TABLE OF CENTIGRADE TO FAHRENHEIT
C CONVERSION FOR 1 TO 100 DEGREES CENTIGRADE
      INTEGER CDEGR, RFDEGR
      REAL FDEGR
      PRINT, '   CENTIGRADE      FAHRENHEIT'
      PRINT, '     DEGREES          DEGREES'
      DO 10 CDEGR = 1, 100
         FDEGR = 1.8 * FLOAT(CDEGR) + 32.0
         RFDEGR = IFIX(FDEGR + 0.5)
         PRINT, CDEGR, RFDEGR
   10 CONTINUE
      STOP
      END
```

The computation is illustrated below for CDEGR = 26:

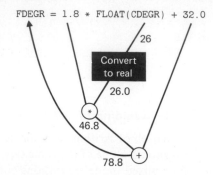

The next assignment statement *rounds* the result to the nearest whole degree; i.e., raises it to the next degree if the fractional part is 0.5 or greater.

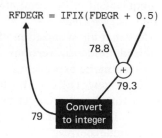

We see that 79 is stored in RFDEGR (rather than 78) as the fractional part of FDEGR is 0.8.

The functions IFIX and FLOAT may also be used to avoid the use of mixed type assignment statements, such as

$$XN = N$$

or

$$I = PSI$$

where XN and PSI are real, and N and I are integers. While Standard FORTRAN does allow the use of such statements, we believe that it is better to consistently avoid assigning a value of one type to a variable of different type. Instead, we recommend that you explicitly represent the conversion indicated by such a mixed assignment:

```
XN = FLOAT(N)
 I = IFIX (PSI)
```

EXERCISE 4.15 Write an assignment statement which rounds a positive real number to two significant decimal places. [*Hint.* You will have to multiply by 100.0.] Generalize your expression to round a positive real number accurate to N decimal places, where N is any positive integer. [*Hint.* 100.0 = 10.0**2.]

EXERCISE 4.16 Assume that you have a program in which the following declarations and data statements appear.

```
INTEGER COLOR, LIME, STRAW, YELLOW, RED, ORANGE
REAL   BLACK, WHITE, GREEN, BLUE, PURPLE, CRAYON
DATA   COLOR, BLACK, CRAYON/2, 2.5, -1.3/
DATA   STRAW, RED, PURPLE/1, -3, +0.3E1/
```

For each of the following assignment statements, eliminate all mixed-mode expressions and assignments and then determine the value that is assigned to the variable appearing on the left-hand side of the equal sign.

a)   `WHITE  = COLOR * 2.5/PURPLE`

b)   `GREEN  = COLOR/PURPLE`

c)   `ORANGE = COLOR/RED`

d)   `BLUE   = (COLOR+STRAW)/(CRAYON+0.3)`

e)   `LIME   = PURPLE**COLOR + RED/CRAYON`

f)   `YELLOW = 1.0 * STRAW/COLOR+0.5`

*4.8 NUMERICAL ERRORS

All of the errors discussed in earlier chapters have been programmer errors. However, even if the program is correct, it is still possible to compute the wrong answer, especially in programs that involve extensive numerical computation. The cause of error is the inherent inaccuracy in the internal representation of floating-point (real) data.

We stated earlier that all information is represented in the memory of the computer as a number. For most computers, data is represented using the binary number system (base 2), rather than the decimal system (base 10). Thus, the representation of information in the memory of the computer is in terms of strings of binary digits (0s and 1s), rather than strings of decimal digits (0–9). However, as shown in the next example, many decimal numbers do not have precise binary equivalents and, therefore, can only be approximated in the binary number system.

---

* This section may be omitted.

Example 4.18 This example lists several binary approximations of the number 0.1. The precise decimal equivalent of the binary number being represented and the numerical error are also shown.

Number of binary digits	Binary approximation	Decimal equivalent	Numerical error
4	.0001	0.0625	0.0375
5–8	.00011000	0.09375	0.00625
9	.000110001	0.09765625	0.00234375
10	.0001100011	.0099609375	0.000390625

We can see from this example that, as the number of binary digits used to represent 0.1 is increased, the precise decimal equivalent represented by the binary number gets closer and closer to 0.1. However, it is impossible to obtain an *exact* binary representation of 0.1, no matter how many digits are used. Unfortunately, the number of binary digits that can be used to represent a real number in the memory of the computer is limited by the size of a memory cell. The larger the cell, the larger the number of binary digits, and the greater the degree of accuracy that can be achieved.

The effect of a statistically small representational error can become magnified in a sequence of computations, or through repetition of an imprecise computation in a loop. Such magnification can sometimes be diminished by the use of functions and careful ordering of the computations. You should be aware that the problem exists, and that it may cause the same FORTRAN program to produce different results when run on computers having memory cells of different size.

Example 4.19:

a) The computation

$$B**2 \quad \text{or} \quad B*B$$

is likely to produce more accurate results than B**2.0, since many compilers will use logarithms to perform the latter computation and multiplication for the former.

b) The computation

$$SQRT(X)$$

is likely to produce more accurate results than X**.5 since most square-root functions produce more accurate results than the logarithm functions required in the latter computation.

c) If we have two real numbers A and B, whose difference is small, and a third number C that is relatively large (compared with A − B), then the calculation

$$(A - B) * C$$

may produce results that are less accurate than

$$A * C - B * C.$$

This is because the percentage of error is greater in a very small number such as $(A - B)$, and additional inaccuracy is introduced when a very small number is multiplied by one that is much larger.

4.9 COMMON PROGRAMMING ERRORS

Errors in type declarations are generally caused by spelling mistakes, or missing commas, or failure to declare a variable used in a program. Spelling errors and failure to declare variables will not be detected by most compilers, and missing commas between short variable names (such as IT and ARE) will also go unnoticed (in this case IT ARE, with a comma missing between the T and the A, will be interpreted as the single variable name ITARE). Such mistakes can often confuse the compiler and cause it to detect additional errors in subsequent program statements. These are really not errors at all, but are considered so by the compiler because of inconsistencies caused by type-declaration errors. Some of these errors may be detected by a compiler, but many will only be reflected in execution-time errors.

The only certain way to avoid the grief that can be caused by type-declaration errors is to check, very carefully, all declarations that you write. There is also no substitute for complete data tables. Such tables can be used in writing program declarations, and can be checked for the correct spelling of variables during the writing of subsequent program statements.

Data-statement errors are usually caused by a mismatch, in type or number, between the variable name list and the constant list. Both kinds of errors are detected by most compilers, which will generate error messages such as

```
INCORRECT TYPE FOR CONSTANT IN DATA STATEMENT
CONSTANT LIST EXCEEDS LENGTH OF VARIABLE LIST, EXTRA CONSTANTS
    IGNORED.
VARIABLE LIST EXCEEDS LENGTH OF CONSTANT LIST.
```

There are two very common errors that are made in the use of format-free input. One of these errors is caused by a discrepancy in the number of items specified for input in a read statement, and the number of items actually available for input in the data deck. This error is detected during the execution of a program when an attempt is made to read data, and no further data is available. At this point, your program execution will be terminated with a message indicating that there is INSUFFICIENT DATA available for the read statement at fault. (In some cases a message is printed indicating that there has been an attempt to read past an *end of file* or *end of record*.) Such a message generally indicates that some data items have been omitted from the data deck. Sometimes, however, the error is caused by the read statement itself, which may be attempting to read more data items than intended. In either case, the discrepancy must be eliminated, thereby restoring the one-to-one correspondence between the number of items in the data-card section and the number of variables in the input lists of the read statements.

INSUFFICIENT DATA errors can also be caused by a loop containing a read statement that does not terminate properly. If such a loop is executed too many times, it will attempt to read more data items than were provided in the data-card section, causing an INSUFFICIENT DATA error.

The other common input error is caused by attempts to read type integer data into type real variables, or vice versa. This error sometimes goes undetected, showing up only in the generation of incorrect program results. The only certain means of easy detection of these errors is to print all data items read into computer memory as they are being entered.

Some of the more common programming errors involving expressions and assignment statements are listed below, along with their remedies. The compiler diagnostics for these errors will be similar in wording to the short descriptions that are given here.

1. *Mismatched or unbalanced parentheses.* The statement in error should be carefully scanned, and left and right parentheses matched in pairs, inside-out, until the mismatch becomes apparent. This error is often caused by a missing parenthesis at the end of an expression.

2. *Missing operator in an expression.* This error is usually caused by a missing multiplication operator, *. The expression in error must be scanned carefully, and the missing operator inserted in the appropriate position.

3. *Logical or character data used with arithmetic operator* or *Logical data used with relational operator.* These errors are examples of mixed-mode expressions; operators which can manipulate data of one type are being used with data of another type. A common error of this sort is a condition of the form (PRIME .EQ. .TRUE.) where PRIME is logical; the correct condition is simply (PRIME).

4. *Arithmetic underflow or overflow* or *Division by zero attempted.* Another type of numerical error is caused by attempts to manipulate very large real numbers or numbers that are very close in value to zero. For example, dividing by a number that is almost zero may produce a number that is too large to be represented (*overflow*). You should check that the correct variable is being used as a divisor and that it has the proper value. On some compilers, a divisor that is undefined would be set to zero and would cause a *division by zero* diagnostic to be printed. Arithmetic *underflow* occurs when the magnitude of the result is too small to be represented in floating point form.

One type of programming error that cannot be detected by a compiler involves the writing of expressions that are syntactically correct, but do not accurately represent the computation called for in the problem statement. All expressions, especially long ones, must be carefully checked for accuracy. Often, this involves the decomposition of complex expressions into simpler subexpressions producing intermediate results. Intermediate results should be printed and compared with hand calculations for a simple, but representative, data sample.

4.10 SUMMARY

The FORTRAN language provides a capability for manipulating a number of different *types* of data. We have introduced four of these types (integer, real, logical, and character strings) in this chapter.

The internal representation of all information in the computer is a *number*. However, this representation takes on a different format depending upon the FORTRAN data type that is represented. In order for the FORTRAN compiler to generate the correct machine-language instructions for a program, it must know the types of all data being manipulated. Thus, the types of all constants and variable names used in a program must be clearly indicated to the compiler. The types of variable names can be specified either by using type-declaration statements, or simply by allowing the compiler to assign a type to each name according to the FORTRAN convention. Under the FORTRAN first-letter implicit type convention, all variable names beginning with the letters A through H and O through Z are automatically typed *real*; names beginning with the letters I through N are automatically typed *integer*.

Constants are typed according to the way in which they are written in a program. Real constants are numbers which contain a decimal point; integer constants do not contain a decimal point. Character-string constants consist of a string of legal FORTRAN characters enclosed in apostrophes. The only two logical constants are .TRUE. and .FALSE..

The DATA statement may be used to load constants of any of the four types into variables of the same type, prior to the start of execution of a program. We encourage the use of this statement primarily for initializing program constants. Program variables, such as counters, should be initialized using assignment statements.

The use of format-free input and output statements requires all input/output format and type information to be determined automatically by special programs. In order for this to be done correctly, all input and output data must agree in type with the variables referenced in the input or output list of a read or print statement For input, this means that all real numbers must contain a decimal point, and all integers must *not* have a decimal point. The input of character strings requires that the strings be enclosed in apostrophes.

The indexed-DO structure provides a most convenient means for representing loops in which execution is controlled by a counter. This structure permits the specification of all loop-control information at the top of the loop. The programmer is freed from having to separately program the counter initialization, increment, and test, but simply tells the compiler what the initial, final, and increment values of the counter are to be, and the compiler does the rest. It treats the counter as the loop-control variable and generates the appropriate instructions for initializing, incrementing, and testing this variable.

Of the basic arithmetic operators $+$, $*$, $/$, and $-$, only the slash (division) produces different results when used with integers instead of reals. This is due to the fact that the internal fixed-point format used for storage of integers does not permit the representation of a fractional remainder.

This chapter has provided some of the rules for forming and evaluating arithmetic expressions. This capability is most useful in numerically oriented problems. Knowledge of these rules will enable you to apply FORTRAN correctly to perform calculations. One useful guideline, which should always be kept in mind when transforming an equation or formula to FORTRAN, is "when in doubt of the meaning, insert parentheses."

The use of functions in arithmetic expressions has also been introduced. Their use will enable you to more efficiently perform numerical calculations, since calling a function to compute a result is much faster and easier than trying to perform the calculation using the basic arithmetic operations.

PROGRAMMING PROBLEMS

4.3   Write a flow diagram for a program to read in a collection of integers and determine whether each is a prime number.

4.4   Let n be a positive integer consisting of up to 10 digits, $d_{10} d_9 \cdots d_1$. Write a program to list in one column each of the digits in the number n. The rightmost digit d_1 should be listed at the top of the column. [*Hint.* If $n = 3704$, what is the value of *digit* as computed according to the following formula?

$$\text{digit} = \text{MOD}(n,10)$$

Test your program for values of n equal to 6, 3704, and 1704985.]

4.5   An integer N is divisible by 9 if the sum of its digits is divisible by 9. Use the algorithm developed for Problem 4.4 to determine whether or not the following numbers are divisible by 9.

$$N = 154168$$

$$N = 62159382$$

$$N = 12345678$$

4.6   Each month a bank customer deposits $50.00 in a savings account. The account earns 6.5 percent interest, calculated on a quarterly basis (one-fourth of 6.5 percent each quarter). Write a program to compute the total investment, total amount in the account, and the interest accrued, for each of 120 months of a 10-year period. You may assume that the rate is applied to all funds in the account at the end of a quarter regardless of when the deposits were made.

The table printed by your program should begin as follows:

MONTH	INVESTMENT	NEW AMOUNT	INTEREST	TOTAL SAVINGS
1	50.00	50.00	0.00	50.00
2	100.00	100.00	0.00	100.00
3	150.00	150.00	2.44	152.44
4	200.00	202.44	0.00	202.44
5	250.00	252.44	0.00	252.44
6	300.00	302.44	4.91	307.35
7	350.00	357.35	0.00	357.35

Keep all computations accurate to two decimal places. How would you modify your program if interest were computed on a daily basis?

4.7 Compute a table of values of $X/(1 + X^2)$ for values of $X = 1, 2, 3, \ldots, 50$. Your table of values should be accurate to four decimal places and should begin as follows:

X	X / (1 + X²)
1.	.5000
2.	.4000
3.	.3000
4.	.2353
5.	.1923
.	.
.	.
.	.

4.8 The interest paid on a savings account is compounded daily. This means that if you start with X dollars in the bank, then at the end of the first day you will have a balance of

$$X \times (1 + rate/365)$$

dollars, where rate is the annual interest rate (0.06 if the annual rate is 6%). At the end of the second day, you will have

$$X \times (1 + rate/365) \times (1 + rate/365)$$

dollars, and at the end of N days you will have

$$X \times (1 + rate/365)^N$$

dollars. Write a program that will process a set of data cards, each of which contains values for X, rate, and N and computes the final account balance.

4.9 (Extension of Exercise 4.14) The program written in Exercise 4.14 finds the square root of the number X (written $\sqrt[2]{X}$ or $\sqrt{X}$) accurate to 4 decimal places. This program can be adapted to find the Nth root $\sqrt[N]{X}$ of a number X, for any positive integer N. The major task required for this change is to generalize the expression for computing YNEW:

$$YNEW = \frac{1}{N} \left((N - 1) \times Y + \frac{X}{Y^{N-1}} \right)$$

(*Note.* In Exercise 4.14, N was equal to 2.). Modify the program given in Exercise 4.14 to read in a number X, a value N, and a value for START, and compute $\sqrt[N]{X}$ accurate to 4 decimal places. Test your program on the following data.

```
    / 7.0    2    2.0
   / 48.0    3    6.0
  / 32.0    5    2.0
 /
```

4.10 Write a name table, flow chart, and computer program to solve the following problem:

Compute the monthly payment and the total payment for a bank loan, given:

1. the amount of the loan (LOAN),
2. the duration of the loan in months (MONTHS),
3. the interest-rate percent for the loan (RATE).

Your program should read in one card at a time (each containing a loan value, months value, and rate value), perform the required computation, and print the values of the loan, months, rate, and the monthly payment (MPAYMT), and total payment (TOTPMT).

Test your program with at least the following data (and more if you want).

Loan	Months	Rate
16000.	300	6.50
24000.	360	7.50
30000.	300	9.50
42000.	360	8.50
22000.	300	9.50
300000.	240	9.25

Don't forget to first read in a card indicating how many data cards you have.

Notes.

i) The formula for computing monthly payment is

$$\text{mpaymt} = \left[\frac{\text{rate}}{1200.} \times \left(1. + \frac{\text{rate}}{1200.}\right)^{\text{months}} \times \text{loan}\right] \bigg/ \left[\left(1. + \frac{\text{rate}}{1200.}\right)^{\text{months}} - 1.\right].$$

ii) The formula for computing the total payment is

$$\text{totpmt} = \text{mpaymt} \times \text{FLOAT (months)}.$$

iii) Don't forget to declare the types of the variables LOAN and MPAYMT.

Also, you may find it helpful to introduce additional variables RATEM and EXPM defined below, and use these to simplify the computation of MPAYMT. You can check the values of ratem and expm to see whether your program's computations are accurate.

$$\text{ratem} = \text{rate}/1200.$$

$$\text{expm} = (1. + \text{ratem})^{\text{months}}$$

4.11 The rate of radioactive decay of an isotope is usually given in terms of the half-life, HL (the time lapse required for the isotope to decay to one-half of its original mass). For the strontium 90 isotope (one of the products of nuclear fission), the rate of decay is approximately .60/HL. The half-life of the strontium 90 isotope is 28 years. Compute and print, in table form, the amount remaining after each year from an initial point at which 50 grams are present. [*Hint.* For each year, the amount of isotope remaining can be computed using the formula

$$r = \text{amount} * C^{(\text{Year}/\text{HL})}$$

where amount is 50 grams (the initial amount), and C is the constant $e^{-0.693}$ ($e = 2.71828$).]

4.12 Write a FORTRAN program to read in a 9-digit Social Security number, such as 219400677, and print this number in the form 219–40–0677. (The problem here is to break the Social Security number into three parts, SSNO1, SSNO2, SSNO3, and to print each part as a separate integer.

4.13 Modify the program in Example 4.16, so that it will generate a table of the form shown below. Each table entry should be the word YES or NO, indicating whether or not that combination of angle and velocity will cause the arrow to go through the window. [*Hint.* Use two indexed-DO loops, one *nested* (completely contained) within the other.]

	VELOCITY					
ANGLE	100.	120.	140.	160.	180.	200.
50.	----	----	----	----	----	----
55.	----	----	----	----	----	----
60.	----	----	----	----	----	----
65.	----	----	----	----	----	----

4.14 Write a program that will read a data card containing two words and store them in the variables FIRST and LAST. The program will then process a set of data cards, each containing a single word, and print that word in column 1 if it precedes FIRST, column 2 if it lies between FIRST and LAST, column 3 if it follows LAST. At the end, print the count of all words in each column.

4.15 An examination with nine questions is given to a group of students. The exam is worth 10 points and everyone turning in an answer sheet receives at least 1 point. Each problem is graded on a no credit, half credit, full credit basis. A data card containing an exam score (SCORE) is punched for each student. Write a program to read the data cards, determine the rank for each score, and print a two column list containing the SCORE, and rank of each student. The ranks are determined as follows:

Score	*Rank*
9.0–10.0	GOOD
6.0– 8.5	FAIR
1.0– 5.5	POOR

The program should also print the number of scores in each rank and the total number of scores.

ARRAYS AND SUBSCRIPTS

5

5.1 Introduction

5.2 Declaring Arrays

5.3 Array Subscripts

5.4 Manipulating Arrays

*5.5 Role of the Translator in Processing Arrays

5.6 Searching an Array

5.7 Processing Selected Array Elements

5.8 Common Programming Errors

5.9 Summary

Programming Problems

5.1 INTRODUCTION

In many applications, we are faced with the problem of having to store and manipulate large quantities of data in memory. In our problems so far, it has been necessary to use only a few memory cells to process relatively large amounts of data. This is because we have been able to process each data item separately and then re-use the memory cell in which that data item was stored.

For example, in Problem 3.4, we computed the maximum value of a set of exam scores. Each score was read into the same memory cell, named SCORE, and then completely processed. This score was then destroyed when the next score was read for processing. This approach allowed us to process a large number of scores without having to allocate a separate memory cell for each one. However, once a score was processed, it was impossible to reexamine it later.

There are many applications in which we may need to save data items for subsequent reprocessing. For example, we might desire to write a program that computes and prints the average of a set of exam scores, and also the difference between each score and the average. In this case, all scores must be processed and the average computed before we can calculate the differences requested. We must therefore be able to examine the list of student exam scores twice, first to compute the average, and then to compute the differences. Since we would rather not provide a duplicate set of data for each of these steps, we will want to save all of the scores in memory during the first step, for subsequent re-use during the second step.

In allocating space for each data item, it would be extremely tedious to have to reference each memory cell by a different name. If there were 100 exam scores to process, we would need 100 read statements to enter each score into its own memory cell.

```
READ, SCR1
READ, SCR2
       .
       .
       .
READ, SCR100
```

In this chapter, we will learn how to use a new feature of FORTRAN, called an *array*, for storing a collection of related data items. Use of the array will simplify the task of naming and referencing the individual items in the collection. Through the use of arrays, we will be able to enter an entire collection of data items with a single read statement. Once the collection is stored in memory, we will be able to reference any of these items as often as we wish without ever having to reenter that item into memory.

5.2 DECLARING ARRAYS

In all prior programming discussed in this text, we have always associated each symbolic name used in a program with a single memory cell, whether the name represented a number, or a character string of a specified length. The association has been handled by the compiler. We simply indicated, via a type declaration, which names we wished to use in a program, and what types of data were to be associated with those names. The compiler then assigned each of these names to a memory cell. If we failed to declare a name, the compiler automatically associated that name with a memory cell as soon as it encountered the name in our program.

An *array* is a collection of two or more adjacent memory cells (called *array elements*) that are associated with a single symbolic name. Whenever we wish to tell the compiler to associate two or more memory cells with a single name, we must use a declaration statement in which we state the name to be used, and the number of elements to be associated with this name.

For example, the declaration statement REAL X(8) instructs the compiler to associate eight memory cells with the name X. The array X is considered to be of *size* 8—i.e., to consist of 8 *array elements*. Each array element may contain a real number.

The association of a collection of memory cells with one variable name poses a problem. How can we refer to the individual elements in the collection if they are all associated with the same name? After all, the computer can manipulate only one data item at a time. Consequently, in writing a program to tell the computer how to manipulate an array of data, we must be able to refer to each and every item in the array. This is accomplished through the use of an array subscript.

For example, if X is a real array of size 8, then we may refer to the elements of the array X as shown in Fig. 5.1.

Array X

X(1)	X(2)	X(3)	X(4)	X(5)	X(6)	X(7)	X(8)
16.0	12.0	6.0	−2.0	−12.0	−24.0	−38.0	−54.0

First   Second Third   Eighth
element   element element   •••   element

Fig. 5.1 The eight elements of the array X.

The *subscripted variable* X(1) can be used to reference the first element of the array X, X(2) the second element, and X(8) the eighth element. The integer enclosed in parentheses is the *array subscript*.

Example 5.1 Let X be the real array shown in Fig. 5.1, and let SUM be a real variable containing the value 34.0 (the sum of the first three elements of X). Then the statement

$$SUM = SUM + X(4)$$

will cause the value −2.0 (the contents of the memory cell designated by X(4)) to be added to SUM.

In the next section, we will study subscripts in more detail, and we will see that integer constants are not the only form of a subscript that is allowed in

FORTRAN. However, first we will describe the complete syntax and interpretation of the FORTRAN array declaration.

Array Declaration

FORTRAN Form:

type name (size)

Interpretation. The "type" may be any one of the four data types INTEGER, REAL, LOGICAL, or CHARACTER * n. The compiler will associate the number of memory elements indicated by size with the variable indicated by name. These elements will be reserved for the storage of data of the indicated type.

Example 5.2 More than one array may appear in a declaration statement. The declarations

```
REAL CACTUS (5), NEEDLE, PINS (6)
INTEGER FACTOR (12), N, INDEX
```

will cause five array elements to be assigned to the real array CACTUS, six to the real array PINS, and twelve to the integer array FACTOR. In addition, separate memory cells will be allocated for storage of the real variable NEEDLE and the integer variables N and INDEX.

Example 5.3 If your compiler permits the character declaration, the statements:

```
CHARACTER * 10 FIRNAM (20), LASNAM (20)
CHARACTER * 40 PARENT (15)
```

will allocate three arrays for storage of character data. Twenty array elements, each capable of storing a character string of length ten, will be assigned to the arrays FIRNAM and LASNAM; fifteen array elements, each capable of storing a character string of length forty, will be assigned to the array PARENT.

5.3 ARRAY SUBSCRIPTS

In the preceding section, we introduced the array subscript as a means of differentiating among the individual elements of an array. We showed that an array element can be referenced by specifying the name of the array followed by a pair of parentheses enclosing a subscript.

In general, FORTRAN allows a special class of arithmetic expressions to be used as the subscript of an array. The compiler can determine the particular array element referenced by evaluating the *subscript expression*, and using the result of this evaluation to indicate the element to be referenced. The rules for the specification and evaluation of array subscripts are summarized below.

Array Subscripts

FORTRAN Form:

array name (subscript)

Interpretation. The subscript may be any one of the following forms of integer expressions:

i) constant

ii) variable

iii) constant * variable

iv) $constant_1$ * variable + $constant_2$

v) $constant_1$ * variable − $constant_2$

The variable in these expressions must be a simple variable; i.e., it cannot be a subscripted array reference as well. During the execution of a program, the subscript is evaluated, and the result is used to indicate the array element being referenced. This value must be within the *range* of the array; it cannot be less than one nor greater than the size of the array as specified in the array declaration.

Note. Many compilers, including WATFIV–S, permit any legal integer expression to be used as a subscript.

Example 5.4 Let ISUB be a memory cell containing the value 3, and let X be an integer array consisting of 10 elements. Then:

X(ISUB) refers to the 3rd element of the array X;
X(4) refers to the 4th element of the array X;
X(2 * ISUB) refers to the 6th element of the array X;
X(5 * ISUB − 6) refers to the 9th element of the array X.

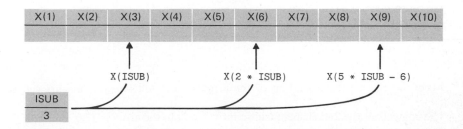

EXERCISE 5.1 In Example 5.4, which elements in the array X are referenced if ISUB is equal to 4 rather than 3?

EXERCISE 5.2 Let I contain the integer 6 and let X be the array in Example 5.4. Which of the following references to elements of X are within the range of X? Which of the subscript expressions listed below do not conform to the standard described in the previous display?

a) X(I)

b) X(3*I−20)

c) X(4+I)

d) X(I*3−12)

e) X(4*I−12)

f) X(I−2*I)

g) X(30)

h) X(I*I−1)

As shown in Exercise 5.2, we will adopt the convention of writing subscript expressions without blanks around the operators *, +, and −.

5.4 MANIPULATING ARRAYS

5.4.1 Manipulating Individual Array Elements

Array elements may be manipulated just as other variables are manipulated in FORTRAN statements. In most cases, we can only specify the manipulation of one array element at a time. For example, each use of an array name in a FORTRAN assignment statement or a condition must be followed by a subscript.

It is important to understand the distinction between the array subscript, the value of the subscript (sometimes called an *index* to the array), and the contents of the array element. The subscript is enclosed in parentheses following the array name. Its value is used to select one of the array elements for manipulation. The contents of that array element is either used as an operand or modified as a result of executing a FORTRAN statement.

Example 5.5 Let G be a real array of 10 elements as shown below.

Array G

G(1)	G(2)	G(3)	G(4)	G(5)	G(6)	G(7)	G(8)	G(9)	G(10)
−11.2	12.0	−6.1	4.5	8.2	1.3	−.7	8.3	9.0	−3.3

According to this representation of the array G, the following statements can be made.

The contents of the 2nd element (subscript value 2) in the array is 12.0.

The contents of the 4th element (subscript value 4) is 4.5.

The contents of the 10th element (subscript value 10) is −3.3.

Remember, the subscript value is used to select a particular array element, but it does not, by itself, tell us what is stored in that element.

Example 5.6 Let G be an array of size 10, as shown in Example 5.5. Then the sequence of instructions

```
J = 1
I = 4
G(10) = 10.0
G(I) = 400.0
G(2 * I) = G(I) + G(J)
```

will alter the contents of the 10th, 4th, and 8th elements of G, as shown in Fig. 5.2.

G(10) = 10.0

Subscript	Value of subscript	Effect
10	10	Store 10.0 in G(10). Destroy old value, −3.3.

G(I) = 400.0

Subscript	Value of subscript	Effect
I	4	Store 400.0 in G(4). Destroy old value, 4.5.

G(2∗I) = G(I) + G(J)

Subscript	Value of subscript	Effect
I	4	Add contents of G(4) and G(1)
J	1	(400.0 + (−11.2)).
2∗I	8	Store result (388.8) in G(8). Destroy old value, 8.3.

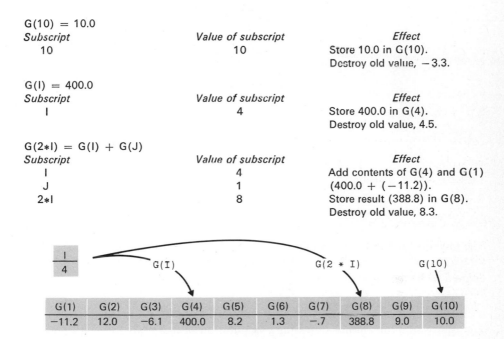

Fig. 5.2 New array G.

EXERCISE 5.3 Given the array G as shown in Fig. 5.2:

a) What is the contents of G(2)?

b) If I = 3, what is the contents of G(2∗I − 1)?

c) What is the value of the logical expression

$$(G(I) .EQ. 8.2)$$

if I is equal to 3; if I is equal to 5?

d) What will be the value of the logical variable FLAG after the statements below are executed?

```
FLAG = .FALSE.
DO 70 INDEX = 1, 10
    IF (G(INDEX) .EQ. 388.8) FLAG = .TRUE.
70 CONTINUE
```

e) What will the array G look like after the following loop is executed?

```
DO 60 IX = 1, 10
   G(IX) = 2.0 * FLOAT(IX)
60 CONTINUE
```

f) If we are given the 4 data cards shown below, describe how the array G would be changed by the following statement sequence.

```
DO 80 INX = 1,4
   READ, G(INX)
80 CONTINUE
```

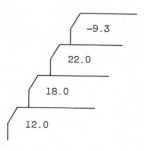

5.4.2 Computing a Table of Factorials

The factorial of a number is often used in formulas for computing the probability that a given event will occur. The factorial of a number N (written as N!) is defined to be the product of N and all integers smaller than N.

$$N! = N \times (N - 1) \times (N - 2) \times \cdots \times 2 \times 1$$

The following problem illustrates the computation of factorials for small positive integers.

PROBLEM 5.1 Compute and print a table of factorials for the integers 1 through 7 and accumulate the sum of the factorials.

DISCUSSION. The factorial of an integer, N, can be computed from the factorial of the next smaller integer, N − 1. As an illustration:

$$5! = 5 \times (4 \times 3 \times 2 \times 1) = 120,$$

and

$$4! = 4 \times 3 \times 2 \times 1 = 24;$$

therefore,

$$5! = 5 \times 4! = 5 \times 24 = 120$$

We can take advantage of this property of factorials to reduce the amount of computation required for this problem. We will compute each factorial, save it in the appropriate element of an array (FACTOR), and use this value in the computation of the next factorial. The data table for this problem follows, and the flow diagrams are given in Fig. 5.3.

Data Table for Problem 5.1

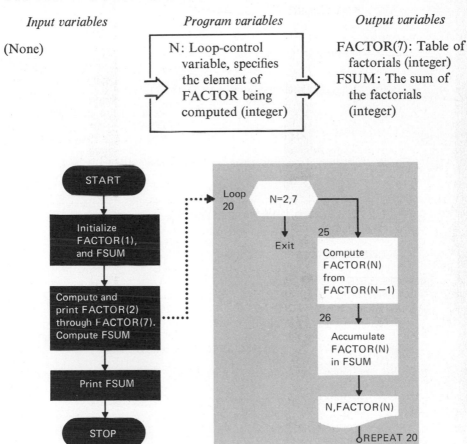

Fig. 5.3 Flow diagrams for computing the factorial table.

    The FORTRAN statement sequence

```
FACTOR(N) = N * FACTOR(N-1)
FSUM = FSUM + FACTOR(N)
```

can be used to implement steps 25 and 26. The effect of these statements is shown in Fig. 5.4, for N = 4.

    The program for the Factorial Problem is shown in Fig. 5.5.

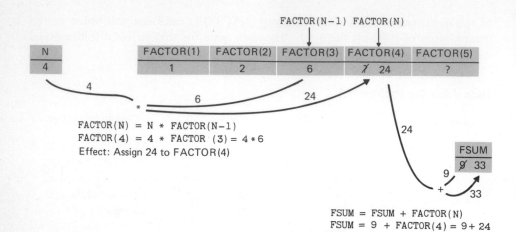

Fig. 5.4 Illustration of the computation of N factorial and FSUM for N = 4.

```
C PROGRAM TO COMPUTE N FACTORIAL FOR N = 1 TO 7
C AND ACCUMULATE FACTORIAL SUMS
C
      INTEGER FACTOR(7), FSUM, N
C
C INITIALIZE
      FACTOR(1) = 1
      PRINT, 'THE FACTORIAL OF ', 1, ' IS ', 1
      FSUM = 1
C
C LOOP TO COMPUTE 2 FACTORIAL THROUGH 7 FACTORIAL
      DO 20 N = 2, 7
C        COMPUTE NEW ARRAY ELEMENT VALUE FROM PREVIOUS ONE
         FACTOR(N) = N * FACTOR(N-1)
C        ACCUMULATE SUM OF FACTORIALS
         FSUM = FSUM + FACTOR(N)
         PRINT, 'THE FACTORIAL OF ', N, ' IS ', FACTOR(N)
20    CONTINUE
      PRINT, 'THE SUM OF THE FACTORIALS 1 THRU 7 IS ', FSUM
      STOP
      END
```

Fig. 5.5 Factorial program.

The final contents of the array FACTOR would be:

FACTOR(1)	FACTOR(2)	FACTOR(3)	FACTOR(4)	FACTOR(5)	FACTOR(6)	FACTOR(7)
1	2	6	24	120	720	5040

The output from the program would appear as follows:

```
THE FACTORIAL OF    1    IS        1
THE FACTORIAL OF    2    IS        2
THE FACTORIAL OF    3    IS        6
THE FACTORIAL OF    4    IS       24
THE FACTORIAL OF    5    IS      120
THE FACTORIAL OF    6    IS      720
THE FACTORIAL OF    7    IS     5040
THE SUM OF THE FACTORIALS 1 THRU 7 IS 5913
```

EXERCISE 5.4 What would be stored in the array FACTOR (Problem 5.1) if the assignment statement

$$FACTOR(N) = N * FACTOR(N-1)$$

in Fig. 5.5 were incorrectly punched as

$$FACTOR(N) = N * (N-1)$$

EXERCISE 5.5 The Fibonacci series is a sequence of numbers with the property that each number in the sequence represents the sum of the two preceding numbers (the first two numbers in the sequence are defined to be one). Write a flow diagram and a program that computes, stores, and prints the first fifteen Fibonacci numbers in the array FIB; e.g.,

```
FIB(1) = 1
FIB(2) = 1
FIB(3) = FIB(1) + FIB(2) = 1 + 1 = 2
FIB(4) = FIB(2) + FIB(3) = 1 + 2 = 3
FIB(15) = FIB(13)+ FIB(14)= 233 + 377 = 610
```

The Fibonacci series has been shown to model the growth pattern of a rabbit colony. Starting with one pair of baby rabbits, there should be 610 pairs of rabbits at the end of fifteen months assuming it takes two months for a rabbit to mature and that each mature pair produces a new pair every month.

5.4.3 Reading, Printing, and Initializing Entire Arrays

We stated previously that an array name cannot appear without a subscript in an assignment statement or a condition. However, an array name can appear without a subscript in read or print statements. In these statements, if the subscript is not included in the array reference, the compiler automatically assumes that all of the array elements are involved in the indicated operation. Some compilers permit array names to be used in this way in data initialization statements as well.

Example 5.7 The statement

```
PRINT, FACTOR
```

will cause all seven elements of the array FACTOR (Problem 5.1) to be printed.

Example 5.8 The following program contains unsubscripted references to the arrays PRES and YEAR.

```
INTEGER YEAR(5)
CHARACTER * 10 PRES(5)     [or INTEGER PRES(5)]
READ, PRES, YEAR
PRINT, PRES
PRINT, YEAR
STOP
END
```

The input list of the read statement contains the names of two arrays of five elements each. Consequently, ten data items will be read into these arrays, as shown below.

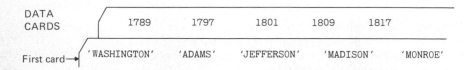

PRES(1)	PRES(2)	PRES(3)	PRES(4)	PRES(5)
WASHINGTON	ADAMS◻◻◻◻◻	JEFFERSON◻	MADISON◻◻◻	MONROE◻◻◻◻

YEAR(1)	YEAR(2)	YEAR(3)	YEAR(4)	YEAR(5)
1789	1797	1801	1809	1817

When you specify the name of an array (without a subscript) in a read statement, as many data cards as necessary will be read until all of the array elements have been filled. As many data items as will fit may be punched on each data card; you may use as many cards as you wish. If you fail to provide sufficient data to fill the entire array, an INSUFFICIENT DATA diagnostic will occur.

The two print statements shown in Example 5.8 would cause the contents of each array to be printed on a single line:

```
WASHINGTON ADAMS    JEFFERSON MADISON    MONROE
    1789         1797        1801        1809         1817
```

The exact spacing of each output line may differ slightly from that shown above, depending upon which FORTRAN compiler you are using.

Although these print statements display all of the information stored in the arrays PRES and YEAR, the form of the printout could be improved upon. It would be more desirable to print the array contents in a table with two columns, one for the name and one for the first year in office. In the next section, we will describe a convenient way to produce such a printout.

If the character data type is not available on your compiler, you should use integer arrays for storing character strings. In this case, you may wish to abbreviate each president's name so that its length does not exceed the character capacity of integer variables for your computer. The excess characters will be truncated from the right of those strings that are too long.

Example 5.9 In compilers which allow the character declaration, the statements

```
CHARACTER * 3 AGE(4)
DATA AGE / 'MY', 'AGE', 'IS', '97' /
```

will cause the four elements of the array AGE to be initialized as shown below.

AGE(1)	AGE(2)	AGE(3)	AGE(4)
MY□	AGE	IS□	97□

The use of the name AGE without a subscript indicates that all of the elements in the array are to be initialized. In general, the number of constants provided in the constant list of a data-initialization statement should be the same as the number of elements in the array. If your compiler does not permit unsubscripted array references in data-initialization statements, you must list separately all of the elements of the array that are to be initialized. For example:

```
DATA AGE(1),AGE(2),AGE(3),AGE(4)/'MY', 'AGE', 'IS', '97'/
```

EXERCISE 5.6

a) Declare and initialize an array called ALFBET which contains each letter of the alphabet in consecutive elements.

b) Declare an array PRIME consisting of ten elements. Prepare a data card and read statement for entering the first ten prime numbers into the array PRIME.

5.4.4 Relationship between the Loop-Control Variable and Array Subscript

In this section, we will examine a loop in which the loop-control variable also serves as the subscript of an array whose elements are manipulated in the loop. This use of the loop control variable is very common in manipulating array elements, since it allows us to easily specify the sequence in which the elements of an array are to be manipulated. As the loop-control variable is incremented, the next array element is automatically selected. (This technique was used earlier in Problem 5.1.)

Example 5.10 The following program segment displays the contents of the arrays PRES and YEAR (see Example 5.8) in tabular form.

```
PRINT, 'NAME          FIRST YEAR IN OFFICE'
DO 10   IX = 1,5
    PRINT, PRES(IX), YEAR(IX)
10 CONTINUE
```

The output list for the print statement in loop 10 references a pair of array elements with subscript IX. As the value of IX goes from 1 to 5, the contents of these arrays will be printed in two columns, as shown on the next page.

```
NAME                FIRST YEAR IN OFFICE
WASHINGTON               1789
ADAMS                    1797
JEFFERSON                1801
MADISON                  1809
MONROE                   1817
```

EXERCISE 5.7 Write a program segment to display the index and the contents of each element of the array PRIME(10) in the tabular form shown below. (See Exercise 5.6.)

N	PRIME(N)
1	1
2	2
3	3
4	5
.	.
.	.
.	.
10	23

5.4.5 Partially Filled Arrays—Implied Indexed-DO Loops

The use of an array name without a subscript in read, print, and data-initialization statements causes the compiler to assume that the entire array is involved in the indicated operation. In many programs, however, we may want to manipulate only a portion of an array, with the exact number of elements involved determined during each execution of the program. In this case, we should declare the size of the array to be large enough to accommodate the largest expected set of data items. Since most executions of the program will require the use of only part of the array, we will not be able to use the name of the array without a subscript in a read or print statement. Instead, we must examine ways to specify that these operations be performed on only part of the array.

Example 5.11 Due to classroom space limitations, the maximum size of a class at the New University is 70. The students at the University are given a series of achievement examinations, and we are asked to write a program to perform some statistical computations on the exam scores on a class-by-class basis. We will be told the size of each class, and will be given a list of the achievement exam scores for the class.

The program segment shown below can be used to read the input data into computer memory for subsequent processing.

```
      INTEGER SCORES(70), COUNT, MAXCNT, IRD
      DATA MAXCNT /70/
C READ IN COUNT OF STUDENTS
      READ, COUNT
      PRINT, 'NUMBER OF SCORES IS ', COUNT
C READ IN SCORES
      DO 10 IRD = 1, COUNT
         READ, SCORES(IRD)
   10 CONTINUE
```

The indexed-DO (loop 10) causes the data items to be read into the array SCORES. Only one data item can be keypunched per card since each execution of the read statement initiates the scanning of a new data card. Only the array elements

SCORES(1), SCORES(2)...SCORES(COUNT)

will be filled with exam scores. If COUNT is not equal to 70, then the remaining elements of SCORES will not be affected by this loop.

Since the need for read and print operations on parts of arrays is so common, the FORTRAN language has been provided with a simple shorthand feature, called an *implied indexed-DO*, which can be used to specify these operations in a concise manner.

Example 5.12 The explicit indexed-DO loop in Example 5.11 may be rewritten using the implied indexed-DO, as shown below.

Explicit DO   *Implied DO*

```
DO 10 IRD = 1, COUNT      →      READ, (SCORES(IRD), IRD = 1, COUNT)
   READ, SCORES(IRD)
10 CONTINUE
```

When an implied indexed-DO is used in a read statement, as many data cards as needed will be read until all of the array elements indicated by the variable list in the read statement are filled. You may keypunch as many items as you wish on each data card. You do not have to keypunch each data item on a separate card as is necessary when the explicit indexed-DO is used.

Example 5.13 If we wished to print the contents of elements 1 through COUNT of the array SCORES, we could also use the implied indexed-DO feature.

```
PRINT, (SCORES(IRD), IRD = 1, COUNT)
```

The rules for specifying the parameters (initial value, end value, and increment) of an implied indexed-DO are identical to the rules that we have learned for the explicit indexed-DO. The implied loop also functions in the same manner as the explicit loop. The general form of the implied indexed-DO is given below.

Implied Indexed-DO

FORTRAN Form:

```
READ, (name(lcv), lcv = iv, fv, sv)
PRINT, (name(lcv), lcv = iv, fv, sv)
```

Interpretation. The name must be the name of an array, and lcv is the loop-control variable for the implied loop. The parameters iv, fv, and sv are the initial value, final value, and step value for the loop. The rules for specifying these parameters and their function are the same as those for the explicit indexed-DO, as explained in Chapter 4.

Note. Many compilers permit the use of the implied indexed-DO with data-initialization statements. However, this use of the implied DO is nonstandard.

Example 5.14 In some compilers, the implied indexed-DO may also be used in a data-initialization statement to initialize portions of an array. For example, the statements

```
INTEGER  X(9)
DATA (X(I), I = 1,5) /5*200/
DATA (X(I), I = 6,8) /3*300/
```

would cause initialization (prior to execution) of the array X as shown below.

X(1)	X(2)	X(3)	X(4)	X(5)	X(6)	X(7)	X(8)	X(9)
200	200	200	200	200	300	300	300	?

EXERCISE 5.8 In Example 5.11, the value of COUNT should be checked after the first read statement to verify that it lies between 1 and 70. Write an IF structure to perform the necessary test on COUNT, and print appropriate diagnostics if COUNT is out of the range 1 to 70. (The program execution should terminate if COUNT is out of range.) Why is this test so important?

EXERCISE 5.9 Rewrite the program segment shown in Example 5.11 using a sentinel card (containing −99) to indicate the end of the data (rather than using a card containing the count of the number of data items.) [*Hint.* Define a loop-control variable NEXT to be used for reading each data item. If the contents of NEXT is not equal to the sentinel value, store NEXT in the next element of the array SCORES, and repeat.]

*5.5 ROLE OF THE TRANSLATOR IN PROCESSING ARRAYS

We have now had a little experience in manipulating arrays of data, and should have a better understanding of the use of the FORTRAN subscript. In this section, we will briefly describe one way in which a compiler might convert a subscripted array reference into a memory-cell address.

The compiler recognizes that it may be dealing with an array reference when it encounters a symbolic name followed by a left parenthesis. The only other symbolic names that may be followed by a left parenthesis are function names. The compiler can distinguish between function and array references, since the names of all arrays must be identified at the beginning of a program through appropriate array-declaration statements.

When the compiler processes an array declaration, it associates a block of adjacent memory cells with the array name, and reserves these cells to be identified with that name. The compiler keeps track of the array size and the address of the

---

* This section may be omitted.

first cell of the block area associated with the array name. When a reference is made to a particular element of an array, the compiler uses the address of the first element of the array as the *base address* for computing the address of the indicated element. The array size is often used to check an array reference to ensure that the subscript value falls within the range of the array.

The calculation of the address of a memory cell indicated by a subscripted array reference is quite straightforward:

Array element address = (base address of array) + subscript value − 1

Example 5.15 Let A be a real array of size 16 with a base address of 3706. Then the address of the tenth element in A, A(10), is 3706 + (10 − 1) or 3715. The address of A(1) is 3706, and the address of A(16) is 3721.

5.6 SEARCHING AN ARRAY

A very common problem in working with arrays of data items is the need to *search* an array to determine whether a particular data item is in the array. We might also want to know how many times the item is present, and where in the array each copy of the item is located.

PROBLEM 5.2 Write a program that searches a real array A of size 30 to determine whether a given item, TARGET, is present. The program should print the subscript of each element of the array A that has the same value as TARGET.

DISCUSSION. We must first read the array element values and TARGET into memory. We will assume enough data items are provided to fill the entire array A. In processing the array A, each element must be examined in sequence and its value compared to TARGET. The subscript of each array element that is equal to TARGET must be printed. The data table for this problem is shown below, and the flow diagrams are shown in Fig. 5.6.

Data Table for Problem 5.2

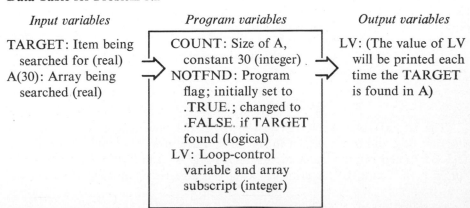

Input variables	*Program variables*	*Output variables*
TARGET: Item being searched for (real)	COUNT: Size of A, constant 30 (integer)	LV: (The value of LV will be printed each
A(30): Array being searched (real)	NOTFND: Program flag; initially set to .TRUE.; changed to .FALSE. if TARGET found (logical)	time the TARGET is found in A)
	LV: Loop-control variable and array subscript (integer)	

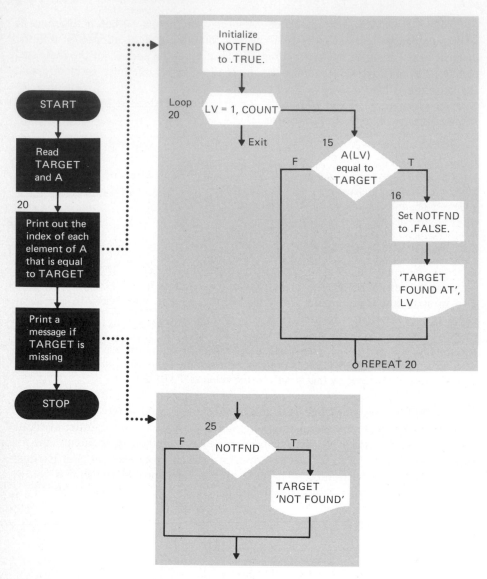

Fig. 5.6 Flow diagrams for searching an array.

The logical variable NOTFND shown in the flow diagrams is used as a program flag, and is initially set to .TRUE.. Each array element is compared to TARGET (step 15); if a match occurs, NOTFND is set to .FALSE. (step 16), and the array subscript, LV, is printed. After the array is completely searched, the value of NOTFND is tested to determine the results of the search (step 25). NOTFND will be .TRUE. only if there were no occurrences of TARGET in the array A.

The search program is provided in Fig. 5.7.

```
C SEARCH AN ARRAY (A) FOR A DATA ITEM (TARGET)
C
      INTEGER TARGET, A(30), COUNT, LV
      LOGICAL NOTFND
      DATA COUNT /30/
C
C READ DATA ITEMS
      READ, TARGET
      PRINT, 'ITEM TO BE FOUND ', TARGET
      READ, A
      PRINT, 'ARRAY BEING SEARCHED ', A
C INITIALIZE PROGRAM FLAG
      NOTFND = .TRUE.
C
C EXAMINE EACH ELEMENT OF ARRAY. IF IT MATCHES TARGET, PRINT SUBSCRIPT
      DO 20 LV = 1, COUNT
         IF (A(LV) .EQ. TARGET) THEN
            NOTFND = .FALSE.
            PRINT, TARGET, ' FOUND IN ELEMENT ', LV, ' OF A'
         ENDIF
 20   CONTINUE
C
C PRINT MESSAGE IF TARGET IS NOT FOUND
      IF (NOTFND) PRINT, TARGET, ' NOT FOUND IN A'
      STOP
      END
```

Fig. 5.7 Program for Problem 5.2.

In this program, the entire array A is entered via a single read statement (READ, A). Once the array has been entered, any element can be manipulated (as shown in decision step 15) by simply using a subscripted reference to A. ∎

EXERCISE 5.10 Explain what is wrong with the proposed refinement of step 20 shown in Fig. 5.8.

EXERCISE 5.11 Re-examine Exercise 5.3, part (d). What does that program segment do?

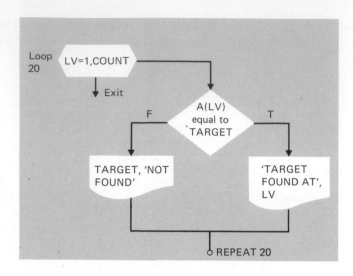

Fig. 5.8 Proposed refinement of Step 20 of Fig. 5.6.

EXERCISE 5.12 Modify the refinement for step 20 in the search flow diagram so that only the first occurrence of TARGET would be found. Is the program flag still needed?

5.7 PROCESSING SELECTED ARRAY ELEMENTS

In the examples seen so far, the loop-control variable of an indexed-DO loop often serves as the array subscript as well. This technique permits us to easily reference the elements of an array in sequential fashion.

There are many programming problems in which only selected elements of an array are to be referenced. In these problems, the selection process involves the computation of a value which is then used as an index for the selection of a specific array element. Usually, the values of one or more input data items are involved in the computations of the index, as shown in the following problem.

PROBLEM 5.3 Write a program that will process up to 120 exam scores and develop a frequency-distribution table that shows the number of A's (90–100), B's (80–89), C's (70–79), D's (60–69) and F's (0–59) given out on the exam.

DISCUSSION. The exam scores are read into the array GRADE. The number of scores, read into COUNT, appears on the first data card. The array FREQ will be used to store the frequency data (the number of scores in each grade category). The number of A's will be stored in FREQ(1), the number of B's in FREQ(2), and so on. The data table for this problem is shown next, and the flow diagrams are given in Fig. 5.9.

Data table for Problem 5.3:

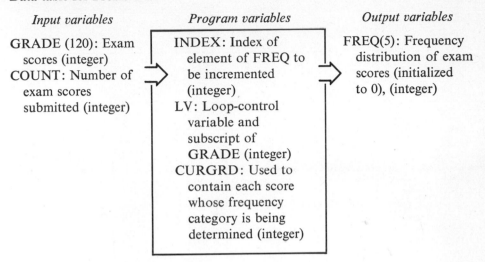

Input variables	*Program variables*	*Output variables*
GRADE (120): Exam scores (integer) COUNT: Number of exam scores submitted (integer)	INDEX: Index of element of FREQ to be incremented (integer) LV: Loop-control variable and subscript of GRADE (integer) CURGRD: Used to contain each score whose frequency category is being determined (integer)	FREQ(5): Frequency distribution of exam scores (initialized to 0), (integer)

The most important parts of the flow diagram shown in Fig. 5.9 are loop 20, and the refinement of step 15 in loop 20. Loop 20 is executed once for each grade. If the grade is not valid (not between 0 and 100, inclusive), an error message is printed, and the grade is not processed; otherwise, the count for one of the frequency classes FREQ(1), ..., FREQ(5) must be updated (incremented by 1). The problem is to determine which of the counts to update, given the value of the current grade being processed (CURGRD). To do this, we must convert the current grade into an index (INDEX) which can then be used to select the particular element of FREQ that is to be updated. The required conversion is summarized in Table 5.1.

Table 5.1   Conversion of grades to indexes

Value of CURGRD	Grade category	Required value of index
Between 90 and 100	A	1
80–89	B	2
70–79	C	3
60–69	D	4
0–59	F	5

We can take advantage of the property of integer division (truncation of the remainder) to write a simple formula that yields the desired conversion in all but two cases:

$$INDEX = 10 - CURGRD / 10$$

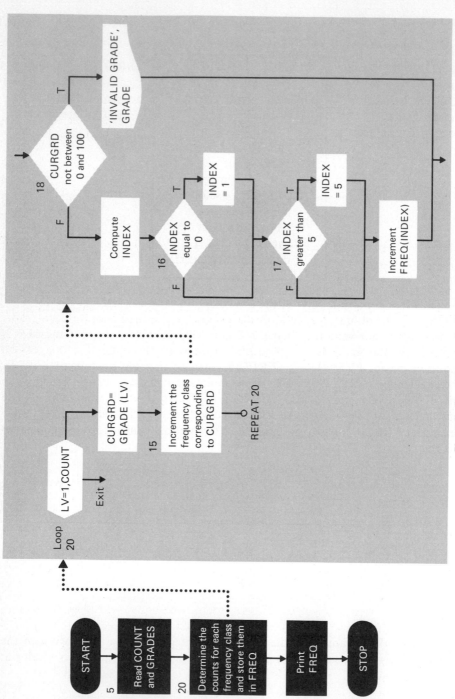

Fig. 5.9 Flow diagrams for Problem 5.3

This formula correctly handles any grade between 50 and 99 inclusive. However, if CURGRD is 100, this formula computes an index of 0; and, if CURGRD is less than 50, the formula computes an index that is larger than 5. Once INDEX has been computed using the above formula, these out-of-range values of INDEX can easily be corrected using the following two conditional statements.

If INDEX is equal to 0, redefine INDEX to be equal to 1.

If INDEX is greater than 5, redefine INDEX to be equal to 5.

Sample computations of INDEX, using the formula and conditional statements just described, are shown in Table 5.2.

Table 5.2 Sample calculations of index

CURGRD	Grade category	INDEX
93	A	$10 - 93/10 = 10 - 9 = 1$
82	B	$10 - 82/10 = 10 - 8 = 2$
79	C	$10 - 79/10 = 10 - 7 = 3$
60	D	$10 - 60/10 = 10 - 6 = 4$
100	A	$10 - 100/10 = 0 \rightarrow 1$
12	F	$10 - 12/10 = 9 \rightarrow 5$

The FORTRAN program for the frequency-distribution problem is shown in Fig. 5.10. Note that step 5 is implemented using a single FORTRAN read statement.

The logical operator .OR. is used in specifying the condition in the decision structure. If either of the conditions "CURGRD less than 0" or "CURGRD greater than 100" is true, then the error message indicating an illegal grade will be printed.

When the operator .OR. is used to connect two conditions, then the entire condition is considered true if either of the connected conditions is true. If both conditions are false, the entire condition is false.

The logical operator .AND. may be used in a similar fashion in specifying conditions. When .AND. is used, both conditions connected by the .AND. must be true in order for the entire condition to be true; otherwise, the entire condition is false. The use of logical operators, and logical expressions in general, will be discussed in more detail in Chapter 9.

EXERCISE 5.13 Hand-simulate the computation of INDEX as specified in the flow diagram in Fig. 5.9 for the following values of CURGRD:

$$\text{CURGRD} = 43, \ 100, \ 99, \ 70.$$

EXERCISE 5.14 Modify the flow diagrams and program for Problem 5.3 to also compute and print the number of grades that are in error (not between 0 and 100 inclusive).

```
C EXAM GRADES FREQUENCY DISTRIBUTION
C
      INTEGER GRADE(120), COUNT, FREQ(5), INDEX, LV, CURGRD
      DATA FREQ /5*0/
C
C READ IN COUNT OF DATA ITEMS, AND ALL DATA
      READ, COUNT, (GRADE(LV), LV = 1, COUNT)
C
C PROCESS EACH EXAM SCORE - DETERMINE FREQUENCY CLASS
      DO 10 LV = 1, COUNT
         CURGRD = GRADE(LV)
         PRINT, CURGRD
         IF (CURGRD .LT. 0 .OR. CURGRD .GT. 100) THEN
            PRINT, 'GRADE ILLEGAL AND IS IGNORED.'
         ELSE
C           COMPUTE INDEX
            INDEX = 10 - CURGRD / 10
            IF (INDEX .EQ. 0) INDEX = 1
            IF (INDEX .GT. 5) INDEX = 5
C           UPDATE FREQUENCY CLASS COUNT
            FREQ(INDEX) = FREQ(INDEX) + 1
         ENDIF
   10 CONTINUE
C PRINT RESULTS
      PRINT, 'DISTRIBUTION OF GRADES'
      PRINT, '     A        B        C        D        F'
      PRINT, FREQ
      STOP
      END
```

Fig. 5.10 Program for Problem 5.3.

EXERCISE 5.15 Suppose a university grading system involved the use of plus (+) and minus (−) grades specified as follows:

A+	96–100	C	75–77
A	93–95	C−	72–74
A−	90–92	D+	69–71
B+	87–89	D	66–68
B	84–86	D−	63–65
B−	81–83	F+	60–62
C+	78–80	F	0–59

Write the double-alternative decision structure for the frequency-distribution program shown in Fig. 5.10, that will compute the frequency counts for the 14 frequency classes listed above. If you begin to get writer's cramp from this exercise, then you should study Problem 5.3 again.

5.7.1 Referencing Array Elements—Review

In the examples we have seen, there have been two methods used to select an array element for manipulation. The first involved the use of a loop to reference a sequence of array elements, and the second involved the computation of an index used to select a single array element for processing.

The second approach was used in Problem 5.3. In this problem, the formula INDEX = 10 − CURGRD/10 was used to compute the index of the element of FREQ to be incremented for each exam score. When we use this approach, the value of the index must be tested and sometimes modified to ensure that it is always within the subscript range of the array being referenced. In the solution shown, we used two decision steps (steps 16 and 17 of Fig. 5.9) to test and modify the value of INDEX.

Problem solutions requiring index computation are very common in programming. Sometimes a good deal of ingenuity on the part of the programmer is required in order to produce a reasonably efficient algorithm for this computation. A little extra effort will often yield a short sequence of statements rather than a complicated nest of decision structures or loops. You are cautioned, however, that ingenuity is no substitute for the care that is required in developing a clean and simple algorithm that works.

The first approach to selecting an array element has been used many times in program solutions. We have read information into array elements in sequential order (Problem 5.3); we have searched array elements in sequential order to find a specific data item (Problem 5.2), etc. For each of these operations, a loop was used in which the loop-control variable also served as the subscript of the array being scanned.

5.8 COMMON PROGRAMMING ERRORS

There are two very common programming errors associated with arrays. One involves the failure to declare a name that is to be used to represent an array, and the other involves the use of subscripts with values exceeding the size of the array being referenced.

1. Failure to Declare an Array

The use of a subscript reference with a symbolic name that has not been declared as an array will cause the compiler to treat the reference as a *function call* rather than an array reference. If this reference occurs at a point where a function call is illegal, then a syntax error will occur. Otherwise, no diagnostic will be given, and the error will not be detected until the program is loaded, or possibly not until execution begins and the erroneous function call is encountered. For example, consider the two statements

```
GRADE(I) = 0
GRDSUM = GRDSUM + GRADE(I)
```

If GRADE is not declared as an array, then the reference in the first statement will be treated as a call to the function GRADE. Since function calls are illegal on the lefthand side of an assignment statement, the FORTRAN Compiler will provide a diagnostic for the statement GRADE(I) = 0. This diagnostic will inform you that you have illegally used a function reference on the left side of an assignment statement. However, the function reference in the second statement is perfectly legal, and no diagnostic will be provided by the compiler. The error will be detected only after compilation, either at load time or execution time, when the erroneously referenced function cannot be found.

Misspelling is a frequent source of the use of undeclared names as array references. When illegal array reference problems occur, the spelling of the array name involved should be carefully compared with the array declaration.

2. Out-of-Range Subscript Values

Out-of-range subscript values (subscripts that are less than one or exceed the declared size of an array) are often caused by errors in index computation, such as those described in Problem 5.3, or by loops that do not terminate properly. These are not syntax errors and cannot be diagnosed during compilation. They may also go undetected during program execution. Such errors can result in the destruction of the contents of memory cells that are adjacent to the array whose subscript reference is in error. This, in turn, may cause unpredictable program results, and sometimes program failure. In either case, before considerable time is spent in debugging, all suspect subscript calculations should be carefully checked for out-of-range errors. This can most easily be done by inserting diagnostic output statements into your program, in order to print subscript values that might be out of range.

Some compilers automatically provide such a subscript checking facility. This facility will print a message indicating an out-of-range subscript, the line number of the program statement at which the error occurred, and the value of the subscript. For example, the message

```
SUBSCRIPT RANGE ERROR AT LINE NO. 28 FOR ARRAY BALANS, IX=0
```

indicates that the subscript IX in the array reference BALANS(IX) (occurring on line 28 of the program) has value 0. When such errors occur, the statements used to define the value of IX must be corrected in order to produce the proper in-range value.

5.9 SUMMARY

In this chapter we introduced a special *data structure* called an *array*, which is a convenient facility for naming and referencing a collection of like items. We discussed how to inform the compiler that an array of elements is to be allocated (by using the type-declaration statement), and we described how to reference an individual array element by writing a parenthesized expression (called a subscript) following the array name, for example, GRADES(I).

Two common programming techniques used to reference array elements were described. The first of these involves referencing each element in sequence. The indexed-DO was shown to be a convenient structure for implementing such sequential references.

The other technique involves references that are determined through the computation of an array index. Such a computation usually involves a program variable whose value follows no predetermined sequence. With this technique, especially, the programmer must be careful not to reference an element that is out of range.

A problem that is frequently encountered when dealing with arrays of data was discussed. This involved searching an array to determine the subscript of a specified data item.

The arrays discussed in this chapter are often called *linear arrays* or *lists*. These arrays are "one-dimensional," in that a single subscript is used to uniquely identify each array element. In Chapter 10, we shall examine a more complex data structure; an array with multiple dimensions.

PROGRAMMING PROBLEMS

5.3 Instructor X has given an exam to a large lecture class of students. The grade scale for the exam is 90–100 (A), 80–89 (B), 70–79 (C), 60–69 (D), 0–59 (F). X has punched the grades for his exams one per card. He now needs a program to perform the following statistical summary for his data.

   i) Count the number of A's, B's, C's, D's, and F's.

   ii) Determine the averages of the A, B, C, D, and F grades, computed on an individual basis—i.e., the average A grade, the average B grade, ..., the average F grade.

   iii) Find the total number of students taking the exam.

   iv) Compute the average and standard deviation* for all of the grades.

5.4 Let A be an array consisting of 20 elements. Write a program to read a collection of up to 20 data items into A, and then find and print the subscript of the largest item in A.

5.5 The Department of Traffic Accidents each year receives accident count reports from a number of cities and towns across the country. To summarize these reports, the Department provides a frequency-distribution report that gives the number of cities reporting accident counts in the following ranges: 0–99, 100–199, 200–299, 300–399, 400–499, 500 or above. The Department needs a computer program to read from a card the number of accidents for each reporting city or town, and to add one to the count for the appropriate accident range. After all the cards have been processed, the resulting frequency counts are to be printed.

---

* The standard deviation is equal to the square root of the variance:

$$S.D. = \sqrt{\frac{\sum_{I=1}^{N} GRADES(I)^2}{N} - AVE^2}$$

5.6 (Improved Bank-Balance Program) The Major Risk Bank has a checking-account program for all of its investors. Each bank member has a different checking-account number. Each month fewer than 20 bank members take advantage of the checking program. Write a program that will be used on a monthly basis to do the following.

i) Read in the account (5 digits) and past month's balance for each bank member using the checking facility (the account and past balance should be punched on one card). Store the account numbers in an array (ACCNS, size 20), and store the past balance in another array (BALANS, size 20).

ii) Read in the transactions for the month. Each transaction card should contain the 5-digit account number and a transaction amount (a positive amount indicates a deposit, and a negative amount indicates a withdrawal).

iii) After all transactions have been read, print each account number and the new bank balance.

Note. There may be many transactions for each account read in during (i) and they need not all be together. For each transaction you will have to search the array ACCNS to find the index of that account. Then you must use this index to alter the contents of the appropriate element in the array BALANS.

5.7 Write a program which, given the *taxable income* for a single taxpayer, will compute the 1975 income tax for that person. Use Schedule X shown in Fig. 5.11. Assume that "line 47", referenced in this schedule, contains the taxable income.

Example If the individual's taxable income is $8192.00, your program should use the tax amount and percent shown in column 3 of line 7 (arrow). The tax in this case is

$$\$1590 + .25(8192. - 8000) = \$1638.00.$$

For each individual processed, print taxable earnings and the total tax.

Hint. Set up three arrays, one for the base tax (column 3), one for the tax percent (column 3), and the third for the excess base (column 4). Your program must then compute the correct index to these arrays, given the taxable income.

5.8 Assume for the moment that your computer has the very limited capability of being able to read and print only single decimal digits at a time; and to add together two integers consisting of one decimal digit each. Write a program to read in two ten-digit integers, add these numbers together, and print the result. Test your program on the following numbers.

$$X = 1487625$$
$$Y = 12783$$

$$X = 60705202$$
$$Y = 30760832$$

$$X = 1234567890$$
$$Y = 9876543210$$

1975 Tax Rate Schedules

SCHEDULE X—Single Taxpayers Not Qualifying for Rates in Schedule Y or Z

Use this schedule if you checked the box on Form 1040, line 1—

If the amount on Form 1040, line 47, is:		Enter on Form 1040, line 16a:	
Not over $500...14% of the amount on line 47.			
Over—	But not over—		of the amount over—
$500	$1,000	$70+15%	$500
$1,000	$1,500	$145+16%	$1,000
$1,500	$2,000	$225+17%	$1,500
$2,000	$4,000	$310+19%	$2,000
$4,000	$6,000	$690+21%	$4,000
$6,000	$8,000	$1,110+24%	$6,000
$8,000	$10,000	$1,590+25%	$8,000
$10,000	$12,000	$2,090+27%	$10,000
$12,000	$14,000	$2,630+29%	$12,000
$14,000	$16,000	$3,210+31%	$14,000
$16,000	$18,000	$3,830+34%	$16,000
$18,000	$20,000	$4,510+36%	$18,000
$20,000	$22,000	$5,230+38%	$20,000
$22,000	$26,000	$5,990+40%	$22,000
$26,000	$32,000	$7,590+45%	$26,000
$32,000	$38,000	$10,290+50%	$32,000
$38,000	$44,000	$13,290+55%	$38,000
$44,000	$50,000	$16,590+60%	$44,000
$50,000	$60,000	$20,190+62%	$50,000
$60,000	$70,000	$26,390+64%	$60,000
$70,000	$80,000	$32,790+66%	$70,000
$80,000	$90,000	$39,390+68%	$80,000
$90,000	$100,000	$46,190+69%	$90,000
$100,000	....	$53,090+70%	$100,000

Fig. 5.11 Schedule X (from IRS Form 1040).

Hints. Store the numbers X and Y in two arrays XAR, YAR, of size 10, one decimal digit per element. If the number is less than 10 digits in length, punch enough *leading zeros* (to the left of the number) to make the number 10 digits long.

Leave a space between each digit punched. (Thus, the first two numbers should be punched as

```
0 0 0 0 0 1 2 7 8 3 ——————Y
1 2 3 4 5 6 7 8 9 10 11 12 13 14 15 16 17 18 19 20

0 0 0 1 4 8 7 6 2 5 ——————X
1 2 3 4 5 6 7 8 9 10 11 12 13 14 15 16 17 18 19 20 21 22
```

Use the statements

```
READ, XAR
READ, YAR
```

to read the numbers into the arrays XAR and YAR respectively.)

You will need a loop to add together the digits in the array elements. You must start with the element with subscript value 10 and work toward the left. Do not forget to handle the carry, if there is one!

Use an integer variable, OFLOW, to indicate if a carry occurred in adding together XAR(1) and YAR(1). OFLOW is set to 1 if a carry occurs here; otherwise, OFLOW will be 0.

5.9 Write a data table, flow diagram, and a program for the following problem. You are given a collection of scores for the last exam in your computer course. You are to compute the average of these scores, and then assign grades to each student according to the following rule.

If a student's score S is within 10 points (above or below) of the average, assign the student a grade of SATISFACTORY. If S is more than 10 points higher than the average, assign the student a grade of OUTSTANDING. If S is more than 10 points below the average, assign the student a grade of UNSATISFACTORY.

Test your program on the following data:

```
'RICHARD LUGAR' 62
'FRANK RIZZO' 31
'DONALD SCHAEFFER' 84
'KEVIN WHITE' 93
'JAMES RIEHLE' 74
'ABE BEAME' 70
'TOM BRADLEY' 84
'WALTER WASHINGTON' 68
'RICHARD DALEY' 64
'RICHARD HATCHER' 82
```

Hint. If your compiler does not allow the use of the character data type, then use the initials of the above listed people in place of their names, and read the initials into a variable of type integer. The output from your program should consist of a labelled 3-column list containing the name, exam score, and grade of each student.

5.10 Write a program to read N data items into each of two arrays X and Y of size 20. Compare each of the elements of X to the corresponding element of Y. In the corresponding element of a third array Z, store:

$+1$ if X is larger than Y

0 if X is equal to Y

-1 if X is less than Y

Then print a three-column table displaying the contents of the arrays X, Y, and Z, followed by a count of the number of elements of X that exceed Y, and a count of the number of elements of X that are less than Y. Make up your own test data, with N less than 20.

5.11 The results of a true–false exam given in a class of Computer Science students has been punched on cards. Each card contains a student identification number, and the students' answers to 10 true–false questions. The data cards are as follows:

Student identification	Answers (1 = true; 0 = false)
0080	0 1 1 0 1 0 1 1 0 1
0340	0 1 0 1 0 1 1 1 0 0
0341	0 1 1 0 1 1 1 1 1 1
0401	1 1 0 0 1 0 0 1 1 1
0462	1 1 0 1 1 1 0 0 1 0
0463	1 1 1 1 1 1 1 1 1 1
0464	0 1 0 0 1 0 0 1 0 1
0512	1 0 1 0 1 0 1 0 1 0
0618	1 1 1 0 0 1 1 0 1 0
0619	0 0 0 0 0 0 0 0 0 0
0687	1 0 1 1 0 1 1 0 1 0
0700	0 1 0 0 1 1 0 0 0 1
0712	0 1 0 1 0 1 0 1 0 1
0837	1 0 1 0 1 1 0 1 0 1
9999	(Sentinel card, punch 10 zeros)

The correct answers are

$$0 \quad 1 \quad 0 \quad 0 \quad 1 \quad 0 \quad 0 \quad 1 \quad 0 \quad 1$$

Write a program to read the data cards, one at a time, and compute and store the number of correct answers for each student in one array, and store the student ID number in the corresponding element of another array. Determine the best score, BEST. Then print a three-column table displaying the ID number, score, and grade for each student. The grade should be determined as follows: If the score is equal to BEST or BEST − 1, give an A; if it is BEST − 2 or BEST − 3, give a C. Otherwise give an F.

5.12 Write a program to read N data items into two arrays X and Y of size 20. Compute the products of the corresponding elements in X and Y and store the result in a third array XY, also of size 20. Print a three-column table displaying the arrays X, Y, and XY. Then compute and print the square root of the sum of the items in XY. Make up your own data, with N less than 20.

5.13 The results of a survey of the households in your township have been punched in cards. Each card contains data for one household, including a four-digit integer identification number, the annual income for the household, and the number of members of the household. Write a program to read the survey results into three arrays and perform the following analyses:

i) Count the number of households included in the survey, and print a three-column table displaying the data read in. (You may assume that no more than 25 households were surveyed.)

ii) Calculate the average household income, and list the identification number and incomes of all households that exceed the average.

iii) Determine the percentage of households having incomes below the poverty level. The poverty level income may be computed according to the formula

$$p = \$3750.00 + \$750.00 * (m - 2)$$

where m is the number of members of each household.

Test your program on the following data.

Identification number	Annual income	Household members
1041	$12,180	4
1062	13,240	3
1327	19,800	2
1483	22,458	8
1900	17,000	2
2112	18,125	7
2345	15,623	2
3210	3,200	6
3600	6,500	5
3601	11,970	2
4725	8,900	3
6217	10,000	2
9280	6,200	1
9999 (Sentinel card)	0	0

6.1 Introduction

6.2 The Multiple-Alternative Decision
     Structure

6.3 The Bowling Problem

6.4 The Indexed-DO and the FOR
     Loop

6.5 Using Structures:
     Part I—Structure Nesting

6.6 Using Structures:
     Part II—Structure Entry and
     Transfers

6.7 Remote Blocks and Top-Down
     Programming

6.8 Common Programming Errors

6.9 Summary

     Programming Problems

ADVANCED CONTROL STRUCTURES

6

6.1 INTRODUCTION

In Chapters 3 and 4 we introduced four fundamental control structures to be used in computer programming. We presented flow-diagram patterns, and described a prototype FORTRAN syntax for each of these structures. These control structures enabled us to write simple programs involving loops and decisions with few, if any, explicit transfers of control.

In this chapter we will present a more general form of the decision structure, called the multiple-alternative decision structure, and a more general form of the indexed-DO loop structure, called the FOR loop.

We will also examine some of the rules for forming combinations or nests of structures. Finally, we will discuss top-down programming as a means of producing more readable, error-free programs, and introduce a new feature, called a *remote block*, that is useful in the application of this technique.

6.2 THE MULTIPLE-ALTERNATIVE DECISION STRUCTURE

6.2.1 How and When To Use It

The problems we have encountered so far have all involved the execution of at most one or two separate decision steps. The solutions to many problems require rather complicated sequences of decisions in order to determine what program statement groups are to be executed.

As an example of this, consider a grading problem similar to Problem 5.3 in which the range of exam scores for each grade category is allowed to vary according to an exam curve specified by the instructor each time the exam is administered. Assuming, as in Problem 5.3, that the range of all exam scores is between 0 and 100, we can solve the new problem by first defining four input variables to be used to determine the grade boundaries.

LOWA   Lowest score in the A grade category
LOWB   Lowest score in the B grade category
LOWC   Lowest score in the C grade category
LOWD   Lowest score in the D grade category

The only restriction on the values of these variables is that LOWD must be less than LOWC, LOWC less than LOWB, and LOWB less than LOWA.

In solving this problem, we cannot use a simple equation for computing the grade category, as we did in Problem 5.3. Instead, we would have to use a sequence of double-alternative decision structures, as shown in Fig. 6.1.

This is a highly nested sequence of considerable complexity, which is not particularly easy to follow, much less program. The necessary decisions for this problem can be more easily written if we generalize the flow-diagram pattern for the IF–THEN–ELSE (double-alternative decision) into a multiple-alternative decision structure, so that more than two alternatives may be represented in a

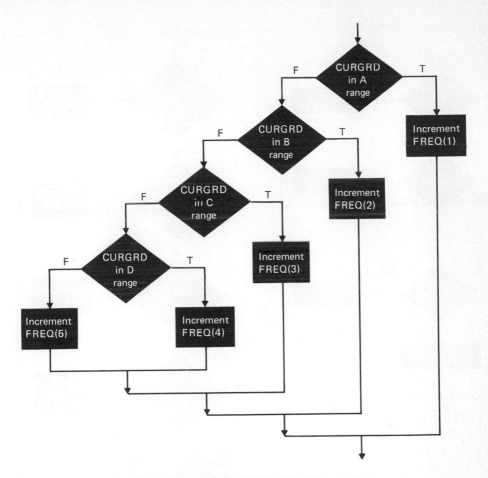

Fig. 6.1 Sequence of IF-THEN-ELSE decision structures.

single structure. The flow-diagram pattern for the multiple-alternative decision structure is shown in Fig. 6.2, along with an example of the structure defined for the new grading problem.

This flow-diagram pattern implies the following program action:

a) The conditions are evaluated from top to bottom.

b) The task ($Task_i$) corresponding to the first condition ($condition_i$) to evaluate to true is performed, and the exit from the structure is taken immediately.

c) If no condition evaluates to true, $Task_E$ is performed.

Thus, the steps in exactly one of the tasks will be performed. More than one condition may actually be true, but only the topmost task will be executed because of the top-to-bottom order of evaluation of conditions, and the fact that the

General form   Example

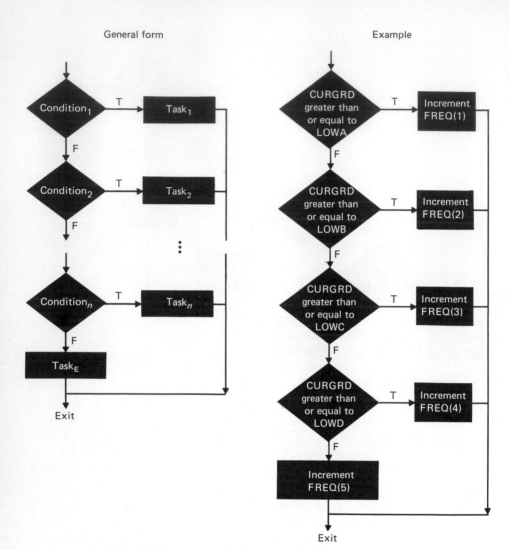

Fig. 6.2 Multiple-alternative decision structure, general form and example.

structure exit immediately follows the execution of the task corresponding to the first true condition.

The bottom task, $Task_E$, may be omitted from this structure. In this case, if all conditions evaluate to false, none of the tasks in the multiple-alternative decision structure will be performed.

The description of the subtasks in a multiple-alternative decision structure should be kept short, and refined, if necessary, in separate flow diagrams. The syntax of the multiple-alternative decision structure (also called the Block–IF) is described next.

Multiple-Alternative Decision Structure (Nonstandard)
Structured FORTRAN Form:

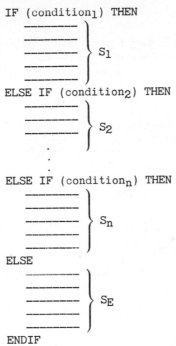

```
IF (condition₁) THEN
        --------- ⎫
        --------- ⎪
        --------- ⎬ S₁
        --------- ⎪
        --------- ⎭
ELSE IF (condition₂) THEN
        --------- ⎫
        --------- ⎬ S₂
        --------- ⎭
           .
           .
           .
ELSE IF (condition_n) THEN
        --------- ⎫
        --------- ⎪
        --------- ⎬ S_n
        --------- ⎪
        --------- ⎭
ELSE
        --------- ⎫
        --------- ⎪
        --------- ⎬ S_E
        --------- ⎪
        --------- ⎭
ENDIF
```

Interpretation. Condition$_1$, condition$_2$, etc., are tested until a condition is reached that evaluates to true. If condition$_i$ is the first condition that evaluates to true, S_i is executed; if none of these conditions evaluates to true, S_E is executed. Regardless of which of the statement groups is carried out, execution next resumes with the first instruction following the ENDIF.

Note. The statement group S_E may be empty (if there is no Task$_E$ in the flow diagram). That is, there may not be any statements between the ELSE and the ENDIF. In this case, the ELSE should be omitted from the FORTRAN structure.

The Structured FORTRAN implementation of the example flow diagram shown in Fig. 6.2 follows.

```
IF (CURGRD .GE. LOWA) THEN
    FREQ(1) = FREQ(1) + 1
ELSE IF (CURGRD .GE. LOWB) THEN
    FREQ(2) = FREQ(2) + 1
ELSE IF (CURGRD .GE. LOWC) THEN
    FREQ(3) = FREQ(3) + 1
ELSE IF (CURGRD .GE. LOWD) THEN
    FREQ(4) = FREQ(4) + 1
ELSE
    FREQ(5) = FREQ(5) + 1
ENDIF
```

Note that for a grade of A, all four of the conditions shown would evaluate to true. However, only the first of these is tested; hence, only FREQ(1) is incremented as desired.

EXERCISE 6.1 You are writing a program to print grade reports for students at the end of each semester. After computing and printing each student's grade point average (GPA) for the semester, you are supposed to use the grade point average to make the following decision:

If the GPA is 3.5 or above, print 'DEANS LIST';
If the GPA is above 1.0 and less than or equal to 1.99, print 'PROBATION WARNING';
If the GPA is less than or equal to 1.0, print 'YOU ARE ON PROBATION NEXT SEMESTER'

Draw a flow diagram and write the FORTRAN program segment for this decision. Use a multiple-alternative decision structure.

EXERCISE 6.2 Replace each set of nested decision structures in Problem 4.1 and Example 4.16 with a multiple-alternative decision structure.

*6.2.2 Compiler Role for the Multiple-Alternative Decision Structure

As was the case with the single- and double-alternative structures, the compiler translates the structure into a sequence of basic computer operations involving

```
IF (CURGRD .GE. LOWA) THEN               IF (CURGRD.LT. LOWA) GO TO 10001
   FREQ(1) = FREQ(1) + 1      ← S₁ →        FREQ(1) = FREQ(1) + 1
                                            GO TO 10005
ELSE IF (CURGRD .GE. LOWB) THEN 10001 IF (CURGRD.LT. LOWB) GO TO 10002
   FREQ(2) = FREQ(2) + 1      ← S₂ →        FREQ(2) = FREQ(2) + 1
                                            GO TO 10005
ELSE IF (CURGRD .GE. LOWC) THEN 10002 IF (CURGRD.LT. LOWC) GO TO 10003
   FREQ(3) = FREQ(3) + 1      ← S₃ →        FREQ(3) = FREQ(3) + 1
                                            GO TO 10005
ELSE IF (CURGRD .GE. LOWD) THEN 10003 IF (CURGRD.LT. LOWD) GO TO 10004
   FREQ(4) = FREQ(4) + 1      ← S₄ →        FREQ(4) = FREQ(4) + 1
                                            GO TO 10005
ELSE
   FREQ(5) = FREQ(5) + 1         10004      FREQ(5) = FREQ(5) + 1
ENDIF                            10005 CONTINUE
   next statement                           next statement
```

Fig. 6.3 Translation example for the multiple-alternative decision structure.

* This section may be omitted.

conditional and GO TO statements. An example of this translation is shown in Fig. 6.3.

Each of the statement groups S_1, S_2, S_3, S_4 is followed by a transfer of control (GO TO 10005) to the first instruction following the structure. Beginning with the first condition, the complement of each condition is tested; if the complement is true, control is transferred to the test of the complement of the next condition in the sequence. If the complement is false, the condition itself must be true; so the associated statement group is executed, and control is transferred to label 10005.

*6.2.3 Implementing the Multiple Alternative Decision Structure

If you are not using Structured FORTRAN, you can implement the multiple-alternative decision structure in standard FORTRAN by imitating the compiler translation shown in the preceding section. If you are using a version of Structured FORTRAN which does not recognize the multiple alternative decision structure (WATFIV–S, for example), you can implement it using a set of nested IF–THEN–ELSE structures as shown in Fig. 6.1.

An alternative approach would be to use a sequence of IF–THEN decision structures, one for each condition and statement group. In order to ensure that only one statement group is executed, the last statement in each structure should transfer control to the next statement following this sequence of structures (see Fig. 6.4).

```
IF (CURGRD .GE. LOWA) THEN           ← S₁ →    IF (CURGRD .GE. LOWA) THEN
    FREQ(1) = FREQ(1) + 1                          FREQ(1) = FREQ(1) + 1
                                                   GO TO 9999
                                               ENDIF
ELSE IF (CURGRD .GE. LOWB) THEN      ← S₂ →    IF (CURGRD .GE. LOWB) THEN
    FREQ(2) = FREQ(2) + 1                          FREQ(2) = FREQ(2) + 1
                                                   GO TO 9999
                                               ENDIF
ELSE IF (CURGRD .GE. LOWC) THEN      ← S₃ →    IF (CURGRD .GE. LOWC) THEN
    FREQ(3) = FREQ(3) + 1                          FREQ(3) = FREQ(3) + 1
                                                   GO TO 9999
                                               ENDIF
ELSE IF (CURGRD .GE. LOWD) THEN      ← S₄ →    IF (CURGRD .GE. LOWD) THEN
    FREQ(4) = FREQ(4) + 1                          FREQ(4) = FREQ(4) + 1
                                                   GO TO 9999
ELSE                                           ENDIF
    FREQ(5) = FREQ(5) + 1            ← Sₑ →         FREQ(5) = FREQ(5) + 1
ENDIF                                     9999 CONTINUE
next statement                                 next statement
```

Fig. 6.4 Translation of a multiple-alternative decision structure into an IF-THEN sequence.

6.3 THE BOWLING PROBLEM

The next problem makes use of the multiple-alternative decision structure.

PROBLEM 6.1 Write a program that will compute a person's tenpin bowling score for one game, given the number of balls rolled, NBALLS, and the number of pins knocked down per ball. Print the score for each frame, as well as the cumulative score at the end of each frame.

DISCUSSION. A bowling *game* consists of 10 *frames*. In ten pin bowling, a maximum of two balls may be rolled in each of the first nine frames, and two or three balls may be rolled in frame ten. Each frame is scored according to the following rules.

1. If the first ball rolled in a frame knocks down all 10 pins (called a *strike*), then the score for the frame is equal to 10 + (the total score on the next two balls rolled). Since all ten pins are down, no other balls are rolled in the current frame.

2. If the two balls rolled in the frame together knock down all 10 pins (called a *spare*), then the score for the frame is equal to 10 + (the score on the next ball rolled).

3. If the two balls rolled knock down fewer than 10 pins (no mark), then the frame score is equal to the number of pins knocked down.

It is immediately clear that a loop will be needed to control the processing of each of the ten frames. The control variable for this loop (FCOUNT) will simply serve to count each frame as it is processed. The array FSCORE (size 10) will be used to save the score for each frame.

The number of pins knocked down by each ball (pin count) will be read into an array called PINS. The variable FIRST will serve as an index to this array. As such, it will be used to select particular elements of PINS, the elements whose values represent the number of pins knocked down by the first ball rolled in each frame. FIRST should be incremented by 1 each time a strike is bowled; otherwise, it should be incremented by 2. (Why?)

An example is given in Fig. 6.5.

This array shows that 10 pins were knocked down by the first ball, 7 by the second, etc. The processing of this array is shown next.

Frame	FIRST	Frame score	Effect
1	1	$10 + 7 + 3 = 20$	STRIKE: Only one ball rolled in frame 1
2	2	$7 + 3 + 5 = 15$	SPARE: Two balls rolled in frame 2
3	4	$5 + 3 = 8$	NO MARK: Two balls rolled in frame 3
4	6	⋮	

PINS(1)	PINS(2)	PINS(3)	PINS(4)	PINS(5)	
10	7	3	5	3	...

Fig. 6.5 Array of pin counts for each ball.

Since PINS(1) is 10, a STRIKE was bowled in the first frame. The frame score (20) is computed by adding 10, PINS(2), and PINS(3); FIRST is then set to 2. In the second frame, balls 2 and 3 are needed to knock down all 10 pins. Adding in the pins knocked down by the next ball, PINS(4), gives a frame score of 15; the index FIRST is then set to 4. Two balls are rolled in the third frame (balls 4 and 5). The frame score is 8, and FIRST is set to 6.

The data table (Fig. 6.6), flow diagrams (Figs. 6.7 and 6.8), and program (Fig. 6.9) follow.

Data Table

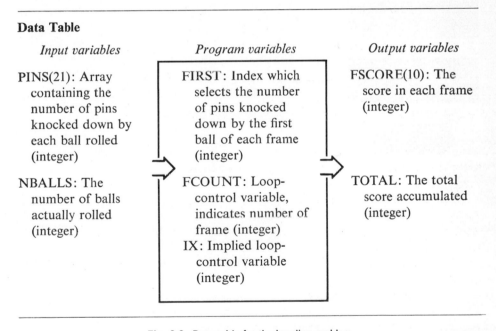

Input variables

PINS(21): Array containing the number of pins knocked down by each ball rolled (integer)

NBALLS: The number of balls actually rolled (integer)

Program variables

FIRST: Index which selects the number of pins knocked down by the first ball of each frame (integer)

FCOUNT: Loop-control variable, indicates number of frame (integer)
IX: Implied loop-control variable (integer)

Output variables

FSCORE(10): The score in each frame (integer)

TOTAL: The total score accumulated (integer)

Fig. 6.6 Data table for the bowling problem.

In Fig. 6.7, the loop-control variable FCOUNT serves as an index to the array FSCORE in loops 10 and 30. Note that the subscript expressions FIRST, FIRST+1, FIRST+2, are used to select elements of the array PINS for testing or for the frame score computation. Since FIRST is the index to the first ball bowled in each frame (anywhere from 1 to 19), FIRST+1 and FIRST+2 serve as indices to the next two balls rolled. The elements in PINS with these indices represent the number of pins knocked down by each ball in the sequence.

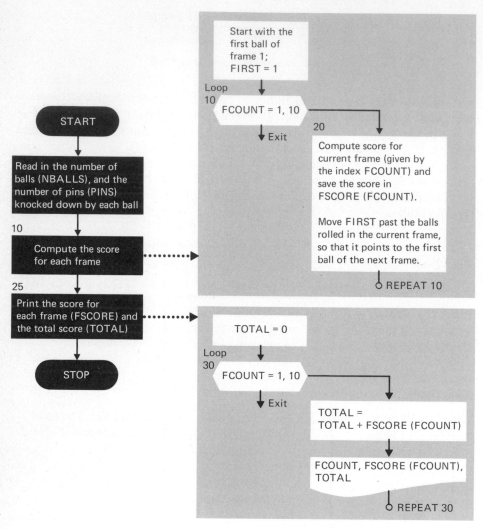

Fig. 6.7 Level one and two flow diagrams for the bowling problem (6.1).

```
C BOWLING PROBLEM
C
      INTEGER NBALLS, FIRST, FCOUNT, IX
      INTEGER FSCORE(10), PINS(21), TOTAL
C
C READ NUMBER OF BALLS AND NUMBER OF PINS KNOCKED DOWN BY EACH BALL
      READ, NBALLS
      READ, (PINS(IX), IX = 1, NBALLS)
      PRINT, 'NUMBER OF BALLS ROLLED IS ', NBALLS
      PRINT, 'SCORES FOR EACH BALL ARE'
      PRINT, (PINS(IX), IX = 1, NBALLS)
```

Fig. 6.9 Bowling problem program.

Refinement of Step 20

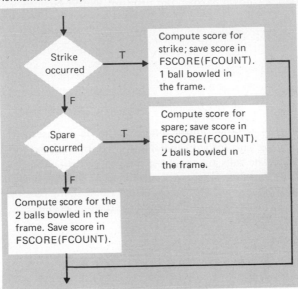

Fig. 6.8   Refinement of step 20 of Fig. 6.7.

```
C INITIALIZE TO FIRST BALL OF FRAME ONE
      FIRST = 1
C COMPUTE SCORE FOR EACH FRAME
      DO 10 FCOUNT = 1, 10
C         TEST FOR A STRIKE OR A SPARE
      IF (PINS(FIRST) .EQ. 10) THEN
C         STRIKE - ONE BALL GETS ALL PINS - TWO BONUS BALLS
          FSCORE(FCOUNT) = 10 + PINS(FIRST+1) + PINS(FIRST+2)
          FIRST = FIRST + 1
      ELSE IF ((PINS(FIRST) + PINS(FIRST+1)) .EQ. 10) THEN
C         SPARE - TWO BALLS GET ALL PINS - ONE BONUS BALL
          FSCORE(FCOUNT) = 10 + PINS(FIRST+2)
          FIRST = FIRST + 2
      ELSE
C         NO MARK - NO STRIKE OR SPARE, TWO BALLS ROLLED
          FSCORE(FCOUNT) = PINS(FIRST) + PINS(FIRST+1)
          FIRST = FIRST + 2
      ENDIF
   10 CONTINUE
C
C PRINT RESULTS
      PRINT, '    FRAME           SCORE           TOTAL'
      TOTAL = 0
      DO 30 FCOUNT = 1, 10
C ACCUMULATE TOTAL BY ADDING IN CURRENT FRAME SCORE
      TOTAL = TOTAL + FSCORE(FCOUNT)
      PRINT, FCOUNT, FSCORE(FCOUNT), TOTAL
   30 CONTINUE
C
      STOP
      END
```

Fig. 6.9 *(continued)*

For the example shown earlier, the printout would be:

FRAME	SCORE	TOTAL
1	20	20
2	15	35
3	8	43
	.	
	.	
	.	

EXERCISE 6.3 They do things a little differently in Massachusetts where Dr. Koffman grew up. The bowling pins (called candlepins) are narrow at the top and bottom and wider in the middle. The balls are about the size of a softball. The rules for a strike and a spare are the same; however, the bowler gets to roll a third ball in each frame if needed. Modify the bowling program to score a candlepin game. (Any pins that fall on the lane are not cleared away in candlepins. This can help the bowler but should not affect your program).

6.4 THE INDEXED-DO AND THE FOR LOOP

6.4.1 The Indexed-DO Revisited

We have been using the indexed-DO as a convenient structure for counter-controlled loops. In most applications to date, both the initial counter value and increment value were one. In this section we will examine other applications of the indexed-DO, discuss its limitations, and introduce an extended form of counter-controlled loops, called the FOR loop.

Example 6.1

```
        NPROD = 1
        DO  60    NTEMP = 2, N, 2
            NPROD = NPROD * NTEMP
    60  CONTINUE
        PRINT, NPROD
        NSUM = 0
        DO  65    NTEMP = 1, N, 2
            NSUM = NSUM + NTEMP
    65  CONTINUE
        PRINT, NSUM
```

In this example, loop 60 computes the product of all even integers less than or equal to N. After this value is printed, loop 65 is used to compute the sum of all odd integers less than or equal to N.

Note that in both loops, NTEMP is used as the loop-control variable, the final expression is N, and the step expression is 2. If N = 7, loop 60 will execute for values of NTEMP equal to 2, 4, and 6 and the value 48 would be printed for NPROD. Loop 65 will execute for values of NTEMP equal to 1, 3, 5 and 7 and the value 16 would be printed for NSUM. You should trace both of these loops and verify that they will indeed perform as just described.

Example 6.2 In Example 4.17, we wrote a program which produced a table showing equivalent Centigrade and Fahrenheit temperatures. This table covered the range of temperatures from 1°C to 100°C in increments of one degree. In general, we might prefer to use input variables for the loop parameters so that any desired table, covering a variety of temperature ranges, could be produced. To do this, we could modify the original program, as shown in Fig. 6.10.

```
C PROGRAM TO PRODUCE A TABLE OF CENTIGRADE TO FAHRENHEIT CONVERSION
C
      INTEGER CDEGR, RFDEGR, TMPST, TMPEND, TMPINC
      REAL FDEGR
C READ LOOP PARAMETERS
      READ, TMPST, TMPEND, TMPINC
      PRINT, '        CENTIGRADE      FAHRENHEIT'
C COMPUTE TABLE ENTRIES AND PRINT
      DO 30 CDEGR = TMPST, TMPEND, TMPINC
         FDEGR = 1.8 * FLOAT(CDEGR) + 32.0
         RFDEGR = IFIX(FDEGR + 0.5)
         PRINT, CDEGR, RFDEGR
   30 CONTINUE
      STOP
      END
```

Fig. 6.10 General Centigrade-to-Fahrenheit conversion program.

This program will accommodate any integer values of **TMPST, TMPEND, TMPINC** which satisfy the general requirements for indexed-DO parameters:

1. TMPEND $\geq$ TMPST > 0

2. TMPINC > 0

Example 6.3 We have the job of writing a program to assist a registrar in updating class lists at the middle of a semester. The following program segment can be used to delete the identification number of any student who has dropped out of class.

Assume the class list is represented by the first N numbers stored in the array CLIST. The variable WHERE represents the index of the number to be deleted. The program segment below accomplishes the deletion by simply rearranging the portion of the array starting at index WHERE + 1. The contents of each element is moved to the element with next smallest index (loop 20). The original and new contents of the array CLIST are shown in Fig. 6.11, followed by the program segment.

If the original list was in numerical order, the new one will be, too. Following the deletion, the value of N is decreased by one, indicating that there is one less item in the list. Thus, the second copy of the last item in the list will be ignored in future manipulations.

Although it is a minor inconvenience to have to introduce a new program variable (START) for storage of the initial value expression, this program is easily implemented using the indexed-DO. However, what if we were faced with the

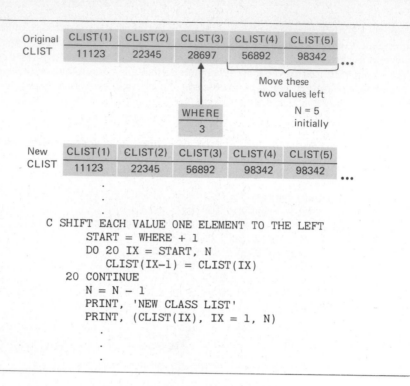

```
C SHIFT EACH VALUE ONE ELEMENT TO THE LEFT
      START = WHERE + 1
      DO 20 IX = START, N
         CLIST(IX-1) = CLIST(IX)
   20 CONTINUE
      N = N - 1
      PRINT, 'NEW CLASS LIST'
      PRINT, (CLIST(IX), IX = 1, N)
```

Fig. 6.11   Deletion of an item from a list.

problem of inserting a new number rather than deleting one? In this case, the program must shift each value that is larger than the new number to the right in order to make room for the new number. This is shown in Fig. 6.12 for IDNUM = 13468 and WHERE = 2.

At first we might try to implement the insertion using the program segment in Fig. 6.13.

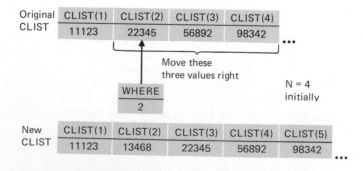

Fig. 6.12   Insertion of an item into a list.

```
                         .
                         .
                         .
    C SHIFT EACH VALUE ONE ELEMENT TO THE RIGHT
          DO 30 IX = WHERE, N
             CLIST(IX+1) = CLIST(IX)
       30 CONTINUE
    C INSERT IDNUM AT WHERE
          CLIST(WHERE) = IDNUM
          N = N + 1
          PRINT, 'NEW CLASS LIST'
          PRINT, (CLIST(IX), IX = 1, N)
                         .
                         .
                         .
```

Fig. 6.13 First attempt at an insertion program.

Unfortunately, the insertion program segment does not work; it produces multiple copies of the item originally at position WHERE (CLIST(3) through CLIST(5) would contain the value 22345). Verify this for yourself by hand-tracing the program segment shown in Fig. 6.12.

To avoid this problem, we must start with the last number in the array and shift it to the right. We should then work backwards (from right to left) through the array until we shift the number at position WHERE. Then we can insert IDNUM. A correct program segment is shown in Fig. 6.14.

```
                         .
                         .
                         .
    C SHIFT EACH VALUE ONE ELEMENT TO THE RIGHT
    C START WITH THE LAST VALUE
          IX = N
          WHILE (IX .GE. WHERE) DO
             CLIST(IX+1) = CLIST(IX)
             IX = IX - 1
          ENDWHILE
    C INSERT IDNUM AT WHERE
          CLIST(WHERE) = IDNUM
          N = N + 1
          PRINT, 'NEW CLASS LIST'
          PRINT, (CLIST(IX), IX = 1, N)
                         .
                         .
                         .
```

Fig. 6.14 Insertion program segment.

Since we must shift the last value first, the loop-control variable is initialized to N and is decremented by one after each shift operation. It is illegal to specify negative parameters for the Standard FORTRAN indexed-DO; consequently, the WHILE loop is used for this particular counter-controlled loop.

Some versions of FORTRAN provide a more general form of the indexed-DO which permits negative values as well as integer expressions for parameters. We call this extended form of the indexed-DO the *FOR loop*; it is described in the next section.

EXERCISE 6.4 As part of the program for the registrar, write program segments which will perform the following 2 tasks.

a) Scan the list of identification numbers to determine the index, WHERE, of a number, NDROP, to be deleted from the class list.

b) Scan the ordered list of identification numbers to determine the index, WHERE, of a number, IDNUM, to be inserted in the class list. WHERE should indicate the array element that currently contains the smallest number larger than IDNUM.

*6.4.2 The Structured FORTRAN FOR Loop

In Chapter 4, we introduced the Standard FORTRAN indexed-DO loop-control structure. We have found it to be a convenient structure even with the limitations imposed on the loop parameters. In this section, we will describe a more general form of counter-controlled loop, the Structured FORTRAN FOR loop.

FOR Loop-Control Structure (Nonstandard)

Structured FORTRAN Form:

```
FOR (lcv = initial, end, step) DO
    ─────
    ─────
    ─────      loop body
    ─────
    ─────
ENDFOR
```

Interpretation. The loop-control parameters initial, end, and step are the *initial value, end value,* and *step value* expressions respectively. The lcv should be an integer variable, and initial, end, and step may be any integer expressions.

The loop body will be repeated once for each value of the lcv, starting with lcv equal to the value of initial, and continuing until lcv "passes" the value of end. After each loop repetition, the value of lcv is updated by the value of step. If the value of step is positive, repetition will continue until lcv becomes greater than end. If the value of step is negative, then repetition will continue until lcv becomes less than end. If step is 1, it may be omitted.

---

* This section may be omitted.

The implementation of the FOR loop is not the same on all compilers. Some compilers have simply extended the indexed-DO by relaxing the restrictions on its parameters rather than introduce a new control structure. Others have provided a new structure with syntactical features that are similar to those described here. Two properties which are true of most implementations are listed below.

Properties of the FOR loop

1. Loop execution is terminated when the value of lcv passes the end value. Thus, after loop repetition terminates, the value of lcv is not the same as it was during the last execution of the loop. If the loop header were

$$\text{FOR } (I = 6, 4, -1) \text{ DO}$$

the loop would be executed for values of I equal to 6, 5, and 4; the value of I after completion of the loop would be 3, not 4.

2. If the loop parameters are such that the loop-control variable initial value has already passed the end value parameter, the loop will not be executed. An example would be: FOR $(I = 4, 6, -1)$ DO.

Example 6.4 The FOR loop could be used to implement the insertion and deletion loops in Example 6.3. The loop headers would be:

Deletion: FOR (IX = WHERE + 1, N) DO
Insertion: FOR (IX = N, WHERE, −1) DO

By using the FOR loop, we eliminate the need for an extra program variable to represent the expression WHERE + 1. We also eliminate the need for a WHILE loop and the extra steps for the explicit specification of the loop-control variable initialization and update in performing the shift operations required in the insertion program.

EXERCISE 6.5 Modify the temperature-conversion program (Example 6.2) so that it will convert Fahrenheit temperatures to Centigrade. Print out a table of conversions for temperatures ranging from 210°F down to −30°F in steps of −10°F. Show how to do this with and without the FOR loop.

EXERCISE 6.6 The formula for the velocity of a body dropped from rest is $v = gt$, where g is the acceleration due to gravity, and t is time (air resistance is ignored here). Write a loop to compute v at 10-second intervals (starting with $t = 0$) for a pickle dropped from a building that is 600 meters tall, with $g = 9.81$ meters/second. [*Hint.* Use the formula $t = \sqrt{2s/g}$ to determine the time, TGRND, it takes for the pickle to hit the ground (s equals 600). Use TGRND to limit the number of repetitions of the loop that is used to produce the table.]

6.5 USING STRUCTURES: PART I—STRUCTURE NESTING

6.5.1 General Comments

Until now, we have been using structures with very little concern for any rules that might govern their use in a FORTRAN program. There are, in fact, only a handful of rules that we must follow. These rules concern the nesting of structures, and the entry into and exit from these structures. More than likely, you have been following these rules ever since you began using these structures. Nevertheless, you should become familiar with the precise statements of the rules before beginning to write more complicated computer programs.

6.5.2 Nested Structures

You have already written and studied programs containing nested structures and encountered little difficulty. To ensure that you have no problems in writing more complicated nests of structures, we will give a precise statement of the rule for nesting structures.

Structure nesting rule

Any structure may be nested within any other, subject to the following rule:

All nested structures must be wholly contained within a single statement group of the structure(s) in which they appear.

To fully understand this rule, you must recall that all loops and the single-alternative decision structure contain a single statement group.

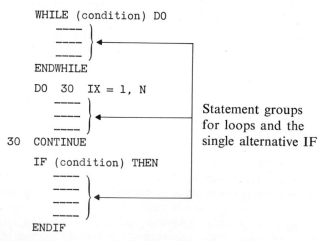

```
WHILE (condition) DO
    ----
    ----
    ----
ENDWHILE
DO   30   IX = 1, N
    ----
    ----
    ----
30   CONTINUE
IF (condition) THEN
    ----
    ----
    ----
    ----
ENDIF
```

Statement groups for loops and the single alternative IF

The double-alternative and multiple-alternative decision structures contain more than one statement group.

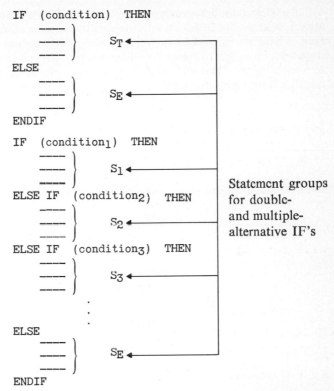

The *structure nesting rule* states that no nested structure may overlap (or be a part of) more than one statement group of each containing structure. All of the programs written in the text are properly nested. See, for example, the bowling problem (Fig. 6.8), in which a multiple-alternative decision structure is nested within an indexed-DO loop.

Example 6.5 The following is an example of illegal structure nesting. The loop nested within the IF structure overlaps both the S_T and S_F statement groups of the IF.

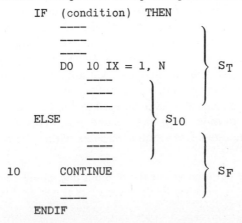

If you carefully draw your first-level flow diagram and then refine each step separately, it is impossible to draw a flow diagram that contains overlapping structures. However, if you are careless in converting your flow diagrams to FORTRAN program statements (or neglect to draw a flow diagram), you may end up with overlapping structures in your program. This will result in a compiler diagnostic since the compiler cannot translate overlapping structures.

EXERCISE 6.7 What is wrong with the following structure nesting?

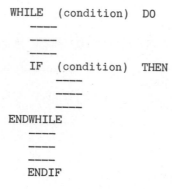

```
WHILE  (condition)  DO
    ----
    ----
    ----
    IF  (condition)  THEN
        ----
        ----
        ----
ENDWHILE
    ----
    ----
    ----
    ENDIF
```

6.5.3 Nested Loops

Nested loops, especially nested indexed-DO's, are perhaps the most difficult of all nested structures to write, read, and debug. For this reason, we will examine some examples involving nested loops which should help clarify the relationship among the loops involved.

A flow diagram of a pair of nested loops is shown in Fig. 6.15. The refinement of step 24 in loop 20 is itself a loop. This means that during each repetition of loop 20 (the outer loop), loop 24 (the inner loop) must also be entered and executed. The number of times loops 20 and 24 are repeated depends on the manner in which their loop-control variables are initialized, updated, and tested. (The initialization steps shown in Fig. 6.15 are not needed if loops 20 and 24 are indexed-DO loops.)

It is permissible to use the loop-control variable of the outer loop as a parameter in the initialization, update, or test of an inner loop-control variable. However, the same variable should never be used as the loop control variable of both an outer loop and an inner loop in the same nest. This would result in an illegal modification of the outer loop-control variable within the loop body.

Example 6.6 We can write out each line of the printout that would be produced by the following program.

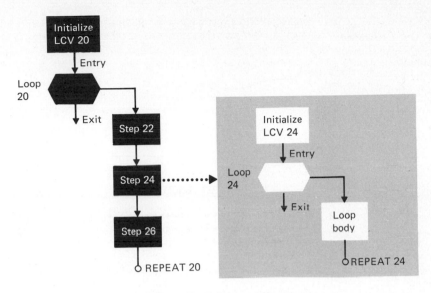

Fig. 6.15 Flow diagram of nested loops.

```
DO   10   I = 1, 3
          PRINT, 'OUTER', I
          DO   20   J = 1, 2
               PRINT, 'INNER', I, J
20           CONTINUE
10   CONTINUE
     STOP
     END
```

For each execution of the outer loop (10), the inner loop (20) would execute twice. Thus, loop 20 would repeat a total of 3 × 2, or 6 times. The output from these loops is

```
OUTER  1
INNER  1  1
INNER  1  2
OUTER  2
INNER  2  1
INNER  2  2
OUTER  3
INNER  3  1
INNER  3  2
```

*Example 6.7** The following program segment plots the contents of the array FREQ in the form of a bar graph (see Fig. 6.16). The data table follows Fig. 6.16 and the program is shown in Fig. 6.17.

---

* If the character data type is not available, this example may be postponed until format statements (Chapter 8) have been introduced.

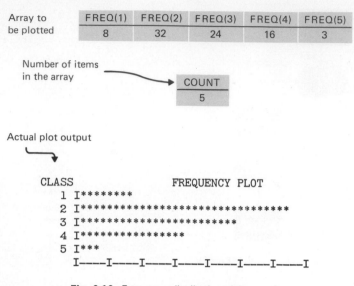

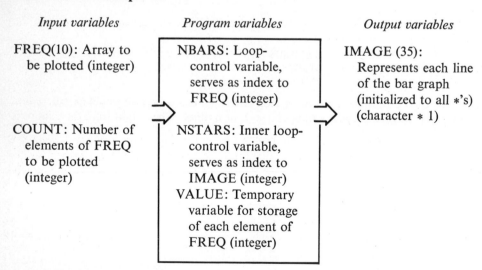

Fig. 6.16 Frequency distribution plot example.

Data table for Example 6.7

Input variables	Program variables	Output variables
FREQ(10): Array to be plotted (integer)	NBARS: Loop-control variable, serves as index to FREQ (integer)	IMAGE (35): Represents each line of the bar graph (initialized to all *'s) (character * 1)
COUNT: Number of elements of FREQ to be plotted (integer)	NSTARS: Inner loop-control variable, serves as index to IMAGE (integer) VALUE: Temporary variable for storage of each element of FREQ (integer)	

The program in Fig. 6.17 has three indexed-DO loops including two implied indexed-DO loops. One implied loop is used for reading data into FREQ. The other implied loop is used for displaying a portion of IMAGE and is nested within loop 10.

NBARS is the outer loop-control variable and is used to cycle through the elements of the array FREQ. NSTARS is the loop control variable for the inner

```
C PLOT THE ARRAY FREQ AS A BAR GRAPH
C
      CHARACTER*1 IMAGE(35)        [or INTEGER IMAGE(35)]
      INTEGER FREQ(10), NBARS, NSTARS, COUNT, VALUE
C
C STORE ALL STARS IN IMAGE PRIOR TO PROGRAM EXECUTION
      DATA IMAGE /35 * '*'/
C
C READ DATA INTO COUNT AND FREQ
      READ, COUNT
      READ, (FREQ(NBARS), NBARS = 1, COUNT)
      PRINT, '      CLASS       FREQUENCY PLOT'
C
C PLOT EACH ELEMENT OF FREQ AS A "BAR"
      DO 10 NBARS = 1, COUNT
C         DISPLAY A PORTION OF IMAGE
          VALUE = FREQ(NBARS)
          PRINT, NBARS, ' I', (IMAGE(NSTARS), NSTARS = 1, VALUE)
   10 CONTINUE
C     BAR GRAPH COMPLETE
      PRINT, '              I----I----I----I----I----I----I----I'
      STOP
      END
```

Fig. 6.17 Program for Example 6.7.

loop of the nest (an implied indexed-DO). Since IMAGE contains all *'s, the statement

```
      PRINT, NBARS, ' I', (IMAGE(NSTARS), NSTARS = 1, VALUE)
```

instructs the computer to print a string of asterisks on each output line. The number of asterisks printed is determined by the value of the element of FREQ being represented on each output line (VALUE = FREQ (NBARS)). This value must be less than or equal to the size of IMAGE.

If your compiler does not have the character data type, the array IMAGE should be type integer. In this case, the format-free output statement in the preceding paragraph may not have the desired effect. If not, it should be replaced by the statements:

```
      PRINT 19, NBARS, (IMAGE(NSTARS), NSTARS = 1, VALUE)
   19 FORMAT (' ', 8X, I2, ' I', 35A1)
```

This is a *formatted output* and associated *format* statement. These statements tell the compiler the following:

' ' —Use single line spacing.

8X —Skip eight print columns.

I2 —Print the value of NBARS as an integer in two print columns.

' I'—Print this character string.

35A1—For each element of the array IMAGE to be printed (up to 35), print the first character only ('*').

We will study formatted input and output in Chapter 8.

EXERCISE 6.8 Write out each line of the printout for the following program.

```
DO   10   I = 1, 2
          PRINT, 'OUTER', I
          DO   20   J = 1, 4, 2
               PRINT, 'INNER J', I, J
     20        CONTINUE
          DO   30   K = 2, 4, 2
               PRINT, 'INNER K', I, K
     30        CONTINUE
     10 CONTINUE
```

6.5.4 Bubble-Sort Problem

The problem that follows is an example of the use of nested loops in sorting, or rearranging in numerical order, the data stored in an array. Sorting programs are used in a variety of applications, and the program developed here could be easily modified to sort alphanumeric data (such as last names) stored in a character array. In this example, we will sort numeric data in ascending numerical order (smallest value first); however it would be just as easy to sort the data in descending order (largest value first).

PROBLEM 6.2 Write a program to sort, in ascending order, an array of integer values.

DISCUSSION. There are many different algorithms for sorting. We will use one of the simplest of these algorithms, the *Bubble Sort*. The Bubble Sort is so named because it has the property of "bubbling" the smallest items to the top of a list. The algorithm proceeds by comparing the values of adjacent elements in the array. If the value of the first of these elements is larger than the value of the second, these values are exchanged, and then the values of the next adjacent pair of elements are compared. This process starts with the pair of elements with indices 1 and 2 and continues through the pair of elements with indices $n - 1$ and n, in an array of size n. Then this sequence of comparisons (called a *pass*) is repeated, starting with the first pair of elements again, until the entire array of elements is compared without an exchange being made. At this point we know that the array is sorted.

As an example, we will trace through the sort of the integer array M as shown in Fig. 6.18. In this sequence of diagrams, diagram (1) shows the initial arrangement of the data in the array; the first pair of values are out of order and they are exchanged. The result is shown in diagram (2).

The above sequence shows all exchanges that would be made during each pass through the adjacent pairs of array elements. After pass one, we see that the array is finally ordered except for the value 25. Subsequent passes through the array will "bubble" this value up one array element at a time until the sort is complete. In each pass through M, the elements are compared in the following order: M(1) and M(2); M(2) and M(3); M(3) and M(4); M(4) and M(5). Note that even though the array is sorted at the end of pass 3, it will take one more pass through the array without any exchanges to complete the algorithm. ∎

Now that we have a general idea of how the algorithm works, we can write the data table and the flow diagrams (Figs. 6.19 and 6.20) for the Bubble Sort.

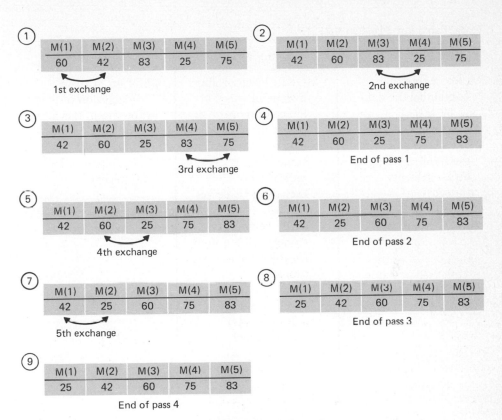

Fig. 6.18 Bubble-sort trace on small array.

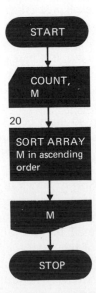

Fig. 6.19 Level-one flow diagram for bubble-sort problem (6.2).

Data Table For Problem 6.2:

Input variables	*Program variables*	*Output variables*
M(10): Array containing the data to be sorted (integer)	MORE: Program flag: a value of true indicates more passes through the data are required; a value of false indicates no exchanges made yet (logical)	M(10): At the conclusion of the program, this array will contain the data sorted in ascending order (integer)
COUNT: Contains the number of array elements (integer)	TEMP: Temporary storage cell required for the exchange (integer)	
	INDEX: Loop-control variable and array index (integer)	
	I: Loop-control variable for all implied loops (integer)	

The variable MORE is used in the outer loop to determine whether or not an exchange has taken place. If no exchange takes place, then MORE will be false upon completion of the operations shown in step 40. The outer loop will then be exited, and the sorted array M will be printed.

As indicated in step 40 (Fig. 6.20), if a pair of array elements is out of order, their values must be exchanged (step 25). We will use a temporary storage cell, TEMP, to hold one of these values to facilitate the exchange. Note that INDEX always points to the first array element of any pair being compared; consequently, the end value expression for loop 40 must be COUNT − 1. We will introduce an additional program variable, NEXLAS, to represent this expression. NEXLAS should be initialized after the value of COUNT is read in and before loop execution begins.

The program for the Bubble Sort is shown in Fig. 6.21.

Whenever nested loops are used, the inner loop is executed from start to finish for *each* repetition or *iteration* of an outer loop. In the program just completed, loop 40 will be executed for all values of INDEX between 1 and COUNT − 1 for each execution of the outer loop.

This kind of repetition can be quite difficult to understand, much less to program. It is, therefore, often extremely helpful to maintain a clear separation among all loops in a program, and to outline the logic of each loop separately,

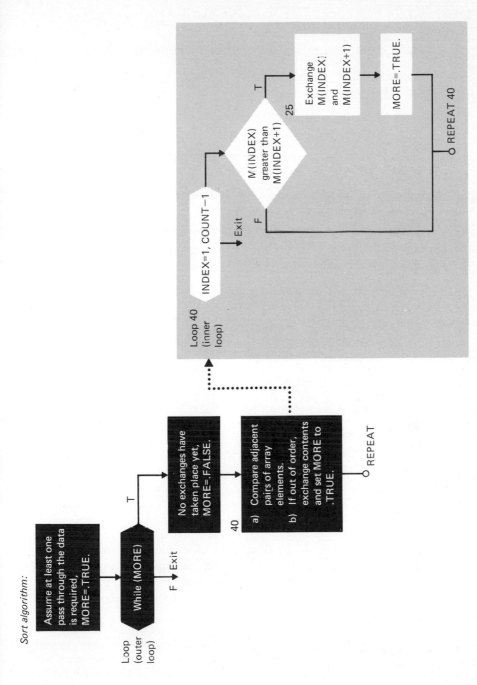

Fig. 6.20 Successive refinements. Step 20, of level-one flow diagram for bubble-sort problem (6.2).

```
C BUBBLE SORT PROGRAM
C ARRANGE A LIST OF INTEGER DATA ITEMS IN ASCENDING ORDER
C
      INTEGER M(10), COUNT, INDEX, I, TEMP, NEXLAS
      LOGICAL MORE
C
C READ AND PRINT DATA TO BE SORTED
      READ, COUNT
      READ, (M(I), I = 1, COUNT)
      PRINT, 'THE NUMBER OF ITEMS TO BE SORTED IS ', COUNT
      PRINT, 'ORIGINAL, UNSORTED LIST --'
      PRINT, (M(I), I = 1, COUNT)
C INITIALIZE
      NEXLAS = COUNT - 1
      MORE = .TRUE.
C
C OUTER LOOP--REPEATED WHILE MORE EXCHANGES NEEDED
      WHILE (MORE) DO
         MORE = .FALSE.
C        INNER LOOP - COMPARE SUCCESSIVE PAIRS OF ITEMS IN M
         DO 40 INDEX = 1, NEXLAS
            IF (M(INDEX) .GT. M(INDEX+1)) THEN
C              EXCHANGE OUT-OF-ORDER PAIRS
               TEMP = M(INDEX)
               M(INDEX) = M(INDEX+1)
               M(INDEX+1) = TEMP
               MORE = .TRUE.
            ENDIF
   40    CONTINUE
      ENDWHILE
C SORT COMPLETE. PRINT SORTED ARRAY
      PRINT, 'FINAL, SORTED LIST IS --'
      PRINT, (M(I), I = 1, COUNT)
      STOP
      END
```

Fig. 6.21 Program for Problem 6.2.

putting the loops together only at the final stage of writing the program. This separation is often most easily maintained by simply summarizing the activity of any loop nested within another (such as has been done for step 40 in Fig. 6.20), and then providing the details of execution of the inner loop in a separate place, possibly on another page.

EXERCISE 6.9 In Fig. 6.18, note that after pass i the ith largest value is in element $M(COUNT - i + 1)$. Hence, it is only necessary to examine elements with indices less than $COUNT - i + 1$ during the next pass. Modify the algorithm to take advantage of this.

EXERCISE 6.10 Modify this program to sort the array M in descending order (largest number first). Trace the execution of your program on the initial array shown in Fig. 6.18.

EXERCISE 6.11 Modify this program so that the median or middle item of the final sorted array is printed out. If COUNT is even, the median should be the average of the two middle numbers, i.e., the average of the elements with subscripts COUNT/2 and COUNT/2 + 1. If COUNT is odd, the median is simply the value of the array element with index COUNT/2 + 1. A number is even if it is divisible by 2. (See Example 4.15.)

*6.6 USING STRUCTURES: PART II—STRUCTURE ENTRY AND TRANSFERS

*6.6.1 Structure Entry Rule

There is one important rule that pertains to all of the structures that have been presented in this text. This rule concerns the manner in which these structures should be entered.

All structures should be entered only "through the top". That is, *no statement within a structure should be executed without prior execution of the header statement of the structure.* Transfers into the middle of a structure from outside the structure should be avoided because unpredictable program behavior may result.

Transfers of control within a structure, or out of an inner structure, are acceptable although you should have little use for them.

*6.6.2 EXIT and NEXT Statements

The only transfer statement we have seen so far is the GO TO statement. Some versions of Structured FORTRAN provide two additional transfer statements for use within loop structures. The *EXIT statement* causes an immediate transfer out of a loop to the first statement following the loop terminator, thereby terminating loop repetition. The *NEXT statement* causes the immediate start of the next iteration of a loop. Both of these statements can be placed anywhere within the body of the loop to be exited or repeated.

The EXIT Statement (Nonstandard)

Structured FORTRAN Form: EXIT [sn]

Interpretation. The label sn is optional. If used, it should be the range label of an indexed–DO or a label associated with the header statement of a WHILE or FOR loop that contains the EXIT statement. Execution of the loop indicated by sn is immediately terminated. If sn is omitted, execution of the innermost loop containing the EXIT statement is terminated. Execution will continue with the first statement following the loop terminator.

---

* This section may be omitted.

The NEXT Statement (Nonstandard)

Structured FORTRAN Form: NEXT [sn]

Interpretation. The label sn is optional. (See discussion of label for EXIT statement.) The next iteration of loop sn is initiated. If sn is omitted, the next iteration of the innermost loop containing the NEXT statement is initiated. For a WHILE loop, this implies the immediate execution of the loop repetition test; for an indexed-DO or FOR loop, this implies the update and test of the loop-control variable. The loop is either repeated or exited depending on the test results.

Example 6.8 The program segment below uses the EXIT statement. This segment is a solution to Exercise 6.4(a); it finds the index (WHERE) of an item (NDROP) to be deleted from an ordered list (CLIST) of N numbers.

```
                   .
                   .
                   .
        FOUND = .FALSE.
        DO 15 IX = 1, N
           IF (CLIST(IX) .EQ. NDROP) THEN
              FOUND = .TRUE.
              WHERE = IX
              EXIT 15
           ENDIF
     15 CONTINUE
                   .
                   .
                   .
```

The loop is exited either because NDROP has been found (EXIT 15 executed) or the end of the list was reached (normal exit). The list deletion should only be performed if the program flag FOUND is true.

Example 6.9 The program segment below processes only the positive elements of the list M. The loop is terminated after the first element larger than 1000.0 has been processed.

```
                   .
                   .
                   .
        DO 10 IX = 1, 125
           IF (M(IX) .LE. 0.0) NEXT
     C PROCESS POSITIVE ELEMENTS OF M
                 _____
                 _____
                 _____
           IF (M(IX) .GT. 1000.0) EXIT
     10 CONTINUE
                   .
                   .
                   .
```

A summary of the properties of the EXIT and NEXT statements is given below. If your compiler does not recognize them (WATFIV–S does not), you should use the implementation suggestions provided.

Table 6.1   EXIT and NEXT statement summaries

EXIT [sn]	NEXT [sn]
Purpose: Used to cause the immediate termination of loop repetition.	*Purpose:* Used to initiate the immediate repetition of a loop. Any increment and test specified in the loop header are first carried out.
Implementation in Standard FORTRAN: Insert a labelled CONTINUE statement as the first statement following the loop terminator. Transfer to that CONTINUE statement.	*Implementation in Standard FORTRAN:* For an indexed-DO loop, transfer to the range label affixed to the terminator statement. For a WHILE or FOR loop, insert a labelled CONTINUE statement just prior to the loop terminator statement; transfer to that CONTINUE statement.

Example 6.9 is implemented below in standard FORTRAN.

```
         .
         .
         .
      DO 10 IX = 1, 125
         IF (M(IX) .LE. 0.0) GO TO 10
         ————
         ————
         ————
         ————
         IF (M(IX) .GT. 1000.0) GO TO 101
   10 CONTINUE
  101 CONTINUE
         .
         .
         .
```

Often you can eliminate the need for a NEXT or EXIT statement by a slight rearrangement of the algorithm. We recommend doing this whenever it is practical.

An EXIT statement in an indexed-DO loop can usually be eliminated by replacing the indexed-DO with a WHILE loop. Loop exit will occur when the WHILE loop-repetition condition evaluates to .FALSE..

The original loop index must be incremented within the WHILE loop.

EXERCISE 6.12 Rewrite the program segments shown in Examples 6.8 and 6.9 so that all transfer statements are eliminated.

*6.7 REMOTE BLOCKS AND TOP-DOWN PROGRAMMING

Early in Chapter 2, we indicated that a desirable goal in problem solving was to break a complex problem into independent subproblems and work on these subproblems separately. We have practiced this technique of problem decomposition throughout the text by drawing a first-level flow diagram outlining the subproblems to be solved. We have then separately refined each of these subproblems to fill in the details of an algorithm, subdividing each subproblem still further when necessary. This technique of specifying algorithms through successive refinement is often referred to as *top-down programming*.

Up to now, the logic, or flow of control, in the programs we have written was relatively straightforward and easy to follow. Most programs consisted of short sequences of structures with little or no nesting. We now have the tools and the ability to write programs that are more complex and may involve several levels of nesting. Such programs can become quite cumbersome and difficult to follow unless proper procedures are followed in the design and implementation of a program.

We have seen how the practice of top-down programming can aid in the description of the flow of control in programs; we have used this technique in designing the algorithms in the text by drawing level-one flow diagrams and successive refinements. Unfortunately, we have not been able to carry this top-down process through to the implementation of our programs. What we would like to do is implement our programs in the same manner in which the flow diagram was designed. This involves writing an initial program segment (the *top-level* or *level one program segment*) which looks much like a first-level flow diagram. Within the top-level program, each of the subproblems to be solved is referenced by name. The specific program statements corresponding to each subproblem are written together as a separate program module called a *remote block*, which is provided in a separate section at the end of the top-level program rather than being imbedded within the top-level program itself. If further problem subdivision is necessary, each of the subproblem program segments may be written top-down as well.

To be able to write programs in the manner just described, we must have a structure available for designating sequences of statements that are to be treated as remote blocks. We must also have a statement that can be used to request the execution of a remote block. One such structure (the REMOTE BLOCK) and statement (the EXECUTE statement) are described next. The REMOTE BLOCK and EXECUTE statements are supported by the WATFIV–S compiler. Other FORTRAN versions may also support these features with slight variations. Neither the REMOTE BLOCK nor the EXECUTE statement are part of Standard FORTRAN.

---

* This section may be omitted.

Remote Block Structure (Nonstandard)

Structured FORTRAN Form:

```
REMOTE BLOCK name
        ----  ⎫
        ----  ⎪
        ----  ⎬   Statements to be executed when
        ----  ⎪   the remote block is referenced
        ----  ⎪
        ----  ⎭
END BLOCK
```

Interpretation. The header statement (REMOTE BLOCK) and the terminator (END BLOCK) serve to bracket a sequence of statements that are to be executed as a group when referenced using an EXECUTE. The name is an identifier of the statement group used in this way in a program. Standard FORTRAN rules for symbolic names should be observed in choosing names, although some FORTRAN compilers may permit the use of longer names.

The EXECUTE Statement (Nonstandard)

Structured FORTRAN Form:

                    EXECUTE name

Interpretation. The remote block named as the operand of the EXECUTE statement is executed. Control is transferred to the first statement in the remote block. After all the statements of the remote block are executed, control is returned back to the next instruction in the top-level program or remote block that contained the EXECUTE.

As an example of how the top-down programming process works, we will rewrite the Bubble Sort Program (Fig. 6.21) using these new features in Fig. 6.22. In Fig. 6.22, the following points should be noted:

1. The top-level program itself is quite compact, giving only an outline of the steps of the solution program (similar to the level one flow diagram). It extends through the STOP statement.

2. All of the remote blocks are inserted between the STOP and END statements of the top-level program.

3. The remote block named SORT references a remote block named COMPAR which, in turn, references a remote block named EXCHNG. SORT and COMPAR are written top-down as well.

```
C BUBBLE SORT PROGRAM WRITTEN WITH REMOTE BLOCKS
C ARRANGE A LIST OF INTEGER DATA ITEMS IN ASCENDING ORDER
C
      INTEGER M(10), COUNT, INDEX, TEMP, NEXLAS
      LOGICAL MORE
C
C READ IN DATA TO BE SORTED
      EXECUTE INPUT
C SORT THE ARRAY
      EXECUTE SORT
C PRINT RESULTS
      PRINT, 'FINAL, SORTED LIST IS --'
      PRINT, (M(I), I = 1, COUNT)
      STOP
C
C
C *** REFINEMENTS OF TOP LEVEL TASKS ***
C
C READ IN DATA
      REMOTE BLOCK INPUT
          READ, COUNT
          READ, (M(I), I = 1, COUNT)
          PRINT, 'THE NUMBER OF ITEMS TO BE SORTED IS ', COUNT
          PRINT, 'ORIGINAL, UNSORTED LIST --'
          PRINT, (M(I), I = 1, COUNT)
      END BLOCK
C
C SORT THE ARRAY
      REMOTE BLOCK SORT
          MORE = .TRUE.
          WHILE (MORE) DO
             MORE = .FALSE.
C            COMPARE ALL ADJACENT PAIRS OF ELEMENTS
             EXECUTE COMPAR
          ENDWHILE
      END BLOCK
C
C *** REFINEMENTS OF SECOND LEVEL BLOCKS
C
C COMPARE ADJACENT PAIRS OF ELEMENTS
      REMOTE BLOCK COMPAR
          NEXLAS = COUNT - 1
          DO 40 INDEX = 1, NEXLAS
             IF (M(INDEX) .GT. M(INDEX+1)) THEN
C                EXCHANGE OUT-OF-ORDER PAIRS
                 EXECUTE EXCHNG
                 MORE = .TRUE.
             ENDIF
   40     CONTINUE
      END BLOCK
```

```
C
C *** REFINEMENTS OF THIRD LEVEL BLOCKS
C
C EXCHANGE OUT-OF-ORDER PAIRS
      REMOTE BLOCK EXCHNG
         TEMP = M(INDEX)
         M(INDEX) = M(INDEX+1)
         M(INDEX+1) = TEMP
      END BLOCK
      END
```

Fig. 6.22 Bubble-sort program using remote blocks.

The use of transfer instructions (GO TO, EXIT, and NEXT) within a remote block is allowed, but transfers into remote blocks from outside are prohibited, as are transfers out of a remote block to statements outside the block. Remote blocks may not be nested within one another, but must be listed separately, as shown in the Bubble Sort example.

As we have indicated, the remote block is not part of standard FORTRAN. However, in the next chapter, we will describe a standard FORTRAN feature, the *subprogram*, which is even more powerful than the remote block and can be used with all versions of FORTRAN in the practice of top-down programming.

EXERCISE 6.13 Rewrite the Bowling Program (see Figs. 6.6 through 6.8) using remote blocks. Use the flow-diagram refinements as a guide for deciding what remote blocks are needed.

6.8 COMMON PROGRAMMING ERRORS

6.8.1 Structure Nesting Errors

Structure-nesting errors are among the most common programming errors that are made. Such errors are more likely to occur when nested decision structures or multiple-alternative decision structures, with lengthy statement groups for each alternative, are used. Most compilers can detect structure-nesting errors and will provide diagnostics informing the programmer that such errors have occurred.

To aid in obtaining the proper structure nesting, we urge you to faithfully follow the process of flow-diagram refinement illustrated in the text. Refine each nested structure as a separate entity, and then carefully implement the refined flow diagram as a FORTRAN program. To retain the proper structure nesting, go back to the flow diagram when making any nontrivial changes to the algorithm. Rearranging structure components without referring to the flow diagram may introduce unexpected program logic and structure-nesting errors.

Remember, too, that the NEXT statement may only be used inside loops, and that its use will cause the immediate start of the *next iteration* of the indicated loop.

Attempts to use the NEXT statement outside the scope of the indicated loop will cause an error message. Similarly, the use of the EXIT statement outside the scope of the indicated loop will cause the generation of a compiler error message. When properly used, the EXIT statement will cause the immediate execution of the first statement following the indicated loop.

6.8.2 Multiple-Alternative Decision Structure Errors

Care must be taken in listing the conditions to be used in a multiple-alternative decision structure. If the conditions are not *mutually exclusive* (that is, if more than one of the conditions can be true at the same time), then the condition sequence must be carefully ordered to ensure the desired results.

Some FORTRAN compilers may require the presence of a list of statements associated with the ELSE portion of the multiple-alternative decision structure. Others may require the ELSE statement to be present, but will allow the ELSE statement group to be empty (contain no statements). It is always a good idea to include an ELSE statement group in every multiple-alternative decision structure, regardless of compiler requirements. Even if the condition list is constructed so as to guarantee that the ELSE group can never be executed, it is nevertheless a good practice to provide for the output of an error message in the ELSE group, should the unexpected happen during the execution of your program.

6.8.3 Indexed-DO and FOR Loop Errors

The most common errors in indexed-DO and FOR loops involve the incorrect definition of loop parameters in the header statement. The Standard FORTRAN indexed-DO loop imposes tight restrictions on the form of its parameters. The FOR loop relaxes these restrictions and permits any integer expression to be used as a parameter.

If the parameter expressions used in a FOR loop header are invalid integer expressions, you will get a diagnostic message. If they are valid but compute the wrong values, you will likely receive no diagnostics. Incorrect expressions will result in the wrong number of loop repetitions, or no repetitions, being performed. This error, in turn, may cause you to run out of input data cards and could result in an INSUFFICIENT DATA diagnostic message. If the loop-control variable is being used in an array subscript expression, you may get a SUBSCRIPT-OUT-OF-RANGE diagnostic if the loop parameters are incorrect. It is desirable to print the value of the loop-control variable if you suspect it is not being manipulated properly.

Whenever practical, you should completely trace the execution of each loop to ensure that the number of repetitions is correct. At a minimum, you should test the "boundary conditions"; i.e., verify that the initial and final values of the loop-control variable are correct. Furthermore, you should verify that all array references which use the loop-control variable in subscript computations are within range at the loop-control variable boundary values.

*6.8.4 Remote Block Errors

Aside from the misuse of transfer statements with remote blocks, the greatest source of difficulty is caused by the misplacement of remote blocks in a program. Each remote block must be isolated from the top-level program, and one remote block may not be nested within another. We suggest that all remote blocks be placed between the STOP and END cards in your program, in order to avoid placement errors.

6.9 SUMMARY

With this chapter, we conclude the discussion of FORTRAN loop and decision control structures. A total of six structures have been presented in the text, and these are listed below.

Available only in Structured FORTRAN
$\begin{cases} \text{Single-alternative decision structure: Chapter 3,} \\ \text{Double-alternative decision structure: Chapter 3,} \\ \text{Multiple-alternative decision structure: This chapter,} \\ \text{WHILE loop structure: Chapter 3,} \\ \text{FOR loop structure: This chapter,} \end{cases}$

Standard FORTRAN Indexed–DO loop structure: Chapter 4 and this chapter.

Of these structures, only the indexed-DO is part of Standard FORTRAN. The others are part of the extended, structured version of FORTRAN that we have been discussing.

The multiple-alternative decision structure introduced in this chapter is extremely useful in describing algorithms containing decisions for which there are more than two alternatives. Such situations could be described using sequences and/or nests of single- and double-alternative decision structures, but these can be extremely difficult to organize, and virtually impossible to understand. The multiple-alternative decision structure should simplify the implementation of decision sequences.

The indexed-DO structure provides a most convenient means for representing loops in which execution is controlled by a counter. This structure permits the specification of all loop-control information in the loop-header statement. The programmer is thereby freed from having to separately program the counter initialization, increment, and test. The FOR loop provides more flexibility and freedom in parameter specification for counter-controlled loops. Any legal integer expression may be used as a parameter in a FOR loop.

All six structures that we have seen may be used in a FORTRAN program,

---

* This section may be omitted.

and any of them may be nested inside another. [There will usually be a limit to the depth of nesting permitted, but this limit is normally large enough that there is little need to be concerned about it.] It is essential, however, that any structure nested inside another structure begin and end within the same statement group. Thus, a loop that begins inside a statement group that is part of an alternative decision structure must end within the same statement group, not another group, of that structure.

All structures must be entered via the execution of the header statement. Transfers into the middle of a structure are highly undesirable and should be avoided. Exit from the middle of any loop structure, to the first statement following that structure, may be accomplished through the use of the EXIT statement.

For loop structures, execution of the NEXT statement will cause the immediate initiation of the next iteration of the loop. Execution of the loop body will be preceded by any increment and test of the loop-control variable specified in the loop header and will be conditional upon the results of this test.

In an optional section at the end of the chapter, we discussed the concept of top-down programming (which we have been practicing throughout the text) and we introduced the remote-block feature of Structured FORTRAN. This feature is a valuable tool for simplifying the flow of control in an otherwise complex program, as it allows us to subdivide the program into separate blocks of statements, or *modules*, which can be referenced anywhere in the program. We will continue the discussion of top-down programming in the next chapter and learn how to use a Standard FORTRAN feature—the subprogram—to construct independent program modules.

PROGRAMMING PROBLEMS

6.3 (*Frequency-distribution problem*) An instructor has just given an exam to a very large class, and has punched the grades onto cards, one grade per card. The grading scale is 90–100 (A), 80–89 (B), 70–79 (C), 60–69 (D), 0–59 (F). The instructor wants to know how many students took the exam, what the average and standard deviation were for the exam (see Problem 3.2), and how many A's, B's, C's, D's, and F's there were. Write a program using a loop and a multiple-decision alternative structure to help the instructor obtain the information that he desires.

6.4 A tax table is used to determine the tax rate for a company employee, based on weekly gross salary and number of dependents. The tax table has the form shown below. An employee's net pay can be determined by multiplying gross salary times the tax rate, and subtracting this product from the gross salary. Write a program to read in the ID number, number of dependents, and gross salary for each employee of a company, and then determine the net salary to be paid to each employee. Your program should also print out a count of the number of employees with gross salary in each of the three ranges shown. [*Hint.* Use a multiple-alternative decision structure to "implement" this table. Note that the increase in rate for each column is constant (0.1 for 0–100, 0.12 for 100–200, 0.13 for ≥ 200).]

		Gross salary		
		0–100	100–200	≥ 200
Number of	0	0.2	0.28	0.38
dependents	1	0.1	0.16	0.25
	≥2	0.0	0.04	0.12

Tax rate table

6.5 (Continuation of the insertion and deletion problem, Example 6.3 and Exercise 6.4) In this chapter, separate program segments were written to maintain a collection of student identification numbers as an ordered list of numbers stored in the array CLIST. Write a single program that will process both deletions and insertions. Assume that all numbers to be inserted are preceded by 'I' and that numbers to be deleted are preceded by 'D'. You will have to test each value read to see whether a deletion or an insertion is required. [*Hints.* The first step in the deletion process involves a search for the student number to be deleted. If the number isn't found, or if the array CLIST is empty, print an error message and ignore the request.]

If the item is found in array element CLIST (ISCH), the deletion process involves moving each element from CLIST (ISCH + 1) through CLIST (N) into elements CLIST (ISCH) through CLIST (N − 1), (see Example 6.3). Use remote blocks (if they are available) to solve this problem. Test your program on the following data:

Read into CLIST (1) through CLIST (17) the numbers:

502	923	1045	2113	4642	8192
10974	14673	21892	33574	33575	33576
41821	44444	58912	71125	88893	

Then process the insertions and deletions given below.

'I'	16891
'D'	33575
'I'	43627
'I'	121
'D'	21212
'I'	91741
'I'	33575
'*'	0 (Sentinel card)

6.6 The equation of the form

(A) $$mx + b = 0$$

(where m and b are real numbers) is called a linear equation in one unknown, x. If we are given the values of both m and b, then the value of x that satisfies this equation may be computed as

(B) $$x = -b/m.$$

Write a program to read in N different sets of values for m and b (punched one set per card), and compute x. Test your program for the following five value sets.

m	b
-12.0	3.0
0.0	18.5
100.0	40.0
0.0	0.0
-16.8	0.0

[*Hint.* There are three distinct possibilities concerning the values of x that satisfy the equation $mx + b = 0$.

1. As long as $m \neq 0$, the value of x that satisfies the original equation (A) is given by equation (B).

2. If both b and m are 0, then any real number that we choose satisfies $mx + b = 0$.

3. If $m = 0$ and $b \neq 0$, then no real number x satisfies this equation.]

6.7 Each year the legislature of a state rates the productivity of the faculty of each of the state-supported colleges and universities. The rating is based on reports submitted by each faculty member indicating the average number of hours worked per week during the school year. Each faculty member is ranked, and the university also receives an overall rank.

The faculty productivity rank is computed as follows:

i) faculty members averaging over 55 hours per week are considered "highly productive";

ii) faculty members averaging between 35 and 55 hours a week (inclusive) are considered "satisfactory";

iii) faculty members averaging fewer than 35 hours a week are considered "over-paid."

The productivity rating of each school is determined by first computing the faculty average for the school:

$$\text{Faculty average} = \frac{\sum \text{hours worked per week for all faculty}}{\text{Number of faculty reporting}}$$

and then applying the faculty average to the category ranges defined in (i), (ii), and (iii).

Use the multiple-alternative decision structure and write a program to rank the following faculty:

HERM	63	
FLO	37	
JAKE	20	
MO	55	
SOL	72	
TONY	40	
AL	12	
ZZZZ	0	(Sentinel card)

Your program should print a three-column table giving the name, hours, and productivity rank of each faculty member. It should also compute and print the school's overall productivity ranking.

6.8 Write a savings-account transaction program that will process the following set of data cards.

'ADAM'	1054.37 ⎫	
'W'	25.00 ⎪	group 1
'D'	243.35 ⎬	
'W'	254.55 ⎭	
'EVE'	2008.24 ⎫	group 2
'W'	15.55 ⎭	
'MARY'	128.24 ⎫	
'W'	62.48 ⎪	group 3
'D'	13.42 ⎬	
'W'	84.60 ⎭	
'SAM'	7.77	group 4
'JOE'	15.27 ⎫	
'W'	16.12 ⎬	group 5
'D'	10.00 ⎭	
'BETH'	12900.00 ⎫	group 6
'D'	9270.00 ⎭	
'ZZZZ'	0.0	(Sentinel card)

The first card in each group (header card) gives the name of an account and the starting balance in the account. All subsequent cards show the amount of each withdrawal (W) or deposit (D) that was made for that account. Each data card that does not contain a W or D as the first item is the header card for the next account. Print out the final balance for each of the accounts processed. If a balance becomes negative, print an appropriate message and take whatever corrective steps you deem proper. If there are no transactions for an account, print a message so indicating.

6.9 (Variation on the mortgage interest problem—Problem 4.10) Use indexed-DO loops to write a program to print tables of the following form.

Home loan mortgage–interest payment tables

Amount_____	Loan duration (Months)_____	
Rate (Percent)	*Monthly payment*	*Total payment*
6.00		
6.25		
6.50		
6.75		
7.00		
7.25		
7.50		
7.75		
8.00		
⋮		
10.00		
10.25		
10.50		
10.75		
11.00		

Your program should produce tables for loans of 30, 40, and 50 thousand dollars, respectively. For each of these three amounts, tables should be produced for loan durations of 240, 300, and 360 months. Thus, *nine* tables of the above form should be produced. Your program should contain three nested loops. Be careful to remove all redundant computations from inside your loops, especially from inside the innermost loop.

6.10 (Quadratic-equation problem) The equation of the form

(A) $ax^2 + bx + c = 0$ (a, b, c real numbers, with $a \neq 0$)

is called a quadratic equation in x. The *real roots* of this equation are those values of x for which

$$ax^2 + bx + c$$

evaluates to zero. (Thus if $a = 1$, $b = 2$, and $c = -15$, then the real roots of

$$x^2 + 2x - 15$$

are $+3$ and -5, since

$$(3)^2 + 2(3) - 15 = 9 + 6 - 15 = 0$$

and

$$(-5)^2 + 2(-5) - 15 = 25 - 10 - 15 = 0.)$$

Quadratic equations of the form (A) have either 2 real and different roots, 2 real and equal roots, or *no* real roots. The determination as to which of these three conditions holds for a given equation can be made by evaluating the discriminant d of the equation, where

$$d = b^2 - 4ac.$$

1. If $d > 0$, then the equation has two real and unequal roots.
2. If $d = 0$, the equation has two real and equal roots.
3. If $d < 0$, the equation has *no* real roots.

Write a program to compute and print the real roots of quadratic equations having the following values of a, b, and c.

a	b	c
1.0	2.0	-15.0
1.0	-1.25	-9.375
1.0	0.0	1.0
1.0	-80.0	-900.0
1.0	-6.0	9.0
0.0	0.0	0.0

You should punch each set of values for a, b, and c on one card, and terminate the program when a value for a of 0.0 is read. If the equation has no real roots for a set of a, b, and c, print an appropriate message, and read the next set. [*Hint*. If the equation has two real and equal roots, then the root values are given by the expression

$$\text{Root } 1 = \text{Root } 2 = -b/2a.$$

If the equation has two real and unequal roots, their values may be computed as

$$\text{Root } 1 = \frac{-b + \sqrt{d}}{2a},$$

$$\text{Root } 2 = \frac{-b - \sqrt{d}}{2a}.$$

6.11 Write a program to solve the following problem:

Read in a collection of N data cards, each containing one integer between 0 and 9, and count the number of consecutive pairs of each integer occurring in the data-card set. (Your program should print the number of consecutive pairs of 0's, of 1's, 2's, ..., and the number of consecutive pairs of 9's found in the data.)

6.13 Write a program which will provide change for a dollar for any item purchased that costs less than one dollar. Print out each unit of change (quarter, dimes, nickels, or pennies) provided. Always dispense the *biggest*-denomination coin possible. For example, if there are 37 cents left in change, dispense a quarter (which leaves 12 cents in change), then dispense a dime, and then 2 pennies. You may wish to use a multiple-alternative decision structure in solving this problem. However, you can also use a four-element array (to store each denominational value 25, 10, 5, and 1), and an indexed-DO.

6.14 (Statistical measurements with functions—a simple linear-curve fit problem)

Scientists and engineers frequently perform experiments designed to provide measurements of two variables X and Y. They often compute measures of central tendency (such as the mean) and measures of dispersion (such as the standard deviation) for these variables, and then attempt to decide whether or not there is any relationship between the variables, and, if so, to express this relationship in terms of an equation. If there is a relationship between X and Y that is describable using a linear equation of the form

$$Y = aX + b,$$

the data collected is said to *fit a linear curve*.

For example, the ACE Computing Company recently made a study relating aptitude-test scores to programming productivity of new personnel. The 6 pairs of scores shown below were obtained by testing 6 randomly selected applicants and later measuring their productivity.

Applicant	Aptitude score (*Variable* X)	Productivity (*Variable* Y)
1	$x_1 = 9$	$y_1 = 46$
2	$x_2 = 17$	$y_2 = 70$
3	$x_3 = 20$	$y_3 = 58$
4	$x_4 = 19$	$y_4 = 66$
5	$x_5 = 20$	$y_5 = 86$
6	$x_6 = 23$	$y_6 = 64$

ACE wants to find the equation of the line which they can use to predict the productivity of workers tested in the future. They are also interested in obtaining means and standard deviations for the variables X and Y. The required computations can be performed as follows:

1. Compute

$$\text{SUMX} \quad = \sum X = x_1 + x_2 + \cdots + x_6$$

$$\text{SUMY} \quad = \sum Y \quad = y_1 + y_2 + \cdots + y_6$$

$$\text{SUMXY} \quad = \sum X \cdot Y = x_1 y_1 + x_2 y_2 + \cdots + x_6 y_6$$

$$\text{SUMXSQ} = \sum X^2 \quad = x_1^2 + x_2^2 + \cdots + x_6^2$$

$$\text{SUMYSQ} = \sum Y^2 \quad = y_1^2 + y_2^2 + \cdots + y_6^2$$

2. Compute

$$\text{MEANX} = \text{SUMX}/\text{N} \qquad \text{where} \qquad N = 6$$

$$\text{MEANY} = \text{SUMY}/\text{N}$$

3. Compute

$$\text{STDDVX} = \sqrt{\text{SUMXSQ}/\text{N} - \text{MEANX}^2}$$

$$\text{STDDVY} = \sqrt{\text{SUMYSQ}/\text{N} - \text{MEANY}^2}$$

4. Compute a and b in $Y = aX + b$ using the equation

$$A = \frac{\text{SUMXY} - \text{N} * \text{MEANX} * \text{MEANY}}{\text{SUMXSQ} - \text{N} * \text{MEANX}^2}$$

$$B = \text{MEANY} - B * \text{MEANX}$$

Write a program to carry out the above computations. The remote block might be useful if it is available in your FORTRAN system. Test your program on the aptitude/productivity data just shown.

7.1   Introduction

7.2   The Program System Chart

7.3   Function Subprograms

7.4   Argument List
      Correspondence

7.5   Top-Down Programming—
      The Relationship Between
      Main Program and
      Subprograms

7.6   Subroutine Subprograms

7.7   Name Independence:
      Subprograms and Remote
      Blocks

7.8   Common Blocks

7.9   Additional Comments
      Concerning Subprograms

*7.10 The Role of the Compiler in
      Processing Subprograms

7.11 Common Programming
      Errors

7.12 Summary
      Programming Problems

SUBPROGRAMS

7

7.1 INTRODUCTION

One of the most fundamental ideas of computer programming and problem solving concerns the subdivision of large and complex problems into smaller, simpler, and more manageable subproblems. Once these smaller tasks have been identified, the solution to the original problem can be specified in terms of these tasks; and the algorithms and programs for the smaller tasks can be developed separately.

We have tried to emphasize this technique of programming in all earlier examples through the use of *algorithm refinement*. In this process, each major part of a problem was identified in a level-one flow diagram, and then further broken down into smaller problems during successive stages of refinement. A number of special control structures were introduced, which enabled us to implement the solution to each of these subproblems in terms of clearly defined groups of FORTRAN program statements.

FORTRAN has still another feature, called a *subprogram*, which facilitates solving problems in terms of their more manageable parts. By using the FORTRAN subprogram features, we can write separate program modules to solve small problems and then reference these modules in the overall solution of the original problem.

In many ways, the purpose of the subprogram is similar to that of the remote block, which was presented in the last chapter. However, many versions of FORTRAN do not permit the use of the remote block. As we shall see, the subprogram provides a mechanism for the totally independent implementation of the algorithms for subproblem solution.

7.2 THE PROGRAM SYSTEM CHART

As an example of the use of subprograms, we will consider a simple statistics problem.

PROBLEM 7.1 Given a collection of N real numbers stored in an array, compute the range, mean (average), and median for this collection.

The level-one flow diagram for this problem is shown in Fig. 7.1. Each box of the diagram represents a major step in the problem solution.

Additional *lower level* subproblems may be identified within each of steps 20, 30, and 40. Each of these subtasks represents a part of the refinement of a task shown at a higher level. We can represent the relationship among the main problem and all of these subproblems using a *program system chart* (Fig. 7.2).

The program system chart identifies the major subproblems of the original problem and illustrates the relationships among them.   The solutions to the

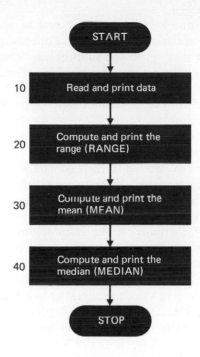

Fig. 7.1 Level-one flow diagram for simple statistics problem (7.1).

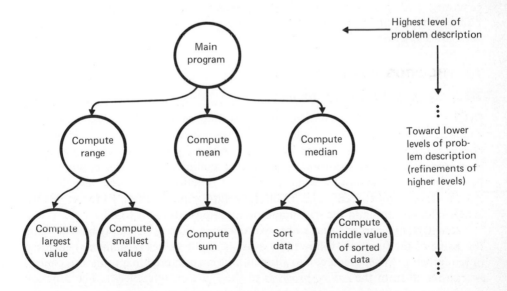

Fig. 7.2 Program system chart for the statistics problem (7.1).

subproblems shown at one level in the chart can be specified in terms of the connected subproblems at the next lower level. For example, the program system chart indicates that the solution to the subproblem "compute median" may be specified in terms of the solution to the subproblems "sort data" and "compute middle value of sorted data." In subsequent sections of this chapter, we will illustrate how this level-by-level algorithm description is implemented for the statistics problem.

There are a number of advantages to using the program-subdivision technique in solving large, complex problems on the computer. It permits us to design and implement the subprograms relating to each subtask on an individual basis, and to test these subprograms separately until we are satisfied that each one performs its prescribed task correctly. If we need to perform a similar task later, we can simply re-use that subprogram by inserting additional statements to reference it in the main program. Furthermore, if the subprogram performs a task that is required in the solution of other problems, it can, if properly written, be easily incorporated into the solution of these problems without alteration or retesting.

In the following sections we will explain how to write (*define*) subprograms and how to reference (*call*) them in a main program or in other subprograms. We will also show how the main program and subprograms communicate with one another, and how data manipulated in one subprogram may be transmitted to another. Finally, we will consider how to recognize when the use of subprograms is desirable, how to decide the best way to divide a large problem into smaller parts, and how to design and implement subprograms so as to achieve the fullest generality and maximum level of independence from other subprograms. Two different types of subprograms will be discussed, *function* subprograms and *subroutine* subprograms.

7.3 FUNCTION SUBPROGRAMS

7.3.1 Review of Library Functions

In Chapter 4 we described a number of special subprograms called *library functions*. These functions are special, independent program modules usually written by computer manufacturers for use by FORTRAN programmers. They enable the programmer to easily incorporate some very common numerical computations into a program. Some of the more standard functions that were described are SQRT (square root), ABS and IABS (absolute value), IFIX, FLOAT, MOD, ALOG (logarithm), and the trigonometric functions SIN and COS.

Recall from Chapter 4 that a library function is referenced simply by specifying the name of the function, followed by a list of input values (arguments) enclosed in parentheses. Whenever a call to a function is encountered in a program, control is transferred from the *calling program* to the function referenced. The function manipulates the arguments, and when the function computation is complete, the result is returned and control is transferred back to the calling program at the point of the call. This process is illustrated in the next example.

Example 7.1

Main program

SQRT subprogram

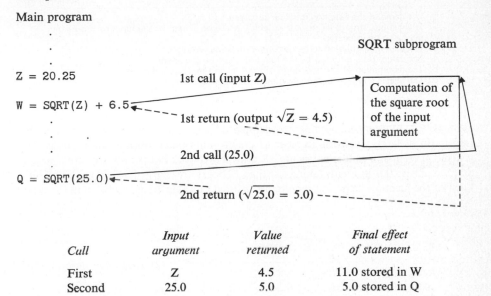

$Z = 20.25$

$W = SQRT(Z) + 6.5$

1st call (input Z)

1st return (output $\sqrt{Z} = 4.5$)

Computation of the square root of the input argument

2nd call (25.0)

$Q = SQRT(25.0)$

2nd return ($\sqrt{25.0} = 5.0$)

Call	Input argument	Value returned	Final effect of statement
First	Z	4.5	11.0 stored in W
Second	25.0	5.0	5.0 stored in Q

The arrows illustrate the transfer of control resulting from two calls to the function SQRT. Each time the function name appears in an expression, the square-root subprogram is executed and a value (the square root of the input argument) is returned to the main program. The variable Z (value 20.25) is the input argument for the first call. The value returned (4.5) is added to 6.5, and this sum (11.0) is stored in W. The constant 25.0 is the input argument for the second call, and the value returned (5.0) is stored in Q.

Example 7.2 The following is an example of the use of an expression as an argument in a function call.

$$X = (-B + SQRT(ABS(B * B - 4.0 * A * C)))/(2.0 * A)$$

The argument of the function SQRT is an expression involving the evaluation of the function ABS, which itself has an expression as its argument.

In this expression, the subexpression $B * B - 4.0 * A * C$ is evaluated first, and the absolute value of this result is computed. Then the square root of the result of the absolute-value calculation is computed, and this value is used in the remaining computation that is specified.

7.3.2 Defining New Functions in FORTRAN

Often, the functions provided in the function library are not sufficient for the solution of a particular problem, and we may wish to write our own. In this section we will see how to write or *define* a new FORTRAN function subprogram.

In specifying the definition of a function, we must satisfy a number of requirements, as shown in Table 7.1.

Table 7.1 Requirements for a function definition

1. The name of the function must be specified.
2. The number, structure (array or variable), and type of each of the function arguments must also be indicated.
3. The data manipulation to be performed must be written.
4. The value to be returned by the function must be specified.
5. The termination of the execution of the function must be indicated.
6. The physical end of the function must be marked.

Example 7.3 Figure 7.3 contains an example of a function that calculates the tuition charge (in dollars), given the number of credit hours taken during one semester by a resident student at a public university. Students taking 12 hours and over are charged a flat rate of $450.00. Students taking less than 12 hours are charged $40.00 per credit hour. Each of the function definition requirements listed in Table 7.1 is indicated in the figure.

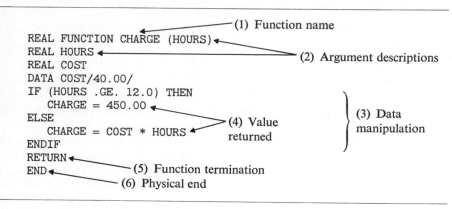

```
                                      (1) Function name
REAL FUNCTION CHARGE (HOURS)
REAL HOURS
REAL COST                             (2) Argument descriptions
DATA COST/40.00/
IF (HOURS .GE. 12.0) THEN
    CHARGE = 450.00
ELSE                                                     (3) Data
                                      (4) Value            manipulation
    CHARGE = COST * HOURS               returned
ENDIF
RETURN
END                    (5) Function termination
                       (6) Physical end
```

Fig. 7.3 A function for computing tuition charge, given credit hours.

As shown in Fig. 7.3, the name of a function and the number of arguments are indicated in a special header statement that must appear at the beginning of each function definition. The form of this header is given in the following display.

Function header statement

FORTRAN Form:

        type FUNCTION name (dummy argument list)

Interpretation. The header must appear as the first statement in a function subprogram. The type indicator is optional, but, if used, it must be REAL, INTEGER, or LOGICAL. The type of function specifies the data type of the result returned by the function. If the type indicator is omitted, the function type is defined by the first letter of the function name. Thus, functions with names beginning with the letters I–N will be typed as integer. All others will be typed as real. The name is the name to be used in calling the function. The argument list is used to identify each of the arguments to be manipulated by the function, and their order of appearance in the calling statements. This list may consist only of the names of variables or arrays, each separated from the others by a comma. There must always be at least one dummy argument listed in a function header statement.

Note. The type of a function must be declared in each program that calls it unless its type is consistent with the first-letter implicit type convention.

The use of the function header fulfills Requirement 1 of Table 7.1. It also provides a means for us to indicate the number of arguments that will appear in any call to the function. We will now see how the rest of the requirements listed in the table are satisfied, by continuing the analysis of the function CHARGE.

The *body of the function* follows the header statement. Within the body, the type of each dummy argument must first be declared. Once the dummy arguments are defined and declared (thus fulfilling Requirement 2 of Table 7.1), any additional program variables, called *local variables*, must be declared. (Local variables are so named because they are defined for use only within the subprogram in which they are declared. The local variable in the function CHARGE is COST.) Next, the algorithm for the data manipulation can be specified in the usual manner, in terms of the local variables and dummy arguments defined in the subprogram. This completes Requirement 3 of Table 7.1.

Requirement 4, the specification of the value to be returned by the function, is satisfied through the use of the statements

```
CHARGE = 450.0
CHARGE = COST * HOURS
```

When a statement that assigns a value to the function name is executed, this value is saved in a special memory cell and represents the result of the function call.

Execution of the statement RETURN causes a transfer of control back to the calling program (Requirement 5). The statement END is not executable, but rather marks the physical end of the function (Requirement 6 of Table 7.1).

The general form of the definition of a function subprogram is shown in Fig. 7.4.

Note that at least one RETURN statement and at least one statement assigning a value to the function name are required. The latter is usually, but not necessarily, an assignment statement of the form

name = expression

(The use of a read statement is another means of assigning a value to a function name.) There are no requirements concerning the placement of these statements within a function, except that at least one RETURN statement, and one statement

---

```
TYPE FUNCTION NAME (DUMMY ARGUMENT LIST)

{ARGUMENT DEFINITIONS AND DECLARATIONS}

{LOCAL VARIABLE DECLARATIONS}

(MANIPULATE DATA AND)
⟨ASSIGN A VALUE TO  ⟩
(FUNCTION NAME      )

RETURN

END
```

Fig. 7.4 General form of a function definition.

assigning a value to the function name must be executed for each call of the function. Usually there is a RETURN statement just before the END statement.

The name HOURS, in the header statement

$$\text{REAL FUNCTION CHARGE (HOURS)}$$

is a *dummy argument* used in the definition of the function. The dummy arguments of a subprogram are used to tell the FORTRAN compiler what is to be done with the *actual arguments* that appear in the call of a subprogram. The actual arguments are not known until the subroutine is called, at which time each dummy argument is replaced by the actual argument it represents.

In the CHARGE function, HOURS represents the number of credit hours taken by a student whose tuition is being computed. For example, if the statement

$$\text{TUITN = CHARGE (10.5)}$$

were used to call CHARGE, HOURS would be replaced by the actual argument 10.5. The value returned from this call to CHARGE would be 10.5×40.00, or 420.00.

As another example, we could write the statements

```
        HOURS = 0.0
        DO 10  I = 1, N
           HOURS = HOURS + SEMHRS (I)
    10 CONTINUE
        TUITN = CHARGE (HOURS)
```

to compute the tuition charge for a student taking N courses in a semester, where N is likely to be between 1 and 6. If SEMHRS contains the number of credit hours for each course, then the call to the function CHARGE would return the tuition cost for the total credit hours taken. In this example, the actual argument is a variable with the same name as the dummy argument used in the function definition. This is not necessary, but it also causes no difficulties.

To further illustrate the definition and use of functions, we now turn our attention from CHARGE, to a function that manipulates an array. Figure 7.5 shows a function LARGE that finds the largest data item in an array. This function has two arguments, A and NRITMS. Argument A represents the array of data that is to be searched for the largest item, and NRITMS represents the number of items in A that are to be examined. In the argument definitions, it is permissible to use the dummy argument NRITMS (instead of an integer constant) to specify the size of the dummy array A. This point will be discussed in the next section.

```
      REAL FUNCTION LARGE (A, NRITMS)
C
C DETERMINE THE LARGEST ITEM IN AN ARRAY
C
C ARGUMENT DEFINITIONS --
C   INPUT ARGUMENTS
C     A - ARRAY CONTAINING THE DATA TO BE PROCESSED
C     NRITMS - NUMBER OF ITEMS IN THE ARRAY
C
      INTEGER NRITMS
      REAL A(NRITMS)
C
C LOCAL VARIABLES
      REAL CURLRG
      INTEGER I
C
C INITIALIZE CURRENT LARGEST ITEM
      CURLRG = A(1)
C LOOK FOR AN ITEM THAT IS LARGER THAN CURLRG
C REDEFINE CURLRG WHEN A NEW LARGEST ITEM IS FOUND
      DO 40 I = 1, NRITMS
         IF (A(I) .GT. CURLRG) CURLRG = A(I)
   40 CONTINUE
C
C RETURN VALUE OF LARGEST ITEM IN A WHEN SEARCH IS COMPLETE
      LARGE = CURLRG
      RETURN
      END
```

Fig. 7.5 Function for finding the largest of a collection of data items.

In the body of the function LARGE, the dummy arguments and then the local variables (CURLRG and I) are declared. The argument declarations are preceded by a short English description of the use of each argument. The data manipulation performed by this function consists of an assignment statement to initialize CURLRG, an indexed-DO loop that searches the array, and the statement

$$LARGE = CURLRG$$

which defines the value to be returned.

7.4 ARGUMENT LIST CORRESPONDENCE

In order to fully understand the concept of a subprogram argument list, we must remember that the arguments listed in the definition of a subprogram serve only to describe to the FORTRAN compiler what is to be done with each of the actual arguments appearing in a call of that subprogram. The actual arguments and their correspondence with the dummy arguments are determined anew each time a subprogram is called, as illustrated in the following example.

Example 7.4 A simple program calling the function LARGE.

```
REAL LARGE
REAL TABLE(10), BIGGST
INTEGER N, I
READ, N, (TABLE(I), I = 1, N)
PRINT, 'THE NUMBER OF DATA ITEMS IS ', N
PRINT, 'LIST OF DATA ITEMS TO BE PROCESSED'
PRINT, (TABLE(I), I = 1, N)
BIGGST = LARGE (TABLE, N)
PRINT, 'THE LARGEST ITEM IS ', BIGGST
STOP
END
```

The function LARGE (see Section 7.3.2) is called by the statement

$$BIGGST = LARGE \ (TABLE, \ N)$$

For this example, we will assume that N is 6, and that the data items are read into TABLE as shown below.

TABLE (1)	TABLE (2)	TABLE (3)	TABLE (4)	TABLE (5)	TABLE (6)	TABLE (7)		TABLE (10)
16.5	22.0	−9.25	0.5	−3.75	8.0	?	•••	?

The argument list correspondence defined in Example 7.4 is illustrated in Fig. 7.6. As shown in this figure, the dummy argument A in the definition of LARGE represents the actual argument TABLE, and NRITMS represents the actual argument N. It is essential that the number of arguments in the call of a subprogram always be the same as the number of arguments in its definition, and that corresponding arguments agree in type and *structure*. (Agreement with respect to structure requires that a dummy argument should be an array if the corresponding actual argument is an array; otherwise, the dummy argument should be a simple variable.) In the above example, both TABLE and A are type-real arrays, and N and NRITMS are integer variables.

When an array is used as a dummy argument in a subprogram, the number of array elements to be manipulated should also be a dummy argument (type integer). This dummy argument is often used in the subprogram to specify the size of the dummy array. In the function LARGE, the dummy argument NRITMS is used as the end-value parameter in loop 40 and in the declaration of the array A. The use of NRITMS in the declaration is possible only because A is not the

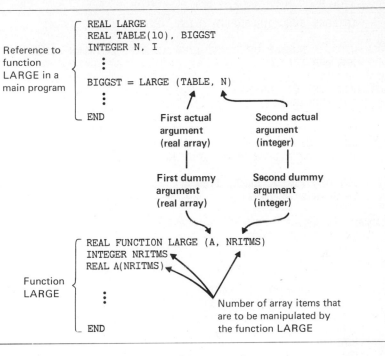

Fig. 7.6 Argument list correspondence.

array that will actually be manipulated by LARGE. The array to be manipulated is not known until the function is called. At that time, both the array and the number of elements to be manipulated (the actual argument corresponding to NRITMS) are determined.

EXERCISE 7.1 The function COUNT computes the number of occurrences of ITEM in an array. (See Fig. 7.7.)

Let ONOFF (an integer array of size 20) and N (an integer variable) be defined as follows:

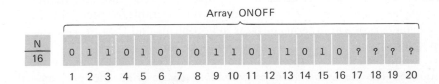

What value will be returned for the following references to COUNT?

a) COUNT (ONOFF, 1, N, 1)

b) COUNT (ONOFF, 5, N − 1, 0)

```
        INTEGER FUNCTION COUNT (LIST, FIRST, LAST, ITEM)
C
C COMPUTE THE NUMBER OF TIMES ITEM APPEARS BETWEEN FIRST AND LAST IN
C     THE ARRAY LIST
C
C ARGUMENT DEFINITIONS --
C   INPUT ARGUMENTS
C     LIST - ARRAY OF ITEMS TO BE EXAMINED
C     FIRST - SUBSCRIPT OF FIRST ELEMENT (IN LIST) TO BE CHECKED
C     LAST - SUBSCRIPT OF LAST ELEMENT (IN LIST) TO BE CHECKED
C     ITEM - DATA ITEM BEING COUNTED IN LIST
C
        INTEGER FIRST, LAST, ITEM
        INTEGER LIST(LAST)
C
C LOCAL VARIABLES
        INTEGER LCV, CNTR
C
C COMPUTE COUNT
        CNTR = 0
        DO 20 LCV = FIRST, LAST
            IF (LIST(LCV) .EQ. ITEM) CNTR = CNTR + 1
    20 CONTINUE
        COUNT = CNTR
        RETURN
        END
```

Fig. 7.7 Program for function COUNT.

c) COUNT (ONOFF, N − 5, N, 0)

d) COUNT (ONOFF, 12, 12, 1)

7.5 TOP-DOWN PROGRAMMING—THE RELATIONSHIP BETWEEN MAIN PROGRAMS AND SUBPROGRAMS

Throughout the text, we have emphasized a specific technique of algorithm development involving the division of complex problems into smaller and more manageable subproblems. We indicated that it is desirable to specify the algorithm for solving a problem in terms of these subproblems and then provide the refinements required for the solution of each subproblem.

Toward the end of Chapter 6, in the optional section on the remote block, we introduced the term *top-down programming* to describe the problem-solving techniques that we have practiced. We discussed, once again, the process of developing a level-one outline of an algorithm, and then refining this algorithm, step by step, until sufficient detail is provided to enable us to write the required program. We then introduced the idea of actually implementing the algorithm with a *main program* that reflected the level-one algorithm. The main program consisted mainly of calls to separate *program modules,* called *remote blocks,* in which the details of each level-one program step were specified. The goal was to construct a program and related modules that would clearly reflect the separate subproblems and refinements given by the flow diagrams. The remote block was introduced as one language feature that could be used to help achieve that goal.

As indicated at the beginning of this chapter, the subprogram feature of standard FORTRAN also can be used to help achieve the goal of top-down programming by enabling us to write separate program modules for solving the subproblems of a large problem. Separate subprogram modules should be provided to represent the respective refinements of each subtask of the initial flow diagram. Where practical, refinements of refinements should also be implemented as separate subprogram modules.

Within the main program, subprograms should be called in the order in which their corresponding subtasks were specified in the initial flow diagram. If a subprogram references other subprogram modules, these calls should be inserted at the appropriate points in the calling subprogram.

In order to compile and execute the main program and the subprograms, all subprogram definitions should be included as part of the program card deck following the END card for the main program and before the control card that separates FORTRAN program statements from input data cards (see Fig. 7.8).

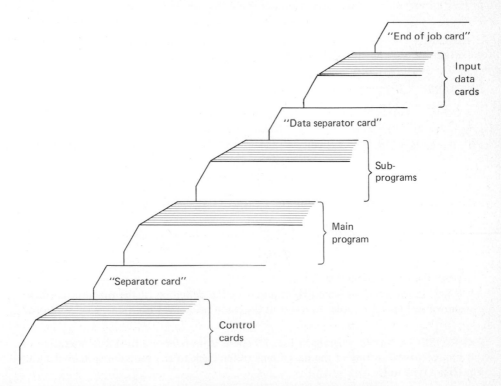

Fig. 7.8 Job-input deck for a main program and subprograms.

Each subprogram must have its own header statement and an END card. In addition, some computers may require additional control cards in front of each subprogram. You should inquire as to which control cards (if any) are needed, and place these cards in front of the header card of each of your subprograms.

Example 7.5 (Continuation of Problem 7.1) In this example, we will write the main program for the simple statistics problem. The program shown (Fig. 7.9) follows directly from the initial flow diagram in Fig. 7.1. We will assume that N (the number of data items) will never exceed 100. TABLE is the name of the array containing the data.

Aside from the input and output statements, the main (top-level) program contains only four executable statements. Three of these statements assign the values of RANGE, MEAN, and MEDIAN, respectively; and the fourth is a program STOP.

Note that subprograms were not used for all of the subproblems shown in the program system chart for the simple statistics problem (Fig. 7.2). In particular, the computation of the range of the data items really did not require the use of a function, since it can be readily accomplished in a single statement using the functions LARGE and SMALL. The computations of the mean and median are carried out by the functions AVERAG and FNDMED (find the median), respectively.

In compiling and executing this program, the complete definitions of all four functions (plus any other subprograms that are needed) should be placed in the program deck following the main program. The order in which they appear is not important, as long as they all precede the data-card section of the input job deck.

EXERCISE 7.2 Write a complete data table for the program in Fig. 7.9. Include the definitions of each function referenced in the program.

EXERCISE 7.3 In the program in Fig. 7.8, replace the two declarations

```
REAL TABLE(100)
INTEGER N, IX
```

with the declarations

```
REAL X(1050)
INTEGER XCOUNT, IX
```

a) Rewrite the two read statements and the three statements beginning

```
RANGE = ...
MEAN = ...
MEDIAN = ...
```

given the new declarations.

b) What, if any, changes would be required to the definition of the function LARGE shown in Fig. 7.5 in order to use it in the main program with the new declarations?

EXERCISE 7.4 In the program in Fig. 7.9 there is no reference to the computation of the sum or to the sorting of the data items (refer back to the program system chart in Fig. 7.2). Why not?

```
C SIMPLE STATISTICS PROBLEM - MAIN PROGRAM
C
C COMPUTE THE RANGE, MEAN, AND MEDIAN OF A COLLECTION OF N DATA ITEMS
C
C
      REAL TABLE(100)
      INTEGER N, IX
      REAL RANGE, MEAN, MEDIAN
C
C FUNCTIONS REFERENCED
      REAL LARGE, SMALL, AVERAG, FNDMED
C
C READ IN DATA
      READ, N
      PRINT, 'THE NUMBER OF DATA ITEMS IS ', N
      READ, (TABLE(IX), IX = 1, N)
      PRINT, 'LIST OF DATA ITEMS TO BE PROCESSED'
      PRINT, (TABLE(IX), IX = 1, N)
C COMPUTE THE RANGE
      RANGE = LARGE (TABLE, N) - SMALL (TABLE, N)
      PRINT, 'THE RANGE IS ', RANGE
C COMPUTE THE MEAN
      MEAN = AVERAG (TABLE, N)
      PRINT, 'THE MEAN IS ', MEAN
C DETERMINE THE MEDIAN
      MEDIAN = FNDMED (TABLE, N)
      PRINT, 'THE MEDIAN IS ', MEDIAN
C
      STOP
      END
```

Fig. 7.9 Main program for Problem 7.1.

EXERCISE 7.5 Write the function AVERAG. Carefully define and declare the arguments with comments. The order and structure of the arguments should conform to the order and structure of the arguments in the call of AVERAG in the program in Fig. 7.9.

EXERCISE 7.6 The following sequence of FORTRAN statements can be used in the function SMALL for determining the smallest item in a real array A containing K data items. Complete the specification of the function SMALL by writing the header statement, the appropriate dummy argument and local variable declarations, the necessary control and value return statements, and appropriate comments.

```
      CURSML = A(1)
      DO 60 I = 1, K
         IF (A(I) .LT. CURSML) CURSML = A(I)
   60 CONTINUE
```

7.6 SUBROUTINE SUBPROGRAMS

7.6.1 Differences between Subroutines and Functions

It is often convenient to be able to write subprograms in which all values are returned by modification of the arguments. Sometimes, it is even desirable to write a subprogram that returns no values, but instead performs some task such as printing the results of a computation. Since a function is always associated with a returned value, it is not appropriate for these purposes and another form of subprogram, called a *subroutine*, is used.

A subroutine is very similar in form to a function. However, a subroutine is not assigned a value and therefore has no type associated with it. Unlike a function, a subroutine cannot be referenced as part of an expression; instead, a special *call statement* is used to reference it. A subroutine may also be defined and referenced with no arguments, whereas functions require at least one argument.

7.6.2 Defining Subroutines in FORTRAN

To illustrate the construction of a subroutine and the differences between functions and subroutines, we will redefine the function LARGE as a subroutine named SLARGE (see Fig. 7.10).

The subroutine SLARGE has two input arguments, A and NRITMS, and one output argument, MAX. In the subroutine, the statement

```
MAX = CURLRG
```

is used to define the value of the output argument. There is no statement in the subroutine that assigns a value to SLARGE; neither is there a type specification in the subroutine header statement. This is because there is no output value, and hence no type, associated with a subroutine. Output values for a subroutine are all returned by modifying the arguments.

The general form of the subroutine header is shown in the next display.

Subroutine Header Statement

FORTRAN Form:

```
         SUBROUTINE name (dummy argument list)
or
         SUBROUTINE name
```

Interpretation. The name by which the subroutine is to be called is given by name. A header of this form is required as the first statement of all subroutines. The argument list may consist only of the names of variables or arrays, each separated from the others by a comma. If the argument list is empty, the parentheses must be omitted.

```
            SUBROUTINE SLARGE (A, NRITMS, MAX)
C
C DETERMINE THE LARGEST ITEM IN AN ARRAY
C
C ARGUMENT DEFINITIONS --
C   INPUT ARGUMENTS
C     A - ARRAY CONTAINING THE DATA TO BE PROCESSED
C     NRITMS - NUMBER OF ITEMS IN THE ARRAY
C   OUTPUT ARGUMENTS
C     MAX - LARGEST VALUE IN THE ARRAY
C
      INTEGER NRITMS
      REAL A(NRITMS), MAX
C
C LOCAL VARIABLES
      REAL CURLRG
      INTEGER I
C
C INITIALIZE THE CURRENT LARGEST ITEM
      CURLRG = A(1)
C LOOK FOR AN ITEM THAT IS LARGER THAN CURLRG
C REDEFINE CURLRG WHEN A NEW LARGEST ITEM IS FOUND
      DO 40 I = 1, NRITMS
          IF (A(I) .GT. CURLRG) CURLRG = A(I)
   40 CONTINUE
C
C RETURN VALUE OF LARGEST ITEM WHEN SEARCH IS COMPLETE
      MAX = CURLRG
      RETURN
      END
```

Fig. 7.10 Subroutine SLARGE used to find largest element of an array.

The form of the definition of a subroutine is shown in Fig. 7.11. As is the case with function definitions, more than one RETURN statement may be used. Normally, a RETURN statement appears just before the END statement.

```
      SUBROUTINE NAME (DUMMY ARGUMENT LIST)

      {ARGUMENT DEFINITIONS AND DECLARATIONS}

      {LOCAL VARIABLE DECLARATIONS}

      {DATA MANIPULATIONS}

      RETURN

      END
```

Fig. 7.11 General form of definition of a subroutine subprogram.

EXERCISE 7.7 Identify the input and output arguments and the local variables in each of the following subroutines. What do subroutines ZERO and BOUND do?

```
a) SUBROUTINE ZERO (X)
   IF (X .LT. 0.0) X = 0.0
   RETURN
   END

b) SUBROUTINE BOUND (M, SIZE, MAX)
   INTEGER SIZE
   REAL M(SIZE), MAX
   DO 10 I = 1, SIZE
      IF (M(I) .GT. MAX) M(I) = 0.0
10 CONTINUE
   RETURN
   END
```

EXERCISE 7.8 Write a subroutine that will compute the sum of the corresponding pairs of items in two integer arrays of equal size, and store the result in a third integer array of the same size.

EXERCISE 7.9 Write a subroutine that will count the number of occurrences of a real item in a real array. Make certain that all of your arguments are carefully defined in comment statements in the subprogram.

7.6.3 The Subroutine Call

The form of a subroutine call is shown next.

Subroutine Call

FORTRAN Form:

```
CALL name (argument list)
```

Interpretation. Subroutine calls, unlike function calls, are not part of an expression. Rather, they are individual FORTRAN statements that begin with the word CALL, followed by the name of the subroutine to be referenced, and the argument list (if any). The arguments may be variable names, array names, or subscripted array element references. Expressions and constants may also be used as input arguments.

The following statement could be used to call the subroutine SLARGE. The largest of the first N items in TABLE would be stored in RMAX at the completion of execution of SLARGE.

```
CALL SLARGE (TABLE, N, RMAX)
```

The correspondence specified by the above call is shown below:

$$\textit{Actual argument} \qquad \textit{Dummy argument}$$

$$\text{TABLE} \longleftrightarrow \text{A}$$
$$\text{N} \longleftrightarrow \text{NRITMS}$$
$$\text{RMAX} \longleftrightarrow \text{MAX}$$

If a similar subroutine, SSMALL, were available to find the smallest number in the array TABLE, then the sequence of statements

```
CALL SLARGE (TABLE, N, RMAX)
CALL SSMALL (TABLE, N, RMIN)
RANGE = RMAX - RMIN
```

could be used to define the value of RANGE as the difference between the largest and smallest values in the array TABLE.

7.6.4 Sorting and Finding the Median of a Collection of Data

In this section, we will complete the statistics problem by writing the function FNDMED, which finds the median of a collection of data items. In the process, we will illustrate many of the points made so far in this chapter, and provide some additional insights concerning the use of subprograms in programming. Although the median problem is a subproblem of the statistics problem, we will treat it as an entirely separate problem in order to illustrate the degree of independence that can be achieved when using FORTRAN subprograms.

PROBLEM 7.2 Write a function to determine the median of a collection of data.

DISCUSSION. Figure 7.12 shows the portion of the program system chart (Fig. 7.2) that is relevant to finding the median, as well as a level-one flow diagram for the problem.

As is so often the case, the level-one flow diagram simply reflects an ordering of the primary steps shown in the program system chart. The information involved in the solution of the problem at this level is shown in the following data table.

Data Table for the Median Function (FNDMED)

Input arguments	*Output arguments*
TABLE (N): Represents the array that contains the data (real)	(None)
N: Represents the number of items in the array (integer)	

The next step in the solution of the problem is to decide how we will deal with steps 10 and 20 in the level-one flow diagram. Since sorting a collection of data is a frequent requirement in many problems and since sorting is a somewhat complicated task, we will perform the sort in a separate subroutine. Once the data

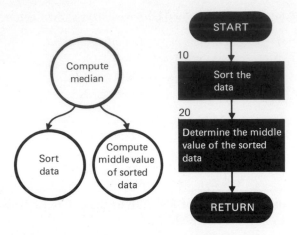

Fig. 7.12 Program system chart and level-one flow diagram for the median problem.

has been sorted, finding the median is rather easy (see Fig. 7.13) so we will not separate this task from the function FNDMED.

We can now make some additions to the data table for FNDMED. These additions reflect the decisions concerning the handling of steps 10 and 20 in the level-one flow diagram. The function FNDMED is shown in Fig. 7.14.

We can now complete Problem 7.2 (and hence also Problem 7.1) by writing the SORT subroutine. We will once again use the bubble-sort algorithm described in Chapter 6 (see Fig. 6.18 and 6.19 for the flow diagrams). The subroutine (shown in Fig. 7.15) uses the same names as those used in the program in Chapter 6. Since we are now writing a subroutine, however, the data table is slightly different.

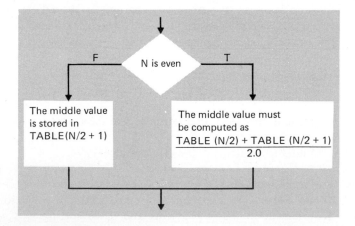

Fig. 7.13 Step 20 refinement—find the middle value in a collection of sorted data items.

Additional data-table entries for FNDMED

Local Variables:

Input variables	*Program variables*	*Output variables*
(None)		(None)

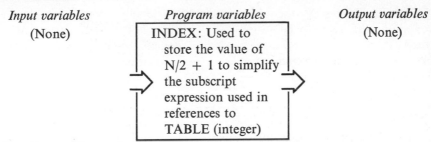

INDEX: Used to store the value of $N/2 + 1$ to simplify the subscript expression used in references to TABLE (integer)

Subprograms referenced:

SORT (subroutine): Sorts a real array in ascending order.

Argument	*Definition*
1	Array containing the data to be sorted (input and output, real)
2	Number of items in the array (input, integer)

```
      REAL FUNCTION FNDMED (TABLE, N)
C
C FIND THE MEDIAN OF A LIST OF REAL DATA ITEMS
C
C ARGUMENT DEFINITIONS --
C   INPUT ARGUMENTS
C     TABLE - ARRAY CONTAINING THE DATA ITEMS
C     N - THE NUMBER OF DATA ITEMS IN THE ARRAY
C
      INTEGER N
      REAL TABLE(N)
C
C LOCAL VARIABLES
      INTEGER INDEX
C
C SORT TABLE
      CALL SORT (TABLE, N)
C
C COMPUTE MEDIAN
      INDEX = N / 2 + 1
      IF (MOD(N,2) .EQ. 0) THEN
C         MEDIAN IS AVERAGE OF TWO MIDDLE ITEMS
          FNDMED = (TABLE(INDEX-1) + TABLE(INDEX)) / 2.0
      ELSE
C         MEDIAN IS THE MIDDLE DATA ITEM
          FNDMED = TABLE(INDEX)
      ENDIF
      RETURN
      END
```

Fig. 7.14 Function MEDIAN for Problem 7.2.

Data table for Sort Subroutine (SORT):

Input arguments	*Output arguments*
M(COUNT): Represents the array containing the items to be sorted (real)	M(COUNT): Also represents the array of sorted items at the completion of the execution of the subroutine (real)
COUNT: Represents the number of data items in the array to be sorted (integer)	

```
        SUBROUTINE SORT (M, COUNT)
C
C SORT AN ARRAY OF REAL DATA IN ASCENDING ORDER
C
C ARGUMENT DEFINITIONS --
C   INPUT ARGUMENTS
C     M - THE ARRAY OF DATA TO BE SORTED
C     COUNT - NUMBER OF DATA ITEMS IN THE ARRAY
C
        INTEGER COUNT
        REAL M(COUNT)
C
C LOCAL VARIABLES
        INTEGER INDEX, NEXLAS
        LOGICAL MORE
        REAL TEMP
C
C PERFORM BUBBLE SORT ON DATA IN M (ASCENDING ORDER)
C
        NEXLAS = COUNT - 1
        MORE = .TRUE.
C       OUTER LOOP - REPEATED WHILE MORE EXCHANGES NEEDED
        WHILE (MORE) DO
           MORE = .FALSE.
C          INNER LOOP - COMPARE SUCCESSIVE PAIRS OF ITEMS IN M
           DO 30 INDEX = 1, NEXLAS
              IF (M(INDEX) .GT. M(INDEX+1)) THEN
C                EXCHANGE OUT-OF-ORDER PAIRS
                 TEMP = M(INDEX)
                 M(INDEX) = M(INDEX+1)
                 M(INDEX+1) = TEMP
                 MORE = .TRUE.
              ENDIF
   30      CONTINUE
        ENDWHILE
C
        RETURN
        END
```

Fig. 7.15 Sort subroutine for Problem 7.2 (and 7.1).

Data table (continued)

Local Variables:

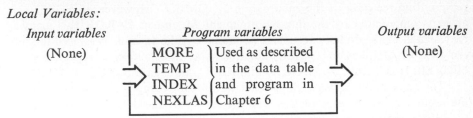

Input variables	Program variables	Output variables
(None)	MORE ⎫ Used as described TEMP ⎬ in the data table INDEX ⎪ and program in NEXLAS ⎭ Chapter 6	(None)

The data tables for the function FNDMED and the Sort subroutine have been described in two sections: arguments first, and then local variables. It is always a good idea to maintain a clear separation between the arguments and the local variables of a subprogram. This aids in the programming and understanding of the subprogram. It also makes it easier to determine how the subprogram should be referenced in any program system in which it is used.

EXERCISE 7.10 Rewrite the search program in Chapter 5 (Problem 5.2, Section 5.6) as a subroutine. Provide a modified data table as well.

7.7 NAME INDEPENDENCE: SUBPROGRAMS AND REMOTE BLOCKS

7.7.1 Name Independence in Subprograms

It is important to realize that each subprogram in a system of programs is compiled separately. Every local variable declared and every statement label used in a subprogram is meaningful only in that subprogram. Thus, the same variables and statement numbers may be used without conflict in different subprograms. This *name independence* feature of FORTRAN means that subprograms may be written in a completely independent fashion either by the same programmer or by different programmers working on the same program system. All that is required is that each programmer know the name of the subprograms in the system, the form of their argument lists, and the effect of each subprogram upon its arguments.

The correct type and structure required for the arguments in a subprogram call are determined solely by the definition of the dummy arguments listed in the subprogram header. No other information about a subprogram, such as how it works or what names or statement numbers are used, is necessary because the communication of information among subprograms is carried out through the argument lists. When a subprogram is called, the actual arguments corresponding to each dummy argument are manipulated as defined in the subprogram. The actual arguments may vary from call to call. Regardless of which argument names are used, they have no meaning to the subprogram except in terms of their correspondence to the dummy arguments of the subprogram.

The subprograms written for the simple statistics problem provide a good illustration of this point. The name given to the array containing the data for this problem is TABLE. This also happens to be the name of the dummy argument representing the data in the subprogram FNDMED. However, in SORT, this array is represented by the dummy argument M, and in LARGE, this array is represented by the dummy argument A. Similarly, the variable N is used to store the number of items in TABLE, but this same information is represented by NRITMS (in LARGE), by COUNT (in SORT), and again by N (in FNDMED).

The association between all of the names for the array is established through the argument list correspondences that are set up by the definitions and calls of the subprograms. Consequently, the same actual array elements are manipulated by all of the subprograms even though the dummy argument names are different.

On the other hand, the variable INDEX has been used as a local variable in both SORT and FNDMED. Since these two uses of the name INDEX are not associated by any argument list correspondence, two distinct memory cells are allocated for these local variables. Thus, these memory cells are entirely unrelated, even though their symbolic names are the same.

Example 7.6 In this example, the effects of a number of references to the subroutine SORT are analyzed. We will assume that C is an array of size 30 and that N1 is defined to be 10.

Call statement	*Effect*
CALL SORT(C, N1)	The first ten elements of C are sorted.
CALL SORT(C, 30)	The entire array C is sorted.
CALL SORT(20, C)	The dummy and calling arguments do not correspond in type of structure. An error diagnostic may be printed; in some FORTRAN versions, this will go undetected and produce unpredictable results.
CALL SORT(C)	The sizes of the argument lists differ. An error diagnostic may be printed; in some FORTRAN versions, this will go undetected and produce unpredictable results.

EXERCISE 7.11 Consider the following function for finding the largest of two real numbers represented by the dummy arguments P1 and P2.

```
REAL FUNCTION MAXVAL(P1, P2)
REAL P1, P2
REAL TEMP
IF (P1 .GT. P2) THEN
   TEMP = P1
ELSE
   TEMP = P2
ENDIF
MAXVAL = TEMP
RETURN
END
```

Let the real array X, and the real variables A, TEMP, and Y be defined in a program that calls MAXVAL, as shown below.

A	TEMP	Y	X(1)	X(2)	X(3)	X(4)	X(5)
16.0	8.2	−6.0	4.0	1.0	−2.0	0.0	.5

a) What value would be stored in Y as a result of the execution of the statement

$$Y = MAXVAL \ (A, \ TEMP)?$$

b) What value would be stored in A as a result of the execution of the statement

$$A = MAXVAL \ (X(3), \ Y)?$$

c) What value would be stored in X(3) as a result of the execution of the following statements?

$$X(1) = MAXVAL(X(4), \ X(5))$$
$$X(3) = MAXVAL(X(1), \ X(2))$$

d) What would be stored in X(5) as a result of the execution of the statement

$$X(5) = TEMP + MAXVAL \ (X(5) + X(2), \ 2.0 * X(3))$$

*7.7.2 Name Independence and the Remote Block

If you studied the remote block in Chapter 6, you may have already noted the major differences between the subprogram and the remote block: A subprogram referenced by another program or subprogram module is compiled separately from that module and the communication of data between modules is through the argument lists. The remote block, however, is compiled together with the module that references it, and therefore requires no argument list for data communication. Thus, the choice of variable names and statement labels to be used in a subprogram can be made independently of the names and labels used in the calling module. The names and labels used in a remote block, however, are considered to be part of the calling module; their use in the remote block must be consistent with the use of names and statement labels in the other parts of the module.

Both the subprogram and the remote block are important in the practice of top-down programming, and unless name independence among the modules of a program system is desirable, the remote block can be used just as effectively as the subprogram.

7.8 COMMON BLOCKS

7.8.1 Fundamentals of Using Common Blocks—Sort/Merge Problem

FORTRAN provides another facility besides argument lists for communicating data among programs and subprograms. This facility, called the *common block*,

---

* This section should be omitted by students who have not studied the remote block.

is useful in programming systems containing several subprograms which must reference a common *data base* of information. In such cases, argument lists can become quite long, introducing the possibility of numerous errors in calling the subprograms involved.

The common declaration can be used to specify that an area of memory called a *common block* is to be set aside so that it can be referenced by two or more program modules. Each of the modules requiring access to the common area must have a description of the information that is stored there which includes the name of each common variable, its type, and size (if an array).

We will illustrate how to define and use common blocks in the following problem.

PROBLEM 7.3 (Sort/Merge) Develop a program system that can be used to read in two lists of real numbers, sort each list in ascending order, and then merge the data in both lists into a single list of numbers, still in ascending order. All duplicate values should be eliminated during the merge. All three sorted lists should be printed in parallel columns at the end of processing.

Example 7.7 Given the data cards shown below

List B
(3 items) → 3   6.3   −1.8   3.1

List A
(5 items) → 5   −1.8   6.3   7.2   −10.5   3.5

the output from the program system would appear as

A	B	C
− 10.5	− 1.8	− 10.5
− 1.8	3.1	− 1.8
3.5	6.3	3.1
6.3		3.5
7.2		6.3
		7.2

DISCUSSION. The program system chart for this problem is shown in Fig. 7.16 together with the level-one flow diagram (for the main program).

Each of steps 10 through 40 will be implemented using subroutines (in fact, step 20 has already been done). Before writing the main program, we must decide how to store the data that is to be manipulated, and provide descriptions of the argument lists for the read, merge, and print subroutines.

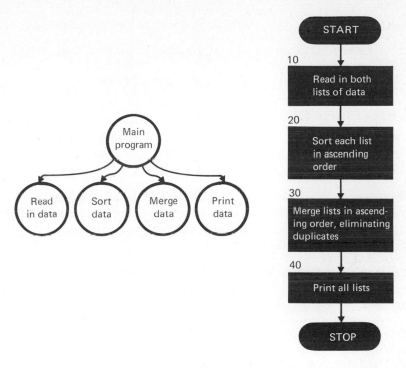

Fig. 7.16 Sort/merge program system chart and level-one flow diagram.

We will use three arrays, A, B, and C, for the storage of list A, list B, and list C, respectively. We will place these arrays, together with some additional variables describing the size of each array and the number of elements to be stored in them, in two common blocks, INBLK and OUTBLK, as indicated in the following data table.

Data table for the Sort/Merge Problem

Input variables	*Program variables*	*Output variables*
A(25), B(25): Arrays containing the lists to be sorted and merged (real)	SIZEAB: Program constant representing maximum size of arrays A and B (integer)	C(50): Array containing the merged lists (real)
NA: Number of items in A (integer)	SIZEC: Program constant representing maximum size of array C (integer)	NC: Number of items in C (integer)
NB: Number of items in B (integer)		

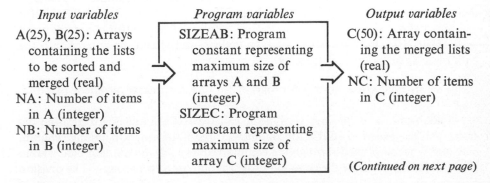

(*Continued on next page*)

Common blocks used:

INBLK: Contains input arrays and information concerning these arrays: NA, NB, SIZEAB, A(25), B(25)
OUTBLK: Contains output information NC, SIZEC, C(50)

Subprograms referenced:

INPUT (subroutine): Reads both lists into the arrays A and B; the subroutine must ensure that NA and NB do not exceed SIZEAB, and if they do, it must print a message and communicate the error back to the main program.

Argument   *Definition*

1   Error flag: If true, indicates that the number of items to be read into
           an array exceeds the size of the array (output, logical)
Common blocks used: INBLK

SORT (subroutine): Sorts a single list of real data in ascending order (see the sort subroutine, Problem 7.2, for argument definitions—neither common block is referenced).

MERGE (subroutine): Merges two lists of real data, eliminating duplicates; the subroutine must ensure that NC (which equals NA + NB) does not exceed SIZEC, and if it does, print a message and communicate the error back to the main program.

Argument   *Definition*

1   Error flag: If true, indicates that the number of items being merged
           exceeds the size of C (output, logical)
Common blocks used: INBLK and OUTBLK

OUTPUT (subroutine): Prints three lists of real data in parallel (no arguments)
Common blocks used: INBLK and OUTBLK

The error flags are used to indicate possible overflow conditions as data is being stored in the arrays A, B, and C. We will use the flags ERRIN (for communication with the subroutine INPUT), and ERRMRG (for communication with MERGE). Both variables are type logical, and should be entered into the data table as program variables. ▌

We can now write the main program for the sort/merge problem (see Fig. 7.17).

Aside from the error flags used in the calls to INPUT and MERGE, and the arguments in the call to SORT, all communication of information among program modules is accomplished through the common blocks. Two common blocks were used in order to separate the common program data into two groups. The division is based on the fact that the data in each group is shared by a different set of

```
C SORT/MERGE PROBLEM
C
C SORT TWO REAL LISTS IN ASCENDING ORDER
C MERGE SORTED LISTS, ELIMINATING DUPLICATE ITEMS
C
C COMMON BLOCK DESCRIPTIONS
      COMMON /INBLK/ NA, NB, SIZEAB, A(25), B(25)
      INTEGER NA, NB, SIZEAB
      REAL A, B
      COMMON /OUTBLK/ NC, SIZEC, C(50)
      INTEGER NC, SIZEC
      REAL C
C·
C PROGRAM VARIABLES
      LOGICAL ERRIN, ERRMRG
C
C INITIALIZE COMMON VARIABLES
      SIZEAB = 25
      SIZEC = 50
C
C READ AND PRINT ORIGINAL LISTS OF DATA
      CALL INPUT (ERRIN)
      IF (ERRIN) THEN
         PRINT, 'ERROR IN INPUT, EXECUTION TERMINATED.'
         STOP
      ENDIF
C
C SORT DATA IN EACH ARRAY AND MERGE THE ARRAYS
      CALL SORT (A, NA)
      CALL SORT (B, NB)
      CALL MERGE (ERRMRG)
      IF (ERRMRG) THEN
         PRINT, 'ERROR IN MERGE, EXECUTION TERMINATED.'
         STOP
      ENDIF
C
C OUTPUT SORTED AND MERGED LISTS
      CALL OUTPUT
      STOP
      END
```

Fig. 7.17 Main program for sort/merge.

program modules. The data in INBLK is shared by the main program, MERGE, INPUT, and OUTPUT; The data in OUTBLK is shared by the main program, MERGE, and OUTPUT. This kind of separation of common data into subblocks helps ensure that each subprogram will contain declarations only for the common information that it manipulates. This can help prevent the introduction and possible misuse of extraneous names in each program module, making the modules easier to read, debug, and maintain.

7.8.2   Additional Comments on the Use of Common Blocks

The form of the common declaration is shown below.

Common Statement

FORTRAN Form:

COMMON /name/ variable list

COMMON variable list

Interpretation. The defined block is treated as one large array of consecutive memory cells containing data in the order indicated by the variables and arrays appearing in the list. Blocks defined using the statement

COMMON /name/ variable list

are called *named common blocks*. The declaration

COMMON variable list

defines a common block with a blank name (*a blank common block*).

Each common statement used in a module should be followed by one or more type declarations defining the type of each of the items listed in the common statement. If arrays are included in a common block, it is good practice to define the array sizes in the common statement and not in the following type declarations. This can help to provide a clearer indication of the organization and structure of the common block.

Although the common declaration must appear in each module requiring access to information in the block, only one block of memory is set aside. The declarations

```
COMMON /INBLK/ NA, NB, SIZEAB, A(25), B(25)
INTEGER NA, NB, SIZEAB
REAL A, B
```

in the sort/merge program specify that one common block named INBLK (of size 53) be set up as shown in Fig. 7.18.

Each of the modules containing the common declaration can reference any or all of the data items stored in the block. In all program modules which reference a particular common block, the common and type declarations for that block should be exactly the same: all names should be the same, array sizes should be the same, and the order in which each name appears in the variable list should be the same.

In the sort/merge system, exact copies of the common statement and type declarations for INBLK (from the main program) must be used in subroutines INPUT, OUTPUT, and MERGE; the description of OUTBLK should be

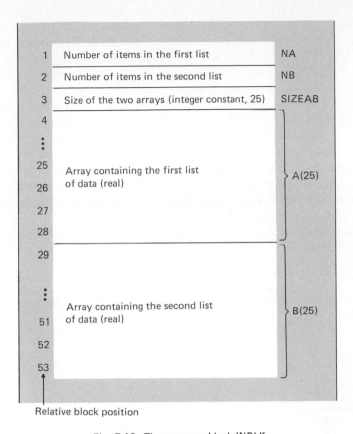

Relative block position

Fig. 7.18 The common block INBLK.

duplicated in MERGE and OUTPUT only. All common declarations should precede any executable program statements. We recommend placing them right after the subprogram argument definitions, if any.

In the sort/merge system, as in most program systems, information is communicated through the use of both argument lists and common blocks. Generally, information (such as ERRIN and ERRMRG) that is directly shared between only two program modules will be communicated through the use of an argument list (unless this list gets too long). Information that is shared among a number of modules (such as the data in INBLK) is placed in a common block.

The generality of a program module also influences the decision as to whether data communication should be via an argument list or not. For example, the subroutines INPUT, OUTPUT, and MERGE were written specifically for the sort/merge problem, and all of the information to be processed by these modules is processed in a single call. SORT, on the other hand, was written as a generalized subroutine to sort in ascending order any single array of real data items. It requires that the particular array to be sorted, and the number of items in that array, be specified as arguments in each call. The sort subroutine, therefore, contains no common declarations. This is as it should be. A common declaration for INBLK in addition to the argument list would be redundant. It might also confuse the compiler: FORTRAN does not allow the name of a dummy argument in a subprogram definition to be used in a common declaration in the subprogram.

One final note concerning the sort/merge program (shown in Fig. 7.17): The variables SIZEAB and SIZEC are both defined using assignment statements, even though both are used to store program constants. This is because Standard FORTRAN does not permit common variables to be initialized using a DATA statement in a main program, function, or a subroutine. (Many compilers have relaxed this restriction for real, integer, and logical variables in named common; a few, including WATFIV-S, even allow real, integer, and logical variables in blank common to be initialized via the DATA statement.)

The completion of the sort/merge problem is left for the student (see Programming Problem 7.7).

EXERCISE 7.12:

a) What values are printed as a result of the execution of the following program and subroutine?

```
COMMON A, B              SUBROUTINE JUMBLE (X)
REAL A, B                REAL X
REAL C                   COMMON A, B
CALL JUMBLE(C)           REAL A, B
PRINT, A, B, C           A = 1.0
STOP                     B = 2.0
END                      X = 4.0
                         RETURN
                         END
```

b) What values will be printed as a result of the execution of the following program and subroutines?

```
COMMON /WHAT/ NEXT(5)    SUBROUTINE DEFINE (ARRAY, SIZE)
INTEGER NEXT             INTEGER SIZE, ARRAY(SIZE)
INTEGER I                INTEGER I
CALL DEFINE (NEXT, 5)    DO 40 I = 1, SIZE
CALL EXCH(1,4)               ARRAY(I) = 2 * I - 1
I = 2                 40 CONTINUE
CALL EXCH(I, I+1)        RETURN
PRINT, NEXT             END
STOP
END                      SUBROUTINE EXCH (S1, S2)
                         INTEGER S1, S2
                         COMMON /WHAT/ NEXT(5)
                         INTEGER NEXT
                         INTEGER TEMP
                         TEMP = NEXT(S1)
                         NEXT(S1) = NEXT(S2)
                         NEXT(S2) = TEMP
                         RETURN
                         END
```

What is the relationship between the variable I in the main program and the variable I in subroutine DEFINE? Why is it not necessary to describe the common block WHAT in subroutine DEFINE?

7.9 ADDITIONAL COMMENTS CONCERNING SUBPROGRAMS

7.9.1 Subprogram Generality

At the beginning of this chapter, we presented a number of ways in which subprograms could be helpful in solving problems on the computer. We discussed the name-independence feature of the subprogram and indicated why name independence was such a vital part of the subprogram concept. Indeed, the utility of the subprogram derives primarily from the name-independence feature. It is this feature that allows the design, implementation, and testing of the subprograms of a large programming system to be carried out individually. Independence also makes it possible for some of these subprograms to be used as the building blocks of a number of programming systems, thereby saving a considerable amount of duplication of effort.

The design and testing of subprograms are topics worthy of considerable study in their own right and entire books have been written on these subjects. In Section 7.11 (Common Programming Errors), we will present a few steps to take in order to reduce the possibility of serious subprogram errors and to help in quickly detecting those errors that do occur. Aside from these comments, there is one aspect of subprogram design which you are urged to keep in mind whenever you are designing and implementing subprograms. This concerns the generality of subprograms.

Subprogram Generality. An important goal in designing subprograms is generality. Attempts should always be made to define the arguments of a subprogram so as to enable it to process a *logically complete set* of potential input values. The exact nature of what constitutes a logically complete set can be deduced only through a careful analysis of the given problem and its possible extensions.

Example 7.8 Given a problem of rounding off employee net-pay computations to the nearest two decimal places, we might initially consider writing a function for rounding off positive real numbers to the nearest two places. However, with just a little additional thought, we would see that we can easily generalize this function to round off any real number (positive or negative) to the nearest n decimal places, where n may be any positive integer. This latter function, while not useful in its fullest generality in the solution of the immediate problem, is certainly far more adaptable to changes in its input than the former. (It is even possible that such a generalized function already exists and that we could use it for the special case just defined, rather than writing a new one.)

7.9.2 Subdividing a Problem

Perhaps the most difficult aspect of the entire problem-solving process involves decisions concerning how a problem is to be subdivided. Such decisions require an in-depth understanding of a problem so that it may be sectioned into a collection of logically meaningful subtasks. In this endeavor, there is little substitute for experience and patience or the ability to recognize design flaws and a willingness to correct them, even when it involves redoing work that may be already under way (or even completed).

In this chapter, and indeed throughout the text, we have presented a number of tools that we feel are helpful in carrying out this kind of problem subdivision. These include the flow diagram and the data table, the concept of flow-diagram refinement, and the program system chart. We have also described a number of features of the FORTRAN language that considerably ease the implementation of a large program. We conclude this section with a brief summary of how all of these tools can be applied in solving one problem. We will use the simple statistics problem as an example.

As a first step, the program system chart shown in Fig. 7.2 is repeated in Fig. 7.19, augmented by a description of the use of relevant data items. Once the

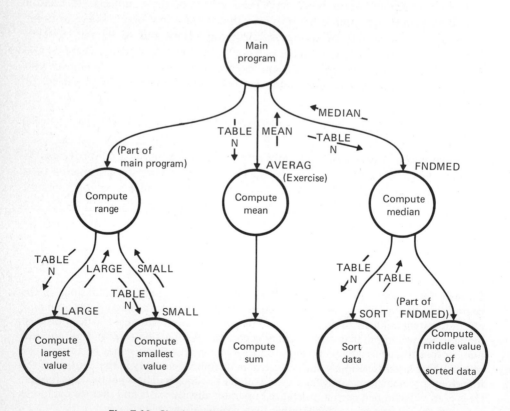

Fig. 7.19 Simple statistics problem (7.1): Program system chart.

program system chart has been completed, a decision must be made as to which subproblems should be implemented using subprograms—which should be functions and which should be subroutines. Generally, most subproblems should be implemented using subprograms. The only exception is in cases such as the computation of the range or of the median (in FNDMED), where a subproblem occurs only once in a system and is rather trivial. In the statistics problem, all of the subtasks except the sort return a single output value and can therefore be written as functions. The sort is implemented as a subroutine because it returns an entire array of values.

When the subprograms are identified, a subprogram table listing the name and purpose of each subprogram should be written. Under each subprogram, the definition of every argument should be listed, in the order specified in the argument list. Once this has been done, the data tables, algorithms, and programs may be developed for each of the defined subproblems. If necessary, the subproblems at the lower levels of the program system chart may be further subdivided, in much the same way that flow-diagram refinement is carried out. Once this work is complete, the subprograms developed can be tested individually and then incorporated into the program system, which can then be verified through additional testing, before being put into use.

Once a programming system is in use, continued verification and spot-checking are essential, especially when modifications are made. This work, and the general maintenance and alteration of the system, can be aided considerably by the documentation provided when the system was originally developed. Of course, this assumes that the documentation is brought up to date whenever changes are made in the system.

EXERCISE 7.13 If we examine the program system chart for the statistics problem (Fig. 7.19), we can see that the subroutine SORT does not enter the picture until the third level, where sorting is required in finding the median of the data items. Yet the sort could have been quite helpful in the computation of the range. Since sorting is needed anyway, we might just as well have sorted the data in the array TABLE as the first step in the main program. Once the data has been sorted in ascending order, the range can be computed simply as

$$RANGE = TABLE(N) - TABLE(1)$$

and the functions LARGE and SMALL are no longer needed.

Rewrite the program system chart and the main program for the statistics problem, with the sort done first.

*7.10   THE ROLE OF THE COMPILER IN PROCESSING SUBPROGRAMS

7.10.1   Introduction

You have probably already written some programs that call the square-root library function SQRT. Yet you didn't write this function; and, in fact, you know

---

* This section may be omitted.

very little about the function aside from its name, the type of its input and output data, and the fact that it somehow computes the square root of a positive real number. How, then, does the computer locate the SQRT function when it is called? How does the function find the argument (its input) and how does it know where to return the result? The answers to these questions can be found by examining the role of the compiler in processing subprograms. We will illustrate this role through the use of an example involving the library function SQRT. The role of the compiler is similar for user-defined functions and for the processing of subroutines. We will point out any differences in this role as we proceed with the example.

7.10.2 The Subprogram Linking Mechanism

Consider the program shown in Example 7.9.

Example 7.9:

```
          REAL X, Y
          READ, X
          PRINT, 'X = ', X
          IF (X .LT. 0.0) THEN
              PRINT, 'X IS NEGATIVE, EXECUTION TERMINATED.'
          ELSE
              Y = SQRT(X)
              PRINT, 'THE SQUARE ROOT OF X IS ', Y
          ENDIF
          STOP
          END
```

This program contains a reference to the library function SQRT with the argument X. Once the program has been translated, it must be loaded into the computer memory for execution. Furthermore, before the function SQRT can be executed, it must also be loaded into memory. Library functions (and user-defined functions and subroutines) are usually stored as machine-language programs on a high-speed auxiliary memory device (such as a disk or drum) and can be loaded from this device into the computer memory whenever they are needed. It is the responsibility of the compiler to ensure that whenever SQRT is loaded into memory, its location can be made known by the loader to the calling program. The compiler must also provide a mechanism that can be used to determine where to transfer control after the SQRT function has finished its task. Exactly how the compiler performs these tasks varies from computer to computer. However, once the appropriate communication mechanisms are set up, execution control can be transferred from the calling program to SQRT and back again, as shown in Fig. 7.20.

C1: The address of the next instruction to be executed in the calling program is saved in a special memory cell. This address is called the *return address* and will be used to return control back to the calling program after the function is executed.

C2: Control is transferred to the address in memory that is associated with the first executable instruction in the SQRT function.

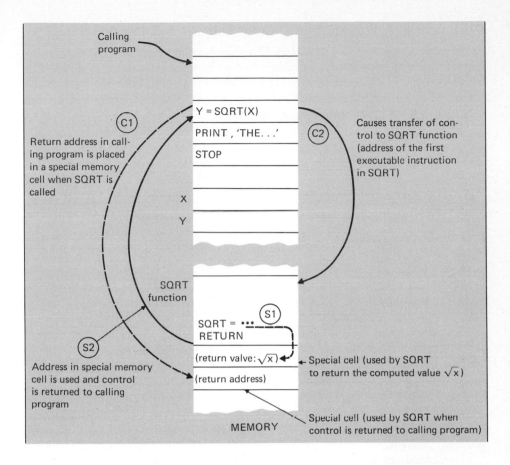

Fig. 7.20 Transfer of control between calling and called subprograms.

The instructions in the function SQRT are then carried out. There are two instructions in the function that have special significance when they are executed:

S1: An assignment statement of the form SQRT = expression causes the indicated expression to be evaluated and its value saved in a particular memory cell.

S2: The statement RETURN causes a transfer of control back to the address which was saved at step C1.

When S2 is carried out, the calling program can continue execution at the point where it left off when the function was called. As part of this instruction sequence, the value returned by the function will be manipulated. The calling program can find the value in the memory cell where the function left it.

The entire mechanism just described, including steps C1, C2, S1, and S2, is set up by the compiler during translation and is invoked during the execution of the calling program.

7.10.3 Establishing the Correspondence between Arguments

In the preceding section we described how the compiler constructs the *transfer-of-control* between subprograms. In addition, we explained the manner in which a function result is returned to a calling subprogram. It is also the role of the compiler to establish the correspondence between the arguments in the subprogram call, and those in the subprogram definition.

In translating a call to a subprogram, the compiler makes certain that the addresses of all of the arguments in the argument list are saved in an *argument address list*. Table 7.2 describes the entries in this table for the various kinds of subprogram arguments that are allowed in FORTRAN.

Table 7.2 Processing the argument address list

Argument type	Address stored in argument address list
Constant	Address of the constant in the calling program
Variable	Address of the variable in the calling program
Expression	The expression is evaluated, and its value stored in a temporary memory cell. The address of this temporary memory cell is placed in the argument address list.
Array	Address of the first element of the array in the calling program
Array element	Address of the particular array element specified in the calling program

The argument address list is used in different ways by different compilers. Some compilers translate a subprogram so that all references to dummy arguments in the subprogram will be replaced by references to the addresses of the actual calling arguments when the subprogram is called.

Other compilers use the argument addresses to obtain copies of the constants, expression values, and the contents of any variables or array elements that are used as calling arguments. These copies are saved in temporary memory cells which are manipulated when the subprogram is executed. Changes in the contents of the temporary cells must then be recorded in the memory cells occupied by the actual arguments at the completion of execution of the subprogram. (If an entire array is specified as a calling argument, it is usually not copied. Instead, the array elements themselves are manipulated as specified in the subprogram.)

Regardless of the details of how the argument list is used, the net effect is the same. To illustrate this, we use a small subprogram EXCH with three arguments, LIST, FIRST, LAST. The purpose of this subprogram is to exchange the contents of two elements of an array represented by LIST. The subscripts of the elements to be exchanged are represented by FIRST and LAST. LAST is also used in the subroutine to specify the array size.

The subroutine EXCH and a portion of a calling program are shown below.

```
REAL TABLE(100)                 SUBROUTINE EXCH (LIST, FIRST, LAST)
INTEGER I1, I2                  INTEGER FIRST, LAST
           .                    REAL LIST(LAST)
           .                    REAL TEMP
           .                    TEMP = LIST(FIRST)
CALL EXCH(TABLE, I1 + I2, 18)   LIST(FIRST) = LIST(LAST)
{next instruction}              LIST(LAST) = TEMP
           .                    RETURN
           .                    END

END
```

In this example, the statement

```
CALL EXCH(TABLE, I1 + I2, 18)
```

is used to call the subroutine. Upon execution of this statement, the steps listed below and shown in Fig. 7.21 are carried out.

1. The address of the first element of TABLE is stored in the argument address list (see arrow Ⓐ in Fig. 7.21).

2. The expression I1 + I2 is evaluated and stored in the temporary location TL. The address of TL is stored in the argument address list (arrow Ⓑ).

3. The address of the constant 18 is stored in the argument address list (arrow Ⓒ).

4. The return address is saved (arrow Ⓓ) as is the address of the first entry of the argument address list (arrow Ⓔ) and control is transferred to subroutine EXCH.

During the execution of EXCH, the values of the expression I1 + I2 and the constant 18 are used as subscripts (FIRST and LAST, respectively) to select the pair of elements of TABLE that are to be exchanged. The actual calling arguments will be manipulated using the addresses in the argument address list (unless copies of these arguments have been saved in temporary memory cells). When RETURN is executed, the return address is used to transfer control back to the calling program. (If the argument copy technique is used the data in the temporary cells is copied back into the actual arguments using the addresses given in the argument address list.)

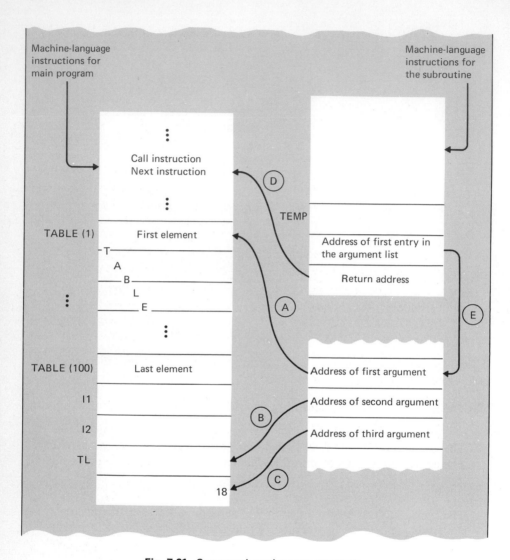

Fig. 7.21 Correspondence between arguments.

7.11 COMMON PROGRAMMING ERRORS

The most frequent and elusive errors that are made in using subprograms involve the specification of the argument list in a subprogram call and the listing of variable names in common declarations. Some compilers may be able to detect argument-list errors, especially those errors that result in too few or too many arguments, or that arise from confusion in the type and structure correspondence between arguments. These compilers can also detect some length ambiguity in common-block declarations.

In most cases, however, the compiler provides little help in the detection of these errors; you must therefore take steps to provide your own means of error detection. Some of these steps are listed below.

i) At least in the debugging stage, the values of all variables input to a subprogram should be printed upon entry to the subprogram. Carefully chosen portions of input arrays might also be printed.

ii) Input arguments and common variables that are integral to the control of execution of a subprogram should always be checked upon subprogram entry to see whether their values fall within a specified range of "meaningful values." Diagnostics should be printed if this range is violated. For example, the argument used to indicate "the number of items" in an array to be manipulated must always be positive, and usually will have some predetermined upper bound associated with it. This argument should be checked at each entry to guarantee that these conditions are met before the remainder of the subprogram is executed. Important output values might also be printed if they fall outside their normal range.

iii) Keep at hand the definition of each common block and descriptive definitions of the argument lists of each subprogram being used. Descriptive definitions of all arguments of a subprogram should be keypunched as comments at the beginning of the subprogram. Double-check each common declaration and argument list before keypunching your program. Make certain that the type and structure of corresponding pairs of arguments are in agreement.

7.12 SUMMARY

Two types of independent, separately compilable subprograms, the function and the subroutine, have been described in this chapter. We discussed how to reference and define these subprograms and showed how data may be communicated among subprograms using argument lists and common blocks.

The importance of the name-independence feature of the FORTRAN subprogram was discussed in some detail. You should remember that the relationships among names used in different subprograms are determined solely by the ordering of the names used in common blocks and in argument lists, and not by the names themselves.

A number of the benefits of using subprograms were presented. Subprograms can be used to identify a sequence of statements that is needed in more than one place in a program. It is convenient to be able to write such a statement sequence only once and to reference it as often as it is needed. The name-independence feature allows us to call a subprogram a number of times in the same program in order to manipulate different input arguments. A subprogram can also be referenced in programs written by people other than the subprogram author. This is often done, and is, in fact, one of the most useful features of subprograms. The only information about a subprogram that a user needs to know is its name, a brief description of what it does (but not how it does it), and a complete description of the data that is communicated between the subprogram and the calling program. This description can be provided through a brief definition of each of the arguments of the subprogram. Once this subprogram documentation is provided, the subprogram may be used by the subprogram author or by other programmers whenever needed.

The independence of subprograms facilitates sectioning complex problems into smaller parts and designing the algorithms and writing and debugging the subprograms for these parts separately. These subprograms can then be put together to solve the original problem. Often, when more than one programmer is assigned to a project, this sectioning facility enables the project manager to assign different sections to different programmers. Each programmer can design and implement assigned sections with little knowledge of what the other programmers are doing. All that is needed is a general description of what will be done in the other program sections and the names and argument lists of the subprograms to be written for these sections.

Regardless of the size or complexity of a problem or the number of programmers involved in its solution, this sectioning technique is a most important concept in programming. The FORTRAN function and subroutine provide the capability of carrying this technique all the way through from the design stage to the final program implementation of an algorithm. By using this technique, we can partition a problem into a collection of logically meaningful sections and concentrate on the design, coding, and debugging of each section separately. This kind of complete problem modularization usually results in programs and programming systems that are easier to implement and debug, easier to understand, and easier to modify.

The use of subroutines will evolve most naturally and be of greatest benefit if the level-by-level discipline of problem analysis and algorithm refinement is followed; in this way, the partitioning of a problem into a collection of subproblems will occur without special effort, at which point the algorithms for solving these problems can be conveniently implemented in the form of subprograms.

PROGRAMMING PROBLEMS

7.4   Two positive integers I and J are considered to be *relatively prime* if there exists no integer greater than 1 that divides them both. Write a logical function RELPRM which has two parameters, I and J, and returns a value of true if and only if I and J are relatively prime. Otherwise, RELPRM should return a value of false.

7.5   The *greatest common divisor*, GCD, of two positive integers I and J is an integer N with the property that N divides both I and J (with 0 remainder), and N is the largest integer dividing both I and J. An algorithm for determinining N was devised by the famous mathematician Euclid; a flow-diagram description of that algorithm, suitable for direct translation into FORTRAN, is provided next.

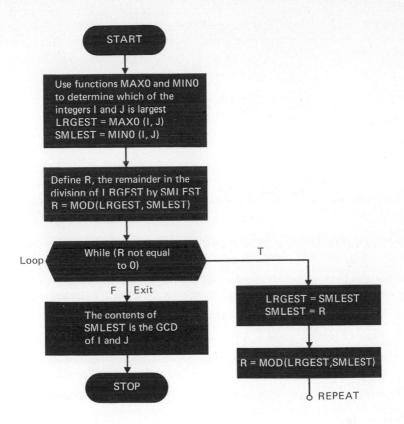

Write a program to read in four positive integers N1, N2, N3, and N4 and find the GCD of all four numbers. [*Hint.* The GCD of the four integers is the largest N that divides all four of them.] Implement the above algorithm as an integer function, and call it as many times as needed to solve the problem.

Note that GCD (N1, N2, N3, N4) = GCD (GCD(N1, N2), GCD(N3, N4)). Print N1, N2, N3, and N4, and the resulting GCD.

7.6 Write a FORTRAN program that will read in a string of up to eighty 0's and 1's, and print out the number of 0's, the number of 1's, and the total number of digits in the string. Use the function COUNT given in Exercise 7.1.

7.7 Complete Problem 7.3 (Sort/Merge). The merge subroutine requires a single simultaneous pass through the arrays A and B. To begin, compare A(1) and B(1), and store the smaller of these two elements in C(1). Then continue with a pairwise comparison of the elements in each array that have not yet been merged, and place the smaller of these elements into successive elements in C. Eliminate duplicate entries as you go along. The process is illustrated below for the data shown in the example at the beginning of Problem 7.3. The numbered lines between arrays A and B indicate the order of comparison of the pairs of elements in A and B.

	A(1)	A(2)	A(3)	A(4)	A(5)
A	−10.5	−1.8	3.5	6.3	7.2

① ② ③ ④ ⑤

	B(1)	B(2)	B(3)
B	−1.8	3.1	6.3

	C(1)	C(2)	C(3)	C(4)	C(5)	C(6)
C	−10.5	−1.8	3.1	3.5	6.3	7.2

When one of the input arrays has been exhausted, do not forget to copy the remaining data in the other array into the array C.

7.8 Write a program system to process a set of exam scores. Each student's score for the exam is keypunched on a data card along with the student's last name.

  a) Determine and print the class average for the exam.

  b) Find the median grade.

  c) Scale each student's grade so that the class average will become 75. For example, if the actual class average is 63, add 12 to each student's grade.

  d) Assign a letter grade to each student based on the scaled grade: 90–100 (A), 80–89 (B), 70–79 (C), 60–69 (D), 0–59 (F).

  e) Print out each student's name in alphabetical order followed by the scaled grade and the letter grade.

  f) Count the number of grades in each letter grade category.

  g) Print a bar chart showing the distribution of exam scores (see Example 6.7).

7.9 Given the lengths a, b, c of the sides of a triangle, write a function to compute the area, A, of the triangle; the formula for computing A is given by

$$A = \sqrt{s(s - a)(s - b)(s - c)}$$

where s is the semi-perimeter of the triangle:

$$s = \frac{a + b + c}{2}$$

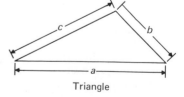

Triangle

Write a program to read in values for a, b, and c, and call your function to compute A. Your program should print A, and a, b, and c.

7.10 Write a type-real function ROUND, which, given a real number X and an integer P, will return the value of X rounded to the nearest P decimal places. (*Example.* If X is 403.7863 ..., then ROUND (X, 2) will return the value 403.79.) Make certain that your function works for negative as well as positive values.

7.11 Write an integer function FACT(N) which will compute the factorial, $n!$, of any small positive integer, n.

7.12 (Continuation of Problem 7.11) The expression for computing $C(n, r)$, the number of combinations of n items taken r at a time, is

$$C(n, r) = \frac{n!}{r! \, (n - r)!}.$$

Assuming that we already have available a function FACT(N) for computing $n!$ (see Problem 7.11), write function CNR(N, R) for computing $C(n, r)$. Write a program which will call CNR for $n = 4, r = 1; n = 5, r = 3; n = 7, r = 7$; and $n = 6, r = 2$.

7.13 Assume the existence of a main program containing a call to a subroutine SEARCH:

```
CALL SEARCH (BUFFER, N, KEY, FOUND, INDEX)
```

Write a subroutine SEARCH to compare each of the N elements in the array BUFFER to the data item in KEY. If a match is found, SEARCH is to set FOUND to true and define INDEX to be the index of the element in the array BUFFER in which the key was located. If no key is found, FOUND is to be set false and INDEX is not to be altered.

7.14 Do Problem 6.5 using subprograms. Provide a program system chart, data tables, and flow diagrams before writing the required program system modules.

7.15 The electric company charges its customers according to the following rate schedule:

8 cents a kilowatt-hour (kwh) for electricity used up to the first 300 kwh;
6 cents a kwh for the next 300 kwh (up to 600 kwh);
5 cents a kwh for the next 400 kwh (up to 1000 kwh);
3 cents a kwh for all electricity used over 1000 kwh.

Write a function to compute the total charge for each customer. Write a program to call this function using the following data:

Customer number	Kilowatt-hours used
123	725
205	115
464	600
596	327
601	915
613	1011
722	47

The calling program should print a three-column table listing the customer number, hours used, and the charge for each customer. It should also compute and print the number of customers, total hours used, and total charges.

7.16 A throw of two dice may produce anywhere from a two (snake-eyes) to a twelve (box-cars). Write a program system to read the 36 two-digit integers representing all possible outcomes (1st digit 1–6, 2nd digit 1–6) into an array ROLLS of size 36, and produce the table shown below.

Roll value	Number of ways of getting this roll	Probability of getting this roll	Probability of a roll greater than or equal to this one
2	1	.028	1.000
3	2	.056	.972
⋮	⋮	⋮	⋮
11	2	.056	.084
12	1	.028	.028

For any roll value, X, the probability of getting that roll is

$$P(roll=X) = tally (X)/36$$

where tally (X) is the number of ways of getting X. Also, the probability of getting a roll greater than or equal to X is

$$P(roll \geq X) = P(roll=X)+P(roll=X+1)+...P(roll=12)$$

Thus

$$P(roll=10) = tally(10)/36.0 = 3.0/36.0 = .083$$

and

$$P(roll \geq 10) = .083 + .056 + .028 = .167$$

Hints. Store the number of ways of getting a roll and the probabilities of each roll, X, and a roll greater than or equal to X, in three arrays NRWAYS, PX, and PGEX, each of size 12 (do not use the first elements of these arrays). Put these arrays in a common block. Your main program should read in the rolls, and call a subroutine TALLY to compute NRWAYS for each roll (TALLY should be called just once). Given the data in NRWAYS, the probabilities of each roll can be determined, and then the data in the last columns can be computed. All computations should be rounded to three decimal places.

For each X, P(roll = X) should be computed using a function. This function should be called 11 times.

Note that for any roll (represented by the two-digit integer *r*) the actual numeric value of the roll can be computed as

$$VALUE = MOD (r, 10) + r/10$$

For example, if r is 36, then the actual value of the roll is

$$\text{VALUE} = \text{MOD}(36,10) + 36/10 = 6 + 3 = 9.$$

7.17 Each week the employees of a local manufacturing company turn in time cards containing the following information:

i) an identification number (a five-digit integer),

ii) hourly pay rate (a real number),

iii) time worked Monday, Tuesday, Wednesday, Thursday and Friday (each a four-digit integer of the form HHMM, where HH is hours and MM is minutes).

For example, last week's time cards contained the following data:

Employee number	Hourly rate	Time worked (hours, minutes)				
		Monday	Tuesday	Wednesday	Thursday	Friday
16025	4.00	0800	0730	0800	0800	0420
19122	4.50	0615	0800	0800	0800	0800
21061	4.25	0805	0800	0735	0515	0735
45387	3.50	1015	1030	0800	0945	0800
50177	6.15	0800	0415	0800	0545	0600
61111	5.00	0930	0800	0800	1025	0905
88128	4.50	0800	0900	0800	0800	0700

NOT IN ORDER — PUT IN ORDER (handwritten note)

Write a program system that will read the above data and compute for each employee the total hours worked (in hours and minutes), the total hours worked (to the nearest quarter-hour), and the gross salary. Your system should print the data shown above with the total hours (both figures) and gross pay for each employee. You should assume that overtime is paid at $1\frac{1}{2}$ times the normal hourly rate, and that it is computed on a weekly basis (only on the total hours in excess of 40.00), rather than on a daily basis. Your program system should contain the following subprograms:

a) A function for computing the sum (in hours and minutes) of two four-digit integers of the form HHMM (*Example.* $0745 + 0335 = 1120$);

b) A function for converting hours and minutes (represented as a four-digit integer) into hours, rounded to the nearest quarter hour (*Example.* $1120 = 11.25$);

c) A function for computing gross salary given total hours and hourly rate;

d) A function for rounding gross salary accurate to two decimal places (see Problem 7.10).

Test your program using the same time cards previously shown.

7.18 A mail order house with the physical facilities for stocking up to 20 items decides that it wants to maintain inventory control records on a small computer. For each stock item, the following data is to be stored on the computer:

 i) the stock number (a five-digit integer);

 ii) a count of the number of items on hand;

 iii) the total year-to-date sales count;

 iv) the price;

 v) the date (month and day) of the last order for restocking an item (a four-digit integer of the form MMDD);

 vi) the number of items ordered.

Both items (v) and (vi) will be zero if there is no outstanding order for an item.

Design and implement a program system to keep track of the data listed in (i) through (vi). You will need six arrays, each of size 20. Your system should contain subprograms to perform the following tasks:

 a) change the price of an item (given the item stock number and the new price);

 b) add a new item to the inventory list (given the item number, the price, and the initial stock on hand);

 c) enter information about the date and size of a restock order;

 d) reset items (v) and (vi) above to zero and update the amount on hand when a restock order is received;

 e) increase the total sales and decrease the count on hand each time a purchase order is received (if the order cannot be filled, print a message to that effect and reset the counts);

 f) search for the array element that contains a given stock number.

The following information should be initially stored in memory (using data initialization (DATA) statements). This information should be printed at the start of execution of your program system.

Stock numbers	On-hand count	Price
02421	12	100.00
00801	24	32.49
63921	50	4.99
47447	100	6.99
47448	48	2.25
19012	42	18.18
86932	3	67.20

A set of typical transactions for this inventory system is given below.

Price Changes

Trans no.	Card ID	Stock no.	New price
2	'PRIC'	19012	18.99
9	'PRIC'	89632	73.90

Add Items

Trans no.	Card ID	Stock no.	Price	On-hand
4	'ADIT'	47447	14.27	36
5	'ADIT'	56676	.15	1500

New Orders

Trans no.	Card ID	Stock no.	Date	Volume
3	'NUOR'	00801	1201	18
8	'NUOR'	47446	1116	15

Orders Received

Trans no.	Card ID	Stock no.	Volume
6	'ORIN'	00801	18

Purchase Orders

Trans no.	Card ID	Stock no.	Number wanted
11	'PRCH'	00801	30
12	'PRCH'	12345	1
7	'PRCH'	56676	150
10	'PRCH'	86932	4

Each transaction should be punched using two cards: a header card, and a data card. The appearance of these cards is shown below.

Header card: Transaction number
              Transaction ID
              Stock number

Data card: Stock number
              Transaction data

For example, transaction four should be punched as

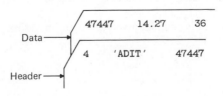

Your main program should process the transactions, one at a time, as shown below.

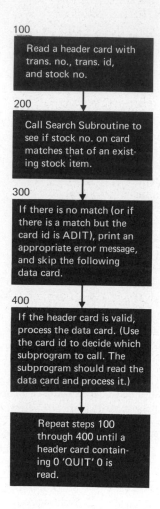

100
Read a header card with trans. no., trans. id, and stock no.

200
Call Search Subroutine to see if stock no. on card matches that of an existing stock item.

300
If there is no match (or if there is a match but the card id is ADIT), print an appropriate error message, and skip the following data card.

400
If the header card is valid, process the data card. (Use the card id to decide which subprogram to call. The subprogram should read the data card and process it.)

Repeat steps 100 through 400 until a header card containing 0 'QUIT' 0 is read.

Each subprogram should print an appropriate informative message for each transaction, indicating whether or not the transaction was processed, and giving other pertinent information about changes in the stored data that were affected by the processing of the data card.

After the quit card is read, all inventory data should be printed in tabular form.

8.1 Limitations of Format-Free
    Input and Output

8.2 The Format Statement: A
    General Discussion

8.3 Format Descriptors

8.4 Common Programming Errors

8.5 Summary
    Programming Problems

FORMATTED INPUT AND OUTPUT

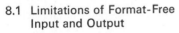

8.1 LIMITATIONS OF FORMAT-FREE INPUT AND OUTPUT

In Chapter 4, Section 4.3, we discussed the role of special format analyzer and data-converter programs in the handling of format-free input and output. The data-converter programs were used to convert data from an external representation (for example, on punched cards) to an internal form; and from the internal form to an external form suitable for output on a high-speed line-printer or terminal.

The format analyzers were used to determine certain descriptive information about the data involved in an input or output operation. This included information concerning the type of the data, the total number of characters (the *width* of the data), and the number of characters to the right of the decimal point in a real number. Also included was information concerning the position on the card of each input data item; or, for output, the position on the printed page in which an item was to be placed.

The use of format-free input and output made it relatively easy for us to program the input and output steps required in our programming problems. However, it prevented us from exercising some important input and output prerogatives. In particular, we had only minimal control over the vertical and horizontal spacing of our output. We were also limited in the complexity of the card and line formats that we could use. Our output data always occupied a prespecified number of print positions, and we had little control over the placement of output items on the printed line. For input, we were required to leave blanks (one or more) between data items appearing in a card and to enclose character strings in apostrophes.

The reason for these limitations is that the format-analyzers impose certain restrictions on the formats that we are permitted to use, and we have no way of overriding these restrictions. In situations in which additional format control is of paramount importance, the only recourse is to abandon the use of the analyzers. This means that the descriptive information previously provided by the analyzers must now come from another source—namely, the programmer. Thus, by abandoning the use of the format analyzers, we gain more control over the input and output operations involved. In return, however, we must learn how to provide the data-converter program with the descriptive information necessary for the input and output desired in our programs. In FORTRAN, this descriptive information is provided through the use of the *format statement*.

8.2 THE FORMAT STATEMENT: A GENERAL DISCUSSION

The FORTRAN statement

```
37 FORMAT (' ', 'I = ', I2, 6X, 'X = ', F7.2)
```

is an example of a format statement. The general form of format statements is described in the next display. The meaning of the symbols enclosed in parentheses is the subject of this chapter.

The Format Statement

FORTRAN Form: sn FORMAT (descriptive information)

Interpretation. The information inside the parentheses provides the data-converter program with all the necessary descriptive information about the input and output operation to be performed. The format statement is a nonexecutable statement and may be placed anywhere in the program. The link between an input or output statement and the format pertaining to that statement is provided by the statement number sn.

Each format used in a program must have its own unique statement number sn, and this number may not be used as a label for any other statement (format or otherwise) in the program. However, a single format may be used to provide descriptive information for more than one input or output statement.

A read (or print) statement that references a format statement is called a *formatted* (rather than format-free) *read* (or *print*) *statement.* Formatted read and print statements used in the text will have the forms

```
         READ sn, list
         PRINT sn, list
```

where sn is the number of the format being referenced.

Example 8.1

```
              READ 25, X
          25 FORMAT ( . . . )
                    .
                    .
                    .
              PRINT 26, Y, X
          26 FORMAT ( . . . )
                    .
                    .
                    .
              READ 25, Z
                    .
                    .
                    .
              PRINT, 'X = ', X
```

Both read statements in this example use the same format statement (sn 25). One of the print statements is formatted (sn 26), and the other is not. Formatted and format-free input and output may be intermixed in the same program.

The read and print statements shown above are nonstandard FORTRAN, but are common abbreviations of the standard statements. The latter require the use of the number of the input or output device involved in an operation, as well as the format statement number. If the short forms just shown are not available on your computer, you will have to find out the numbers that designate the input and output devices you are using. For most computers, the number 5 is used for the card reader and the number 6 is used for the line printer. In this case, the standard FORTRAN statements are:

```
READ (5, sn) list
WRITE (6, sn) list
```

where the command WRITE is used instead of PRINT.

It is important to remember that even with formatted input and output the variable name list in a read or print statement still controls the transfer of information in and out of computer memory. In a read statement, the list indicates the variables or arrays in which the input data is to be stored. In a print statement, the list dictates which variables or arrays are to be printed.

The format statement is only descriptive in nature. When used with a read operation, the format tells the computer the precise form in which to expect the input data. With a print operation, the format completely describes the form in which all items are to be printed and contains any character strings denoting the headings or labels that are to accompany the printed data. These points are summarized next.

A formatted read or print statement specifies which variables are to be used for data transmission and indicates the number of an associated format statement. No descriptive information (headings, labels, etc.) may be specified in a read or print statement. The format statement is used for descriptive purposes—for specifying the appearance of information on a data card or for indicating the layout of the line to be printed.

8.3 FORMAT DESCRIPTORS

The information enclosed within the parentheses of a format statement provides the descriptive information needed by the data converter. This information cannot be written in English, but rather must be coded in such a way as to keep the descriptions as short and precise as possible. These codings are called *format descriptors*, and it is our purpose, in the ensuing sections, to describe how these descriptors are used and what they mean. Only the most common descriptors available in FORTRAN will be discussed. We will examine the use of the descriptors for output first, and then for input.

8.3.1 Output Formats

It is often necessary to print information stored in memory in a form that is more readable and better organized than that allowed by format-free output. This form frequently takes on the appearance of a table or a graph and requires precise column-by-column, line-by-line control over the appearance of the information that is printed. This control over the printing of information can be accomplished by using format statements to describe the appearance of each line of information to be printed. Each line usually consists of from 120 to 132 distinct *print positions*, which can be grouped together as specified by the format descriptors to form *output fields*.

There are two classes of output format descriptors. One class, the *space descriptors*, is used to control horizontal and vertical spacing of printed data and to control the printing of *quoted character strings* that provide descriptive information to accompany this data. The other class, the *data descriptors*, is used to describe the external appearance of the data in the memory of the computer that is to be printed. We will use examples to illustrate the differences between these classes and define the rules for using output format descriptors.

Example 8.2

```
      PRINT 37, J, X
   37 FORMAT (' ', 'J = ', I3, 6X, 'X = ', F6.2)
```

Assume J contains 125 and X contains -35.69. The output line would appear as follows:

```
 J = 125     X = -35.69
```

The meaning of each of the format descriptors used in Example 8.2 is described below.

Format Descriptor	*Meaning*
' '	This descriptor defines a quoted character string consisting of a single blank. This blank will not be printed because it is the first character of the line being formed. It will be used instead for vertical spacing or line control. Vertical spacing will be discussed in more detail later in the chapter.
'J = '	This descriptor defines a quoted character string of length 4 which is placed in the output line being formed exactly as it appears.
I3	This descriptor specifies that the first variable in the output list (J in this case) is an integer which is to occupy the next 3 print positions in the output line.
6X	This descriptor indicates that blanks are to be printed in the next six print positions.
'X = '	The quoted character string of length 4 is placed in the output line exactly as it appears, following the six blanks.

Format
descriptor   *Meaning*

F6.2   This descriptor specifies that the second variable in the output list, X, is type real (floating point) and will occupy the next six print positions. The 2 in this descriptor indicates that the value of X is to be rounded to two decimal places before printing. The number six represents the total number of print positions to be used, and includes the decimal point and a sign (if any).

When the line control character is followed by a quoted character string in a format, the character is usually combined with the string as shown below.

37 FORMAT (' J = ', I3, 6X, 'X = ', F6.2)

Example 8.3 (Home-Loan Mortgage Interest/Payment Tables)   The Raisem Higher Home Loan Association maintains lists of home-loan mortgage interest payments. A sample page of these lists is shown below.

```
RAISEM HIGHER HOME LOAN ASSOCIATION            07-04-76
HOME LOAN MORTGAGE INTEREST PAYMENT TABLES
AMOUNT = $30000.00          LOAN DURATION (MONTHS) = 300
RATE (PERCENT)    MONTHLY PAYMENT    TOTAL PAYMENT
     6.50            XXX.XX           XXXXXX.XX
     6.75            XXX.XX           XXXXXX.XX
      .                 .                 .
      .                 .                 .
      .                 .                 .
     9.50            262.11           78632.70
      .                 .                 .
      .                 .                 .
      .                 .                 .
    12.00            XXX.XX           XXXXXX.XX
```

The person who wrote the program to print this table used six variables.

DATE: The date the list was made (a character string of length 8)
AMOUNT: The amount of the loan (real)
MONTHS: Period of time (in months) for loan repayment (integer)
RATE: Interest rate (percent) applied to the loan (real)
MPAYMT: Monthly payment required from borrower (real)
TPAYMT: Total amount to be paid over entire loan period (real)

The program contains the three print statements shown in Fig. 8.1.

Together these three statements produce the sample page of output just shown. Statement (a) prints the three lines of page-heading information that appears at the top of the page. The values of the variables DATE, AMOUNT, and MONTHS are included as part of the heading. Statement (b) prints the column heading labels, and statement (c) is used inside a loop in the program to print the numbers appearing in each row of output that is shown. (The values of RATE, MPAYMT, TPAYMT.)

a)   PRINT 26, DATE, AMOUNT, MONTHS
      26 FORMAT ('1RAISEM HIGHER HOME LOAN ASSOCIATION', 10X, A8/
         A 'OHOME LOAN MORTGAGE INTEREST PAYMENT TABLES'/
         B 'OAMOUNT = $', F8.2, 10X, 'LOAN DURATION (MONTHS) = ', I3)
          PRINT 27
b)   27 FORMAT (' RATE (PERCENT)', 3X, 'MONTHLY PAYMENT', 3X,
         A 'TOTAL PAYMENT')
c)   PRINT 28, RATE, MPAYMT, TPAYMT
      28 FORMAT (6X, F5.2, 10X, F6.2, 10X, F9.2)

Fig. 8.1 Print statements for sample output page in home mortgage problem.

You should convince yourself that formats 26, 27, and 28 do indeed produce the output shown in Example 8.3. To aid you in this effort, we will provide a detailed tabular, step-by-step description of the formation of the three output lines defined in format 26. (See part (a) of Fig. 8.1.) Additional explanations will follow this listing.

	Format descriptor	*Corresponding variable list item*	*Meaning*
Line 1 of format 26	'1RAISEM... ASSOCIATION'	None	Indicates that a field of width 36, consisting of the 36 character quoted string 1RAISEM... ASSOCIATION, is to be entered into the line being formed. (The "1" is not printed; it is used for vertical line control.)
	10X	None	Indicates that a field of 10 blanks is to be entered into the line being formed.
	A8	DATE	Indicates that a field of width 8 (8 print positions) is to be used to print the character string stored in DATE.
	/	None	Indicates the end of the output line being formed.
Continuation line A	'OHOME... TABLES'	None	Indicates that a field of width 43, consisting of the 43 character quoted string 0HOME... TABLES, is to be entered into the line being formed. (The "0" is not printed; it is used for vertical line control.)
	/	None	Indicates the end of an output line.

	Format descriptor	Corresponding variable list item	Meaning
Continuation line B	'OAMOUNT = $'	None	Indicates that a field of width 11, consisting of the 11-character quoted string 0AMOUNT = $, is to be entered into the line being formed. (The "0" is not printed; it is used for vertical line control.)
	F8.2	AMOUNT	Indicates that a field of width 8 is to be used to print the real number stored in AMOUNT (two digits will appear to the right of the decimal point).
	10X	None	(as defined above)
	'LOAN... MONTHS) = '	None	Indicates that a field of width 25, consisting of the 25-character quoted string LOAN... (MONTHS) = , is to be entered into the print line being formed.
	I3	MONTHS	Indicates that a field of width 3 is to be used to print the integer stored in MONTHS.

The format descriptors used in Examples 8.2 and 8.3 are summarized in Table 8.1.

Table 8.1 Format descriptors for output

Spacing descriptors	Data descriptors
X for specifying horizontal spacing	I: For describing a field of integer output
'' (apostrophes) for printing quoted character strings	F: For describing a field of real output
/ for specifying vertical spacing	A: For describing a field of character output

There are many rules governing the use and function of format descriptors and some of them are rather complicated. We do not intend to discuss all of the intricacies of formats. Rather, we will limit our discussion to the more fundamental aspects of format specification. In the remainder of this section, we will discuss the rules pertaining to the print statements and formats of Examples 8.2 and 8.3. In subsequent sections we will describe some additional fundamental rules of format specification.

Item 1. In a format statement, all descriptors except the slash should be separated from the others by a comma. The entire format must be enclosed in parentheses. Continuation cards may be used for long formats, but caution should be used when continuing character strings from one card to another. To avoid such continuation, it is advisable to break the string into two parts (each enclosed in apostrophes), put a comma after the first, and place the entire second part on the next card.

Item 2. Data descriptors I, F, and A: Width-specification and output-list correspondence. Each variable appearing in the list portion of a print statement must have associated with it a data descriptor of the same type. This association is summarized in Table 8.2.

Table 8.2 **Variable and format descriptor type association**

Variable type	Descriptor form	
Integer	Iw	⎫
Character	Aw	w and d must be
(or an integer containing		positive integer
a character string)		constants
Real	Fw.d	⎭

The width specification w shown in the table describes the width of the field (the number of print positions) to be used for printing the contents of the indicated variable.

Example 8.4 This example illustrates the required correspondence between variable names and data descriptors.

```
CHARACTER*4  LASTNA        [or INTEGER LASTNA]
REAL   HOURS
INTEGER   AGE
         .
         .
         .
```

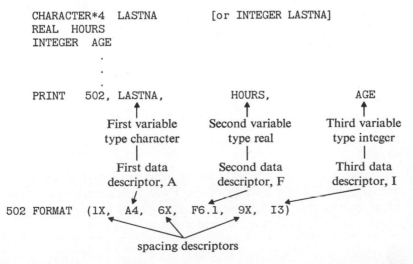

The PRINT 27 statement shown in Fig. 8.1 has no list of variables for printing. The print statement is used to print only a *quoted character string*, with no variable contents specified for printing. Format 27, of course, contains no data descriptors, because no variables appear in the output list.

The following comments pertain to field width specifications in output formats.

---

1. For integer and real variables, if the data to be printed does not fit within the indicated field width, an error indication may be given. (Usually, the error indication consists of a string of one or more asterisks appearing in the field.) For character data, if the string is too long, the excess characters at the right end of the string will not be printed. No error indication will be given.

2. Integer and real variables that do not completely fill a field will be printed in the rightmost print positions (right-adjusted) in the field, and the left portion of the field will be padded with blanks.

3. The length of a character string to be printed is equal to the character capacity, c, of the variable containing the string. If c exceeds the field width specification, w, in the format descriptor corresponding to the variable, then only the leftmost characters in the string will be printed:

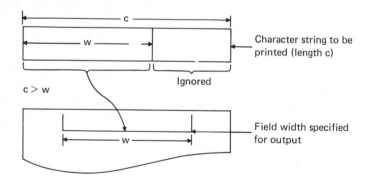

This rule is followed by most FORTRAN versions regardless of whether the character string involved is stored in a variable of type character or type integer.

4. The width specification w for a real number includes the sign (if any) and the decimal point. The d portion of the Fw.d descriptor indicates the number of decimal digits to be printed to the right of the decimal point. This count is included as part of the field width w.

Example 8.5 Let W contain the real value − 647.928. Then the statements

```
        PRINT 16, W
   16 FORMAT (1X, F7.2)
```

will result in the printing of the number − 647.93. (Note that real numbers are always printed rounded to the specified number of decimal places.) The statements

```
        PRINT 17, W
   17 FORMAT (1X, F7.3)
```

will cause an error because the number to be printed now requires 8 print positions (to achieve three-decimal-place accuracy), and only 7 were indicated.

$$-647.928$$
$$\text{Positions} \quad 12345678$$

Example 8.6 On a computer with an integer variable character capacity of 6, the 8-character string 07-04-06 is too long to fit in one integer variable. Two integer variables, DATE1 and DATE2 might be used, as shown below.

DATE1	DATE2
07-04	760000

In this case the print statement and its accompanying format for Example 8.3 should be written:

```
     PRINT 26, DATE1, DATE2, AMOUNT, MONTHS
  26 FORMAT ('1RAISEM....ASSOCIATION', 10X, A6, A2/
```

.
.
.

Item 3. Horizontal spacing—The X descriptor. The use of an X format descriptor in an output format causes blanks to be inserted in a line to be printed. The general form of this descriptor is nX, where n is the number of blanks to be inserted in the line. Note that with the X descriptor, the field width is indicated to the left of the descriptor rather than to the right, as is the case with the data descriptors I, F, and A.

Item 4. The line-terminator descriptor, slash. Often, we may want to use a single format to describe the appearance of more than one line of output (format 26, for example, describes 3 separate lines). The character slash, /, may be used to indicate that we have reached the end of the formation of one line of output, and wish to go on to describe the next line.

A string of consecutive slashes has the effect of causing blank lines to appear on a page. The number of blank lines will be one less than the number of consecutive slashes if the slashes are in the middle of the format. The number of blank lines will be equal to the number of slashes if the slashes appear at the very beginning or very end of the format. Commas are not required to separate consecutive slashes nor to separate slashes from other format descriptors. Large numbers of consecutive slashes may be indicated using the descriptor form n(/), where n is a positive integer constant indicating the number of slashes to be used.

Example 8.7 The statements

```
      PRINT 18, X, Y
   18 FORMAT (1X, F8.2///// 1X, F8.2)
      PRINT 19, X, Y
   19 FORMAT (1X, F8.2, 5(/), 1X, F8.2)
```

will cause 4 blank lines to appear between the values of X and Y.

Item 5. Line control (vertical spacing control). Each execution of a print statement initiates the printing of information beginning at print position one of an output line. The use of the slash in an output format serves the same purpose; it specifies the termination of one line and the start of a new line. Consecutive slashes may be used for vertical spacing or *line control,* as shown previously. In addition, FORTRAN has another feature that may be used to specify line control on the high-speed line-printer.

The first character of every line that is formed for printing on the high-speed line-printer is actually not printed but is used for line control instead. There are four common line-control characters in FORTRAN, and their effects are summarized in the following table.

Line-control character	*Effect*
Blank	Single line space
0 (zero)	Double line space
1	Skip to the top of a new page
+	Suppress line spacing

Other characters may have special line-control meaning on different computers, but these four characters are standard. We repeat, for emphasis, that these characters are effective for line control only on the high-speed line-printer and typically not on other output devices such as a teletype or display scope.

Double spacing is like double-spaced typewriter text. It is often useful when headings are being printed or when text material is being produced on the computer. Line suppression can be used to achieve line overprints for underlining, dark and light contrasts, or for graphical or picture effects. We will have little occasion to use line suppression in this text.

You should be certain to explicitly indicate a line-control character at the beginning of every line that is to be printed on the high-speed printer. This can be done in a number of different ways, as illustrated in the following examples.

Example 8.8 (continuation of Example 8.3)

a) The quoted character string 1RAISEM....ASSOCIATION is specified as the first printed information in format 26. The character 1 is therefore taken as the first character of the line; it is not printed but is used for line control, causing a skip to the top of the next page.

b) The identification label 'OHOME...TABLES' (also in format 26) is specified as the first information to be printed following the line terminator, /. The zero, 0, is taken as the first character of the line; it is not printed but causes a double line space.

c) Format 28 provides an example of another method of specifying that a blank is to be used for carriage control. The 6X indicates that the line being formed for printing is to begin with 6 blanks. The first of these blanks will be used for carriage control (causing a single line space), and only 5 blanks will actually appear in the printed line (see Example 8.5 also).

Example 8.9 The formats

$$(1X, \ldots) \text{ and } (' ', \ldots)$$

both specify that a blank is to be used as the carriage-control character of a line.

Item 6. Quoted character strings. Formats 26 and 27 of Example 8.3 contain strings of characters enclosed in apostrophes. Anything written in this manner in a format will be copied directly into the output line. It does not describe the form of output of other data but is itself the data to be printed. Such data must always be enclosed in apostrophes.

A blank included in quoted character strings is treated the same as any other character in the string. (Recall that blanks are ignored in most other places in FORTRAN statements.)

EXERCISE 8.1 Which of the following format statements are correct, and which contain syntax errors? Correct the syntax errors that you find.

a) 35   FORMAT (1X, 3X, I4, F12.2)   4 ✗

b)   FORMAT (4I, 2X, F12.1)   I4, 2 ✗ F 12. '

c) 16   FORMAT (F16.35X)   ? 5 ✗

d) 142 FORMAT (I2)

e) 127 FORMAT (A2, F3.3, X6, I2)

f) 128 FORMAT (A3, 'X = , I3)

g) 129 FORMAT (A3, 'X = , ' F3.1)

EXERCISE 8.2 Let K contain the value 1234, and ALPHA contain the value 555.4567. What would be printed by the statement

PRINT 500, K, ALPHA

for each of the following formats?

a) 500 FORMAT (1X, I4, F8.4)
b) 500 FORMAT ('0', I4///1X, F12.4)
c) 500 FORMAT (' K = ', I5/' ALPHA = ', F6.2)
d) 500 FORMAT ('1', 'K = ', I5, 10X, 'ALPHA = ', F10.3)
e) 500 FORMAT (6X, 'K IS ', I5,
   A   'ALPHA IS ', F10.4)

Your descriptions should be as precise as possible.

EXERCISE 8.3 One of the problems of using formats for describing data to be printed is that the width parameter w places an upper limit upon the number of characters that can be printed for a given variable. Writing a format specification therefore requires that we know the maximum absolute value that can be stored in a real or integer variable. In Example 8.3, we used the data descriptor I3 to describe the output field for the variable MONTHS. This would have caused an error if a loan period of more than 999 months were ever to be considered by the Loan Association. What are the maximum values of the variables AMOUNT, RATE, MPAYMT, and TPAYMT that can be processed without error by the statements shown in Fig. 8.1?

EXERCISE 8.4 Consider the variable definitions shown below.

SSN01	SSN02	SSN03	LAST	FIRST	HOURS	RATE	PAY
219	40	9677	DOG␣	HOT␣	40.00	4.50	180.00

Write a segment of a FORTRAN program (including declarations) to produce the following output:

```
Line 1    SOCIAL SECURITY NUMBER 219-40-9677
Line 2
Line 3    DOG, HOT
Line 4
Line 5    HOURS   RATE    PAY
Line 6    40.00   4.50    180.00
```

EXERCISE 8.5 Modify the formats given in Exercise 8.4 so that each line of output is printed centered on a line of 132 print positions.

8.3.2 Input Formats

The function of an input format is analogous to that of an output format. Output formats can be used to provide a line-by-line description of the external appearance of data that is to be printed in a meaningful and readable form. Input formats, on the other hand, can be used to describe the card-by-card appearance of information that is to be read into the computer from punched cards.

As was the case with format-free input, each execution of a read statement causes at least one new data card to be read. The data items in these cards are placed into the memory cells designated by the list portion of the input statement. For example, the statement

(i)   READ,   FIRST, LAST, IDEMPL, HOURS, RATE, OTHRS

```
'JOHN'  'CAGE'  37458   35.0 6.75   0.0
1 2 3 4 5 6 7 8 9 10 11 12 13 14 15 16 17 18 19 20 21 22 23 24 25 26 27 28 29 30 31 32 33 34 35 36 37 38 39 40 41 42 43 44 45 46 47 48 49          •••              80
```

will cause the card above to be read, and its contents to be placed in the named memory cells, as shown below.

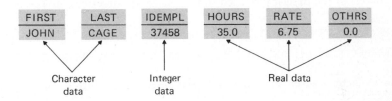

Using format-free input, the format analyzer must examine the card, determine the necessary descriptive information about the data (such as type, width, number of decimal digits, and position in the card), and pass this information to the data converter program.

Given a similar card,

the statements

(ii)   READ 25, FIRST, LAST, EMPLNO, HOURS, RATE, OTHRS

         25 FORMAT (1X, A4, 3X, A4, 2X, I5, 1X, F5.1, 1X, F4.2, 1X, F4.1)

will have precisely the same effect as statement (i). In contrast to (i), all descriptive information in (ii) has been provided by the programmer through the use of the format statement, and the apostrophes around JOHN and CAGE have been deleted.

In order to see why the statements (ii) have the same effect as the statement in (i), it is necessary to understand the meaning of the descriptors listed in format 25. There are four descriptors used in this format: the X descriptor, the I descriptor, the F descriptor, and the A descriptor. These descriptors are used to partition a card into a number of separate fields according to the following rules.

Descriptor	Form	Meaning
X	nX	Indicates that a field of n columns is to be skipped.
I	Iw	Indicates that a field of width w (w columns) is to be treated as an integer.
A	Aw	Indicates that a field of width w is to be treated as a character string.
F	Fw.d	Indicates that a field of width w is to be treated as a real number with d digits to the right of the decimal point.

The meanings of the descriptors used in format 25 are described in Table 8.3.

```
READ 25, FIRST, LAST, EMPLNO, HOURS, RATE, OTHRS

25 FORMAT (1X, A4, 3X, A4, 2X, I5, 1X, F5.1, 1X, F4.2, 1X, F4.1)
```

Table 8.3 Actions specified by sample format descriptor codes in an input format

Format descriptor	Corresponding variable list item	Meaning
1X	None	Skip the first column in the card.
A4	FIRST	Indicates that the next four columns in the card (2–5 in this case) are to be treated as a field containing a character string JOHN, which is to be stored in the variable FIRST.
3X	None	Skip the next three columns in the card (columns 6, 7, and 8).
A4	LAST	The next four columns in the card (9–12) are to be treated as a field containing a character string CAGE, which is to be stored in the variable LAST.
2X	None	Skip the next two columns in the card (columns 13, 14).
I5	EMPLNO	The next five card columns (15–19) are to be treated as containing a 5-digit integer 37458, to be stored in variable EMPLNO.
1X	None	Skip the next column in the card (column 20).
F5.1	HOURS	The next five card columns (21–25) are to be treated as containing a real number (35.0) with one digit (0) to the right of the decimal point. This number is to be stored in variable HOURS.
1X	None	Skip the next column in the card (column 26).
F4.2	RATE	The next four columns (27–30) are to be treated as containing a real number (6.75) with two digits (75) to the right of the decimal point. This number is to be stored in variable RATE.
1X	None	Skip the next column in the card (column 31).
F4.1	OTHRS	The next four columns (32–35) are to be treated as containing a real number (0.0), with one digit to the right of the decimal point. This number is to be stored in the variable OTHRS.

The following points should be noted in your analysis of the previous example.

Item 1. The format statement determines which card columns are to be skipped and which are to be read. It also describes the type and width (number of columns) of the information contained in each field to be read and the number of decimal places in each type real data item.

Item 2. As is the case with output formats, all descriptors in an input format except the slash should be separated from one another using a comma. The correspondence between variable names and data descriptors applies to input formats as well as to output formats.

Item 3. The field-width (w) information for each data descriptor immediately follows the type indication:

Aw: The A indicates that a string of characters is to be read into one
       memory cell; the w indicates the total width (or number of characters)
       contained in the string. Any legal FORTRAN character may appear
       in the string. If the length of the character string to be read is less
       than the character capacity, c, then most FORTRAN versions will
       store the string in the leftmost portion of the corresponding variable,
       and blanks will be padded on the right:

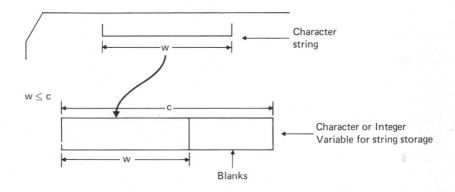

Iw: I indicates that a type integer value is to be read. The w indicates
       the width (the number of decimal digits) contained in the integer.

Fw.d: F indicates that a type real value is to be read. The w indicates the
       total width (including the sign and decimal point); the d indicates the
       number of decimal digits in the real number that are assumed to be
       to the right of the decimal point.

It is often desirable to print data being read into the computer immediately following the read statement. In such cases, it is tempting to try to use the same format statement for both the read and the print statements. This temptation should be avoided because there is no guarantee that the first character read from the card will be suitable for use as a carriage-control character. Unless you can be certain of the carriage-control character, a separate format, with the explicit specification of the carriage-control character, should be used for printing.

Example 8.10 If we punch the date 07-04-76 in columns 1–8 of a card and wish to read this date into the integer variables DATE1 and DATE2 on a computer with a character capacity of 6 (see Example 8.6), then the statements

```
       READ 62, DATE1, DATE2
    62 FORMAT (A6, A2)
```

will result in the storage of the 8-character date in the variables DATE1 and DATE2 exactly as shown in Example 8.6.

Item 4. The field-width specification n for the X descriptor indicates that a field of n columns is to be *skipped*. These columns need not contain blanks. They will be skipped regardless of what they contain.

Item 5. It is not necessary that the data occupying a character, integer, or real input field fill the entire field. However, if the data does not take up all of the columns in the field, the following guidelines should be followed:

a) Integer values must be punched in the rightmost portion of the field;

b) Real values may be punched anywhere in the field as long as the decimal point is included (if the decimal point is not punched, the number must be punched in the rightmost portion of the field, and the decimal point will be assumed to be placed as indicated by the d parameter of the format descriptor; if the decimal point is punched, then it overrides the d parameter in the Fw.d format descriptor);

c) Character-string values should be punched in the leftmost portion of the field.

The rules pertaining to reading reals without a decimal point and integers are important. If the numbers read do not fill the entire field width (indicated by w in the format descriptor) in the card, then extra blanks (if any) in the right portion of the field will be treated as zeros. Thus, if reals (punched without a decimal point) and integers are not punched right-adjusted, this will affect the values read, as shown in the next example.

Example 8.11

a)
```
    INTEGER  ME, YOU
    REAL HIM
          .
          .
          .
    READ 30, ME, YOU, HIM
 30 FORMAT (I5, I5, F4.1)
```

This statement sequence produces the result

ME	YOU	HIM
387	14000	350.0

because the blanks in columns 8, 9 and 10, and in columns 13 and 14 are treated as zeros.

b)   REAL X, Y, Z

        READ 672, X, Y, Z
    672 FORMAT (F4.1, F4.2, F4.2)
This yields the following:

X	Y	Z
−2.5	6.3	.623

In the first field, the decimal point is assumed to be between the 2 and the 5, according to the format descriptor F4.1. In the last field, the keypunched decimal point overrides the format descriptor.

Item 6. A single format statement may be used to describe the layout of more than one card. The format descriptor slash, /, can be used to mark the end of the description of one card, and the start of the description of a new card, as shown in the following example.

Example 8.12 The format
                562 FORMAT (A8/F10.4/I6, I4)
describes the appearance of three cards. The first card is described as containing one field that is to be treated as a character string of width 8. The second card is described as having a field of width 10 containing a real number. If the decimal point is not punched in this number, it will be assumed to be located to the left of the fourth decimal digit (counting from the right). The third card is described as containing two integer fields, the first of width 6 and the second of width 4.

EXERCISE 8.6 You are given a card with the following format:

Card columns	Contents	Sample data
1–11	Social Security Number	552–63–0179
12–31	Last name	BROWN
32–44	First name	JERRY
45	Middle initial	L
46–48	Blanks	
49–50	Age	38
51–54	Blanks	
55–59	Total years of education	23
60–63	Blanks	
64–66	Code of occupation	12
67–80	Blanks	

Assign variable names to the data in each of the nonblank fields. Give these names appropriate types, and write a read statement and appropriate format for reading such a card. Draw a picture of the card, and show how the sample data would be arranged in each field (left-adjusted, right-adjusted, and so on).

EXERCISE 8.7 Design a card layout for an account records program. For each account, the following information must appear on a single card.

Information	*Form*
Account number	a 6-digit integer
Name of firm	character string (maximum width of 25)
Previous accounts balance	a real number between -9999.99 and 9999.99
Charges for current month	a real number between 0.0 and 999.99
Credits for current month	a real number between 0.0 and 999.99
Total amount due	a real number between -999.99 and 999.99

You should ensure that there is at least one space between each of the six data items listed. Write the appropriate variable name declarations, read statement, and format statement for reading in the card that you designed.

EXERCISE 8.8 (continuation of 8.7): Suppose you decided that you did not want to have to keypunch the decimal points in the four real values in Exercise 8.7 and that you didn't want to bother punching zero entries (if any) for these four values. Will your FORTRAN statements for Exercise 8.7 still work? Why? If not, change them.

EXERCISE 8.9 You are given the following data declarations and read statement

```
REAL   ALPHA, BETA
INTEGER GAMMA, EPS
CHARACTER*4  DELTA         [or INTEGER DELTA]
          .
          .
          .
READ 30, ALPHA, GAMMA, DELTA, BETA, EPS
```

Write format 30 so that the information in the three cards shown below (on the left) will be read in as indicated below (on the right).

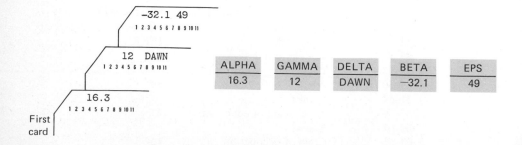

EXERCISE 8.10 (continuation of Exercise 8.9): How would you punch the data shown in Example 8.9 if format 30 appeared as shown below?

                30 FORMAT (F3.1, I2, A4, F4.1, 3X, I3)

8.3.3 Additional Format Features

Array Input and Output

The input and output of arrays using formats is handled in a similar manner as format-free array processing. Care must be taken, however, to ensure that there is a data descriptor in the format statement for each array element specified in a read or print list. This is especially important when an unsubscripted array name appears in a list, indicating that the entire array is involved in an input or output operation.

Example 8.13 Given the declaration

                        INTEGER K(4)

and the read statement

                        READ 10, K

the format statement 10 must have four data descriptors of type I.

In the next section we will explain a format feature which is an indispensable aid in specifying large or variable numbers of format descriptors.

Descriptor Repetition—List Control of Input and Output

It is often convenient to be able to specify the repetition of format descriptors, either individually or in groups. FORTRAN provides very simple facilities for indicating both types of repetition.

Example 8.14 Let W be a real array consisting of 200 elements. We wish to print the elements of W in columns, 10 per line. We can do this using the following print and format statements:

                    PRINT 62, W
                    62 FORMAT (20(1X, 10F12.3/))

As shown in the example, individual format data descriptors may be repeated simply by writing a positive integer constant *repeat count* in front of the descriptor (for example, 10F12.3). Space descriptors or groups of descriptors may be repeated by enclosing them in parentheses and placing the repeat count in front of the left parenthesis, as was done with 20(1X, ...). The portion of the format

                        1X, 10F12.3/

describes a single line consisting of ten real numbers, each of width 12, with three digits to the right of the decimal point. The slash / is used to mark the end of the line. Without the slash, it would be assumed that all 200 real elements of W are to be printed in F12.3 format on the same line. It is not likely that a printer exists that can accommodate such a long line—of 2,400 characters. The repeat count 20 will cause the line description 1X, 10F12.3/ to be repeated 20 times during the printing of the array W. Each time, the blank indicated by 1X will be used for carriage control resulting in single line spacing.

In addition to the explicit format repetition feature described in Example 8.14, FORTRAN also provides an automatic format repetition if the number of variables in an input or output list exceeds the number of I, F, or A data descriptiors. This feature can be extremely useful when arrays are involved in an input or output operation and the exact number of elements to be processed depends upon a value that is determined during program execution.

Example 8.15 Again let W be an array of 200 elements, and let N be an integer variable used to indicate the number of data items to be stored in W. If the value of N is punched on one data card (in I3 format), and the N values to be read into W are punched on successive cards (8 items per card in F10.3 format), then the statements

```
      READ 40, N
   40 FORMAT (I3)
      READ 50, (W(I), I = 1, N)
   50 FORMAT (8F10.3)
```

can be used to read in N and the items to be stored in W. The format (50) will work regardless of the size of N (as long as N is positive and does not exceed 200, of course). Each time the format is exhausted during the execution of the READ 50 statement, a new card will be read and the format will be repeated automatically. The format still describes a single card layout, but it will be repeated as often as necessary, until all N elements of W have been filled with data.

The statements

```
      PRINT 60
   60 FORMAT ('1THE DATA IN W IS')
      PRINT 70, (W(I), I = 1, N)
   70 FORMAT (1X, 12F10.3)
```

can be used to print a short heading at the top of a page, and then print the data in the array W, twelve items per line. Format 70 describes a single line of output, but the format will be repeated as often as necessary, until all N elements in W have been printed. Each time the format is repeated, a new line is started, and the blank specified by the 1X descriptor is used for carriage control.

The input or output list in a read or print statement completely determines the number of data items to be processed regardless of the number of data descriptors in the associated format statement. During processing, each item in the input or output list is matched with the corresponding data descriptor. If there are more data descriptors than items in the input or output list, any extra data descriptors are ignored (although left-over space descriptors, including quoted strings, are processed up to the next data descriptor). If there are more items than data descriptors, the format statement is repeated as many times as necessary until the list of input or output items is satisfied.

*The E Format Descriptor

Another method for reading real numbers is to use the E format descriptor (rather than F). A number to be read under E format must be punched in exponential notation, using the letter E. The E descriptor also contains a total-width specification, w, and a count of the number of decimal digits to the right of the decimal point, d. In this case, however, the width specification must not only include the sign and the decimal point (if present), but also the letter E and the sign and the value of the integer exponent. Thus in the E format descriptor, w should normally be larger than d + 5.

For example, the number

$$-6.245E-6$$

could be read using a format descriptor of E9.3. Here again, if the decimal point is punched in the card, it overrides the d parameter of the E descriptor.

The E format descriptor may also be used for printing real data. It is often convenient to use the E descriptor when the magnitude of a real number is not known, or is so large that the use of the F format descriptor is impractical. Real data printed using the E format descriptor will usually appear in the form

$$\pm 0.X_1 X_2 \ldots X_d E \pm \exp$$

where the X_i are the d most significant digits of the number (after rounding) and exp is the base 10 exponent. When the E descriptor is used for output, w must include the zero (if present), the two signs, the decimal point, the E, the width of the exponent as well as the d digits to the right of the decimal point. Therefore, w should always be greater than d + 7 when Ew.d is used in output (the exponent cannot exceed two digits in width).

Example 8.16:
```
          READ 37, INDEX, A, B, C
       37 FORMAT (I5, E10.3, E10.3, E10.3)
```
This read statement will cause the information in the following card

```
   36 6.107E+02   3.993E+4   -92.6E-3
 1 2 3 4 5 6 7 8 9 10 11 12 13 14 15 16 17 18 19 20 21 22 23 24 25 26 27 28 29 30 31 32 33 34 35 36 37 38 39 40 41 42 43 44
```

to be placed in the named variables as shown below:

INDEX	A	B	C
36	610.7	39930.0	-.0926

---

* This section may be omitted.

Additional Exercises

EXERCISE 8.11 Describe the information input by the following statements for the
card images shown. For b) and c), remember that multiple format descriptors are required when an array name (without a subscript) appears in the input list. (You may
assume that the variables involved in each operation have been declared consistent with
the type of the data that is punched.)

a)   READ 527, COLOR, ID, COST
    527 FORMAT (3X, A4, 5X, I5, 3X, F6.2)

```
      BLUE      37288      672.25
1 2 3 4 5 6 7 8 9 10 11 12 13 14 15 16 17 18 19 20 21 22 23 24 25 26 27 28 29 30 31 32 33
```

b)   READ 65, NAME, FLIGHT, AIRLIN, DATE
    65 FORMAT (A3, 3X, I3, A6, I2, 1X, I2, 1X, I2)
       Assume DATE is an array of size 3.

```
DEBBIE698UNITED06/13/75
1 2 3 4 5 6 7 8 9 10 11 12 13 14 15 16 17 18 19 20 21 22 23 24 25 26 27 28
```

c)   READ 2231, NAME, AB, RUNS, HITS, RBI, AVE
   2231 FORMAT (A4, A4, I3, I3, I3, I3, F5.3)
        Assume NAME is an array of size 2.

```
ELIEKOFF6241262140420.312
1 2 3 4 5 6 7 8 9 10 11 12 13 14 15 16 17 18 19 20 21 22 23 24 25 26 27 28 29 30 31 32 33 34 35 36 37 38
```

EXERCISE 8.12

a) Let WCF be an integer array of size 12 containing values ranging from $-130°F$
   to $+50°F$, and TEMP be an integer variable whose values range from $-50°$ to
   $+50°$. Write the PRINT and FORMAT statement to output the contents of TEMP
   and WCF in one row:

             TEMP   WCF(1)   WCF(2) . . . WCF(12)

   The value of TEMP should be separated from WCF(1) by at least five blanks, and
   the contents of the elements of WCF should be separated from one another by at
   least two blanks.

b) Suppose you wished to put your PRINT statement from part (a) into a loop in which TEMP ranges from -50 to $+50$ in increments of 5, and the contents of WCF are recomputed for each of these 21 values of TEMP. Would any changes be required in either your PRINT or your FORMAT statement? What would be the result of the execution of such a loop containing your PRINT statement?

c) Write one print and one format statement to display the following heading:

```
WIND CHILL FACTOR TABLE (DEGREES F)
TEMPERATURE                 WIND VELOCITY (MILES PER HOUR)
READING (DEG F)      0    5    10    15 . . .   60
```

EXERCISE 8.13 Write the print and format statements needed to produce the output described below. Start each new line described by your format with the descriptor 1X. This will indicate a blank for line control for these lines.

a) Let X be a real array of 20 elements each containing positive real numbers ranging in value from 0 to 99999.99. Print the contents of X, accurate to two decimal places, 4 elements per line.

b) Do the same as for part (a), but print the contents of the variable N (containing an integer ranging in value from 1 to 20) on one line, and then print the contents of the first N elements of the array X, four per line.

c) Let QUEUE be a 1000-element array of real numbers whose range of values is not easily determinable but is known to be very large. Print the contents of QUEUE, six per line, accurate to six decimal places.

d) Let ROOM and TEMP be 120-element arrays. ROOM contains the numbers of the rooms in a 9-story building (these range from 101 through 961). TEMP contains the temperatures of these rooms on a given day, accurate to one decimal place. Print two parallel columns of output, one containing all room numbers, and the other containing the temperature of each room.

8.4 COMMON PROGRAMMING ERRORS

There are a number of very common errors that can be made in working with formatted input and output. Some of the errors are described in the list below. Errors 1, 4, and 6 are not unique to formatted input and output but can just as easily be made in working with format-free input and output.

1. Type mismatches in the correspondence between variable names and format descriptors will result in execution-time errors. A diagnostic message may be printed, and many FORTRAN versions will immediately terminate execution of your program. Unintentional failure to provide a sufficient number of descriptors to accommodate an input or output variable list may have a number of possible disastrous effects, including subsequent type mismatches, or a format repetition that could result in a huge waste of computer paper.

2. If an integer is not right-justified in its card field, the blanks on the right may be interpreted as trailing zeros during input. This may change the value of the

input data. Similarly, embedded blanks in an integer field will be input as zeros. These comments also apply to real numbers that are punched without a decimal point.

3. If apostrophes in character strings are not carefully paired, the format descriptor list will not be interpreted correctly, and a compile-time syntax error will occur.

4. Attempting to print a number in a field that is too small will result in an execution-time error. The specified field will either be filled with asterisks, or will contain one asterisk followed by the least significant digits of the number. No other diagnostic will be printed.

5. Not providing sufficient data to satisfy the input-variable list will result in an execution-time error. The diagnostic message will indicate that there was insufficient input data or the end of the *input file* was reached.

6. Failure to provide a line-control character (1, +, 0, or blank) in an output format for the high-speed line-printer will produce unpredictable program output results. This failure may be noted by a warning diagnostic but usually will go undetected during compilation.

8.5 SUMMARY

A detailed description of the meaning and use of the more frequently used FORTRAN format descriptors has been given. The discussion was confined to punch-card input and line-printer output.

The descriptors X, I, F, E, A, /, and ' were described. The advantages and disadvantages of using formatted versus format-free input and output were discussed. The use of formatted input is advantageous only when the space used by apostrophes (for character-string input) or input item separators (blanks) is vital, or when data that has been prepunched or formatted must be read. In most cases, format-free input is highly recommended. It frees the data-deck keypuncher from having to punch each data item in specific field columns and from having to worry about the maximum field-width designation for all input variables. There is little or no sacrifice of flexibility in using format-free input in FORTRAN. Furthermore, there is considerable advantage in allowing the format analyzer to determine all descriptive information about the input data rather than forcing the programmer to do it himself.

Such is not the case with format-free output, however. No format-free output facility allows the degree of horizontal and vertical space control that can be achieved with formats. Formatted output permits direct control over the use of every print position of every line printed on a page. When such detailed control is necessary for the generation of precisely spaced output, formats must be used, and the programmer must provide all details of spacing, data types, and data widths.

In both input and output, the separation of situations that require the use of formats from those that do not is extremely beneficial. Formatted and format-free input and output can be intermixed, and you should take advantage of this to obtain, with the least amount of effort, the level of format descriptive precision required in a program.

The rules for using the space descriptors (nX, /, and ') and the data descriptors (Fw.d, Ew.d, Aw, and Iw) for both input and output were discussed. Not all of the intricacies of format processing were described, but the fundamental features of format usage have been presented.

Format features for line control and descriptor repetition were described. In the latter connection, we emphasized that the number of data items transmitted in an input or output operation was totally dependent upon the length of the variable-name list in the input or output statement, and not the number of data descriptors in the corresponding format. Associated with each name in the variable list should be a format descriptor of the correct type: A for character data, I for integers, and F or E for reals. If your version of FORTRAN does not have the character declaration facility, then it will permit the use of the A descriptor for reading or printing operations with integer variables (and perhaps real variables).

PROGRAMMING PROBLEMS

8.1 Write a program to read in a deck of cards containing the addresses of all the students in the class, and print each address on an envelope. You may assume that a "skip to the top of the next page" operation implies that the next envelope is put in position for the first line of an address.

Each address will consist of three lines. The information to be printed on the first line is in columns 1–20 of each input card. The second line of information is in columns 21–40, and the third line is contained in columns 41–80. For example:

MR. JOHN JONES	325 CEDAR ST.	PHILADELPHIA	PA. 19122
1 •••	20 21 •••	40 41 •••	60 61 ••• 80

8.2 Especially during the colder months of the year, weather forecasters frequently will inform us not only of the degrees F temperature (TEMP) reading at a given hour, but also of the wind-chill factor (WCF) at that time. This factor is used to indicate the relative degree of coldness that we are likely to experience if we are outside, and its calculation is based not only on the thermometer reading (TEMP), but also upon the velocity (V) of the wind at the time. Write a program to compute the wind-chill factor for temperatures ranging from $-50°$ to $+50°$ in increments of $5°$, and for wind velocities of from 5 to 60 miles per hour, also in increments of 5. Your output should appear similar to the following table.

```
WIND CHILL FACTOR TABLE (DEGREES F)
TEMPERATURE                          WIND VELOCITY (MILES PER HOUR)
READING (DEG F)              5 10 15 20 25 30 35 . . .
      -50
      -45
      -40
       .                                      .
       .                                      .
       .                                      .
       0
       5
       .
       .
       .
      20            . . .                  -16
       .
       .
       .
      50
```

The formula for computing the wind-chill factor is

$$WCF = 91.4 - (.486 + .305\sqrt{V} - .020V) \times (91.4 - TEMP)$$

Your answers should be rounded to the nearest whole degree. The WCF of -16 has been given as a test value. It is the WCF when TEMP is 20 degrees and V is 25. (You might wish to use the print and format statements from Exercise 8.12.)

8.3 (Base 2 addition, using the multiple-alternative decision structure) Write a program to read two 15-digit binary numbers (strings of 0's and 1's) into the arrays I and J (both of size 15), using the 15I1 format. Then compute the decimal (base 10) representation of these numbers, and print both the binary and decimal representations.

Next, compute the column-by-column sum of these two numbers, moving *right to left*. Use the variable CARRY to indicate whether or not a previous addition contained a CARRY. A zero value for CARRY should indicate that the previous addition had no carry; a one value should be used when a carry occurs. (Initially, CARRY is 0.) Store the column-by-column sum in the array SUMIJ of size 16. The value of each element SUMIJ $(L+1)$ and the next value of CARRY is determined by adding the values of elements I(L), J(L), and CARRY as shown next.

For all L from 15 to 1:

If only one of I(L), J(L), or CARRY is 1, then

SUMIJ$(L+1)$ is 1, and CARRY must be set to 0.

If all three of I(L), J(L), and CARRY are 1, then

SUMIJ$(L+1)$ is 1 and CARRY must be set to 1.

If any two of I(L), J(L), or CARRY are 1, then

SUMIJ$(L+1)$ is 0 and CARRY must be set to 1.

Otherwise, SUMIJ$(L+1)$ is 0 and CARRY must be set to 0.

This will define the values of SUMIJ(16) through SUMIJ(2), from I(15), J(15) through I(1) and J(1), respectively. SUMIJ(1) can be defined directly from CARRY, once the other "additions" are done. Compute the decimal representation of the SUM, and print the binary and decimal representations.

Test your program on the following strings:

```
I = 00000 00010 11011
J = 00000 01010 11110
I = 00000 00010 00110
J = 00000 00001 11101
I = 10001 00010 00100
J = 11100 11101 11001
```

Your output, for example, for the second set of data, might appear as follows:

```
    I = 00000 00010 00110      70
    J = 00000 00001 11101      61
SUMIJ =000000 00100 00011     131
```

Use functions and subroutines as needed, and draw a program system chart.

8.4 (Determining the collating sequence on your computer) On a single card, punch the following character string (starting in column 1):

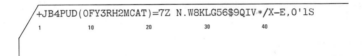

```
+JB4PUD(OFY3RH2MCAT)=7Z N.W8KLG56$9QIV*/X-E,O'1S
 1       10        20        30        40
```

There should be a total of 48 characters in your card. Write a program that will read these characters into an array CHARS, one character per array element, and sort them. Print the string before the sort and after. The result will tell you the exact collating sequence for these characters on the computer you are using. [*Hint.* Use the subroutine SORT shown in Chapter 7, Fig. 7.15, or an equivalent subroutine of your own to perform the sort. Remember to change the declarations in this subroutine: you will be using it to sort character strings and not real numbers. Use the format descriptor A1. *WARNING to instructors:* For desired results, these hints may require modification on some computers.]

8.5 (Questionnaire tabulation) Complete the questionnaire shown in Fig. 8.2, by filling in the blanks as instructed. Each blank shown has a number below it. These numbers indicate the columns of the card in which your responses will be keypunched for processing by the computer. Write a program which will read in the responses to the questionnaire for all students in your class and tabulate the results as follows:

Compute and print the total number of responses, and a breakdown according to class and according to age: less than 18; 18–22; over 22.

Compute and print the number of Yes and No answers to each of questions 4–10.

Label all output appropriately, and use formats for all input and output.

POLITICS AS USUAL—A PREFERENCE POLL

1. Name:
   $\overline{1}$ $\overline{2}$ $\overline{3}$ $\overline{4}$ $\overline{5}$ $\overline{6}$ $\overline{7}$ $\overline{8}$ $\overline{9}$ $\overline{10}$ $\overline{11}$ $\overline{12}$ $\quad$ $\overline{14}$ $\overline{15}$ $\overline{16}$ $\overline{17}$ $\overline{18}$ $\overline{19}$ $\overline{20}$ $\overline{21}$ $\quad$ $\overline{23}$
   $\qquad$ Last $\qquad\qquad\qquad\qquad$ First $\qquad\qquad\qquad$ M.I.

2. Academic year:
   $\overline{25}$ $\overline{26}$

   (Fr, So, Jr, Sr, Use 0 for other)

3. Age:
   $\overline{28}$ $\overline{29}$

   For items 4. through 10., answer yes (Y) or no (N).

4. Have you ever voted in a presidential election?
   $\overline{31}$

5. Do you think that most politicians are basically honest?
   $\overline{32}$

6. Do you think that most politicians are responsive to the needs of their constituents?
   $\overline{33}$

7. Do you think that the Federal government has taken steps sufficient to prevent another Watergate?
   $\overline{34}$

8. Have you ever taken a Political Science course?
   $\overline{35}$

9. Are you very interested in national politics?
   $\overline{36}$

10. Have you ever paid any Federal income taxes?
    $\overline{37}$

Fig. 8.2 Questionnaire for Problem 8.5.

Hint. Read the answers to questions 4 through 10 into an array (ANSWER) of size 7, using 7A1 format. To compare the responses to the letter Y, use a statement such as

```
IF (ANSWER(I) .EQ. Y) THEN
```

where Y is initialized using the statement

```
DATA Y /'Y'/
```

8.6 Write a program to print a table (with headings) for values of i, i^2, i^3, and $\sqrt{i}$ and $\sqrt[3]{i}$, where i is an integer that ranges from 1 to 100 in steps of 1. Use formats.

8.7 Write a program which, given the size of an angle in degrees, computes the size in radians, and then computes the sine, cosine, and tangent of the angle. The program should print a neatly arranged, appropriately labelled 5-column table for degrees, radians, sine, cosine, and tangent of angles from $-90°$ to $+90°$ in steps of $1°$. Note that the SIN, COS, and TAN functions all require real arguments in radians, and that tan $90°$ and tan $-90°$ are not mathematically defined. You should note undefined computations in a meaningful way in your table. Keep your answers accurate to 5 decimal places, and use the following formula for degrees-to-radians conversion:

Number of radians = 0.01745 * Number of degrees.

8.8 We can consider a single sheet of printer paper as a piece of graph paper containing a grid of 50 × 100—50 rows and 100 columns (with space left over).

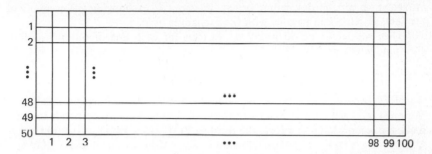

We can use this grid to plot a function f on x,y-axes, in much the same way as we would plot f on a piece of graph paper. To do this, we set up two 100-element real arrays, Y and XLIST, and a CHARACTER∗1 array LINE of size 100. (If you do not have the character-declaration facility, use the integer array LINE (100). LINE will be used to define 50 lines of 100 print positions each. Initially, LINE is to contain all blanks. Y will be used to store 100 values of f (one for each of 100 values of x along the x-axis). XLIST will be used to define the index of each x in the 100-item list used to compute $f(x)$. Thus, initially, XLIST$(i) = i$ for all values of i between 1 and 100. These indices will be used to indicate which of the 100 horizontal grids corresponds to each value of x for which $f(x)$ was computed.

Now proceed as shown in the following diagram.

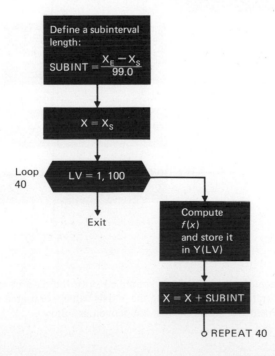

This will compute a value of f for each of the 100 values of X used. Each x index and the corresponding value $f(x)$ will be stored in corresponding elements of XLIST and Y, respectively.

Next we sort, in descending order, the array Y, exchanging the contents of the elements in XLIST in parallel with the exchanges in Y.

Then we determine 50 y-axis values (one for each line of output) as follows: Compute YINT as

$$YINT = \frac{Y(1) - Y(100)}{49.0}$$

where Y(1) now contains the largest value of f, and Y(100) contains the smallest value. We must print each of the 50 lines of the grid. The first line corresponds to the value Y(1), the second Y(1) $-$ YINT, the third to Y(1) $-$ 2 $*$ YINT, ..., and the 50th to Y(1) $-$ 49 $*$ YINT, or Y(100). (For example, if Y(1) $=$ 1000.0 and Y(100) $=$ 100., then the lines would correspond to

$$1000.00, 981.63, 693.26, \ldots, 136.74, 118.37, 100.00.$$

Note that 900./49. $=$ 18.37.)

We do this as follows.

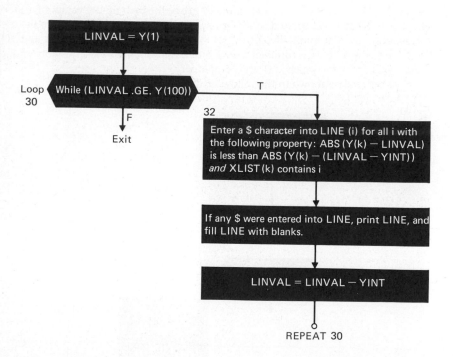

The implementation of box 32 is simplified since the data in array Y has been sorted. We illustrate by example, using the Y-axis values computed earlier. Suppose the first few elements in Y and XLIST are defined as follows.

XLIST(1)	XLIST(2)	XLIST(3)	XLIST(4)	XLIST(5)
37	53	36	54	35

Y(1)	Y(2)	Y(3)	Y(4)	Y(5)
996.3	992.2	987.3	980.1	970.5

The first time through loop 30, LINVAL will be equal to 1000. Since both 996.3 and 992.2 are closer in value to 1000. than to 981.63, a $ will be entered into LINE(37) and LINE(53). The next time through loop 30, LINVAL will be 981.63. Since 987.3 and 980.1 are closer to 981.63 than to 963.26, a $ will be placed in LINE(36) and LINE(54). Therefore, the test for the condition

        ABS (Y(k) − LINVAL) < ABS(Y(k)−(LINVAL − YINT))

must be made only upon consecutive elements in Y, starting where the previous test failed, and continuing until the test fails again.

Write a program to implement the above algorithms. Use subroutines whenever practicable. Test your program on the function

$$f(x) = (x - 1)^4/(x - 6),$$

where x ranges from -1 to $+6$ ($[-1,6]$). Provide a program system chart to describe the components of your system.

9.1 Introduction

9.2 Logical Expressions

9.3 Character-String Manipulation

9.4 Character Manipulation—
Sample Problems

9.5 Common Programming Errors

9.6 Summary
Programming Problems

USING LOGICAL AND CHARACTER-STRING DATA

9

9.1 INTRODUCTION

We have already introduced the character and logical data types in Chapter 4. The character and logical declarations have been explained, and we have seen examples of the use of integer variables for storing character strings (or Hollerith data) when the character declaration is not available.

We have also used both character and logical data in many of the programs we have written. Character-string constants have been used in print statements to provide labels for output data. Simple logical expressions have been used as conditions in WHILE loops and decision statements, and logical variables have been used as program flags.

In this chapter, we will describe the syntax of more complex logical expressions, and learn how to evaluate logical expressions containing the logical operators .AND., .OR., and .NOT.. We will also learn how to manipulate character strings in FORTRAN, and study some typical character-string manipulation problems.

9.2 LOGICAL EXPRESSIONS

9.2.1 Syntax Rules for Logical Expressions

Since the beginning of the text, we have been using logical expressions to specify the condition in IF statements, decision structures, and WHILE loops. In addition, we have used logical variables as program flags to signal to one program segment the results of the prior execution of another. Examples of statements we have used that involve logical expressions are listed below.

```
FOUND = .TRUE.
MORE = .FALSE.
IF (FOUND) THEN
WHILE (MORE) DO
IF (COUNTR .LE. NRITMS) GOTO 20
IF ((PINS(FIRST) + PINS(FIRST+1)) .EQ. 10) THEN
IF (GRADE .LT. 0.0 .OR. GRADE .GT. 100.0) THEN
```

As shown in these examples, logical expressions consist of logical constants (.TRUE. or .FALSE.), logical variables used by themselves, or arithmetic operands connected by the relational operators (.LT., .LE., .NE., .EQ., .GT., .GE.). As introduced in Chapter 5, compound logical expressions may also be formed from simple logical expressions using the logical operators .AND. and .OR.. In this chapter we will introduce a third logical operator, .NOT., which computes the complement of a logical value, and we will learn more about the use and evaluation of logical expressions and logical operators. We begin by presenting the formation rules for logical expressions.

Rules of Formation for Logical Expressions

1. A logical expression may be a logical constant (.TRUE., .FALSE.) or a logical variable.

2. A logical expression may be an expression of the form:

$$e_1 \quad \text{relop} \quad e_2$$

where e_1 and e_2 are both arithmetic expressions or both character variables, and relop is a relational operator (.GT., .GE., .LT., .LE., .EQ., .NE.).

3. A compound logical expression may be formed by using the logical operators in combination with simpler logical expressions which may be enclosed in parentheses. The binary logical operators .AND., .OR. may be used to write logical expressions of the form:

$$\text{lex}_1 \quad \text{.AND.} \quad \text{lex}_2$$

$$\text{lex}_1 \quad \text{.OR.} \quad \text{lex}_2$$

where lex_1, lex_2 are logical expressions.

The unary logical operator .NOT. may be used to write logical expressions of the form

$$\text{.NOT.} \quad \text{lex}$$

Example 9.1 Let X, Y, and Z be of type real, NAME and KEY are of type character, and FLAG is of type logical. The following are all legal logical expressions:

1. `(X .GT. 2.0) .AND. (Y .GT. 2.0)`
2. `(X + Y/Z) .LE. 3.5`
3. `.NOT.((X .GT. Y) .OR. (X .GT. Z))`
4. `.NOT. FLAG .OR. ((Y + Z) .LE. (X - Z))`
5. `.NOT. FLAG`
6. `NAME .NE. KEY`
7. `(0.0 .LT. X) .AND. (X .LT. 1.0)`
8. Any combination of (1) through (7) combined with the logical operators .AND. and .OR.—for example:

```
((X+Y/Z).LE. 3.5) .AND. (.NOT.((X .GT. Y) .OR. (X.GT.Z)))
        (2)                          (3)

(.NOT. FLAG) .OR. (NAME .NE. KEY)
      (5)              (6)
```

The major points illustrated in this example are:

a) Only two arithmetic expressions of the same type or two character variables may be used as operands with a relational operator. (Using logical operands with relational operators or mixing arithmetic and character data with the same relational operator is not permitted.)

b) Only logical expressions (having values .TRUE. or .FALSE.) may be used as operands with the logical operators.

Any deviation from these rules will result in the construction of illegal expressions, examples of which follow.

9. `FLAG .EQ. .TRUE.`

Logical expressions (including logical constants or variables) cannot be used as operands of a relational operator (the expression, FLAG, is sufficient here).

10. `X .GE. NAME`

Real and character data may not be mixed as operands of a relational operator.

11. `0.0 .LT. X .LT. 1.0`

The logical expression `0.0 .LT. X` cannot be used as an operand of the second relational operator .LT.. (See (7) above for the correct form of the condition "X lies between 0.0 and 1.0".)

12. `X .AND. Y .GT. 2.0`

Real variable X cannot be used as an operand of the logical operator .AND.. (See (1) above for the correct form of the condition "X and Y are both greater than 2.0".)

13. `.NOT. (X .GT. Y .OR. Z)`

Real variable Z cannot be an operand of the logical operator .OR..
(See (3) above for the correct form.)

14. `(X+Y/Z) .LE. (X * Z + Y .OR. FLAG)`

An arithmetic expression cannot be the operand of the logical operator .OR.. (If the right parenthesis following FLAG were inserted between Y and .OR., the logical expression would be legal.)

EXERCISE 9.1 Identify and correct the errors in the following illegal expressions. (Assume X, Y, Z are type real, I is type integer, and FLAG1, FLAG2 are type logical.)

a) `I .LT. 1 .AND. 2 .AND. 3`

b) `X .EQ. Y .OR. Z`

c) `X .OR. Y .LT. Z`

d) `FLAG1 .OR. (FLAG2 .EQ. .TRUE.)`

e) `(FLAG1 .EQ. FLAG2) .OR. (X .EQ. Y)`

9.2.2 Evaluating Logical Expressions

We know how to evaluate simple logical expressions involving only a relational operator. In order to evaluate compound logical expressions, we must understand the properties of the logical operators and learn something about the relative order of application of the different kinds of operators.

Figure 9.1 summarizes the properties of the logical operators. The second display (Fig. 9.2) describes the order in which the operators in a logical expression are evaluated. These rules are similar to the ones listed in Section 4.6.1, *Evaluation of Arithmetic Expressions*. Only Rule (b) has been expanded to include all operators.

Properties of the Logical Operators

All logical expressions have values of .TRUE. or .FALSE..

a) A logical expression involving the .AND. operator evaluates to .TRUE. only if both its operand expressions are .TRUE.. In all other cases, the expression evaluates to .FALSE..

b) A logical expression involving the .OR. operator evaluates to .TRUE. if either or both of its operand expressions are .TRUE.. If both operand expressions are .FALSE., the entire expression evaluates to .FALSE..

c) A logical expression involving the .NOT. operator evaluates to .TRUE. if its operand expression is .FALSE. and vice versa. (The .NOT. operator forms the complement of its operand expression.)

Fig. 9.1   Properties of logical operators.

Rules for Evaluation of Expressions

a) All parenthesized subexpressions must be evaluated first. Nested parenthesized subexpressions must be evaluated inside-out, with the innermost expression evaluated first.

b) Operators in the same subexpression are translated according to the following hierarchy.

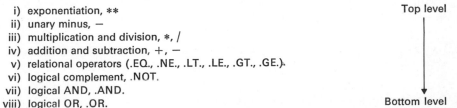

i) exponentiation, **		Top level
ii) unary minus, −		
iii) multiplication and division, *, /		
iv) addition and subtraction, +, −		
v) relational operators (.EQ., .NE., .LT., .LE., .GT., .GE.)		
vi) logical complement, .NOT.		
vii) logical AND, .AND.		
viii) logical OR, .OR.		Bottom level

c) Operators in the same subexpression at the same hierarchical level (such as .EQ. and .LT.) are translated left to right. (Exception: Some compilers evaluate A**B**C as A**(B**C).)

Fig. 9.2   Evaluation rules for expressions.

As is the case with arithmetic expressions, when in doubt it is best to use parentheses to clearly specify the desired grouping of operands and operators.

Example 9.2 The evaluation of a sample logical expression is given in Fig. 9.3. For each operator circle, the evaluation order number is shown on the left, and the dominant evaluation rule is shown on the right. The value of each subexpression is written as T or F on the line coming out of the operator circle. We will assume that X and Y are real variables containing 2.0 and 3.0, respectively:

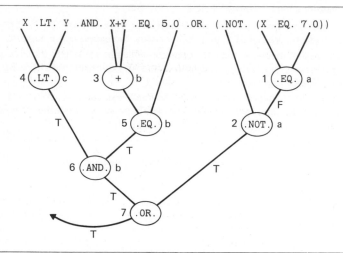

Fig. 9.3 Evaluation of a logical expression.

EXERCISE 9.2 Evaluate the above expression for X = 3.0, Y = 2.0; for X = 7.0, Y = 12.0.

EXERCISE 9.3 Evaluate all of the legal expressions in Example 9.1 for X = 1.0, Y = 2.5, Z = −1.0, FLAG = .TRUE., NAME = 'JOHN' and KEY = 'KING'.

9.2.3 Application of Logical Expressions

Logical expressions are most frequently used to specify conditions in WHILE loops or decision statements. They can also be used in assignment statements in which the variable on the left side of the assignment operator '=' is of type logical.

Example 9.3 In this example, use of the logical variables L1, L2, and L3 simplifies the listing of conditions in the multiple-alternative decision statement.

```
LOGICAL L1, L2, L3
READ, X, Y
PRINT, 'X = ', X, 'Y =   ', Y
L1 = (X .GT. Y)
L2 = (X .GT. 0.0)
L3 = (Y .GT. 0.0)
IF (L1 .AND. L3) THEN
    PRINT, 'X BIGGER THAN Y. BOTH POSITIVE'
ELSE IF (L1 .AND. L2) THEN
    PRINT, 'X BIGGER THAN Y. X-POSITIVE, Y-NEGATIVE OR ZERO'
ELSE IF (L1) THEN
    PRINT, 'X BIGGER THAN Y. X-NEGATIVE OR ZERO, Y-NEGATIVE'
ELSE
    PRINT, 'Y GREATER THAN OR EQUAL TO X'
ENDIF
STOP
END
```

L1, L2, and L3 are assigned the values .TRUE. or .FALSE., depending on the values of X, Y, prior to executing the multiple-alternative decision structure. Based on these values, one of the four messages in the multiple-alternative structure will be printed.

Another common use of logical variables is as a program flag to communicate to one program segment the results of the execution of another. This application has been illustrated earlier (Sections 4.4.2. and 6.5.4.)

Example 9.4 To provide another example of the use of logical variables as problem flags, we will rewrite the program for searching an array (Section 5.6) as a subroutine. The program flag, FOUND, is used to communicate the results of the search to the calling program.

We will use a WHILE loop to control the search process (rather than an indexed-DO, as shown in Section 5.6). This loop is repeated as long as the array has not been exhausted and the target item has not been located.

Data Table for Search Subroutine (SEARCH)

Input arguments

ARRAY: Represents the array being searched (integer)

SIZE: Represents the number of elements of ARRAY that are to be searched (integer)

ITEM: Represents the item to be located (integer)

Output arguments

FOUND: Represents a program flag; set to .TRUE. if the item is found; set to .FALSE. if the item is not found (logical)

WHERE: Represents the value of the subscript of the element of ARRAY that contains ITEM if it is found (integer)

Local program variables

NEXT: Subscript of the next element in ARRAY to be compared to ITEM

The flow diagram and subroutine for SEARCH are shown in Figs. 9.4 and 9.5, respectively.

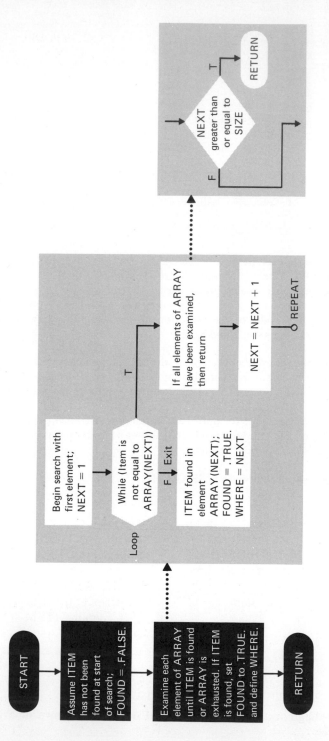

Fig. 9.4 Flow diagram for search subroutine (Example 9.4).

```
      SUBROUTINE SEARCH (ARRAY, SIZE, ITEM, FOUND, WHERE)
C
C SEARCH AN INTEGER ARRAY FOR A SPECIFIED DATA ITEM
C
C ARGUMENT DEFINITIONS
C   INPUT ARGUMENTS
C     ARRAY - ARRAY TO BE SEARCHED
C     SIZE - NUMBER OF ELEMENTS OF ARRAY TO BE EXAMINED
C     ITEM - ITEM TO BE FOUND
C   OUTPUT ARGUMENTS
C     FOUND - DEFINED TO BE TRUE IF ITEM FOUND - OTHERWISE FALSE
C     WHERE - SUBSCRIPT OF ARRAY ELEMENT CONTAINING ITEM (IF FOUND)
C
      INTEGER SIZE
      INTEGER ARRAY(SIZE), ITEM
      LOGICAL FOUND
      INTEGER WHERE
C
C LOCAL VARIABLES
      INTEGER NEXT
C
C INITIALIZE - ASSUME ITEM NOT FOUND - START SEARCH WITH FIRST ELEMENT
      FOUND = .FALSE.
      NEXT = 1
C
C SEARCH UNTIL ITEM FOUND (OR ARRAY IS EXHAUSTED)
      WHILE (ARRAY(NEXT) .NE. ITEM) DO
         IF (NEXT .GE. SIZE) RETURN
         NEXT = NEXT + 1
      ENDWHILE
C ITEM FOUND IN ARRAY(NEXT)
      FOUND = .TRUE.
      WHERE = NEXT
      RETURN
      END
```

Fig. 9.5 Search subroutine (Example 9.4).

EXERCISE 9.4 Add a fourth input argument, START, to subroutine SEARCH, to permit a calling program to indicate where the search is to begin. (In the current version of SEARCH, the search always begins with the first element of the array.) What changes must be made to the search subroutine shown in Fig. 9.5 to accommodate the change? Note that START must always be less than or equal to SIZE and larger than 0.

9.3 CHARACTER-STRING MANIPULATION

9.3.1 Introduction

So far, we have seen limited use of character data. Character variables (or integer variables used to store character data) have appeared in the list portion of data-initialization, read, and print statements. They also have been used for the storage of character strings which were later displayed to identify program output (see

Problem 4.1). Character constants have been used in print statements as labels for data printed by a program (see Problem 3.3, Fig. 3.12), and as column headings (see Problem 6.1, Fig. 6.9). Simple character assignment statements and comparisons were also illustrated in Chapter 4.

In the remainder of this chapter, we will provide numerous examples of how character strings can be manipulated in FORTRAN. We will assume that all character strings are stored in A1 format—one character per variable or array element. Unless memory space is limited, this is the most convenient form for storing character data that is to be manipulated (not just read and printed) by the computer.

We will begin with a discussion of reading and printing character strings using 80A1 format. We will then write two short subprograms for manipulating character strings stored in integer arrays, one character per array element. We will write a function (GETLEN) for determining the length of a character string, and a subroutine (COPY) for copying a string from one array to another. These subprograms will then be used in Section 9.4, as integral parts of the algorithms for solving three typical character-manipulation problems.

Since not all compilers provide the character declaration, we will continue our practice of writing declarations for character variables and arrays as:

```
        CHARACTER * n list              [or INTEGER list]
```

where n represents the length of the character variable. The manipulations performed will be the same regardless of whether integer or character variables are used for character-string storage. If your compiler provides specialized character string operations such as explicit substring specification and character string concatenation, we recommend that you study the material provided in the appendix on character-string manipulation instead of the rest of this chapter.

9.3.2 Character-String Reading and Printing in A1 Format

Figure 9.6 shows an example of a program that reads a character string into an array (TEXT), one character per array element, replaces each blank in the string with an asterisk, and then prints the new string.

The format descriptor 80A1 used in format 20 indicates that the input card is partitioned into 80 separate fields, each consisting of a character string of length one. Each of the 80 elements of the array TEXT will therefore be filled with a single character from the corresponding card column, as shown in Fig. 9.7.

The loop (10) in the program examines each element of the array TEXT and replaces all blanks with asterisks. The conditional statement involves the comparison of two variables, (TEXT(I) and BLANK), that contain character data. The dependent assignment statement redefines the value of TEXT(I) only if the characters stored in each of these variables are the same. Note that some compilers do not permit the use of apostrophes for character constant representation. For these compilers, the data initialization statement would appear as

```
        DATA BLANK, STAR/1H , 1H*/
```

```
          CHARACTER * 1 TEXT(80), BLANK, STAR        [or INTEGER...]
          DATA BLANK, STAR /' ', '*'/
C READ EACH SYMBOL INTO AN ELEMENT OF TEXT
          READ 20, TEXT
    20 FORMAT (80A1)
C REPLACE EACH BLANK WITH *
          DO 10 I = 1, 80
             IF (TEXT(I) .EQ. BLANK) TEXT(I) = STAR
    10 CONTINUE
          PRINT 21, TEXT
    21 FORMAT (1X, 80A1)
          STOP
          END
```

Fig. 9.6 Program to replace blanks with asterisks.

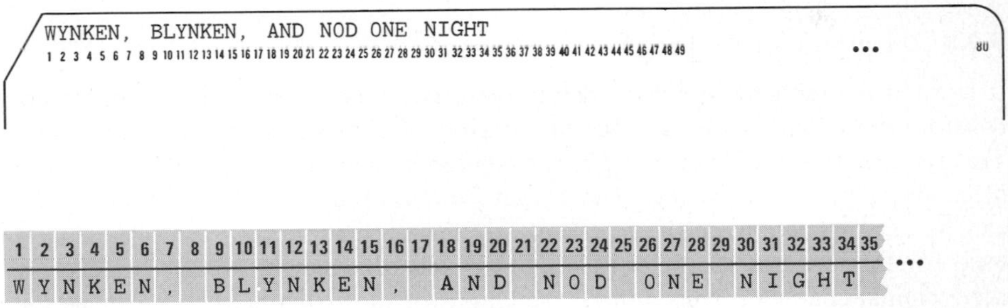

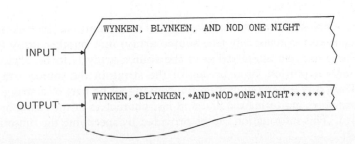

Array TEXT

Fig. 9.7 Reading character strings in 80A1 format.

The print statement is associated with format statement 21:

$$21 \quad \text{FORMAT (1X, 80A1)}$$

This format statement specifies that the characters in TEXT should be printed one after another across the next eighty print positions of the output line. The output line would be identical to the input data card except that all blanks would be replaced by asterisks:

The main points illustrated in the program in Fig. 9.6 are summarized in the following display.

---

1. Character strings may be read in and stored, one character per memory cell, by punching the characters in consecutive columns of a card, and reading the card using the 80A1 format descriptor. If the string is longer than 80 characters, a larger array and additional cards may be used. The 80A1 descriptor, as used in format 20, will be repeated as often as needed, to fill the entire list of variables indicated in the read statement. (See section 8.3.3.)

2. A character string stored one character per memory cell may be printed in consecutive positions of a print line using the A1 format descriptor.

9.3.3   Determining the Length of a String

It is often desirable to be able to determine the number of meaningful characters (without extra blanks on the end) of a string of characters read into an array. This requires that the input string be terminated by a special character that cannot otherwise appear in the string. The integer function (GETLEN) shown in Fig. 9.8 can be used to determine the length of any string in an array. A dollar sign is used for the terminal character (TRMCHR), but this can be changed easily. If the terminal character is not found, the length of the string is assumed to be the maximum, usually the size of the array containing the string.

EXERCISE 9.5 Compare the function GETLEN and the subroutine SEARCH, and explain the differences. Modify GETLEN to call the subroutine SEARCH to find the terminal character.

EXERCISE 9.6 Write a short program which will read in, one at a time, a collection of N cards each containing a character string terminated with a dollar sign, and print out the string and its length. Use the function GETLEN.

EXERCISE 9.7 In the function GETLEN (Fig. 9.8), if the terminal character is found, GETLEN is set equal to $I - 1$. Why shouldn't we have set GETLEN equal to I instead?

9.3.4   Copying Strings

One of the simplest and most often used string manipulations involves the copying of a string stored in one array (the source array) into another array (the target array). Sometimes an entire string in the source array is to be copied. Often, however, only a portion, or *substring*, of the string in the source array is to be copied. Thus, any general algorithm for copying all or part of a string would require information indicating the first and last characters of the string or substring to be copied. This information can be provided by specifying the subscripts of the

```
      INTEGER FUNCTION GETLEN (STRING, SIZE)
C
C DETERMINES THE LENGTH OF A STRING STORED IN AN ARRAY
C
C ARGUMENT DEFINITIONS (ALL ARE INPUT ARGUMENTS)
C     STRING - ARRAY CONTAINING THE CHARACTER STRING
C     SIZE - MAXIMUM POSSIBLE LENGTH OF THE STRING
      INTEGER SIZE
      CHARACTER * 1 STRING(SIZE)        [or INTEGER STRING(SIZE)]
C
C LOCAL VARIABLES - INCLUDING TERMINAL CHARACTER (TRMCHR)
      INTEGER I
      CHARACTER * 1 TRMCHR       [or INTEGER TRMCHR]
      DATA TRMCHR /'$'/
C
C SEARCH STRING FOR TERMINAL CHARACTER - SET GETLEN IF FOUND
      DO 10 I = 1, SIZE
         IF (STRING(I) .EQ. TRMCHR) THEN
            GETLEN = I - 1
            RETURN
         ENDIF
   10 CONTINUE
C CHARACTER NOT FOUND
      GETLEN = SIZE
      RETURN
      END
```

Fig. 9.8 Function for finding the length of a character string.

source array elements containing the first and last characters (the lower and upper bounds, respectively). It would also be necessary to indicate the subscript of the target array element in which the first character of the copied string is to be stored. These points are illustrated in Fig. 9.9. In this figure, the substring in elements 24 through 27 of the source array is copied into the target array beginning at element 90. Note that all elements in the target array preceding element 90, and following element 93, are not altered by this operation.

The steps required to actually perform the copy can be specified in a single indexed-DO loop. However, it is inadvisable to attempt such a copy before ensuring that a minimum number of constraints upon the upper and lower bounds of the source array and the target array have been satisfied. These minimal constraints are:

1. The lower bound for the source array should be positive and less than or equal to the upper bound.

2. The lower bound for the target array should be positive and less than or equal to the upper bound.

3. The bounds for the target array must fall within the range of allowable subscripts for that array. (If this constraint is not met, it is likely that valuable program information stored outside the array will be destroyed.)

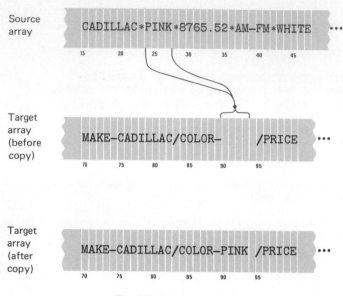

Fig. 9.9 The copy operation.

The copy steps and the steps required to validate the array bounds, are of sufficient length as to make a copy subroutine a virtual necessity.

Example 9.5 (A subroutine (COPY) to copy a string from one array to another)

Data Table for the Copy Subroutine (COPY):

Input arguments

SOURCE: Represents the array containing the string to be copied (character∗1)

SRFRST: Represents the subscript of the first element in SOURCE that is to be copied (integer)

SRLAST: Represents the subscript of the last element in SOURCE that is to be copied (integer)

TRGMAX: Represents the maximum number of elements that can be stored in TARGET (integer)

TRFRST: Represents the subscript of the element of TARGET into which the first SOURCE string character is copied (integer)

Output arguments

TARGET: Represents the array into which the source is to be copied (character∗1)

COUNT: Represents a count of the number of characters copied (integer)

Data Table (continued)

Local variables

LCV: Loop-control variable for copy
loop (integer)

TRLAST: Represents the subscript of
the element of TARGET into which
the last SOURCE string character
is copied (integer)

The flow diagram for subroutine COPY is given in Fig. 9.10. Before going on to this diagram, we suggest that you examine the following figure, so that you will have a clear understanding of the meaning of the parameters just defined.

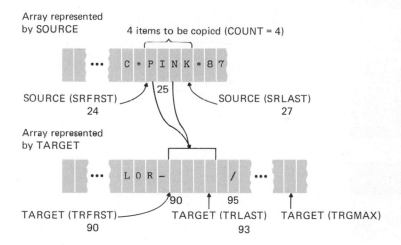

The copy subroutine is listed in Fig. 9.11. Note that this routine can be used to copy all or part of one array to another regardless of the array contents. You should verify for yourself that the boundary conditions are satisfied, i.e., that the first element of SOURCE is copied when LCV is one; and the last element is copied when LCV equals COUNT.

EXERCISE 9.8 In certain types of problems it may be necessary to move a substring in an array either to the right or to the left of its current position. For example, we may wish to alter the string in the array NEWS on the next page.

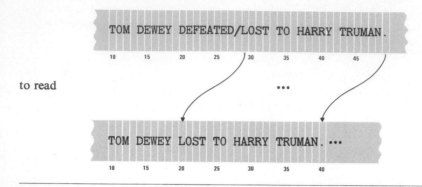

to read

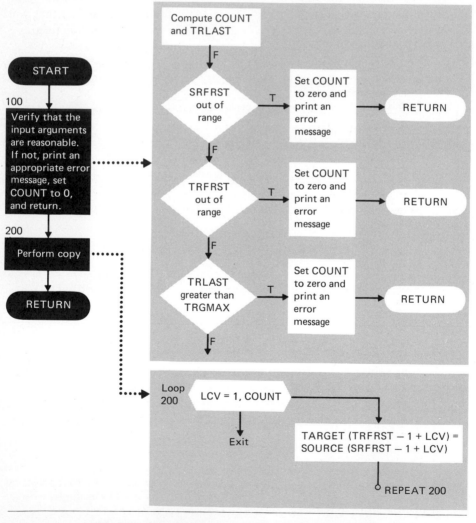

Fig. 9.10 Flow diagrams for subroutine COPY (Example 9.5).

```
            SUBROUTINE COPY(SOURCE,SRFRST,SRLAST,TARGET,TRGMAX,TRFRST,COUNT)
C
C COPY A STRING FROM ONE ARRAY TO ANOTHER
C
C ARGUMENTS DEFINITIONS
C    INPUT ARGUMENTS
C       SOURCE - ARRAY CONTAINING STRING TO BE COPIED
C       SRFRST - SUBSCRIPT OF FIRST ELEMENT TO BE COPIED
C       SRLAST - SUBSCRIPT OF LAST ELEMENT TO BE COPIED
C       TRGMAX - MAX NUMBER OF ITEMS THAT CAN BE PUT IN TARGET
C       TRFRST - SUBSCRIPT OF TARGET ELEMENT TO GET FIRST SOURCE ELEMENT
C
C    OUTPUT ARGUMENTS
C       TARGET - ARRAY TO WHICH STRING IS COPIED
C       COUNT - NUMBER OF CHARACTERS COPIED (ZERO IF COPY NOT PERFORMED)
C
        INTEGER TRGMAX, SRFRST, TRFRST, SRLAST, COUNT
        CHARACTER * 1 SOURCE(SRLAST), TARGET(TRGMAX)       [or INTEGER...]
C
C LOCAL VARIABLES
        INTEGER LCV, TRLAST
C
C INITIALIZE COUNT AND TRLAST
        COUNT = SRLAST - SRFRST + 1
        TRLAST = TRFRST + COUNT - 1
C VALIDATE INPUT PARAMETERS
        IF (SRFRST .LE. 0 .OR. SRFRST .GT. SRLAST) THEN
            PRINT, 'SOURCE ARRAY RANGE ERROR'
            PRINT, 'SRFRST = ', SRFRST, ' SRLAST = ', SRLAST
            COUNT = 0
            RETURN
        ELSE IF (TRFRST .LE. 0 .OR. TRFRST .GT. TRLAST) THEN
            PRINT, 'TARGET ARRAY RANGE ERROR'
            PRINT, 'TRFRST = ', TRFRST, ' TRLAST = ', TRLAST
            COUNT = 0
            RETURN
        ELSE IF (TRLAST .GT. TRGMAX) THEN
            PRINT, 'TARGET UPPER BOUND TOO LARGE '
            PRINT, 'TRLAST = ', TRLAST, ' TRGMAX = ', TRGMAX
            COUNT = 0
            RETURN
        ENDIF
C
C PERFORM COPY
        DO 200 LCV = 1, COUNT
            TARGET(TRFRST-1+LCV) = SOURCE(SRFRST-1+LCV)
    200 CONTINUE
        RETURN
        END
```

Fig. 9.11 Subroutine COPY, Example 9.5.

by shifting the substring in positions NEWS (29) through NEWS (49) to the left 9 positions. This left shift can be accomplished using the subroutine COPY:

```
CALL COPY (NEWS, 29, 49, NEWS, NEWSMX, 20, COUNT)
```

where the array NEWS serves as both the source and the target array.

    Unfortunately, this use of COPY may not work if the substring is to be moved to the right rather than the left. Why not? (See Example 6.3.) Write a subroutine REVCOP, patterned after COPY, that can be used to copy a string from one array to another and to move a substring in an array to the right of its current position. *Hint.* The copy operation will have to start at the rightmost position of the string to be copied. Use the FOR loop if it is available to you. Otherwise use the standard indexed-DO (be careful to use legal parameters) or the WHILE.

9.4 CHARACTER MANIPULATION—SAMPLE PROBLEMS

9.4.1 Introduction

In the previous sections, we wrote subprograms for several often-used character manipulation operations. We will now illustrate the application of these operations in the solution of three sample problems.

9.4.2 Scanning an Indexed-DO Header

The first problem involves scanning a character string and extracting designated substrings.

PROBLEM 9.1 We can consider the indexed-DO structure header statement as a character string of the form

$$\text{DO sn lcv} = \text{initval, endval, stepval}$$

For example,

```
DO 35 I = FIRST,LAST,5
```

One of the tasks of a compiler, in translating this statement, is to identify the symbols representing the loop parameters initval, endval, and stepval, and to store them in consecutive elements of three separate arrays (IVPAR, EVPAR, and STPAR, respectively) for later reference.

    For the example given, the result of this process is shown next.

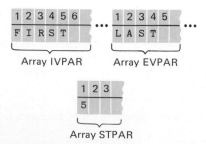

We will write a program to perform this substring separation.

DISCUSSION. The task of our program is to identify and copy each of the DO loop parameters initval, endval, and stepval into IVPAR, EVPAR, and STPAR, respectively.

The most difficult subtask for our program involves the location of the starting and ending positions of the loop parameter strings. This, in turn, requires the identification of the positions in the header string of the equal sign (POSEQL) and the first and second commas (POS1CM and POS2CM). If the second comma (and third parameter) in the header statement is missing, the character '1' is stored in STPAR. If either the equal sign or the first comma is missing, an error message is printed. For simplicity, we will assume that the DO statement header requires no continuation cards.

The positions of the equal sign and the commas can be determined using the subroutine SEARCH as modified in Exercise 9.4. Once these positions have been located, the substrings delimited by them (including all blanks) can be copied into IVPAR, EVPAR, and STPAR. These tasks can be carried out using the subroutine COPY (Example 9.5). The data table and flow diagrams for the program are shown in Figs. 9.12 and 9.13, respectively. The program appears in Fig. 9.14. ∎

Data Table for Indexed-DO Header Processor:

Input variables	*Program variables*	*Output variables*
HEADER (80): Array for storage of the indexed-DO header (character∗1)	EQUAL: The symbol '=' (character∗1) COMMA: The symbol ',' (character∗1) ONE: The symbol '1' (character∗1) POSEQL: Index of symbol '=' in HEADER (integer)	IVPAR (40): Array containing the initial-value parameter (character∗1)
LENGTH: The number of elements of HEADER used (integer)	POS1CM: Index of first comma in HEADER (integer) POS2CM: Index of second comma in HEADER (integer) FOUND: program flag. Set .TRUE. if desired symbol is located; otherwise, .FALSE. (logical)	EVPAR (40): Array containing the end-value parameter (character∗1)
	PARMAX: Maximum size of parameter arrays (integer program constant, 40) BEGIN: Index of first element of HEADER to be examined (integer) IVSIZE, EVSIZE, STSIZE: Number of characters in the initial-, end-, and step-value parameters, respectively. (Output from copy subroutine— all are integers)	STPAR (40): Array containing the step-value parameter (character∗1)

Subprograms Referenced:

COPY: (See Example 9.5 for argument definitions)
SEARCH: (See Example 9.4 for argument definitions)

Fig. 9.12   Data table for Problem 9.1.

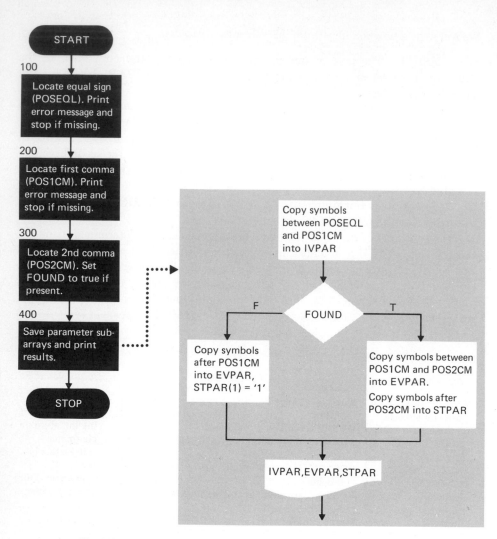

Fig. 9.13 Flow diagrams for indexed-DO header processor (Problem 9.1).

In this program, we are assuming that the length of the DO header is provided as input data, and need not be determined by scanning the header string actually read. The header is read using an 80A1 format, so that each of the characters in the 80 card columns will be stored in separate elements of the array HEADER. Note that the same format, 21, was used to print the four character strings HEADER, IVPAR, EVPAR, and STPAR. The repetition factor, 80, will accommodate the maximum number of characters to be printed from any of these arrays. The actual number of characters printed is determined by the list portion of each of the PRINT 21 statements. ∎

```
C SEPARATE AND SAVE PARAMETER SUBSTRINGS IN INDEXED-DO HEADER
      CHARACTER * 1 HEADER(80)                      [or INTEGER...]
      CHARACTER * 1 IVPAR(40), EVPAR(40), STPAR(40)  [or INTEGER...]
      CHARACTER * 1 COMMA, EQUAL, ONE               [or INTEGER...]
      INTEGER LENGTH, POSEQL, POS1CM, POS2CM, BEGIN, PARMAX
      INTEGER EVSIZE, STSIZE, IVSIZE
      LOGICAL FOUND
      DATA COMMA, EQUAL, ONE, PARMAX /',', '=', '1', 40/
C ENTER INPUT DATA
      READ, LENGTH
      READ 20, (HEADER(I), I = 1, LENGTH)
   20 FORMAT (80A1)
      PRINT, 'INDEXED-DO HEADER'
      PRINT 21, (HEADER(I), I = 1, LENGTH)
C SEARCH FOR EQUAL SIGN - SET POSEQL
      BEGIN = 1
      CALL SEARCH (HEADER, LENGTH, EQUAL, BEGIN, FOUND, POSEQL)
C PRINT ERROR MESSAGE IF EQUAL SIGN IS MISSING
      IF (.NOT. FOUND) THEN
          PRINT, 'EQUAL SIGN MISSING IN INDEXED-DO HEADER'
          STOP
      ENDIF
C SEARCH FOR FIRST COMMA AFTER EQUAL SIGN
      BEGIN = POSEQL + 1
      CALL SEARCH (HEADER, LENGTH, COMMA, BEGIN, FOUND, POS1CM)
C PRINT ERROR MESSAGE IF FIRST COMMA MISSING
      IF (.NOT. FOUND) THEN
          PRINT, 'COMMA MISSING IN INDEXED-DO HEADER'
          STOP
      ENDIF
C SEARCH FOR SECOND COMMA
      BEGIN = POS1CM + 1
      CALL SEARCH (HEADER, LENGTH, COMMA, BEGIN, FOUND, POS2CM)
C SAVE SUBARRAYS - FORM IVPAR
      CALL COPY (HEADER,POSEQL+1,POS1CM-1,IVPAR,PARMAX,1,IVSIZE)
C CHECK IF STEP VALUE IS SPECIFIED - FORM EVPAR AND STPAR
      IF (FOUND) THEN
          CALL COPY (HEADER,POS1CM+1,POS2CM-1,EVPAR,PARMAX,1,EVSIZE)
          CALL COPY (HEADER,POS2CM+1,LENGTH,STPAR,PARMAX,1,STSIZE)
      ELSE
          CALL COPY (HEADER,POS1CM+1,LENGTH,EVPAR,PARMAX,1,EVSIZE)
          STPAR(1) = ONE
          STSIZE = 1
      ENDIF
C PRINT RESULTS
      PRINT, 'INITIAL VALUE PARAMETER'
      PRINT 21, (IVPAR(I), I = 1, IVSIZE)
      PRINT, 'END VALUE PARAMETER'
      PRINT 21, (EVPAR(I), I = 1, EVSIZE)
      PRINT, 'STEP VALUE PARAMETER'
      PRINT 21, (STPAR(I), I = 1, STSIZE)
   21 FORMAT (1X, 80A1)
      STOP
      END
```

Fig. 9.14 Main program for Problem 9.1.

EXERCISE 9.9 Rewrite the "ENTER INPUT DATA" portion of the program in Fig. 9.14, assuming that the length of the header is not given, but that the header is terminated by a dollar sign if it does not fill the entire card.

9.4.3 Searching for a Substring

In the solution of Problem 9.1, there were three separate instances in which a character string (the indexed-DO header) was searched for a single character (an equal sign or a comma). In many character-string manipulation problems, it is necessary to search a character string for a substring of arbitrary length (between 1 and the length of the original string). As you may have already surmised, we can generalize the SEARCH subroutine (Example 9.4) to perform this task.

PROBLEM 9.2 Write a subroutine (FNDSTR) to find a specified substring of characters in an array containing a string stored one character per element. If the substring is found, FNDSTR should return as output the subscript of the array element which contains the first (leftmost) character of the substring.

DISCUSSION. The data table for this subroutine is shown in Fig. 9.15.

Data Table for the "Find String" Subroutine (FNDSTR)

Input arguments

ARRAY: Represents the array used to store the character string to be searched (character*1)

SIZE: Represents the number of elements of ARRAY that are to be searched (integer)

SUBSTR: Represents the array used to store the string to be found (character*1)

SUBLEN: Represents the length of SUBSTR (integer)

START: Represents the position in ARRAY where the search is to begin (integer)

Output arguments

FOUND: Represents a flag used to indicate whether or not SUBSTR is found. FOUND is set to true if SUBSTR is found; otherwise, FOUND is set to FALSE (logical)

WHERE: Represents the value of the subscript of the element of ARRAY in which the substring starts, if it is found (integer)

Local program variables

NEXT: Position of first character of the next substring in ARRAY that is to be compared to SUBSTR (integer)

Fig. 9.15 Data table for FNDSTR subroutine.

This table is quite similar to the data table for Example 9.4. However, now a substring of characters (represented by SUBSTR), rather than a single item, is to be searched for in ARRAY. We must, therefore, add to the data table an additional input argument (SUBLEN) to indicate the length of the substring to be found.

The flow diagram for this problem is virtually identical to the diagram for Example 9.4 (see Fig. 9.4), and is shown in Fig. 9.16.

Unfortunately, the task of determining whether or not the specified substring appears in ARRAY is more difficult than the task for a single character. One possible search technique is outlined next.

1. Beginning with the substring at element ARRAY (START), we must compare each substring of length SUBLEN in ARRAY to the string in SUBSTR. This process is depicted in Fig. 9.17, with SUBLEN assumed to be 4. Here, a total of six string comparisons are made, before the string 'BABY' is matched.

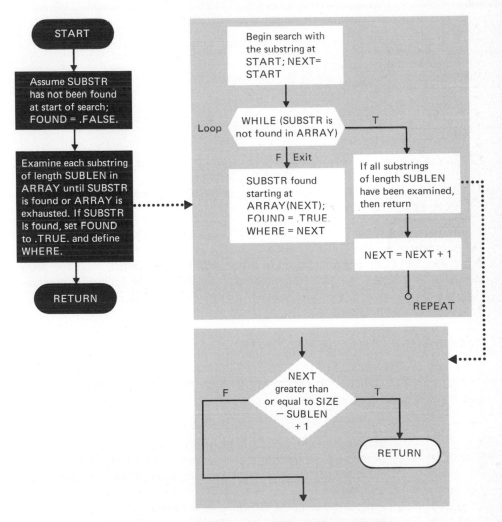

Fig. 9.16 Flow diagrams for the character-string search problem.

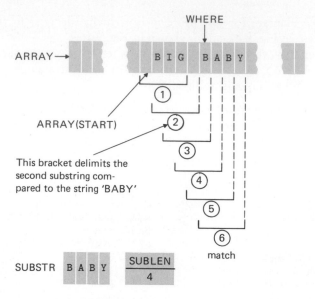

Fig. 9.17 Searching an array for a substring.

2. If the comparison is successful at any point, we can set FOUND equal to
   true, and define the value of WHERE, as shown in Fig. 9.16. If none of the
   substrings in ARRAY match the string in SUBSTR, then FOUND is defined
   to be false, and WHERE is left undefined.

We can use a logical function, MATCH, to compare a substring in ARRAY to
the contents of SUBSTR. If a match is found, MATCH returns the value true;
otherwise MATCH returns the value false. MATCH is called once for each
substring in ARRAY that is to be compared to SUBSTR. The following information must be added to the data table for FNDSTR in order to complete the
definition of the function MATCH.

Additional Data Table Entries for FNDSTR:

Subprograms referenced. MATCH (logical function): used to compare a substring in an array (first argument) to see if it matches an equal-length string in
another array (fourth argument)

Argument	Definition
1	array containing substring to be tested for a match
2	number of elements in the array passed as argument 1
3	subscript of first element to be compared in the array passed as argument 1
4	array containing the string to be matched
5	length of the string to be matched

```
      SUBROUTINE FNDSTR (ARRAY,SIZE,SUBSTR,SUBLEN,START,FOUND,WHERE)
C
C SEARCHES AN ARRAY FOR A SUBSTRING
C
C ARGUMENT DEFINITIONS
C   INPUT ARGUMENTS
C     ARRAY - ARRAY TO BE SEARCHED
C     SIZE - NO. OF ELEMENTS OF ARRAY TO BE EXAMINED
C     SUBSTR - ARRAY CONTAINING STRING TO BE FOUND
C     SUBLEN - LENGTH OF THE STRING IN SUBSTR
C     START - SUBSCRIPT OF ARRAY ELEMENT AT WHICH SEARCH STARTS
C   OUTPUT ARGUMENTS
C     FOUND - DEFINED TO BE TRUE IF SUBSTRING IS FOUND. OTHERWISE,
C             FALSE.
C     WHERE - SUBSCRIPT OF ARRAY ELEMENT CONTAINING FIRST
C             CHARACTER OF SUBSTRING (IF FOUND).
C
      INTEGER SIZE, SUBLEN, START, WHERE
      CHARACTER * 1 ARRAY(SIZE), SUBSTR(SUBLEN)        [or INTEGER...]
      LOGICAL FOUND
C FUNCTIONS REFERENCED
      LOGICAL MATCH
C
C LOCAL VARIABLES
      INTEGER NEXT
C
C VALIDATE START
      IF (START .LE. 0 .OR. (START + SUBLEN - 1) .GT. SIZE) THEN
         PRINT, 'SEARCH START ARGUMENT ', START, ' IS INVALID.'
         FOUND = .FALSE.
         RETURN
      ENDIF
C
C INITIALIZE - ASSUME ITEM NOT FOUND. BEGIN SEARCH AT START
      FOUND = .FALSE.
      NEXT = START
C
C SEARCH AS LONG AS SUBSTRING NOT FOUND AND ARRAY NOT EXHAUSTED
      WHILE (.NOT. MATCH (ARRAY, SIZE, NEXT, SUBSTR, SUBLEN)) DO
C        RETURN WITH FOUND SET FALSE IF ARRAY EXHAUSTED
         IF (NEXT .GE. SIZE - SUBLEN + 1) RETURN
         NEXT = NEXT + 1
      ENDWHILE
C SUBSTRING FOUND STARTING AT ARRAY(NEXT)
      FOUND = .TRUE.
      WHERE = NEXT
      RETURN
      END
```

Fig. 9.18 Subroutine for finding a string (Problem 9.2).

Given this definition of the function MATCH, the subroutine FNDSTR now can be written directly from the flow diagram. (See Fig. 9.18.)

EXERCISE 9.10 Given the variables and arrays used in Problem 9.2, the statements required to compare the contents of SUBSTR to a substring in ARRAY (beginning at ARRAY(NEXT)) are as follows:

```
C ASSUME NO MATCH
      MATCH = .FALSE.
C COMPARE EACH CHARACTER IN SUBSTR TO CORRESPONDING CHARACTER IN ARRAY
C RETURN IMMEDIATELY IF THERE IS A MISMATCH
      DO 10 J = 1, SUBLEN
          IF (SUBSTR(J) .NE. ARRAY(NEXT+J-1)) RETURN
   10 CONTINUE
C MATCH SUCCESSFUL
      MATCH = .TRUE.
      RETURN
```

Using these statements as the function body, complete the specification of the function MATCH. Be sure your argument list and definitions are consistent with the call to MATCH in subroutine FNDSTR (Fig. 9.18). Insert all appropriate comments and make certain that $NEXT + SUBLEN - 1$ is less than or equal to SIZE.

EXERCISE 9.11 Why is NEXT compared to $SIZE - SUBLEN + 1$ in FNDSTR rather than SIZE in order to determine if ARRAY has been completely searched?

9.4.4 Text Editing Problem

PROBLEM 9.3 There are many applications for which it is useful to have a computerized text-editing program. For example, if you are preparing a laboratory report (or a textbook), it would be convenient to edit or modify sections of the report (improve sentence and paragraph structure, change words, correct spelling mistakes, etc.) at a computer terminal and then have a fresh, clean copy of the text typed at the terminal without erasures or mistakes.

A Text Editor System is a relatively sophisticated system of subprograms which can be used to instruct the computer to perform virtually any kind of text alteration you might think of. At the heart of such a system is a subprogram that replaces one character substring in the text with another substring. As an example, consider the following sentence prepared by an overzealous member of the Addison-Wesley advertising group.

```
'THE BOOK BY FRIEDMEN AND KOFFMAN
     IN FRACTURED PROGRAMING IS GRREAT?'
```

To correct this sentence we would want to specify the following edit operations:

1. Replace 'MEN' with 'MAN'
2. Replace 'IN' with 'ON'
3. Replace 'FRAC' with 'STRUC'
4. Replace 'AM' with 'AMM'
5. Replace 'RR' with 'R'
6. Replace '?' with '!'

The result is now at least grammatically correct.

```
'THE BOOK BY FRIEDMAN AND KOFFMAN
 ON STRUCTURED PROGRAMMING IS GREAT!'
```

We will write the text replacement program module as a subroutine called REPLAC. The argument portion of the data table is shown next.

Data Table for Subroutine REPLAC:

Input arguments

OLD (OLDLEN): Substring to be removed (character * 1)
OLDLEN: Length of OLD (integer)
NEW (NEWLEN): Substring to be inserted (character * 1)
NEWLEN: Length of NEW (integer)

Since many of the subprograms in the Text Editing System will be referencing the character string stored in TEXT, we will assume that TEXT is in a common block. Two other data items, CURLEN and MAXLEN, defined as shown below, will be stored in a second common block. (The reason for two is that some compilers do not permit data declared as type character to be in the same common block as data of other types.)

Additional Data-Table Entries for REPLAC:

Common blocks used:

Name	Description
TXTBLK	TEXT (1000): The text string (character * 1)
LENBLK	CURLEN: Current length of the string in TEXT (integer)
	MAXLEN: Maximum possible length of the string in TEXT (integer)

MAXLEN is a Text Editor System constant which is defined to be equal to the maximum length of the text string (1000). CURLEN would be defined when the string to be edited is first placed in TEXT (probably in the main program), and would be re-defined each time a change was made to TEXT. (Remember that some compilers do not permit variables in common blocks to be initialized in a main program or subprogram using a data statement.)

The initial task to be performed by REPLAC is to locate the first occurrence of the string to be replaced (OLD) in TEXT (only the first occurrence will be replaced). This can be accomplished using the subroutine FNDSTR from Section 9.4.3. Remember, FNDSTR was generalized to locate the first-character position of any substring in another string. We can now take advantage of this generalization in writing REPLAC.

The flow diagrams are shown in Fig. 9.19; additional data-table entries required for REPLAC are given on the next page.

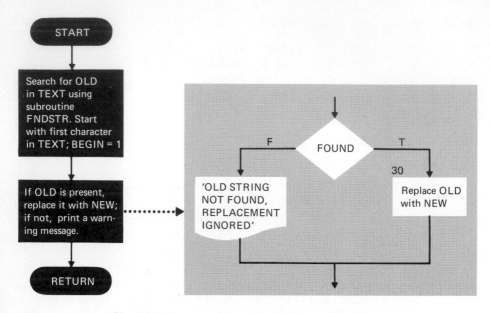

Fig. 9.19   Flow diagrams for string replace problem (9.3).

Additional Data Table Entries for REPLAC

Local program variables

BEGIN: Input argument in call of FNDSTR (program constant, integer 1—all searches will start in position 1 of TEXT)

FOUND: Output argument in call of FNDSTR; FOUND will be true if OLD is in TEXT; otherwise, FOUND will be false (logical)

POSOLD: Output argument in call of FNDSTR; POSOLD contains the position of the first character of OLD in TEXT if OLD is found (integer)

Subprograms referenced: FNDSTR: (See Problem 9.2 for argument definitions.)

Before we can write the subroutine, a further refinement of step 30 is needed. If NEWLEN is larger than OLDLEN, it is possible that the length, REVLEN, of the revised version of TEXT would exceed MAXLEN.   In this case, an error message should be printed and the replacement operation ignored; otherwise, a new version of TEXT can be made by using the COPY subroutine to *concatenate* (join together) the substring in TEXT that precedes OLD (the *head*), the replacement string (NEW), and the substring in TEXT following OLD (the *tail*). The refinement of step 30 is shown in Fig. 9.20.   The additional data table entries are given below.

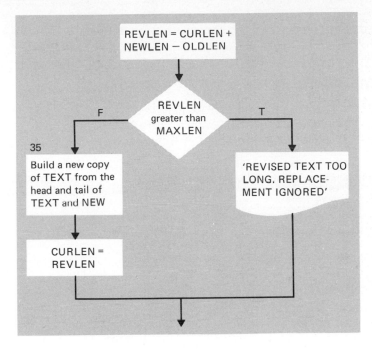

Fig. 9.20 Refinement of Step 30 in subroutine REPLAC.

Additional Data Table Entries for REPLAC:

Local program variables

TAIL (1000):   Output argument in call of COPY; TAIL will contain the section of TEXT which follows OLD (character * 1)

TAILEN: Output argument in call of COPY; TAILEN will contain the length of TAIL (integer)

REVLEN: Length of revised TEXT (integer)

Subprograms referenced: COPY: (See Example 9.5 for argument definitions.)

    In forming the new version of TEXT, the first step is to save the tail of TEXT in TAIL. Next, the string in NEW is copied into TEXT, starting at the array element where OLD was located (subscript POSOLD). Finally, TAIL is copied back into TEXT starting at the first element following NEW (subscript POSOLD + NEWLEN). Since the characters preceding OLD in TEXT are not changed, the head of TEXT remains intact.

    The subroutine REPLAC can now be written as in Fig. 9.21. ∎

```
        SUBROUTINE REPLAC (OLD, OLDLEN, NEW, NEWLEN)
C
C REPLACE SUBSTRING OLD WITH STRING NEW
C
C ARGUMENT DEFINITIONS (ALL ARE INPUT ARGUMENTS)
C   OLD - ARRAY CONTAINING STRING TO BE REPLACED
C   OLDLEN - LENGTH OF STRING TO BE REPLACED
C   NEW - ARRAY CONTAINING REPLACEMENT STRING
C   NEWLEN - LENGTH OF REPLACEMENT STRING
C
        INTEGER OLDLEN, NEWLEN
        CHARACTER * 1 OLD(OLDLEN), NEW(NEWLEN)          [or INTEGER...]
C
C COMMON BLOCKS
        COMMON /TXTBLK/ TEXT(1000)
        CHARACTER * 1 TEXT          [or INTEGER TEXT]
        COMMON /LENBLK/ CURLEN, MAXLEN
        INTEGER CURLEN, MAXLEN
C
C LOCAL VARIABLES
        INTEGER BEGIN, POSOLD, REVLEN
        INTEGER TAILEN
        LOGICAL FOUND
        CHARACTER * 1 TAIL(1000)          [or INTEGER TAIL(1000)]
C
C SEE IF OLD IS IN TEXT. IF SO, REPLACE IT. IF NOT, IGNORE REQUEST
C
        BEGIN = 1
        CALL FNDSTR (TEXT, CURLEN, OLD, OLDLEN, BEGIN, FOUND, POSOLD)
        IF (FOUND) THEN
C           CHECK REVISED LENGTH BEFORE REPLACEMENT
            REVLEN = CURLEN + NEWLEN - OLDLEN
            IF (REVLEN .GT. MAXLEN) THEN
                PRINT, 'REVISED TEXT TOO LONG. REPLACEMENT IGNORED'
            ELSE
C           FORM NEW VERSION OF TEXT - UPDATE CURLEN
C           SAVE THE TAIL OF TEXT
                CALL COPY (TEXT,POSOLD+OLDLEN,CURLEN,TAIL,MAXLEN,1,TAILEN)
C           COPY NEW INTO TEXT WHERE OLD WAS
                CALL COPY (NEW, 1, NEWLEN, TEXT, MAXLEN, POSOLD, NEWLEN)
C           COPY TAIL BACK INTO TEXT FOLLOWING NEW
                CALL COPY (TAIL,1,TAILEN,TEXT,MAXLEN,POSOLD+NEWLEN,TAILEN)
                CURLEN = REVLEN
            ENDIF
        ELSE
            PRINT, 'OLD STRING NOT FOUND, REPLACEMENT IGNORED'
        ENDIF
        RETURN
        END
```

Fig. 9.21 The subroutine for Problem 9.3.

EXERCISE 9.12 The algorithm for the replace subroutine makes no provision for either of the following two situations:

1. the length of the new string (NEWLEN) is equal to the length of the old string (OLDLEN);
2. the length of the tail is zero—that is, the last element of the string to be replaced is TEXT (CURLEN), the last character in the text.

In both cases, all that is required to build a revised version of the text is to copy the new string into TEXT in place of the old string. Nothing need be done with the tail of TEXT. (In case 1, the tail does not have to be moved, and in case 2, there is no tail). Modify the subroutine in Fig. 9.21 to test for these two situations, and take the appropriate action.

EXERCISE 9.13 The algorithm used in Problem 9.3 requires the use of a local array (TAIL) of 1000 elements for the temporary storage of the tail of TEXT. If the subroutine REVCOP (see Exercise 9.8) were used in this algorithm, this array could be eliminated. Discuss the reasons for this: why is TAIL needed in the current algorithm, and how can the use of REVCOP eliminate the need for TAIL? Rewrite the subroutine REPLAC (step 35 *only*) using REVCOP and COPY.

EXERCISE 9.14 Should the common blocks TXTBLK and LENBLK be declared in FNDSTR or COPY?

EXERCISE 9.15 The REPLAC subroutine shown in Fig. 9.22 always begins its search for OLD at position one of TEXT. In many instances, it is useful to be able to provide REPLAC with an additional piece of information—namely, the position in TEXT where the search is to begin. Such flexibility can be provided in REPLAC simply by changing BEGIN from a local variable to an argument. By providing REPLAC with a starting point that is closer to the sequence of characters to be replaced, we can cut down on the amount of searching that needs to be done. We may also be able to reduce the amount of *contextual information* required in order to have the correct replacement done.

For example, if BEGIN is the fifth argument in REPLAC, then the statement

```
CALL REPLAC (OLD, 1, NEW, 1, 5)
```

where OLD and NEW contain the letters 'E' and 'A' respectively, could be used to correct the spelling error in 'FRIEDMAN' instead of

```
CALL REPLAC (OLD, 3, NEW, 3)
```

where OLD and NEW are shown below:

The original contextual information 'M' and 'N' was needed to prevent the first occurrence of 'E' in the array TEXT from being changed to 'A'.

For each of the editing operations listed below, write two call statements to REPLAC. Write the first call statement using four arguments, and the second call using five arguments, with BEGIN as the fifth. Show the character strings stored in the arrays NEW and OLD for each call. In determining the value of the fifth argument, assume any prior replacements in the list have been performed.

a) replace 'FRAC' with 'STRUC'

b) replace the 'O' in 'ON' with an 'I'

c) replace 'BOOK' by 'TEXT'

d) insert an extra 'M' into 'PROGRAMING'

e) delete an 'R' from 'GRREAT'

EXERCISE 9.16   From Exercise 9.15 (parts (d) and (e)) it is clear that REPLAC can be used to perform both insertions into and deletions from TEXT simply by providing enough contextual information in the arguments representing the new and the old strings. Nevertheless, we might wish to write subroutines DELETE and INSERT to handle all deletions and insertions.

a) Using the REPLAC subroutine as a guide, write a subroutine DELETE (OLD, OLDLEN, BEGIN) to delete a string (OLD) of length OLDLEN from TEXT. The search for OLD will start at BEGIN.

b) We can write a subroutine INSERT to insert a character string NEW of length NEWLEN into TEXT. In addition to NEW and NEWLEN, this subroutine will need a third input argument, BEGIN, which in this instance marks the exact position in TEXT in which the insertion is to be performed. For example, the statement

```
CALL INSERT (NEW, 7, 26)
```

would insert the string of length 7 stored in NEW before 'KOFFMAN' in the original TEXT. Again using REPLAC as a guide, write the subroutine INSERT (NEW, NEWLEN, BEGIN).

9.5 COMMON PROGRAMMING ERRORS

Now that we know how to manipulate different types of data, we must be especially careful not to misuse these data types in expressions. Only logical constants and variables can appear as operands of logical operators (.AND., .OR., .NOT.). Character and integer variables and array elements used to store character strings should not be used as operands for any arithmetic operations, although they may be used with the relational operators (.EQ., .NE., etc.).

A frequent source of disastrous errors in manipulating character strings, especially where large numbers of subprograms are used, involves the use of invalid array subscripts. As we mentioned in Chapter 5, some compilers can detect these errors during execution, but many others cannot. It is essential that you provide at least minimum validation of subprogram input arguments that are used as subscripts. Failure to do so can increase program debugging time considerably.

Misspelling the name of a logical or character variable (or neglecting to declare it) may result in compiler detection of syntax errors. This is because the type declaration intended for that variable will not be recognized if the variable name is spelled incorrectly. Consequently, the compiler will follow the implied type convention and assume that the variable is type integer or real; since arithmetic variables cannot be operands of logical operators, diagnostic messages may be generated.

If you do not have the character data type available, we strongly urge you to consistently use integer variables and arrays to store character strings, as shown in this chapter (avoid the use of real variables and arrays for this purpose). Remember that arithmetic operations performed on integer variables used in this manner are meaningless. Carefully constructed data tables are of critical importance in helping to keep straight the different uses of the variables named in your program.

9.6 SUMMARY

In this chapter, we have provided a description of logical and character data manipulation. We explained how compound logical expressions may be formed and evaluated, and we have expanded on the use of program flags to communicate information between the subprogram and main program.

We also implemented a number of subprograms for use in character-string manipulation problems, and illustrated the use of these subprograms. All character-string manipulation examples presented assumed that the character strings were stored in A1 format—one character per memory cell.

In solving the character-manipulation problems, we applied all the FORTRAN tools and programming techniques we have learned to date. Loop structures were used to scan the individual characters of a character string. Decision structures with logical expressions involving character data were used to test for the presence of particular substrings in larger strings of characters.

The top-down approach we have taken throughout this textbook is still central to the problem-solving process, as it helps facilitate the design of correct algorithms for nonnumerical as well as numerical problems.

PROGRAMMING PROBLEMS

9.4 Let FIRST, LAST, and WORD be arrays of size 10, with FIRST and LAST defined as follows:

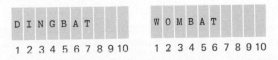

Write a program to read in a set of words (given below) represented as character strings of 10 characters or less, and determine whether or not each word falls between the words in FIRST and LAST. The words DINGBAT and WOMBAT should be considered as falling between the words in FIRST and LAST. Print the words in FIRST and LAST and print each word read in (except the last) along with the identifiers 'BETWEEN' or 'NOT BETWEEN,' whichever applies. Use the following data:

```
HELP
ME
STIFLE
THE
DINGBAT
AND
THE
WOMBATS
BEFORE
IT
IS
TOO
LATE
ZZZZZZZZZZ
```

9.5 Let BUFFER be an integer array of size 20, and let ITEM be an integer array of size 4. Write a program to read a character string of length 20 into BUFFER and a character string into ITEM. Then search BUFFER for the string contained in ITEM. Print

```
                       STRING FOUND
```

if the string in ITEM is found in *consecutive* elements of BUFFER. Print

```
                     STRING NOT FOUND
```

if the string in ITEM does not occur in the BUFFER in consecutive elements. Print all information read in. Test your program on the following strings:

```
        BUFFER:  IS A MAN IN THE MOON
        ITEMS:   MAN , NUT , N T , MEN , I

        BUFFER:  IS DUST ON THE MOON
        ITEMS:   THEM, UST , DUST , IN  , ON  ,O
```

9.6 (Modification of 9.5). Alter the program for Problem 9.5 to read strings of from 1 to 4 characters (terminated by a dollar sign) into ITEM. Use the function GETLEN (Fig. 9.8) to determine the length of each string.

9.7 Assume a set of data cards is to be processed. Each card contains a single character string which consists of a sequence of words, each separated by one or more blank spaces. Write a program which will read these cards and count the number of words with one letter, two letters, etc., up to ten letters. (*Hint.* You will need a subroutine to find blanks in an array.)

9.8 Write a subroutine which will scan an array TEXT of size N and replace all multiple occurrences of a blank with a single occurrence of a blank. You may assume that

TEXT and N are input arguments. You should also have an output argument, COUNT, which will be used to return the number of occurrences of multiple blanks found in each call of the subroutine.

9.9 Write a program to read in a collection of cards containing character strings of length less than or equal to 80 characters. These character strings are to be made up solely of letters (A–Z), digits (0–9), and the special characters ., ( ). The input string on each card will be terminated by a dollar sign $, unless the string is exactly 80 characters. For each card read, your program should do the following:

i) Count and print the length of the string (use the integer function GETLEN to determine the length count);

ii) Count the number of occurrences of four-letter words in each string;

iii) Replace each four-letter word with a string of four asterisks, ****;

iv) Print the string read in, without the four-letter words, and without the dollar sign.

9.10 (A simple payroll problem). Write a data table, flow diagram, and program that will process the employee record cards described in Table 9.1 below, and perform the following tasks.

a) For each employee compute the gross pay:
$$\text{Gross pay} = \text{Hours worked} * \text{Hourly pay} + \text{Overtime hours worked} * \text{Hourly pay} * 1.5$$

b) For each employee compute the net pay as follows:
$$\text{Net pay} = \text{Gross pay} - \text{Deductions}$$

Deductions are computed as follows:

$$\text{Federal Tax} = (\text{gross pay} - 13 * \text{no. of dependents}) * .14$$

$$\text{FICA} = \text{gross pay} * .052$$

$$\text{City Tax} = \begin{cases} \$0.00 \text{ if employee works in the suburbs} \\ 4\% \text{ of gross pay if employee works in city} \end{cases}$$

$$\text{Union Dues} = \begin{cases} 0.00 \text{ if employee not a union member} \\ 6.75\% \text{ of gross pay otherwise} \end{cases}$$

Table 9.1 Employee record card for Problem 9.10

Columns	Data description
1–6	Employee number (an integer)
7–19	Employee last name
20–27	Employee first name
28–32	Number of hours worked (to the nearest $\frac{1}{2}$ hour) for this employee
33–37	Hourly pay rate for this employee
38	Contains a C if employee works in the City Office and an S if he works in the Suburban Office
39	Contains an M if the employee is a union member
40–41	Number of dependents
42–46	Number of overtime hours worked (if any) (also to the nearest $\frac{1}{2}$ hour)

For each employee, print a line of output containing:

1. Employee number
2. First and last name
3. Number of hours worked
4. Hourly pay rate
5. Overtime hours
6. Gross pay
7. Federal tax
8. FICA
9. City wage tax (if any)
10. Union dues (if any)
11. Net pay

Also compute and print:

1. Number of employees processed
2. Total gross pay
3. Total federal tax withheld
4. Total hours worked
5. Total overtime hours worked

Use formats and provide appropriate column headings for employee output, and labels for totals.

9.11 (Student grade reports). Shown below is the layout of a card that the registrar uses as input for a program to print the end-of-the-semester final grade report for each student.

Card columns	Data description
1–6	Student number
7–19	Last name
20–27	First name
28	Middle initial
29	Academic year:
	1 = Fr, 2 = So, 3 = Jr, 4 = Sr
30–32	First course—Department ID (3 letters)
33–35	First course—Number (3 digits)
36	First course—Grade A, B, C, D, or F
37	First course—Number of credits: 0–7
40–42	
43–45	
46	Second course: data as described above
47	

$$
\left.\begin{array}{l} 50\text{--}52 \\ 53\text{--}55 \\ 56 \\ 57 \end{array}\right\} \quad \text{Third course data}
$$

$$
\left.\begin{array}{l} 60\text{--}62 \\ 63\text{--}65 \\ 66 \\ 67 \end{array}\right\} \quad \text{Fourth course data}
$$

$$
\left.\begin{array}{l} 70\text{--}72 \\ 73\text{--}75 \\ 76 \\ 77 \end{array}\right\} \quad \text{Fifth course data}
$$

Write a data table, flow diagram, and program to print the following grade report sheet for each student.

```
Line    1          MAD RIVER COLLEGE
Line    2          YELLOW GULCH,   OHIO
Line    3
Line    4      GRADE REPORT, SPRING SEMESTER 1976
Line    5
Line    6 (student number)        (year)   (student name)
          - - - - - - - - -        - -     - - - - - - - - - - -
Line    7
Line    8               GRADE SUMMARY
Line    9        COURSE
Line   10    DEPT   NMBR           CREDITS       GRADE
Line   11 1. ---    ---              -             -
Line   12 2. ---    ---              -             -
Line   13 3. ---    ---              -             -
Line   14 4. ---    ---              -             -
Line   15 5. ---    ---              -             -
Line   16
Line   17  SEMESTER GRADE POINT AVERAGE = - - - -
```

Compute the grade-point average as follows:

i) Use 4 points for an A, 3 for a B, 2 for a C, 1 for a D, and 0 for an F

ii) Compute the product of points times credits for each course

iii) Add together the products computed in (ii)

iv) Add together the total number of course credits

v) Divide (iii) by (iv) and print the result rounded off to two decimal places. [*Hint.* Rounding is easy when formats are used for printing.]

Use formats for all input and output. Your program should work for students taking anywhere from 1 to 5 courses. You will have to determine the number of courses taken by a student from the input data.

9.12 (Roman numeral conversion). Write a program to read in a string of up to 10 characters representing a number in the form of a Roman numeral. Print the Roman numeral form and then convert to Arabic form (a standard FORTRAN integer). The character values for Roman numerals are

M	1000
D	500
C	100
L	50
X	10
V	5
I	1

Test your program on the following input.

LXXXVII	87
CCXIX	219
MCCCLIV	1354
MMDCLXXIII	2673
MDCDLXXVI	?

Use formats for all input and output.

9.13 (Continuation of 9.12). Write a program to read in an integer and print the integer and its Roman numeral representation.

9.14 Write an arithmetic-expression translator which compiles fully-parenthesized arithmetic expressions involving the operators $*$, $/$, $+$, and $-$. For example, given the input string

$$((A+(B*C))-(D/E))$$

the compiler would print out:

$$Z = (B*C)$$
$$Y = (A+Z)$$
$$X = (D/E)$$
$$W = (Y-X)$$

Assume only the letters A through F can be used as variable names. [*Hint.* Find the first right parenthesis. Remove it and the four characters preceding it and replace them with the next unused letter (G–Z) at the end of the alphabet.] Print out the assignment statement used. For example, the following is a summary of the sequence of steps required to process expression (i).

Expression status	*Print*
$((A+(B*C))-(D/E))$	$Z = (B*C)$
$((A+Z)-(D/E))$	$Y = (A+Z)$
$(Y-(D/E))$	$X = (D/E)$
$(Y-X)$	$W = (Y-X)$

9.15 Write a subprogram, BLNKSP which removes all of the blanks from a character string and "compacts" all nonblank characters in the string. Assume the last character of the input string is a dollar sign. You should only have to scan the input string once from left to right.

9.16 Write a program system (with appropriate documentation) which reads a FORTRAN program or subprogram and classifies each statement according to the following statement types:

1. Subroutine or function header
2. Type declaration (INTEGER, REAL, LOGICAL, or CHARACTER)
3. Data-initialization statement
4. Comment statement
5. Assignment statement
6. Decision-structure header IF (——) THEN
7. Loop-structure header (indexed DO or WHILE)
8. Structure terminator (CONTINUE, ENDIF, ENDWHILE)
9. IF statement
10. Transfer statement (GOTO, NEXT, EXIT, RETURN, STOP)
11. END statement
12. Decision-structure alternative header (ELSE, ELSEIF(——) THEN)
13. Input/output statement (READ or PRINT)
14. Subroutine call
15. None-of-the-above (possible error)

Assume that each statement fits on a single card. Print each statement and its type in a legible form. [*Hint.* You may find the BLNKSP subroutine (Problem 9.15) helpful here.]

9.17 (Continuation of 9.16). Add a collection of subroutines to your program system for Problem 9.16. These subroutines should each break up the statements of types 1–15 into their basic parts, as shown below. Omit types 4, 8, 10, 11, and, of course, 15.

1. SUBROUTINE name (argument list)
                 A   B
    type FUNCTION name (argument list)
                   A   B

2. type variable list
           A

3. DATA name list / constant list /
           A   B

5. variable or array element name = expression
                   A   B

6. IF (condition) THEN
          A

7. DO sn loop-control variable = initial, end, step
                 A   B   C   D
    WHILE (condition) DO
              A

9. IF (condition) dependent statement
          A   B

12. ELSEIF (condition) THEN
          $\underbrace{}_{A}$

13. READ, list or PRINT, list
          $\underbrace{}_{A}$ $\underbrace{}_{A}$

14. CALL name (argument list)
          $\underbrace{}_{A}$ $\underbrace{}_{B}$

Warning. This problem is best done by small groups of people rather than by one person. For students working alone, 2 or 3 of the subroutines required should be more than sufficient.

9.19 (Text Editor problem). Use the subroutine REPLAC (Problem 9.3), and subroutines DELETE and INSERT (Exercise 9.16), and any other subprogram that you need, and write a simple Text Editor system to perform the following tasks:

a) Delete the first occurrence of a character string from TEXT;

b) Replace the first occurrence of a character string with another string;

c) Insert a character string at a specified position of TEXT.

The program system chart for the Text Editor is as follows:

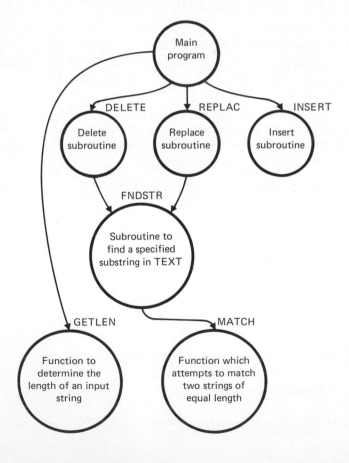

```
THE ORGANIZATION OF A PROGRAM IS A VERY MISERABLE EXPERIENCE.  EVERY PROGRAMMER
HAS HIS OWN INEFFICIENT WAY OF GOING ABOUT THE DEVELOPMENT PROCESS.    PROGRAMMING
IS STILL A WASTE OF TIME, BUT EVEN TEACHERS WASTE TIME.
216
REPLACE
MISERABLE$ ⎫
           ⎬ data associated with REPLACE directive
PERSONAL$  ⎭
DELETE
THIS IS NONSENSE$ ⎫ data associated with DELETE directive
INSERT
DESIGN AND $ ⎫
             ⎬ data associated with INSERT directive
5
REPLACE
A WASTE OF TIME$
AN ART$
DELECTABLE$
DELETE
INEFFICIENT$
INSERT
WELL STRUCTURED PROGRAMS ARE OBTAINED BY WORKING IN A TOP-DOWN FASHION$
470
INSERT
WELL STRUCTURED PROGRAMS ARE OBTAINED BY WORKING IN A TOP-DOWN FASHION$
74
REPLACE
TEACHERS WASTE TIME$
ARTISTS HAVE RULES OF COMPOSITION AND STYLE$
QUIT
```

Fig. 9.22 Input data for text editor problem.

The subroutines COPY and REVCOP should be added to this chart to describe their use in DELETE, REPLAC, and INSERT.

Test your system with the input given in Fig. 9.22 (each line represents one card of input).

For this problem, TEXT should be an integer array of size 240. The main program should begin by reading the character string in the first three cards into TEXT. The length of this string (216) is given on the fourth card.

Next, the main program should enter a loop in which text-edit directives, REPLACE, INSERT, DELETE, and QUIT are processed. The main program should read a directive, then read the data associated with that directive (see Fig. 9.23), and call the appropriate subroutine to perform the indicated edit. If QUIT is read, the program should terminate.

The main program should also call the function GETLEN to determine the length of each data string (except the TEXT string) that is read in. In each such string, the dollar sign marks the end.

There are several deliberate errors in the input data above (such as insertion points beyond the end of TEXT and incorrect commands). Make sure your main program detects these.

10.1 Introduction

10.2 Declaration of
      Multidimensional Arrays

10.3 Manipulation of
      Multidimensional Arrays

*10.4 Compiler Role for
      Multidimensional Arrays

10.5 Multidimensional Arrays as
      Subprogram Arguments

10.6 Applications of
      Multidimensional Arrays

10.7 Common Programming
      Errors

10.8 Summary
      Programming Problems

MULTI-DIMENSIONAL ARRAYS

10

10.1 INTRODUCTION

We have been introduced to several types of data: real, integer, logical, and character. In addition, we have used one data structure, the array, for the identification and referencing of a collection of data items of the same type. The array enables us to save a list of related data items in memory. All of these data items are referred to by the same name, and the array subscript is used to distinguish among the individual array elements.

In this chapter, the use of the array will be extended to facilitate the convenient organization of related data items into tables and lists of more than one dimension. For example, we will see how a two-dimensional array with three rows and three columns can be used to represent a tic-tac-toe board. This array has nine elements, each of which can be referenced by specifying the row subscript (1, 2, or 3) and column subscript (1, 2, or 3), as shown in Fig. 10.1. Similarly, we shall see that arrays of three or more dimensions can be used to represent collections of data items that can be conveniently described in terms of a multidimensional picture.

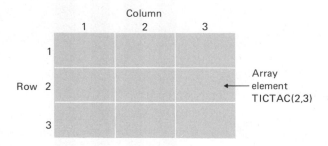

Fig. 10.1 Representation of a tic-tac-toe board as a two-dimensional array, TICTAC

10.2 DECLARATION OF MULTIDIMENSIONAL ARRAYS

The general form of an array declaration can be expanded to handle arrays of two or more dimensions, as shown in the display at the top of page 365.

Example 10.1

```
CHARACTER * 1 TICTAC (3, 3)
REAL RECORD (7, 5, 6)
```

The array TICTAC is a two-dimensional array consisting of nine elements (3 × 3). Both subscripts may take on the values 1, 2, or 3. The array RECORD consists of three dimensions: The first subscript may take on values from 1 to 7; the second, from 1 to 5; and the third from 1 to 6. There are a total of 7 × 5 × 6 or 210 elements in the array RECORD.

Array Declaration (for Multidimensional Arrays)

FORTRAN Form: (for an n-dimensional array)

type name (range $_1$, range$_2$, . . . , range$_n$)

Interpretation. Type is any of the four data types INTEGER, REAL, CHARACTER $* n$, or LOGICAL. Range$_i$ represents the range of dimension i. Range$_i$ can be specified by an integer constant or by a dummy argument if name is a subprogram dummy argument.

Note 1. Range$_i$ specifies the range of permissible subscript values for dimension i. The total number of array elements (array size) is determined by the product

$$\text{range}_1 \times \text{range}_2 \times \dots \times \text{range}_n$$

Note 2. For a two-dimensional array, range$_1$ refers to the number of *rows* and range$_2$ to the number of *columns* in the array.

10.3 MANIPULATION OF MULTIDIMENSIONAL ARRAYS

10.3.1 Manipulation of Individual Array Elements

Since the computer can manipulate only individual memory cells, we must be able to identify the individual elements of a multidimensional array. This is accomplished by using a subscripted reference to the array, as shown next.

Subscripted Array Reference (Multidimensional Arrays)

FORTRAN Form:
$$\text{array name } (S_1, S_2, , \dots, S_n).$$

Interpretation. Each of the S_i is a subscript expression. The forms permitted in standard FORTRAN are discussed in Section 5.3. Some compilers permit any valid integer expression to be used.

In the case of two-dimensional arrays, the first subscript of an array reference is considered the *row subscript* and the second subscript the *column subscript*. Consequently, the subscripted array reference

TICTAC (2,3)

selects the element in row 2, column 3 of the array TICTAC shown in Fig. 10.1. (This row/column convention is derived from the area of mathematics called *matrix algebra*. A *matrix M* is a two-dimensional arrangement of numbers. Each element in M is referred to by the symbol M_{ij}, where i is the number of its row and j is the number of its column.)

Example 10.2 Consider the array TICTAC drawn below.

This array contains three blank elements (TICTAC(1, 2), TICTAC(2, 1), TICTAC(2, 3)); three elements with value 'X' (TICTAC(1, 1), TICTAC(3, 1), TICTAC(3, 2)); and three elements with value 'O' (TICTAC(1, 3), TICTAC(2, 2), TICTAC(3, 3)).

Example 10.3 A university offers 50 courses at each of five campuses. We can conveniently store the enrollments of these courses in an array declared as

```
INTEGER  ENROLL (50,5)
```

This array consists of 250 elements; ENROLL(I, J) represents the number of students in course I at campus J.

If we wish to have this enrollment information broken down further according to student rank (freshman, sophomore, junior, senior), we would need a three-dimensional array with 1000 elements:

```
INTEGER  ENRANK (50, 5, 4)
```

The subscripted array reference ENRANK(I, J, K) would represent the number of students of rank K taking course I at campus J (see Fig. 10.2). We will assume that K must have a value between 1 and 4 and that rank 1 is associated with freshmen, rank 2 with sophomores, rank 3 with juniors, and rank 4 with seniors.

In Fig. 10.2, the circled element, ENROLL (1, 3), has a value of 33. The numbers shown in the array ENRANK represent the number of students of each rank in course 1 on campus 3. The following program segment computes the total number of students in course 1 at campus 3 regardless of rank. You should verify that CSUM will have the value 33 at the completion of the execution of this loop.

```
        CSUM = 0
        DO 10 K = 1, 4
           CSUM = CSUM + ENRANK(1,3,K)
     10 CONTINUE
```

EXERCISE 10.1 Given the array ENRANK shown in Fig. 10.2, write program segments to perform the following operations:

a) Find the number of juniors in all classes at campus 3. Students will be counted once for each course in which they are enrolled.

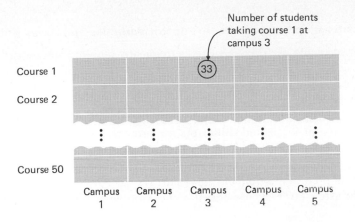

(a) Two-dimensional Array ENROLL

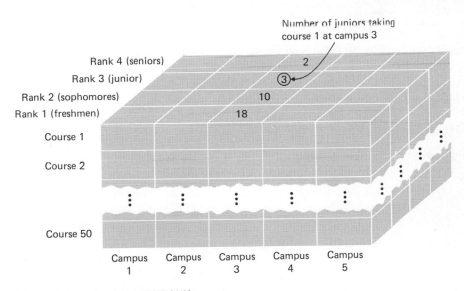

(b) Three-dimensional array ENRANK

Fig. 10.2 (a) Two-dimensional array ENROLL. (b) Three-dimensional array ENRANK.

b) Find the number of sophomores on all campuses who are enrolled in course 25.

c) Compute and print the number of students at campus 1 enrolled in each course and the total number of students at campus 1 in all courses. Students will be counted once for each course in which they are enrolled.

d) Compute and print the number of upper-class students in all courses at each campus, as well as the total number of upper-class students enrolled. (Upper-class students are juniors and seniors.) Again, students will be counted once for each course in which they are enrolled.

10.3.2 Relationship between Loop-Control Variables and Array Subscripts

Sequential referencing of array elements is frequently required when working with multidimensional arrays. This process often requires the use of nested loops, since more than one subscript must be incremented in order to process all or a portion of the array elements. It is very easy to become confused in this situation and interchange subscripts, or nest the loops improperly. If you are in doubt as to whether or not your loops and subscripts are properly synchronized, you should include extra print statements to display the subscript and array element values.

Exercise 10.1 (especially parts (c) and (d)) provides some experience in writing nested loops to process multiple-dimension arrays. The following problem, which processes the array TICTAC (described earlier), provides further illustration.

PROBLEM 10.1 Write a subprogram which will be used after each move is made in a computerized tic-tac-toe game to see if the game is over. When the game is over, the subprogram should indicate the winning player or the fact that the game ended in a draw.

DISCUSSION. To see whether a player has won, the subprogram must check each row, column, and diagonal on the board to determine if all three squares are occupied by the same player. A draw occurs when all squares on the board are occupied but neither player has won. The flow diagrams for this problem are shown in Fig. 10.3 The data table follows.

Data Table for Tic-Tac-Toe Problem:

Input arguments

TICTAC (3, 3): Represents an array which shows the current state of the tic-tac-toe board after each move (character * 1)

Output arguments

OVER: Represents a flag used to indicate whether the game is over (OVER will be defined as true if the game is over; otherwise it will be false) (logical)

WINNER: Represents an indicator used to define the winner of the game ('X', 'O', or 'D' for draw when the game is over (character * 1)

Local variables

IR: Row subscript for array TICTAC; used as lcv (integer)

IC: Column subscript for array TIC-TAC; used as lcv (integer)

DRAW: Program constant, 'D' (character * 1)

BLANK: Program constant, ' ' (character * 1)

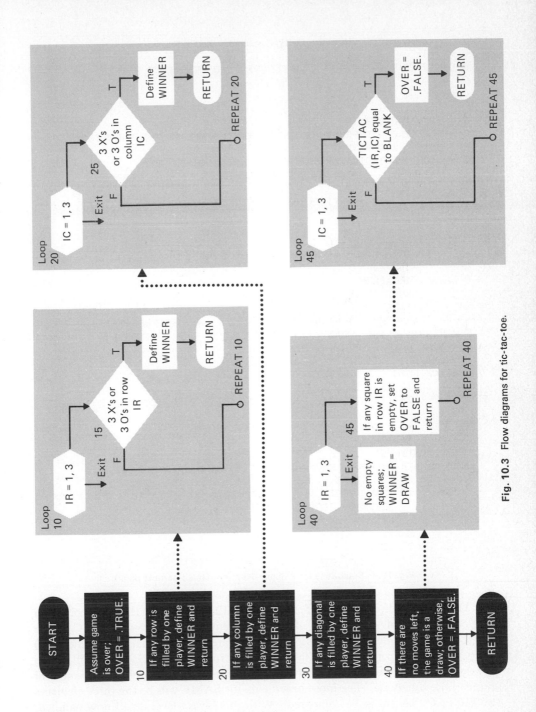

Fig. 10.3 Flow diagrams for tic-tac-toe.

```
              SUBROUTINE CHKOVR (TICTAC, OVER, WINNER)
C
C CHECK IF TIC-TAC-TOE GAME IS OVER AND DETERMINE WINNER (IF ANY)
C
C ARGUMENT DEFINITIONS
C
C   INPUT ARGUMENTS
C     TICTAC - REPRESENTS THE CURRENT STATE OF THE GAME BOARD
C   OUTPUT ARGUMENTS
C     OVER - INDICATES WHETHER OR NOT GAME IS OVER
C     WINNER - INDICATES THE WINNER (O OR X) OR A DRAW (D)
C
      CHARACTER * 1 TICTAC(3,3), WINNER        [or INTEGER...]
      LOGICAL OVER
C
C FUNCTIONS REFERENCED
      LOGICAL SAME
C
C LOCAL VARIABLES
      LOGICAL DSAME
      INTEGER IR, IC
      CHARACTER * 1 BLANK, DRAW         [or INTEGER...]
      DATA BLANK, DRAW /' ', 'D'/
C ASSUME GAME IS OVER AT START
      OVER = .TRUE.
C CHECK ROWS FOR A WINNER
      DO 10 IR = 1, 3
         IF (SAME(TICTAC(IR,1), TICTAC(IR,2), TICTAC(IR,3))) THEN
            WINNER = TICTAC(IR,1)
            RETURN
         ENDIF
   10 CONTINUE
C NO WINNER BY ROWS, CHECK COLUMNS FOR A WINNER
      DO 20 IC = 1, 3
         IF (SAME(TICTAC(1,IC), TICTAC(2,IC), TICTAC(3,IC))) THEN
            WINNER = TICTAC(1,IC)
            RETURN
         ENDIF
   20 CONTINUE
```

Fig. 10.4 Subroutine for Problem 10.1 (continued on next page).

The refinements of steps 15, 25, and 30 (Fig. 10.3) all involve the same operation —a comparison of the contents of three elements of the array TICTAC to see whether they are identical. (In step 30, there are two diagonals to be checked.) To perform this operation, we will use a logical function SAME which will return a value of true if the three array elements are the same (and not blank), and will return false otherwise. The input arguments for SAME will be the three elements of TICTAC that are to be compared. With this lowest-level detail now handled, we can write the subroutine for Problem 10.1 (see Fig. 10.4). Additional data-table entries are shown on the following page.

```
C NO WINNER BY ROWS OR COLUMNS. CHECK DIAGONALS
      DSAME = SAME(TICTAC(1,1), TICTAC(2,2), TICTAC(3,3))
    X  .OR. SAME(TICTAC(1,3), TICTAC(2,2), TICTAC(3,1))
      IF (DSAME) THEN
          WINNER = TICTAC(2,2)
          RETURN
      ENDIF
C
C NO WINNER AT ALL. SEE IF GAME IS A DRAW
C CHECK EACH ROW FOR AN EMPTY SPACE
      DO 40 IR = 1, 3
          DO 45 IC = 1, 3
              IF (TICTAC(IR,IC) .EQ. BLANK) THEN
                  OVER = .FALSE.
                  RETURN
              ENDIF
   45     CONTINUE
   40 CONTINUE
C NO BLANK FOUND, GAME IS A DRAW
      WINNER = DRAW
      RETURN
      END
```

Fig. 10.4 Completion of subroutine CHKOVR.

Additional Data-table Entries (Problem 10.1):

Local variables

DSAME: Defined to be true when a diagonal is filled with 3 X's, or 3 O's. (logical)

Subprograms referenced

SAME (logical function): Tests a row, column, or diagonal; returns a value of true if all three elements are the same ('X' or 'O'); otherwise, returns a value of false.

Argument	*Definition*
1, 2, 3	The arguments are the elements of a row, column, or diagonal of TICTAC. The order in which these elements are specified is immaterial.

For versions of FORTRAN in which the character declaration is not available, TICTAC(3, 3), WINNER, BLANK, and DRAW can be declared as integers. The subroutine will otherwise remain unchanged.

EXERCISE 10.2 Write the function SAME (include all appropriate comments). *Note.* Make sure SAME properly handles the situation in which all three items being compared are blank; the value returned should be true only if all three items are 'X' or all three are 'O'.

10.3.3 Reading, Printing, and Initializing Multidimensional Arrays

The use of an array name without subscripts in an input list causes the entire array to be filled with data items. Similarly, if the array name appears in an output list without subscripts, the entire array contents will be printed. A subscripted reference to an array in a read or print statement will affect only one element of the array.

If a two-dimensional array appears in an output list without subscripts, this array will be printed on a column-by-column basis (first column, second column, etc.). This means that the statement

PRINT, TICTAC

would cause the elements of the array TICTAC to be printed as:

```
TICTAC(1,1), TICTAC(2,1), TICTAC(3,1)  TICTAC(1,2), TICTAC(2,2), TICTAC(3,2)  TICTAC(1,3), TICTAC(2,3), TICTAC(3,3)
```

| Column 1 | Column 2 | Column 3 |

The compiler will position as many of these values as it can fit on each line in the order shown. The board in Example 10.2 would be printed as:

X   X   O   X   O   O

| Column 1 | Column 2 | Column 3 |

where the blanks represent empty spaces in the board.

Usually, however, we would prefer the contents of an array to be printed on a row-by-row basis. This, too, can be done fairly easily. The program segment shown below displays the array contents in the form of a tic-tac-toe board.

```
      PRINT, '--------'
      DO 10 ROW = 1, 3
          PRINT 30, (TICTAC(ROW,COL), COL = 1, 3)
          PRINT, '--------'
   30     FORMAT (1X, 3(1X, A1))
   10 CONTINUE
```

The print statements in loop 10 will be executed once for each value of the row subscript, ROW. The implied indexed-DO loop causes the three elements of each row to be printed across the output line. The program output is shown in Fig. 10.5.

A similar problem exists in entering data. Normally, we prefer to punch one row of values per data card. However, the compiler stores data items on a column-by-column basis if an unsubscripted array reference appears in an input list.

Fig. 10.5 Printing the array TICTAC.

Therefore, explicit and/or implied loops will be required to enter data on a row-by-row basis.

Example 10.4 The subroutine below reads data items into one row of an integer array at a time and echoes these values back.

```
        SUBROUTINE ENTER (ARRAY, NROWS, NCOLS)
C ENTER DATA INTO MEMORY ON A ROW BY ROW BASIS
C
C ARGUMENT DEFINITIONS
C    INPUT ARGUMENTS
C       NROWS - NUMBER OF ROWS
C       NCOLS - NUMBER OF COLUMNS
C    OUTPUT ARGUMENTS
C       ARRAY - ARRAY TO RECEIVE DATA ITEMS
C
        INTEGER NROWS, NCOLS
        INTEGER ARRAY(NROWS, NCOLS)
C
C LOCAL VARIABLES
        INTEGER I, J
C
C READ CARDS ON A ROW BY ROW BASIS
        DO 10 I = 1, NROWS
           READ, (ARRAY(I,J), J=1, NCOLS)
           PRINT, (ARRAY(I,J), J=1, NCOLS)
     10 CONTINUE
        RETURN
        END
```

Example 10.5 In Example 10.3, the array ENROLL (50 rows, 5 columns) is used for storing the course enrollment figures for each of fifty courses at five branch campuses of a large university. If a separate data card is keypunched for each course, with the enrollment figures broken down by campus, the statement

```
        CALL ENTER (ENROLL, 50, 5)
```

would properly process the data cards shown at the top of page 374.

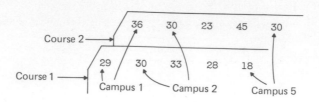

If the enrollment figures are keypunched by campus instead of by course, then the statement

READ, ENROLL

would suffice. The data cards should be prepared as follows:

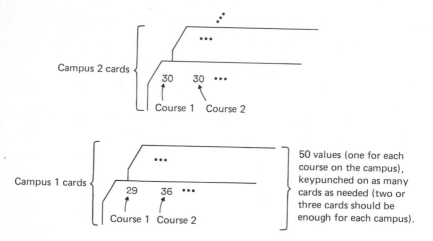

The points illustrated in these examples are summarized in the next display.

In general, if a multidimensional array appears unsubscripted in a variable list of a read or print statement, the compiler will assume that the first subscript changes first and most often, then the second, then the third, etc. To alter this sequence, the programmer must utilize a suitable combination of implied or explicit indexed-DO loops.

What we mean by the statement "the first subscript changes first and most often" is that the compiler processes the array as if the first subscript were the innermost loop-control variable in a nest of loops, and the last subscript were the outermost loop-control variable. Consequently, while all other subscripts are still set at their initial values, the first subscript cycles through all of its values. The second subscript is then incremented, and the first subscript cycles through all of its values again. This continues until subscript 2 reaches its final value. Then subscript 3 is incremented to its next value and the process repeats, with subscripts 1 and 2 cycling through their respective ranges.

Example 10.6 The processing just described also applies for a data-initialization statement. The statements:

```
DATA TICTAC /'X', ' ', 'X', ' ', 'O', 'X', 'O', ' ', 'O'/
DATA ((TICTAC (I,J), J = 1,3), I = 1,3)
Z          /'X', ' ', 'O', ' ', 'O', ' ', 'X', 'X', 'O'/
```

will both initialize the array TICTAC to the configuration shown in Fig. 10.6. The first statement initializes the array on a column-by-column basis. (The row subscript changes first and most often.) The second statement initializes the array on a row-by-row basis, using a pair of nested implied indexed-DO loops. The column subscript, J, is considered the inner loop-control variable (J changes first and most often); the row subscript, I, is considered the outer loop-control variable. The use of implied indexed-DO loops in data-initialization statements is nonstandard and may not be allowed by your compiler.

EXERCISE 10.3 Given a square array TABLE with M rows and M columns, describe the effect of the following program segments. (Does every element get printed at least once? Do any elements get printed more than once?)

a)   PRINT, (TABLE(I,I), I = 1, M)

b)   DO 10 I = 1, M
          PRINT, (TABLE(I,J), J = 1, I)
   10 CONTINUE

c)   DO 20 I = 1, M
          PRINT, (TABLE(I,J), J = I, M)
   20 CONTINUE

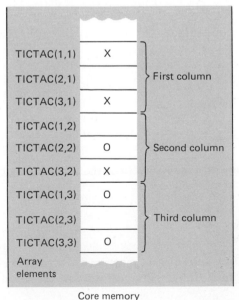
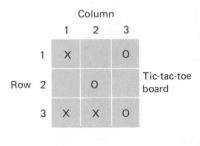

Fig. 10.6 Storage of a two-dimensional array in a contiguous memory block.

*10.4 COMPILER ROLE FOR MULTIDIMENSIONAL ARRAYS

Certainly the compiler has no capability to modify the physical configuration of memory or reorganize memory cells into a rectangular pattern in order to represent a two-dimensional array. Memory consists of a linear sequence of individual memory cells. The compiler allocates a block of adjacent cells for storing a multidimensional array, and must associate each element of the array with a particular cell, as shown in Fig. 10.6. The allocation of the block of memory is done on a column-by-column basis, so that the first column of the array occupies the first subblock of cells, the second column occupies the next subblock, and so on.

The actual location in memory of each array element is determined by computing its *offset* from the *base address*. (The base address is the address of the memory cell assigned to the first element of the array.) The formula for this computation is

$$\text{array element address} = \text{base address of array} + \text{offset}.$$

The offset for TICTAC (I, J) is determined from the formula

$$\text{offset} = (I - 1) + (J - 1) * 3,$$

where 3 represents the number of rows in TICTAC. In general for two-dimensional arrays, the formula for computing the offset for element (I, J) is

$$\text{offset} = (I - 1) + (J - 1) * (\text{range}_1)$$

where range_1 represents the number of rows. A similar formula can be derived for arrays of dimensions greater than two.

From either of these formulas, we can compute the offsets as shown in the following table.

Array element	Offset	Address
TICTAC (1, 1)	$0 + 0*3 = 0$	Base
TICTAC (2, 2)	$1 + 1*3 = 4$	4th cell after base
TICTAC (3, 3)	$2 + 2*3 = 8$	8th cell after base

A comparison of the offsets in this table with Fig. 10.6 verifies the correctness of these formulas.

10.5 MULTIDIMENSIONAL ARRAYS
AS SUBPROGRAM ARGUMENTS

Any array that is used as an argument in a subprogram must be declared in the subprogram as well as in the calling program. In the initial declaration, the range

---

* This section may be omitted.

of each subscript must be specified using an integer constant. However, within the subprogram it is possible to use an integer dummy argument to specify the range of a subscript.

When using an argument to define the range of a multidimensional array subscript, there is one very important rule that must be followed.

Any dummy argument used in the declaration of a dummy array should be passed the same value as the corresponding integer constant used in the initial declaration of the actual array.

This rule, which does not apply to one-dimensional arrays, must be followed when using multidimensional arrays, even when only a portion of an array is to be processed by a subprogram.

The reason for this rule is that subprograms are compiled separately and the translations will involve instructions for computing the address of each memory cell corresponding to an array reference. As shown in the preceding section, the memory cell address for a particular element in a two-dimensional array is a function of the range of the row subscript for that array. Consequently, the correct value of this range must be available to all subprograms that reference the array.

Example 10.7 The subroutine EXCHNG creates a modified version of any array such that row one of the original will be column one of the new array, column one of the original will be row one of the new array, etc. If the array represents a matrix, the modified version is called the *transpose* of the original matrix. A matrix and its transpose are shown in Fig. 10.7. Note that the old array (matrix) has two rows and four columns, while the new array (transpose) has four rows and two columns.

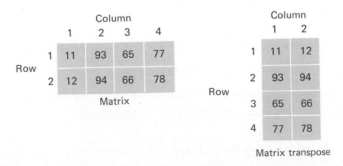

Fig. 10.7 A matrix and its transpose.

```
              SUBROUTINE EXCHNG (OLD, NEW, M, N)
C
C FORM THE TRANSPOSE OF MATRIX OLD
C ARGUMENT DEFINITIONS
C   INPUT ARGUMENTS
C      OLD - ORIGINAL ARRAY (M x N)
C      M, N - RANGE OF ARRAY SUBSCRIPTS
C   OUTPUT ARGUMENTS
C      NEW - TRANSPOSE OF OLD (N x M)
C
          INTEGER M, N
          INTEGER OLD(M, N), NEW(N, M)
C
C LOCAL VARIABLES
          INTEGER I, J
C
C FORM EACH ROW OF NEW
          DO 10 I = 1, N
C COPY A COLUMN OF OLD INTO A ROW OF NEW
             DO 20 J = 1, M
                NEW(I, J) = OLD(J, I)
   20        CONTINUE
   10 CONTINUE
          RETURN
          END
```

Fig. 10.8   Subroutine EXCHNG for transposing a matrix.

The subroutine EXCHNG is provided in Fig. 10.8.

Within loop 20 of EXCHNG, I serves as the row subscript for NEW and the column subscript for OLD; J serves as the column subscript for NEW and the row subscript for OLD. Column I of OLD is copied into row I of NEW, as J is sequenced from 1 to M in inner loop 20. This subroutine will transpose any two-dimensional integer array.

10.6 APPLICATIONS OF MULTIDIMENSIONAL ARRAYS

To further illustrate the use of multidimensional arrays we will present two solved problems in which this data structure plays a central role.

PROBLEM 10.2 (The Schedules and Space Problem):   The little red high-school building in Sunflower, Indiana, consists of three floors each with five classrooms of various sizes. Each semester the high school runs fifteen classes which must be scheduled for the rooms in the building. We will write a program which, given the capacity of each room in the building (shown in the table), and the size of each class to be run, will attempt to find a satisfactory room assignment that will accommodate all 15 classes in the building. For those classes that cannot be satisfactorily placed, the program will print an error message.

Capacity of
room 202   Room number

Floor	01	02	03	04	05
1	30	30	15	30	40
2	25	(30)	25	10	110
3	62	30	40	40	30

Room capacities for Sunflower High

DISCUSSION. The input data for the program will consist of 15 cards, each containing a four character course identification and course enrollment.

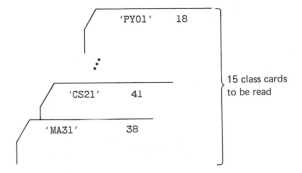

'PY01'   18

'CS21'   41

'MA31'   38

15 class cards
to be read

The program should process each class card and find a room that is large enough to hold it if one is available. (The ideal situation would be to find a room whose capacity exactly matched the class size.) For each class, we will print, in tabular form, the class id and size and the number and capacity of the room assigned to the class.

As part of the data-table definition, we must decide how the table of room capacities is to be represented in the memory of the computer. Since the building may be pictured as a two-dimensional structure with 3 floors (vertical dimension) and 5 rooms (horizontal dimension), a two-dimensional array should be a convenient structure for representing the capacities of each room in the building. We will use the 3 × 5 integer array RMCAP to store the room capacities. Note that the use of the two-dimensional array will enable us to determine the number of the room assigned to each class directly from the indices of the array element that represents that room. For example, if a class is placed in a room with capacity given by RMCAP (2, 4), we know that the number of this room is 204. In general, RMCAP (FLOOR, NR) represents the capacity of the room whose number is the value of the expression:

$$FLOOR * 100 + NR$$

Data Table for Problem 10.2:

Input variables	*Program variables*	*Output variables*
CLID: Identification code for each class (character * 4) CLSIZE: Size of each class (integer)	RMCAP: a 3 × 5 array used to store the capacities for each room. RMCAP (I, J) contains capacity for room number I * 100 + J (integer) CLASS: Loop control variable for loop to process each class card (integer) NUMROW: The number of rows in RMCAP (integer) NUMCOL: The number of columns in RMCAP (integer)	ROOMNO: Number of the room assigned to each class (integer) (Also required as output are the capacity of the room assigned, and CLID and CLSIZE.)

The basic algorithm for this problem is outlined in the flow diagrams shown in Fig. 10.9. Steps 10, 30, and 50 require further refinement. We will handle step 10 through the use of a subroutine PRTCAP which, given as input the name and size of the room capacity table, will print the table in a readable form.

Step 30 will be carried out using a subroutine, ASSIGN, which given the name and size of the room capacity table and the size of a class to be assigned as input, will search the table and return the subscripts FLOOR and NR of an assigned room if one is found. A logical variable, FOUND, will be used to indicate whether or not a room was available. These considerations are summarized in the following list of additions to the Data table for Problem 10.2. The program system chart is shown in Fig. 10.10.

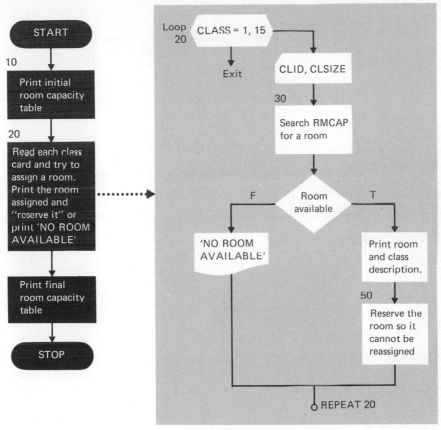

Fig. 10.9   Flow diagrams for schedules and space problem (10.2).

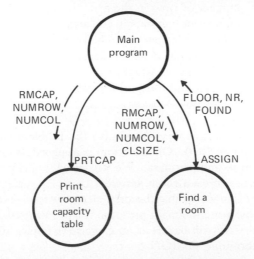

Fig. 10.10   Program system chart for Problem 10.2.

Additional Data-table Entries for Problem 10.2:

Program variables

FOUND: Defined by subroutine
ASSIGN. Set to true if a room is
available for a class; set to false
otherwise (logical)
FLOOR) Indices indicating room to
NR   ∫ be assigned to a class; returned by ASSIGN if a room
is found (integer)

Subprograms referenced:

PRTCAP (subroutine): Used to print contents of the two-dimensional array
RMCAP.

Argument	Definition
1	array RMCAP (input, integer)
2	number of rows in RMCAP (input, integer)
3	number of columns in RMCAP (input, integer)

ASSIGN (subroutine): Searches a two-dimensional array to find the indices of an
element that is greater than or equal to a specified value. If no such element is
found, a flag is set to false.

Argument	Definition
1	array to be searched (input, integer)
2	number of rows in the array (input, integer)
3	number of columns in the array (input, integer)
4	value that is being searched for (input, integer)
5 (6)	row (column) index of element selected (output, integer)
7	flag: indicates whether or not a satisfactory array element was found (output, logical)

There are probably many ways to resolve the problem indicated in step 50
of the flow diagram (Fig. 10.9). Once a room is assigned, we must ensure that it
cannot be reassigned to another class. We will provide this protection simply by
negating the capacities of each room assigned to a class when the assignment is
made. Exactly why this works may become clearer when subroutine ASSIGN is
written. We can now write the main program for Problem 10.2 (see Fig. 10.11).

Subroutine PRTCAP will be left as an exercise (Exercise 10.5). We now turn
our attention to subroutine ASSIGN.

```
C SCHEDULES AND SPACE PROGRAM
C
      CHARACTER * 4 CLID              [or INTEGER CLID]
      INTEGER CLSIZE, RMCAP(3,5), CLASS, NUMROW, NMCOL, ROOMNO
      INTEGER FLOOR, NR
      LOGICAL FOUND
      DATA RMCAP /30, 25, 62, 30, 30, 30, 15, 25, 40, 30, 10, 40, 40,
     X 110, 30/
      DATA NUMROW, NUMCOL /3, 5/
C PRINT CAPACITY TABLE AND OUTPUT TABLE HEADER
      CALL PRTCAP (RMCAP, NUMROW, NUMCOL)
      PRINT, 'ROOM ASSIGNMENT TABLE'
      PRINT, '      CLASS ID     CLASS SIZE     ROOM NUMBER',
     X       '     ROOM CAPACITY'
C
C PROCESS EACH CLASS CARD
      DO 20 CLASS = 1, 15
         READ, CLID, CLSIZE
C        SEARCH FOR A SUITABLE ROOM - SET FOUND, FLOOR, AND NR
         CALL ASSIGN (RMCAP, NUMROW, NUMCOL, CLSIZE, FLOOR, NR, FOUND)
         IF (FOUND) THEN
C           COMPUTE NUMBER AND RESERVE ROOM
            ROOMNO = FLOOR * 100 + NR
            PRINT, CLID, CLSIZE, ROOMNO, RMCAP(FLOOR, NR)
            RMCAP(FLOOR, NR) = - RMCAP(FLOOR, NR)
         ELSE
            PRINT, 'NO ROOM AVAILABLE FOR CLASS', CLID, 'REQUEST IGNORED.'
         ENDIF
   20 CONTINUE
      PRINT, 'FINAL ROOM ASSIGNMENT TABLE'
      CALL PRTCAP (RMCAP, NUMROW, NUMCOL)
      STOP
      END
```

Fig. 10.11 Main program for Problem 10.2.

Data Table for Subroutine ASSIGN:

Input arguments	*Output arguments*
RMCAP: Represents a two-dimensional integer array to be searched (size determined by arguments NUMROW and NUMCOL)	FOUND: Represents a flag used to indicate whether or not a room has been found. FOUND is set to true if a room is found and false otherwise (logical)
NUMROW: Represents the number of rows in RMCAP (integer)	
NUMCOL: Represents the number of columns in RMCAP (integer)	FLOOR⎫ Represent the indices of NR ⎭ the entry in RMCAP corresponding to the room in which the class will be placed (integer)
SIZE: Represents the size of the class to be assigned to a room (integer)	

The algorithm that we will use to find a room for a class of size SIZE may be summarized as follows:

Search RMCAP and find the smallest room that is greater than or equal to SIZE and is still not assigned.

This is called the *best fit* algorithm because the unassigned room with the least excess capacity is chosen for each class. The ideal situation is to find a room which fits exactly. This algorithm assigns as many classes to suitable rooms as is physically possible without requiring a later juggling of room assignments. The implementation of this search requires two nested loops with loop-control variables ROW and COL (the only two local variables in the subprogram):

Local program variables for ASSIGN

  ROW: Inner loop-control variable (row subscript, integer)
  COL: Outer loop-control variable (column subscript, integer)

The flow diagrams shown in Fig. 10.12 use the following criteria to locate the room with smallest capacity that is larger than SIZE.

1. If a room is found with a capacity equal to SIZE, this room is chosen as the best-fit room, and the search is complete (step 26).
2. When the first room with capacity larger than SIZE is found, it is (perhaps temporarily) chosen to be the best-fit room (step 27). If, subsequently, a room of sufficient capacity is located that is smaller than the current best-fit room, the new room becomes the best-fit room (step 28). We will implement steps 26, 27, and 28 using a multiple-alternative decision structure.

The program for subroutine ASSIGN is shown in Fig. 10.13. We have introduced an additional local variable, TEMP1 (type logical), to simplify the logical expressions used to implement steps 27 and 28 of the flow diagram.

Additional local program variable for ASSIGN

  TEMP1: represents the value of the condition

  RMCAP (ROW, COL) is greater than SIZE

TEMP1 is type logical.

EXERCISE 10.4 Rewrite the data statement for RMCAP (main program, Fig. 10.11) to initialize RMCAP on a row-by-row basis.

EXERCISE 10.5 Complete the program system for Problem 10.2 by writing the subroutine PRTCAP. Your subroutine should produce a nicely labelled, two-dimensional table with each line representing the capacities of the rooms on one floor of the school building. A data table and a flow diagram should be provided.

EXERCISE 10.6 Modify the main program so that the final contents of the array RMCAP can be used to determine the number of empty seats in each classroom. Make sure that it is not possible to assign a large room to 2 small classes after your modification.

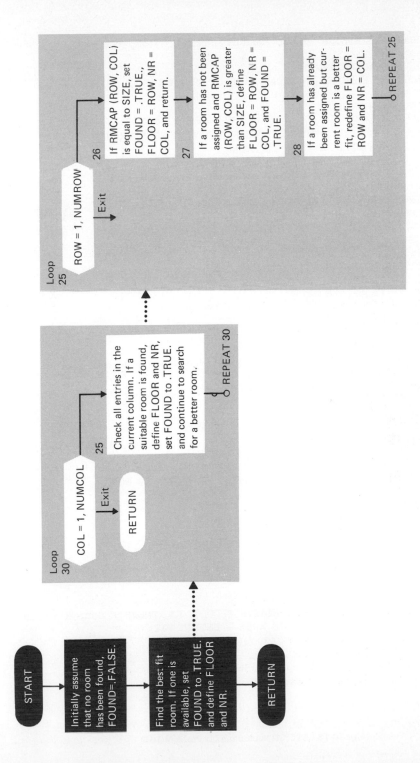

Fig. 10.12 Flow diagrams of ASSIGN subroutine for schedules and space problem (10.2).

```
         SUBROUTINE ASSIGN (RMCAP, NUMROW, NUMCOL, SIZE, FLOOR, NR, FOUND)
C
C USE BEST FIT ALGORITHM TO
C FIND SMALLEST ELEMENT IN RMCAP THAT IS GREATER THAN OR EQUAL TO SIZE
C
C ARGUMENT DEFINITIONS
C   INPUT ARGUMENTS
C     RMCAP - TWO DIMENSIONAL INTEGER ARRAY TO BE SEARCHED
C     NUMROW - NUMBER OF ROWS IN RMCAP
C     NUMCOL - NUMBER OF COLUMNS IN RMCAP
C     SIZE - SIZE OF CLASS TO BE ASSIGNED TO A ROOM
C   OUTPUT ARGUMENTS
C     FOUND - TRUE IF A ROOM IS FOUND, FALSE OTHERWISE
C     FLOOR - INDICATES ROW OF RMCAP ENTRY CONTAINING BEST CAPACITY
C     NR - INDICATES COLUMN OF RMCAP ENTRY CONTAINING BEST CAPACITY
C
         INTEGER NUMROW, NUMCOL, SIZE
         INTEGER RMCAP(NUMROW, NUMCOL)
         LOGICAL FOUND
         INTEGER FLOOR, NR
C
C LOCAL VARIABLES
         INTEGER ROW, COL
         LOGICAL TEMP1
C
C ASSUME NO ROOM FOUND AT START
         FOUND = .FALSE.
C OUTER LOOP, CHECK COLUMN ENTRIES
         DO 30 COL = 1, NUMCOL
C          INNER LOOP, CHECK ROWS OF EACH COLUMN
           DO 20 ROW = 1, NUMROW
             TEMP1 = RMCAP(ROW, COL) .GT. SIZE
             IF (RMCAP(ROW, COL) .EQ. SIZE) THEN
C              SIZE MATCH.  MAKE ASSIGNMENT OF BEST FIT ROOM
               FOUND = .TRUE.
               FLOOR = ROW
               NR = COL
               RETURN
             ELSE IF (TEMP1 .AND. (.NOT. FOUND)) THEN
C              FIRST AVAILABLE ROOM FOUND
               FOUND = .TRUE.
               FLOOR = ROW
               NR = COL
             ELSE IF (TEMP1 .AND. RMCAP(ROW,COL). LT. RMCAP(FLOOR,NR)) THEN
C              SUBSEQUENT AVAILABLE ROOM - BETTER FIT
               FLOOR = ROW
               NR = COL
             ENDIF
   20      CONTINUE
   30    CONTINUE
         RETURN
         END
```

Fig. 10.13 ASSIGN subroutine for Problem 10.2.

EXERCISE 10.7 The algorithm used in subroutine ASSIGN is called a *best-fit* algorithm, because the room having the capacity that was closest to class size was assigned to each class. Another algorithm that might have been used is called a *first-fit* algorithm. In this algorithm, the first room having a capacity greater than or equal to class size is assigned to the class (no further searching for a room is carried out). Modify the flow diagram (Fig. 10.12) and program (Fig. 10.13) to reflect the first-fit algorithm. (You will see that this algorithm is simpler than best-fit.) Apply both algorithms using the room capacities shown earlier and the following 15 class sizes: 38, 41, 6, 26, 28, 21, 25, 97, 12, 36, 28, 27, 29, 30, 18. Exactly what is wrong with the first-fit algorithm?

10.6.1 Introduction to Computer Art: Drawing Block Letters

Many of you have seen examples of computer art or calendars "drawn" by the computer. Normally the picture consists of lines of numbers or symbols printed so as to depict a pattern. The pattern is composed of different layers of shading and the degree of shading is determined by the density of symbols printed in a given area. (See Fig. 10.14).

Since the line-printer prints one line at a time, the "computer artist" must organize the picture as a sequence of print lines of constant width. If the character declaration is not available on the compiler you are using, a two-dimensional integer array is required to store the lines of the picture. The size of the second dimension is determined by the width of the picture and the character capacity of integer variables on your computer.

Example 10.8

Part (A) (for those who use the character declaration):

The program below enters a picture into an array (PICTUR) and then draws N copies of the picture. The number of lines in the picture is given by the variable HEIGHT (HEIGHT ≤ 100); the width is 60 characters. Each character string keypunched on a data card must be enclosed in apostrophes.

```
        C COMPUTER ART PROGRAM
                INTEGER N, HEIGHT, NCOPY, NLINE
                CHARACTER * 60 PICTUR(100)
        C ENTER DATA
                READ, N, HEIGHT
                READ, (PICTUR(NLINE), NLINE = 1, HEIGHT)
        C DRAW N COPIES
                DO 10 NCOPY = 1, N
        C           DRAW ONE LINE OF PICTURE AT A TIME
                    DO 20 NLINE = 1, HEIGHT
                        PRINT, PICTUR(NLINE)
           20       CONTINUE
        C           SEPARATE EACH COPY WITH BLANK LINES
                    PRINT 30
           30       FORMAT (/////)
           10   CONTINUE
                STOP
                END
```

Fig. 10.14 Computer art.

Part (B) (for those who cannot use the character declaration):

If the character declaration is not permitted by your compiler, each line of the picture could be stored in a row of a two-dimensional integer array. The number of array elements needed to store a line—i.e., the size of the second dimension—is determined by dividing the picture width by the character capacity of an integer variable (represented by C). If C = 4 and the picture width is 60, fifteen array elements (or columns) are required to store a line of the picture.

The program below enters a picture into an array (PICTUR) and then draws N copies of the picture. The number of lines in the picture is determined by the variable HEIGHT (HEIGHT ≤ 100); the width is 60 characters. Each data card should contain a character string of length 60 keypunched in columns 1 through 60 without apostrophes.

```
C COMPUTER ART PROGRAM
       INTEGER N, HEIGHT, NCOPY, NLINE, NGROUP
       INTEGER PICTUR (100, 15)
C ENTER DATA
       READ, N, HEIGHT
C ENTER EACH LINE OF THE PICTURE SEPARATELY
       DO 5 NLINE = 1, HEIGHT
          READ 18, (PICTUR(NLINE, NGROUP), NGROUP = 1, 15)
    5 CONTINUE
   18 FORMAT (15A4)
C DRAW N COPIES
       DO 10 NCOPY = 1, N
C         DRAW ONE LINE OF PICTURE AT A TIME
          DO 20 NLINE = 1, HEIGHT
             PRINT 19, (PICTUR(NLINE, NGROUP), NGROUP = 1, 15)
   20     CONTINUE
   19     FORMAT (1X, 15A4)
C         SEPARATE EACH COPY WITH BLANK LINES
          PRINT 30
   30     FORMAT (//////)
C DRAW NEXT COPY
   10 CONTINUE
       STOP
       END
```

Two important points illustrated in Example 10.8 are:

1. A character string of length ℓ can be stored in type integer variables if the character declaration is not available. The number of integer variables required is given by the integer quotient $q = \ell/c$ when c is an exact division of ℓ or $q = (\ell/c) + 1$ otherwise. Thus, using integer variables to store character data adds one dimension to the data structure being used unless ℓ is less than or equal to c.

2. A format statement used for reading or printing the character string should contain the descriptor qAc.

In the next problem, we will write a program which draws large block letters on the line printer. You may have already seen examples of the output of such a program in signs or announcements printed by the computer. Block letters are also often used in identifying the name of the owner of a program listing.

The solution of this block-letter problem is initially given using the character declaration. The solution discussed can be implemented using integer variables for character string storage if the character capacity for integers is five or greater. The modifications required to implement a block-letter program when the character capacity is less than five will be presented in the section that follows.

PROBLEM 10.3 Develop a program which prints a sequence of letters, provided as input data, in large block letters across a page. Each letter should be printed as a 6 × 5 grid pattern of X's and blanks (6 rows and 5 columns). We will skip two print columns between letters. If your line printer provides 120 print columns of output, a maximum of 17 letters can be displayed (17 × 7 = 119).

For example, given the input:

```
      /
     /   DRAW ME
    |
    |
```

the program should produce:

```
XXX    XXXX     X    X   X        X X   XXXXX
X  X   X   X   X X   X   X       X X X  X
X   X  XXXX    X   X  X  X   X    X X X  XXXX
X   X  X X    XXXXX  X X X X     X   X  X
X  X   X  X    X    X   X X X    X   X  X
XXX    X   X  X   X   X   X X     X   X  XXXXX
```

DISCUSSION. We will use a two-dimensional character array to store all of the block letters including a space (blank). Each line of a letter will be stored as a character string of width five in the array BLOCK declared as

$$\text{CHARACTER} * 5 \quad \text{BLOCK} \ (6,27)$$

In referencing BLOCK, the second subscript denotes a particular letter of the alphabet (1 for A, 2 for B, 3 for C, . . . 26 for Z, and 27 for the space), and the first subscript denotes a line of the block letter. The first subscript has an upper bound of six since there are six lines in each block letter.

The block diagram patterns for each letter will be defined through the use of a rather lengthy list of 27 data statements. Some examples of these statements follow; the storage arrangement that they produce is shown in Fig. 10.15. An analysis of this figure should provide a clear picture of the way in which the information in BLOCK will be arranged.

Data Statements:

```
    DATA (BLOCK(I, 1), I = 1, 6)/  '  X  ',
  Z                                ' X X ',
  Z                                'X   X',
  Z                                'XXXXX',        ←——BLOCK(4, 1)
  Z                                'X   X',
  Z                                'X   X' /
    DATA (BLOCK(I, 2), I = 1, 6)/  'XXXX ',
  Z                                'X   X',
  Z                                'XXXX ',
  Z                                'X   X',         ←——BLOCK(4, 2)
  Z                                'X   X',
  Z                                'XXXX ' /
```

Data Table for Block-Letter Program

Input variables	Program variables	Output variables
STRING (17): Contains the string of characters to be printed in block form (character * 1)	BLOCK (6, 27): Array of block letters– program constant (character * 5) XLIST (17): Represents the index in the alphabet of each element of STRING. Each of these indices will select the column of BLOCK that contains the block letter pattern of the corresponding character in STRING (integer). VALID: Indicate whether or not all characters in STRING are valid—i.e., are letters and/or blanks (logical)	Selected elements from the array BLOCK

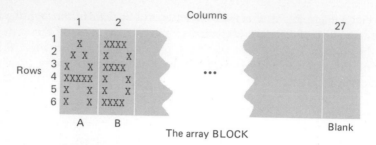

Fig. 10.15 Data-initialization statements for the array BLOCK.

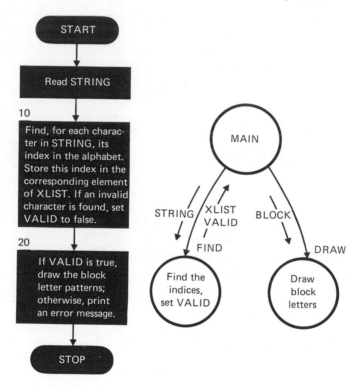

Fig. 10.16 Level-one flow diagram and program system chart for block letter problem (10.3).

Caution. The implied indexed DO in data statements is not standard. Your compiler may require explicit mention of each array element being initialized. In this case, it would be easier to keypunch the block-letter patterns on data cards and read them in as explained in the next section.

Now that we have an understanding of the main data structure to be used in solving the problem, we can begin writing a level-one algorithm for producing the desired block-letter output. The data table is on page 391; the level-one flow diagram for this algorithm and program system chart are shown in Fig. 10.16.

We will implement this algorithm using the two subroutines, FIND and DRAW. The data table entries for these subroutines are as follows:

Additional Data Table Entries for Problem 10.3

Subprograms referenced:

FIND: (for step 10) Processes each character in STRING to determine its index in the alphabet and stores these indices in XLIST. If any characters are invalid, FIND communicates this back to the main program.

Argument	Definition
1	Array STRING (input, character * 1)
2	Array XLIST (output, character * 1)
3	error flag; if false, indicates that an invalid character was stored in STRING (output, logical)

DRAW: (for step 20) Draws the block letters corresponding to the characters in STRING as selected by XLIST.

Argument	Definition
1	Array BLOCK (input, character * 5)
2	Array XLIST (input, integer)

If the input string is:

STRING

1	2	3	4	5	6	7	8		17
D	R	A	W		M	E		...	

FIND will store the indices in XLIST as shown below:

XLIST(1)	XLIST(2)	XLIST(3)	XLIST(4)	XLIST(5)	XLIST(6)	XLIST(7)	XLIST(8)		XLIST(17)
4	18	1	23	27	13	5	27	...	27
D	R	A	W		M	E			

DRAW would then print the letters in rows 1 through 6 of columns 4, 18, 1, 23, 27, 13, and 5 of the array BLOCK (followed by 10 copies of the entry in column 27 of BLOCK (the blank)).

The main program is given in Fig. 10.17.

To determine the index for each character in STRING, FIND searches an array ALFBET which contains the letters of the alphabet in sequence (one letter per element) and the blank character. The index of the element of ALFBET which matches each character in STRING is stored in the corresponding element of XLIST. The data table for FIND is listed on page 395; the flow diagrams are shown in Fig. 10.18.

```
C MAIN PROGRAM TO DRAW BLOCK LETTERS
      CHARACTER * 1 STRING(17)              [or INTEGER STRING(17)]
      CHARACTER * 5 BLOCK(6, 27)            [or INTEGER BLOCK(6, 27)]
      INTEGER XLIST(17)
      LOGICAL VALID
C
C DATA STATEMENTS TO INITIALIZE BLOCK
      DATA (BLOCK(I, 1), I = 1, 6) / '  X  ',
     Z                                '  X X ',
     Z                                'X   X',
     Z                                'XXXXX',
     Z                                'X   X',
     Z                                'X   X' /
      DATA (BLOCK(I, 2), I = 1, 6) / 'XXXX ',
     Z                                'X   X',
     Z                                'XXXX ',
     Z                                'X   X',
     Z                                'X   X',
     Z                                'XXXX ' /


                        .
                        .
                        .
      DATA (BLOCK(I,27), I = 1, 6) / '     ',
     Z                               '     ',
     Z                               '     ',
     Z                               '     ',
     Z                               '     ',
     Z                               '     ' /
C
C ENTER STRING TO BE DRAWN
      READ 19, STRING
   19 FORMAT (17A1)
C DEFINE ARRAY OF INDICES
      CALL FIND (STRING, XLIST, VALID)
C DRAW BLOCK DIAGRAM IF ALL CHARACTERS IN STRING ARE VALID
      IF (VALID) THEN
         CALL DRAW (BLOCK, XLIST)
      ELSE
         PRINT, 'STRING CONTAINS INVALID CHARACTER'
      ENDIF
      STOP
      END
```

Fig. 10.17 Main program for Problem 9.3.

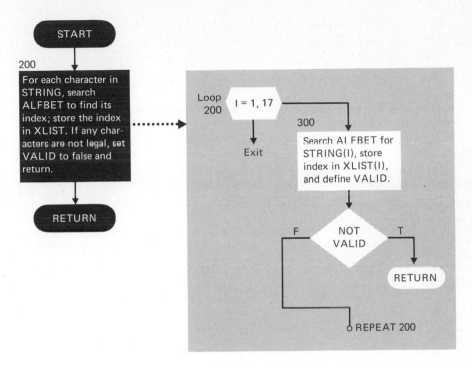

Fig. 10.18   Flow diagrams for FIND (Problem 10.3).

Data Table for Subroutine FIND:

Input arguments	*Output arguments*
STRING (17): Represents the array of characters whose indices are to be found (character ∗ 1)	XLIST (17): Represents the index in ALFBET for each character of STRING (integer) VALID: Program flag which indicates whether or not STRING contains all legal symbols (logical)

Local program variables

ALFBET (27): Contains the 26 letters of the alphabet and the blank symbol (character ∗ 1)

I: Loop-control variable and subscript for STRING (integer)

Subprograms referenced:

SEARCH (subroutine): (See Example 9.4 for argument definitions; change the declarations for ARRAY and ITEM to type character if that data type is available.)

The variable I is introduced into the data table when loop 200 is specified in the algorithm. Step 300 can be implemented by calling the subroutine SEARCH written in Chapter 9 (Fig. 9.5). The arguments required in the call are listed below.

```
CALL SEARCH (ALFBET,27,STRING(I), VALID, XLIST(I))
```

where ALFBET is the string to be searched, and 27 is its length. STRING (I) is the character to be located in ALFBET. If the character is found, XLIST (I) is defined as its index in ALFBET and VALID will be set to true; otherwise, VALID will be false.

The program for subroutine FIND is given in Fig. 10.19.

Subroutine SEARCH can be added to the program system chart in Fig. 10.16 as follows:

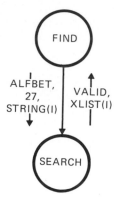

We can now turn our attention to subroutine DRAW. This subroutine prints seventeen block letters on a line-by-line basis. The contents of seventeen elements of the array BLOCK are printed across each line. The second subscript of each of these elements is determined by the corresponding element of the array XLIST; the first subscript is the number of the line being printed.

For the example shown earlier, the following array elements are printed as indicated below:

	position 1	position 2	position 3	position 17
Line 1	BLOCK(1,4),	BLOCK(1,18),	BLOCK(1,1),...BLOCK(1,27)	
Line 2	BLOCK(2,4),	BLOCK(2,18),	BLOCK(2,1),...BLOCK(2,27)	
.		.	.	.	.
.		.	.	.	.
.		.	.	.	.
Line 6	BLOCK(6,4),	BLOCK(6,18),	BLOCK(6,1),...BLOCK(6,27)	

```
      SUBROUTINE FIND (STRING, XLIST, VALID)
C
C BUILD XLIST (LIST OF CHARACTER INDICES) FROM STRING
C
C ARGUMENT DEFINITIONS
C   INPUT ARGUMENTS
C     STRING - ARRAY OF CHARACTERS TO BE DRAWN
C   OUTPUT ARGUMENTS
C     XLIST - ARRAY OF INDICES CORRESPONDING TO CHARACTERS IN STRING
C     VALID - SET FALSE IF INVALID CHARACTER IN STRING
C
      CHARACTER * 1 STRING(17)                    [or INTECER STRING(17)]
      INTEGER XLIST(17)
      LOGICAL VALID
C
C LOCAL VARIABLES
      INTEGER I
      CHARACTER * 1 ALFBET(27)                    [or INTEGER ALFBET(27)]
      DATA ALFBET/'A', 'B', 'C', 'D', 'E', 'F', 'G', 'H', 'I',
     Z     'J', 'K', 'L', 'M', 'N', 'O', 'P', 'Q', 'R', 'S',
     Z     'T', 'U', 'V', 'W', 'X', 'Y', 'Z', ' '/
C
C DETERMINE INDEX OF EACH CHARACTER IN STRING
      DO 200 I = 1, 17
          CALL SEARCH (ALFBET, 27, STRING(I), VALID, XLIST(I))
          IF (.NOT. VALID) RETURN
C         TARGET FOUND - LOCATE NEXT CHARACTER
  200 CONTINUE
      RETURN
      END
```

Fig. 10.19 Subroutine FIND (Problem 10.3).

Data Table for Subroutine DRAW

Input arguments

XLIST (17): Indices (second subscript values) of elements of BLOCK to be printed (integer)

BLOCK (6, 27): Block-letter patterns (character * 5)

Local program variables

VERT: Loop-control variable and first subscript for BLOCK (integer)

HORIZ: Loop-control variable and subscript for XLIST (integer)

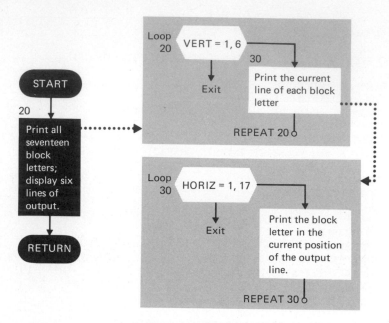

Fig. 10.20 Flow diagrams for DRAW.

Figures 10.20 and 10.21 show the flow diagram and the program, respectively, for the subroutine DRAW.

In the above program, note that loop 30 is implemented as an implied indexed-DO loop nested within loop 20. This is to ensure that all of the character strings that correspond to a particular row of a block-letter pattern are displayed on the same line of computer printout. If an explicit DO were used instead, these character strings would be printed on separate lines. Format 29 specifies single spacing between lines and two blank print columns between letters.

EXERCISE 10.8 Describe how you would modify the program system to eliminate printing trailing blanks characters.

Block-Letter Program without the Character Data Type

If the character data type is not available and the character capacity, c, for integer variables on your computer is less than five, then a three-dimensional array will have to be used to store each row of a block letter. We would define the array BLOCK as:

                    INTEGER BLOCK (q, 6, 27)

where the value of q represents the number of elements needed to store five characters:

$$q = (5/c) + 1$$

```
      SUBROUTINE DRAW (BLOCK, XLIST)
C
C DISPLAY BLOCK LETTER PATTERN
C
C ARGUMENT DEFINITIONS (ALL ARE INPUT)
C     BLOCK - TWO DIMENSIONAL ARRAY OF BLOCK LETTER PATTERNS
C     XLIST - INDICES OF BLOCK LETTER PATTERNS TO BE PRINTED
C
      CHARACTER * 5 BLOCK(6, 27)              [or INTEGER BLOCK(6, 27)]
      INTEGER XLIST(17)
C
C LOCAL VARIABLES
      INTEGER HORIZ, VERT
C
C PRINT 6 LINES OF OUTPUT
      DO 20 VERT = 1, 6
C         PRINT 17 LETTERS ACROSS A LINE. THE COLUMN SUBSCRIPT
C         OF EACH ELEMENT OF BLOCK PRINTED IS FOUND IN XLIST. THE ROW
C         SUBSCRIPT IS THE NUMBER OF THE LINE BEING PRINTED.
      PRINT 29, (BLOCK(VERT, XLIST(HORIZ)), HORIZ = 1, 17)
   20 CONTINUE
   29 FORMAT (1X, 17(A5, 2X))
      RETURN
      END
```

Fig. 10.21 Program for subroutine DRAW.

(since there are no exact divisors of 5 (except 1 and 5).) Of course, each statement that referenced BLOCK would have to be changed; specifically, the data-initialization statements in the main program and the print statement in DRAW.

It would be better, in this case, to read in the array block. The first six data cards should each contain a row of the block letter pattern for A keypunched in columns 1 through 5 without apostrophes, the next six cards should each contain a row of the block letter pattern for B, etc. The statements:

$$\text{READ 39, BLOCK}$$
$$\text{39 FORMAT (A4, A1)}$$

would read the set of 162 data cards ($27 \times 6 = 162$) into BLOCK if $c = 4$ ($q = 2$). If $c = 2$ ($q = 3$), the format statement should be:

$$\text{39 FORMAT (A2,A2,A1)}$$

EXERCISE 10.9 Provide the correct data cards for the letter A. Also, modify the print statement and format statement 29 in the subroutine DRAW so that they will work correctly on your computer.

10.7 COMMON PROGRAMMING ERRORS

The errors encountered using multidimensional arrays are similar to those encountered in processing one-dimensional arrays. The most frequent errors are likely to be subscript range errors. These errors may be more common now because multiple subscripts are involved in an array reference, introducing added complexity and confusion.

Some compilers will check every subscript to see whether it is within range; some will check only to see whether the address computed is within the area of storage allocated to the array; and some will do no checking. Consequently, it is important to verify for yourself that all subscripts are correct by printing any suspect subscript values. This is especially important in subprograms that are passed subscripts as arguments.

Other kinds of errors arise because of the complex nesting of indexed-DO and implied indexed-DO loops when they are used to manipulate multidimensional arrays. Care must be taken to ensure that the subscript order is consistent with the nesting structure of the loops. Inconsistent usage will not result in an error diagnostic but should produce incorrect program results.

An additional source of error involves the use of subprogram arguments in dummy array declarations. If the range of a subscript is passed through the argument list, care must be taken to ensure that the value passed is correct. Otherwise, the address computation performed within the subroutine will cause the wrong array elements to be manipulated and out-of-range errors may occur.

10.8 SUMMARY

In this chapter, we have introduced a more general form of the array. This form is useful in representing data which is most naturally thought of in terms of multidimensional structures. The multidimensional array is convenient for representing rectangular tables of information, matrices, game-board patterns, n-dimensional spaces, and tables involving data with multiple category decompositions (such as that found in the university enrollment example, Example 10.3).

We have seen examples of the manipulation of individual array elements through the use of nests of indexed-DO loops. The correspondence between the loop-control variables and the array subscripts determines the order in which the array elements are processed.

Reading, printing, and initializing multidimensional arrays were also described in this chapter. Specifically, we saw that an unsubscripted reference to a two-dimensional array in a read or print statement causes data to be manipulated on a column-by-column basis. We have written nested loops which can be used to read and write data on a row-by-row basis instead.

PROGRAMMING PROBLEMS

10.4 Write a program which reads in a tic-tac-toe board and determines the best move for player X. Use the following strategy: Consider all squares which are empty and evaluate potential moves into them. If the move fills the third square in a row, column, or diagonal which already has two X's, add 50 to the score; if it fills the third square in a row, column, or diagonal with two O's, add 25 to the score;

for each row, column, or diagonal containing this move which will have 2 X's and one blank, add 10 to the score; add 8 for each row, column, or diagonal through this move which will have one O, one X, and one blank; add 4 for each row, column, or diagonal which will have one X and the rest blanks. Select the move which scores the highest.

The possible moves for the board below are numbered. Their scores are shown to the right of the board. Move 5 is selected.

1	O	X
2	X	3
O	4	5

1—10 + 8 = 18
2—10 + 8 = 18
3—10 + 10 = 20
4—8
⑤—10 + 10 + 8 = 28

10.5 Each card of a poker deck will be represented by a pair of integers: the first integer represents the suit; the second integer represents the value of the card. For example, 4, 10 would be the 10 of spades, 3, 11 the jack of hearts, 2, 12 the queen of diamonds, 1, 13 the king of clubs, 4, 14 the ace of spades. Read five cards in and represent them in a 4 × 14 array. A mark should be placed in the five array elements with row and column indices corresponding to the cards entered. Evaluate the poker hand. Provide subroutines to determine whether the hand is a flush (all one suit), a straight (five consecutive cards of different suits), a straight flush (five consecutive cards of one suit), 4 of a kind, a full house (3 of one kind, 2 of another), 3 of a kind, 2 pair, or 1 pair.

10.6 Represent the cards of a bridge check by a pair of integers, as described in Problem 10.5. Read the thirteen cards of a bridge hand into a 4 × 14 array. Compute the number of points in the hand. Score 4 for each ace, 3 for a king, 2 for a queen, 1 for a jack. Also, add 3 points for any suit not represented, 2 for any suit with only one card which is not a face card (jack or higher), 1 for any suit with only two cards, neither of which is a face card.

10.7 (Continuation of Problem 10.2.) If, in the Schedules and Space Problem (10.2), we removed the restriction of a single building, and wished to write the program to accommodate an entire campus of buildings, each with varying numbers of floors and varying numbers of available rooms on each floor, the choice of a two-dimensional array for storing room capacities may prove inconvenient. Instead, it might be easier to use two *parallel arrays*, RMID and RMSIZE to store the identification of each room (building and number) and its size. In fact, we may wish to represent the building ID and room number in separate arrays, RMIDBL, RMIDNO. (This will certainly be the case if the character declaration is not available.) Write a program, with appropriate subroutines, to solve the Schedules and Space Problem using the 15 class sizes given in Exercise 10.7, and the campus room table shown at the top of page 402.

10.8 Implement the block-letter program using only the letters A through E as characters which may be printed.

10.9 Instead of block letters, store a collection of stick-figures in an array. Assign each stick figure a single-digit identification number. Your input data cards should indicate the stick figure to be drawn and its relative placement on the output page. (*Hint.* You should not need the FIND subroutine.)

Room ID

Building	Number	Room size
HUMA	1003	30
MATH	11	25
MUSI	2	62
LANG	701	30
MATH	12	30
ART	2	30
EDUC	61	15
HUMA	1005	25
ART	1	40
ENG	101	30
MATH	3	10
EDUC	63	40
LANG	702	40
MUSI	5	110
HUMA	1002	30

Example For the data cards below,

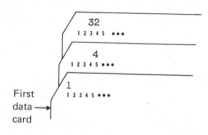

Figure 1 will be drawn above and to the left of Fig. 4. Figures 3 and 2 will be placed next to each other at the bottom of the drawing. Their horizontal displacement will be such that they will be drawn between Figs. 1 and 4.

10.10 Write a set of subroutines to manipulate a pair of matrices. You should provide subroutines for addition, subtraction, and multiplication. Each subroutine should validate its input arguments (i.e., check all matrix dimensions) before performing the required data manipulation.

10.11 The results from the mayor's race have been reported by each precinct as follows, one input card per precinct:

Precinct	Candidate A	Candidate B	Candidate C	Candidate D
1	192	48	206	37
2	147	90	312	21
3	186	12	121	38
4	114	21	408	39
5	267	13	382	29

Write a program to do the following:

A.   Print out the table with appropriate headings for the rows and columns.

B.   Compute and print the total number of votes received by each candidate and the percent of the total votes cast.

C.   If any one candidate received over 50% of the votes, the program should print a message declaring that candidate the winner.

D.   If no candidate received over 50% of the votes, the program should print a message declaring a run-off between the two candidates receiving the largest number of votes; the two candidates should be identified by their letter names.

E.   Run the program once with above data and once with candidate C receiving only 108 votes in precinct 4.

The card format is as follows:

Card column 1: precinct number
Card columns 3–5: candidate A's votes
Card columns 7–9: candidate B's votes
Card columns 11–13: candidate C's votes
Card columns 15–17: candidate D's votes

10.12 The game of Life, invented by John H. Conway, is supposed to model the genetic laws for birth, survival, and death. (See *Scientific American*, October 1970, p. 120.) We will play it on a board consisting of 25 squares in the horizontal and vertical directions. Each square can be empty or contain an X indicating the presence of an organism. Every square (except the border squares) has eight neighbors. The small square shown in the segment of the board drawn below connects the neighbors of the organism in row 3, column 3.

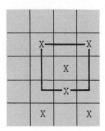

Generation 1

The next generation of organisms is determined according to the following criteria:

1. *Birth:* An organism will be born in each empty location that has exactly three neighbors.

2. *Death:* An organism with four or more organisms as neighbors will die from overcrowding. An organism with fewer than two neighbors will die from loneliness.

3. *Survival:* An organism with two or three neighbors will survive to the next generation.

Generations 2 and 3 for the sample follow:

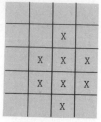

Generation 2

Generation 3

Read in an initial configuration of organisms. Print the original game array, calculate the next generation of organisms in a new array, copy the new array into the original game array, and repeat the cycle for as many generations as you wish. Provide a program system chart. [*Hint.* Assume that the borders of the game array are infertile regions where organisms can neither survive nor be born; you will not have to process the border squares.]

APPENDIX
THE MANIPULATION OF
CHARACTER-TYPE DATA

A.1. Introduction
A.2. The Length of a Character String
A.3. Character Substrings
A.4. The Concatenation Operator
A.5. Use of Character Expressions
A.6. The Character-String Length Function
A.7. Character Manipulation—Sample Problems
A.8. Common Programming Errors
Programming Problems

A.1. INTRODUCTION

The character data declaration

CHARACTER * n   list

and some character data-manipulative features have been included in the 1976
FORTRAN Standard. These features have been implemented and are available
for use on a few FORTRAN compilers. In this appendix, we will describe the
fundamentals of the manipulation of character type data as described in the 1976
Standard. This material is not applicable to compilers that do not allow the character declaration. In fact, many compilers that do have a character data-
declaration feature have not yet included these manipulative features. If you are
using a compiler that does allow these features, you should be reading this appendix, rather than the material in Chapter 9 (from Section 9.3 on).

In the sections that follow, we will introduce three basic operations that
can be performed on character-type data. We will describe how to reference a

character *substring,* and how to *concatenate* (or join) two strings. We will also discuss the use of the function LEN, which computes the length of its character-string argument. Finally, we will see how to write expressions involving character-type data.

In studying this material it is important to remember that character-type data can be manipulated only in conjunction with other character-type data. FORTRAN does not permit the mixing of character-type data with arithmetic (type real or integer) or logical-type information.

A.2. THE LENGTH OF A CHARACTER STRING

The notion of the length of a character string is important to the discussion of character-type data. We will introduce this concept by defining what is meant by the length of a character-string constant and a character variable. The definition of the length of other character entities will be given as they are introduced in later sections.

Length of Character-String Constants and Variables

1. The length of a character-string constant is equal to the number of characters in the constant (excluding the apostrophes used to delimit the constant) except that adjacent pairs of apostrophes within the constant are counted as a single character.

2. The length of a character variable is defined to be the length given to the variable when it is declared. The length of a character variable is, therefore, completely independent of the information that is stored in the variable.

Note. The length of any character entity is a positive number. Zero-length character strings are not permitted in FORTRAN.

FORTRAN provides a library function LEN which can be used to determine the length of its character-string argument. We will describe this function and provide examples of its use in Section A.6. These examples will help provide a better understanding of the length properties of character entities.

A.3. CHARACTER SUBSTRINGS

Character-string manipulations frequently require references to substrings of a character string. A *character substring* is a contiguous portion of a character data item. We can use the character-substring feature of FORTRAN to break a character string into sections or to extract part of a character string.

To specify a substring of a character variable or character array element, we must write the substring name in the form shown below.

Substring References

FORTRAN form:

$$\text{cname} \; (\exp_1: \; \exp_2)$$

Interpretation. cname is a character variable or character array element, and $\exp_1$, $\exp_2$ are *substring expressions*. The values of $\exp_1$ and $\exp_2$ should be type integer. $\exp_1$ and $\exp_2$ are used to specify which substring of cname should be referenced. The value of $\exp_1$ indicates the position in cname of the first character of the substring; the value of $\exp_2$ indicates the position in cname of the last character of the substring.

Note. The reference cname $(\exp_1: \exp_2)$ is called the *substring name*. The integer values of $\exp_1$ and $\exp_2$ must satisfy the following constraints:

$$1 \leq \exp_1 \leq \exp_2 \leq \text{length of cname}$$

If $\exp_1$ is omitted, it is considered to be 1; if $\exp_2$ is omitted, it is considered to be the same as the length of cname. The length of a substring cname $(\exp_1: \exp_2)$ is defined as $\exp_2 - \exp_1 + 1$.

Example A.1 The names of three substrings of the character variable PRES are shown below:

```
CHARACTER * 18 PRES
DATA PRES/'ADAMS, JOHN QUINCY'/
```

```
      PRES(1:5)  │   PRES(13:)
            PRES(8:11)
```

Example A.2

```
CHARACTER * 11  SOSSEC
CHARACTER * 3   SSN1
CHARACTER * 2   SSN2
CHARACTER * 4   SSN3
READ, SOSSEC
SSN1 = SOSSEC (1:3)
SSN2 = SOSSEC (5:6)
SSN3 = SOSSEC (8:11)
```

If the data card

'042–30–0786'

is read, this program segment breaks the Social Security number in this card into substrings as shown below:

SOSSEC	SSN1	SSN2	SSN3
042-30-0786	042	30	0786

The assignment statements in this program are *character assignment statements;* they assign a character string to a character variable. We will discuss character assignments in more detail in Section A.5.

Example A.3 In this example, we will use a character array, FIELD, for storing substrings.

```
        CHARACTER * 10 FIELD(4)
        CHARACTER * 40 SAYING
        READ, SAYING
C BREAK SAYING INTO 4 SUBSTRINGS
        DO  10  I = 1, 4
            FIELD(I) = SAYING((10*I-9): 10*I)
   10   CONTINUE
        PRINT, (FIELD(I)(1:1), I =  1, 4)
        STOP
        END
```

This program segment reads one large character string (length 40) into memory. It then breaks the string into 4 substrings of ten characters each, which are stored in successive elements of FIELD as shown below.

Data Card

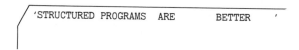

'STRUCTURED PROGRAMS   ARE   BETTER   '

Substrings Referenced in loop 10 for Each Value of I

I	Value of exp_1 $10 \cdot 1 - 9$	Value of exp_2 $10 \cdot 1$	FIELD(I)
1	1	10	'STRUCTURED'
2	11	20	'PROGRAMS '
3	21	30	'ARE '
4	31	40	'BETTER '

The array FIELD (after the execution of loop 10)

FIELD(1)	FIELD(2)	FIELD(3)	FIELD(4)
STRUCTURED	PROGRAMS□□	ARE□□□□□□□	BETTER□□□□

The print statement following loop 10 displays the first character in each element of FIELD. The output from this program segment would be the letters SPAB.

EXERCISE A.1 Given the character variables SSN1, PRES, and FIELD (defined in Examples A.1 through A.3), list the characters that would be printed by the statements:

1)   PRINT, SSN1(1:3)

2)   PRINT, PRES(6:)

3)   PRINT, FIELD(1)(3:9)

A.4. THE CONCATENATION OPERATOR

The only character-string operator available in FORTRAN is the binary operator for *concatenation* (joining strings), written using two consecutive slashes, //.

The Concatenation Operator

FORTRAN form

$$X_1 \; // \; X_2$$

Interpretation. The character string X_2 is concatenated with the character string X_1. This means the string X_2 is joined to the right end of the string X_1. The length of the resulting string is equal to the sum of the lengths of X_1 and X_2.

Example A.4

a) The assignment statement

$$ALFBET = 'ABC' \; // \; 'DE'$$

concatenates the strings 'ABC' and 'DE' together to form one string of length 5, 'ABCDE', which is stored in ALFBET. ALFBET should be a character variable of length 5 or larger.

b) Given the string

'ADAMS, JOHN QUINCY'

stored in the character variable PRES (length 18), the statement

$$\text{NAME} = \text{PRES}(8{:}12) \; // \; \text{PRES}(13{:}13) \; // \; \text{'. '} \; // \; \text{PRES}(:5)$$

will result in the storage of the string

JOHN Q. ADAMS

in the character variable NAME (length at least 13).

c) Given the array FIELD as defined in Example A.3, the statement:

$$\text{REMEDY} = \text{FIELD}(4)(1{:}7) \; // \; \text{FIELD}(1)(1{:}9) \; // \; \text{'S'}$$

will cause the string

'BETTER STRUCTURES'

to be stored in the character variable REMEDY (length at least 17).

EXERCISE A.2   Given PRES and FIELD as defined in Examples A.3 and A.4, evaluate the following:

1)   PRES(8:11) // ' ' // FIELD(2)(1:8)
2)   PRES(1:5) // PRES(7:8) // '.' // PRES(13:13) // '.'

A.5. USE OF CHARACTER EXPRESSIONS

Character expressions may be used in FORTRAN in character assignment statements, as operands of relational operators in logical expressions, and as arguments in subprogram calls. In this section we will describe the rules for the first two uses of character strings mentioned; character-string arguments will be discussed in Section A.7.2.

A.5.1. Character Assignment Statements

The rules of formation of the character assignment statement are summarized below.

Character Assignment Statement

FORTRAN form

variable = expression

Interpretation. Both the variable and the expression must be of type character. A character expression consists of a sequence of character-string constants, character variables, character array elements, or substrings connected by the character operator, //.

Notes. If the length of the variable being assigned exceeds the length of the expression, the expression will be padded on the right with blanks and then stored. If the length of the variable is smaller than the length of the expression, the extra characters on the right will be truncated. If the variable is a substring name, only the character positions specified are defined by the assignment. The definition status of character positions not included in the substring name is unchanged.

Example A.5

```
CHARACTER * 8 NAME, HERS
CHARACTER * 4 FIRST, FIRSTA, FIRSTB, INITLS
CHARACTER * 9 LSTFST
NAME = 'JOHN DOE'
FIRST = 'JOHN'
FIRSTA = NAME(1:4)
FIRSTB = NAME
LSTFST = NAME(6:)// ', '//FIRST
INITLS = NAME(1:1)//'.'//NAME(6:6)//'.'
HERS = NAME
HERS(3:3) = 'A'
```

The execution of these assignment statements will result in the following string assignments.

NAME	FIRST	FIRSTA	FIRSTB	LSTFST	INITLS
JOHN␣DOE	JOHN	JOHN	JOHN	DOE,␣JOHN	J.D.

HERS
JOAN␣DOE

Example A.6

```
CHARACTER * 17 BIGGER
CHARACTER * 8 SMALLR
CHARACTER * 12 SAME
BIGGER = 'EXTRASENSORY'
SMALLR = BIGGER
SAME = BIGGER
```

The result of executing the above character assignments is shown below:

BIGGER	SAME	SMALLR
EXTRASENSORY␣␣␣␣␣	EXTRASENSORY	EXTRASEN

The assignment statement:

$$BIGGER = SMALLR (1:5)//SAME$$

would change BIGGER as shown below.

```
             BIGGER
      EXTRAEXTRASENSORY
```

It would appear that the statement:

$$BIGGER = SMALLR (1:5)//BIGGER$$

would have the same effect as the preceding character assignment statement. However, this statement is illegal since the variable being assigned a value is also referenced in the character expression. FORTRAN does not allow any of the character positions being defined in an assignment statement to appear in the character expression used in the definition. Thus, the statement

$$BIGGER(4:8) = BIGGER(1:5)$$

is illegal because positions 4 and 5 are referenced on both sides of the assignment operator. However,

$$BIGGER(13:17) = BIGGER(1:5)$$

is legal since there is no overlap between the character positions in BIGGER being defined (13 to 17) and the positions being referenced (1 to 5). The effect of this statement is shown next.

```
             BIGGER
      EXTRASENSORY  EXTRA
```

EXERCISE A.3 Let HIPPO, QUOTE1, QUOTE2, and BIGGER be declared and initialized as:

```
CHARACTER * 12 HIPPO, BIGGER
CHARACTER * 30 QUOTE1
CHARACTER * 24 QUOTE2, QUOTE
DATA HIPPO, BIGGER/ 'HIPPOPOTAMUS', 'SMALL' /
DATA QUOTE1/ 'STRUCTURED PROGRAMS ARE BETTER' /
```

Carry out each of the following assignment statements. Indicate if any are illegal.

a)   QUOTE(:24) = QUOTE1(21:24)//QUOTE1(:20)

b)   QUOTE2 = QUOTE(21:24)//QUOTE(:20)

c)   QUOTE(1:24) = QUOTE2

d)   HIPPO(4:) = 'S'

e)   BIGGER = 'LARGE'

f)   BIGGER = 'EXTRA'//BIGGER

g)   BIGGER(6:7) = 'ST'

A.5.2. Character Data in Logical Expressions

The use of character data in logical expressions is governed by rules that are similar to those for arithmetic data. Besides the concatenation operator, character data may be used only as operands of the relational operators .GE., .LT., etc. The result of the indicated comparison of character strings is either .TRUE. or .FALSE.

Character Data in Logical Expressions

FORTRAN form

$$string_1 \text{ relop } string_2$$

Interpretation. $string_1$ and $string_2$ are evaluated. If $string_1$ and $string_2$ are not the same length, the shorter string is padded on the right with blanks until their lengths are equal. The two equal-length strings are then compared as specified by the relational operator, relop.

The result of a character-string comparison depends solely upon the collating sequence of the particular version of FORTRAN that you are using. The *collating sequence* defines the relationships between the characters in the FORTRAN character set. The collating sequence specified in the 1977 FORTRAN Standard is summarized below.

Collating Sequence (1977 Standard)

1. The collating sequence for the letters A–Z corresponds to their normal alphabetical order. (Thus, A is less than B–Z, B is less than C–Z, and so on.)

2. The collating sequence for the characters 0–9 corresponds to their normal numerical order.

3. The blank character precedes both A and 0 in the collating sequence. Thus, the blank is considered to be less than all characters A–Z and 0–9.

This standard collating sequence guarantees that if a word w_1 precedes another word w_2 in the dictionary, then w_1 will be less than w_2 in FORTRAN. (Also, if a person's name, n_1 precedes a name n_2 in the phone book, then n_1 will be less than n_2 in FORTRAN.)

It is important to note that very little else is specified by the new standard collating sequence. In particular:

1. The collating sequence for special characters (not A–Z, 0–9, or blank) is not specified, nor are the relationships between these characters and A–Z, 0–9, and blank specified.

2. The relationships between the letters A–Z and the characters 0–9 are not specified.

All relationships not specified in the Standard are defined separately for each version of FORTRAN, and hence may differ from one version to the next. It is important that you learn the collating sequence defined for the FORTRAN version that you are using.

Example A.7 The relationships between the pairs of character strings shown below are not specified in the 1977 Standard.

'ALLEN, R.'   and   'ALLEN, RICHARD'   (collating sequence of the period is not specified)

'X123'   and   'XYZ'   (collating sequence of 0–9 is not specified in relation to A–Z)

'./*'   and   '.*//*='   (collating sequence for special characters is not specified)

'***'   and   '*'   (collating sequence for a blank, in relation to the special characters, is not specified)

Example A.8 If the character variable WORD contains the string 'PROGRAMS', then the following logical expressions evaluate to true.

```
WORD .GT. 'PROG'
WORD (1:4) .EQ. 'PROG'
WORD (1:1) .LT. 'PR'
WORD (1:1) .EQ. 'P'
WORD (6:10) .LT. 'A' // WORD (1:4)
```

In the last expression, the character expression 'A' // WORD(1:4) is evaluated first because // is above .LT. in the operator hierarchy. (The concatenation operator (//) is between the arithmetic and relational operators in the operator hierarchy (see Fig. 9.2).) The resulting string 'APROG' is then compared to the string 'AMS □□'. 'AMS □□' is less than 'APROG' because M precedes P in the collating sequence.

EXERCISE A.4 Evaluate the following logical expressions assuming that the character variable WORD contains the character string 'PROGRAMS □□'.

a)   WORD (2:4) .GT. 'RO'

b)   WORD (2:4) .GT. 'ROP'

c)   WORD (1:4) // WORD(6:) .LT. 'PROGRAM'

A.6. THE CHARACTER-STRING LENGTH FUNCTION—LEN

The FORTRAN library function LEN accepts character-type data as its argument and determines the length (number of characters) of its argument.

FORTRAN Library Function LEN

FORTRAN form

$$\text{LEN (string)}$$

Interpretation. String may be any character expression (including character-string constants and variables). The value returned is an integer denoting the length of the string.

Note. If the argument is a substring, string (exp_1: exp_2), then LEN will return the value $exp_2 - exp_1 + 1$. If the argument is a variable or array element, its length is defined by the corresponding declaration statement regardless of the length of the string last stored there.

Example A.9

a) LEN ('ABCDE') returns a value of 5.

b) LEN ('MY'//' NAME') returns a value of 7.

c) If WORD is declared as a character variable of length 10, LEN(WORD) always returns a value of 10. Thus the sequence of statements

```
WORD = 'ABCDE'
I = LEN(WORD)
PRINT, I
```

would result in the printing of the value 10, the length of the string (after padding with 5 blanks) that is stored in WORD.

EXERCISE A.5   Assume I is an integer; BIGGER is a character variable of length 20, and SMALER is a character variable of length 5. Evaluate the following:

1)
```
        BIGGER = 'EXTRASENSORY'
        I = LEN (BIGGER)
```
2)
```
        SMALER = 'EXTRASENSORY'
        I = LEN(SMALER)
```
3)
```
        I = LEN(SMALER(1:2) // BIGGER(10:11))
```
4)
```
        (LEN('ABCDE') .EQ. LEN('AB') + LEN('CDE'))
```

A.7. CHARACTER MANIPULATION—SAMPLE PROBLEMS

A.7.1. Scanning an Indexed–DO Header

In the previous sections, we introduced the FORTRAN character manipulation operations. We will now illustrate the application of these operations in the solution of two sample problems. The first problem involves scanning a character string and extracting substrings.

PROBLEM A.1   We can consider the indexed–DO structure header statement as a character string of the form

```
        DO sn lcv = initval, endval, stepval
```

For example,

```
        'DO 35 I = FIRST, LAST, 5'
```

One of the tasks of a compiler in translating this statement might be to separate the substrings representing the loop parameters initval, endval, and stepval from the rest of the string and to save these substrings in separate character variables, IVSTR, EVSTR, and STSTR for later reference. We will write a program to perform this substring separation.

DISCUSSION.   The task of our program is to identify and copy each of the indexed–DO parameters—initval, endval, and stepval—into IVSTR, EVSTR, and STSTR, respectively.

The most difficult subtask for our program involves determining the starting and ending positions of the loop parameter strings. This, in turn, requires the identification of the positions in the header string of the equal sign (POSEQL) and the first and second commas (POS1CM and POS2CM). If the second comma (and third parameter) in the header statement is missing, the character '1' is stored in STSTR. If either the equal sign or the first comma is missing, an error message is printed and program execution is terminated. For simplicity, we will assume that the indexed–DO parameters contain no array element or function references.

Once the positions of the equal sign and the commas have been located, the substrings *delimited* by them (including all blanks) must be copied into IVSTR, EVSTR, and STSTR. In each case, the copy can be performed using a simple character assignment statement.

To locate the equal sign and the commas, we will use a search subroutine similar to the one written for Example 9.4, as modified in Exercise 9.4. The difference is that this subroutine (SRCHAR) searches a character string of length SIZE for a specified substring instead of searching an integer array of size SIZE for an integer value. A logical variable (FOUND) will communicate the results of the search to the main program as before.

The data table for the main program follows; the flow diagram is shown in Fig. A.1.

Data table for scanning indexed-DO header

Input variables	*Program variables*	*Output variables*
HEADER: Indexed–DO header (character*80)	EQUAL: Symbol '=' (character*1)	IVSTR: Initial value loop parameter (character*40)
LENGTH: Number of characters in the indexed–DO header (integer)	COMMA: Symbol ',' (character*1)	EVSTR: End-value loop parameter (character*40)
	ONE: Symbol '1' (character*1)	STSTR: Step-value loop parameter (character*40)
	POSEQL: Position of '=' in HEADER (integer)	
	POS1CM: Position of first ',' in HEADER (integer)	
	POS2CM: Position of second ',' in HEADER (integer)	
	FOUND: Program flag; Set true if desired symbol is located; otherwise, false (logical)	
	BEGIN: Represents the position in HEADER where the search should start. (integer)	

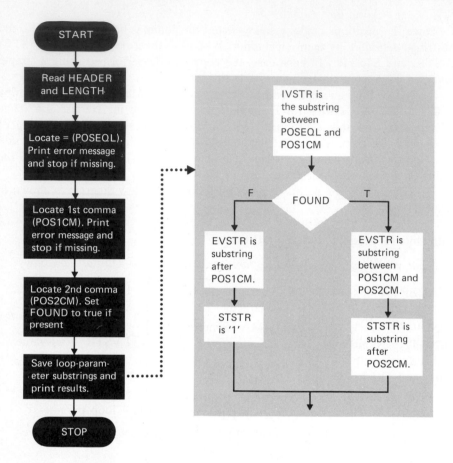

Fig. A.1 Flow diagrams for the indexed-DO scanner (Problem A.1).

Data table (continued)

Subprograms referenced:

SRCHAR (subroutine): Searches a character string for a specified substring.

Argument	Definition
1	String to be searched (input, character)
2	Length of argument 1 (input, integer)
3	Substring to be found (input, character)
4	Length of argument 3 (input, integer)
5	Position in argument 1 where search begins (input, integer)
6	Program flag to communicate search results (output, logical)
7	Starting position in argument 1 of substring if found (output, integer)

The main program is shown in Fig. A.2.

```
C SEPARATE AND SAVE PARAMETER SUBSTRINGS OF INDEXED-DO HEADER
        CHARACTER * 80 HEADER
        CHARACTER * 1 COMMA, EQUAL, ONE
        CHARACTER * 40 IVSTR, EVSTR, STSTR
        INTEGER LENGTH,POSEQL, POS1CM, POS2CM, BEGIN
        LOGICAL FOUND
        DATA COMMA, EQUAL, ONE/',', '=', '1'/
C ENTER INPUT DATA
        READ, HEADER, LENGTH
C SEARCH FOR EQUAL SIGN - SET POSEQL
        BEGIN = 1
        CALL SRCHAR (HEADER, LENGTH, EQUAL, 1, BEGIN, FOUND, POSEQL)
C PRINT ERROR MESSAGE IF = SIGN MISSING
        IF (.NOT. FOUND) THEN
            PRINT, ' = SIGN MISSING'
            STOP
        ENDIF
C SEARCH FOR FIRST COMMA FOLLOWING = SIGN
        BEGIN - POSEQL + 1
        CALL SRCHAR (HEADER, LENGTH, COMMA, 1, BEGIN, FOUND, POS1CM)
C PRINT ERROR MESSAGE IF FIRST COMMA IS MISSING
        IF (.NOT. FOUND) THEN
            PRINT, 'COMMA IS MISSING'
            STOP
        ENDIF
C SEARCH FOR SECOND COMMA FOLLOWING FIRST COMMA
        BEGIN = POS1CM + 1
        CALL SRCHAR (HEADER, LENGTH, COMMA, 1, BEGIN, FOUND, POS2CM)
C
C SAVE PARAMETER STRINGS
        IVSTR = HEADER (POSEQL + 1 : POS1CM - 1)
C       SAVE ENDVALUE AND STEP PARAMETERS
        IF (FOUND) THEN
            EVSTR = HEADER(POS1CM + 1 : POS2CM - 1)
            STSTR = HEADER(POS2CM + 1 : LENGTH)
        ELSE
            EVSTR = HEADER(POS1CM + 1 : LENGTH)
            STSTR = ONE
        ENDIF
C
C PRINT RESULTS
        PRINT, 'FOR INDEXED DO HEADER: ', HEADER
        PRINT, 'INITIAL VALUE EXPRESSION: ', IVSTR
        PRINT, 'FINAL VALUE EXPRESSION: ', EVSTR
        PRINT, 'STEP VALUE EXPRESSION: ', STSTR
        STOP
        END
```

Fig. A.2 Program to extract indexed-DO parameters.

EXERCISE A.6 Of what relevance is the assumption made in the discussion of Problem A.1 that no array element or function references could appear in the indexed–DO loop control parameters?

A.7.2. Character Strings as Subroutine Arguments

We can complete Problem A.1 by writing the subroutine SRCHAR. However, before doing this, we will present guidelines for the use of character strings as subprogram arguments.

Character arguments in a subprogram call can be character expressions as well as character string constants or character variables. Character arguments used in a subprogram call must, of course, correspond to subprogram dummy arguments which are declared to be of type character as well. As part of the type declaration of a character dummy argument, the programmer must specify its length. This is accomplished by using a declaration of the form

```
CHARACTER * (*) STRING
```

within the subprogram. The symbol (*) is used to indicate that the length of the dummy argument STRING is variable, and will be defined to match the length of its corresponding argument at each call of the subprogram. Only character dummy arguments can be declared using the length specifier (*); all local character variables must have integer constants as length specifiers.

A.7.3. Searching for a Substring

We are now ready to write the subroutine SRCHAR as defined in the data table for Problem A.1. We will generalize this subroutine to search for any substring, SUBSTR, of length SUBLEN. The data table follows; the flow diagrams are found in Fig. A.3.

Data Table for Subroutine SRCHAR

Input arguments

STRING: Represents the string to be searched (character)

LENGTH: Represents the length of STRING (integer)

SUBSTR: Represents the substring to be found (character)

SUBLEN: Represents the length of SUBSTR (integer)

START: Represents the position in STRING where the search is to begin (integer)

Output arguments

FOUND: A flag used to indicate whether or not SUBSTR is found. FOUND is set to true if SUBSTR is found; otherwise, FOUND is set to false (logical)

POS: Represents the position in STRING where the substring starts if found (integer)

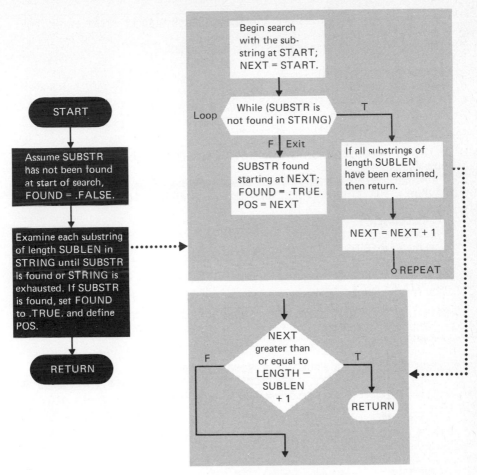

Fig. A.3 Flow diagrams for SRCHAR subroutine.

Data table (continued)

Local variables

NEXT: Position of the first character
of the substring in STRING that is
to be compared to SUBSTR (integer)

The subroutine can now be written directly from the flow diagram (see Fig. A.4).

EXERCISE A.7   Why is NEXT compared to LENGTH − SUBLEN + 1 rather than simply LENGTH in order to determine whether STRING has been completely searched?

```
      SUBROUTINE SRCHAR (STRING,LENGTH,SUBSTR,SUBLEN,START,FOUND,POS)
C
C SEARCHES A CHARACTER STRING FOR A SUBSTRING
C
C ARGUMENT DEFINITIONS
C   INPUT ARGUMENTS
C      STRING - STRING TO BE SEARCHED
C      LENGTH - LENGTH OF STRING
C      SUBSTR - SUBSTRING TO BE FOUND
C      SUBLEN - LENGTH OF SUBSTR
C      START - POSITION IN STRING WHERE SEARCH IS TO START
C   OUTPUT ARGUMENTS
C      FOUND - FLAG - SET TRUE IF SUBSTR FOUND. ELSE FALSE
C      POS - POSITION OF FIRST CHARACTER OF SUBSTR IN STRING
C
      CHARACTER * (*)STRING, SUBSTR
      INTEGER LENGTH, START, POS, SUBLEN
      LOGICAL FOUND
C
C LOCAL VARIABLES
      INTEGER NEXT
C
C INITIALIZE - ASSUME SUBSTR NOT FOUND - BEGIN SEARCH AT START
      FOUND = .FALSE.
      NEXT = START
C
C SEARCH UNTIL SUBSTR FOUND OR STRING EXHAUSTED
      WHILE (STRING(NEXT : NEXT+SUBLEN-1) .NE. SUBSTR(1 : SUBLEN)) DO
         IF (NEXT .GE. LENGTH-SUBLEN+1) RETURN
         NEXT = NEXT + 1
      ENDWHILE
C SUBSTR FOUND IN STRING STARTING AT POSITION NEXT
      FOUND = .TRUE.
      POS = NEXT
      RETURN
      END
```

Fig. A.4 Character-string search subroutine.

A.7.4. Text Editing Problem

PROBLEM A.2   There are many applications for which it is useful to have a computerized text-editing program.   For example, if you are preparing a laboratory report (or a textbook), it would be convenient to edit or modify sections of the report (improve sentence and paragraph structure, change words, correct spelling mistakes, etc.) at a computer terminal and then have a fresh, clean copy of the text typed at the terminal without erasures or mistakes.

DISCUSSION   A Text Editor System is a relatively sophisticated system of subprograms that can be used to instruct the computer to perform virtually any kind of text alteration.   At the heart of such a system is a subprogram that replaces one substring existing in the text with another substring. As an example, consider the following sentence prepared by an overzealous member of the Addison-Wesley advertising group.

```
'THE BOOK BY FRIEDMEN AND KOFFMAN
 IN FRACTURED PROGRAMING IS GRREAT?'
```

To correct this sentence we would want to specify the following edit operations:

1) Replace 'MEN' with 'MAN'
2) Replace 'IN' with 'ON'
3) Replace 'FRAC' with 'STRUC'
4) Replace 'AM' with 'AMM'
5) Replace 'RR' with 'R'
6) Replace '?' with '!'

The result is now at least grammatically correct.

```
'THE BOOK BY FRIEDMAN AND KOFFMAN
 ON STRUCTURED PROGRAMMING IS GREAT!'
```

We will write the replacement program module as the subroutine REPLAC. The argument portion of the data table is shown below.

Data table for REPLAC

Input arguments

OLD: Character string
   to be replaced
   (character)

OLDLEN: Length of OLD
   (integer)

NEW: Character string
   to be inserted
   (Character)

NEWLEN: Length of NEW
   (integer)

Since many of the subprograms in the Text Editing System will be referencing the string in TEXT, we will assume that TEXT is in a common block. Two other data items, CURLEN and MAXLEN, defined as shown below, will be in a second common block. (Two common blocks are used because the 1976 FORTRAN Standard specifies that a common block containing character-type data may not contain data of any other type.)

Additional data table entries for REPLAC

Common blocks used:

Name	*block contents*
TXTBLK	TEXT: The text string (character*1000)
LENBLK	CURLEN: Current length of string in TEXT (integer)
	MAXLEN: Maximum possible length of string in TEXT (integer)

MAXLEN is a Text Editor System constant which is defined to be equal to the maximum length of the text string (1000). CURLEN would be defined when the string to be edited is first placed in TEXT (probably in the main program) and would be redefined each time a change was made to TEXT.

The first task to be performed by REPLAC is to locate the first occurrence of the string to be replaced (OLD) in TEXT (only the first occurrence will be replaced). This can be accomplished using the subroutine SRCHAR from Section A.7.3. Remember, SRCHAR was generalized to locate the first character position of any substring in a larger string. We can now take advantage of this generalization in writing REPLAC.

The additional data-table entries required for REPLAC are shown next. The flow diagrams are drawn in Fig. A.5.

Additional data table entries for REPLAC

Local variables

BEGIN: Input argument in call of SRCHAR (program constant, integer 1—all searches will start in position 1 of TEXT)

FOUND: Output argument in call of SRCHAR; FOUND will be true if OLD is in TEXT; otherwise, FOUND will be false (logical)

POSOLD: Output argument in call of SRCHAR; POSOLD contains the position of the first character of OLD in TEXT if OLD is found (integer)

Subprograms referenced:

SRCHAR: (see Section A.7.3)

Before we can write the subroutine, a further refinement of step 30 is needed. If NEWLEN is larger than OLDLEN, it is possible that the length of the revised version of TEXT, REVLEN, would exceed MAXLEN. In this case, an error message should be printed and the replacement operation ignored; otherwise, a copy of TEXT can be made by concatenating the substring preceding OLD (the *head*), NEW, and the substring following OLD (the *tail*). The new data-table entries are at the top of page A22. The refinement of step 30 is shown in Fig. A.6; the subroutine is given in Fig. A.7.

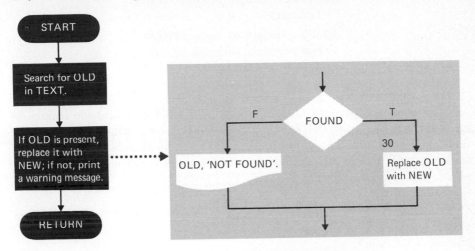

Fig. A.5 Flow diagrams for string replacement subroutine.

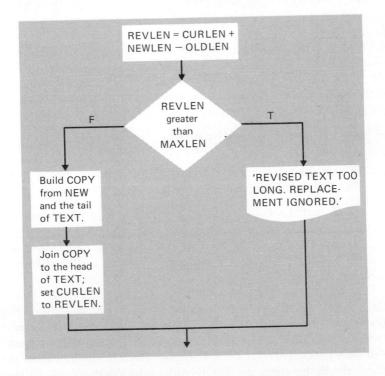

Fig. A.6 Refinement of Step 30 in subroutine REPLAC.

Additional local variables

REVLEN: Length of edited text
(integer)

COPY: Temporary copy of NEW
concatenated with the tail of
TEXT (character*1000)

The dummy arguments OLDLEN and NEWLEN represent the lengths of the substrings OLD and NEW, respectively. Since the declared length of the actual argument corresponding to NEW may be greater than NEWLEN, the reference to NEW in Fig. A.7 should be in the form of a substring name:

```
COPY = NEW(1:NEWLEN)//TEXT(POSOLD+OLDLEN:CURLEN)
```

This statement concatenates the string represented by NEW and the tail of TEXT (part following OLD) as desired.

EXERCISE A.8   Consider the subroutine in Fig. A.7. Why is the character variable COPY needed in this program? Is it necessary that the length of this variable be 1000?

EXERCISE A.9   Will the common blocks TXTBLK and LENBLK have to be declared in SRCHAR?

EXERCISE A.10   The algorithm for the replace subroutine makes no provision for either of the following two situations:

1. The length of the new string (NEWLEN) is equal to the length of the old string (OLDLEN);
2. The length of the tail is zero—that is, the last character of the string to be replaced is also the last character in the text.

In both cases, all that is required to build a revised version of the text is to copy the new string into TEXT in place of the old string. Nothing need be done with the tail of TEXT. (In case 1, the tail does not have to be moved, and in case 2, there is no tail.) Modify the subroutine in Fig. A.7 to test for these two situations and take the appropriate action.

EXERCISE A.11   The REPLAC subroutine shown in Fig. A.7 always begins its search for OLD at position one of TEXT. In many instances, it is useful to be able to provide REPLAC with an additional piece of information—namely, the position in TEXT where the search is to begin. Such flexibility can be provided in REPLAC simply by changing BEGIN from a local variable to an argument. By providing REPLAC with a starting point that is closer to the sequence of

```
      SUBROUTINE REPLAC (OLD, OLDLEN, NEW, NEWLEN)
C
C REPLACE SUBSTRING OLD WITH STRING NEW
C
C ARGUMENT DEFINITIONS (ALL ARE INPUT ARGUMENTS)
C     OLD - STRING TO BE REPLACED
C     OLDLEN - LENGTH OF STRING TO BE REPLACED
C     NEW - REPLACEMENT STRING
C     NEWLEN - LENGTH OF REPLACEMENT STRING
C
      CHARACTER * (*) OLD
      CHARACTER * (*) NEW
      INTEGER OLDLEN, NEWLEN
C
C COMMON BLOCKS
      COMMON /TXTBLK/ TEXT
      CHARACTER * 1000 TEXT
      COMMON /LENBLK/ CURLEN, MAXLEN
      INTEGER CURLEN, MAXLEN
C
C LOCAL VARIABLES
      INTEGER BEGIN, POSOLD, REVLEN
      LOGICAL FOUND
      CHARACTER * 1000 COPY
C
C SEE IF OLD IS IN TEXT. IF SO, REPLACE IT. IF NOT, IGNORE REQUEST.
C
      BEGIN = 1
      CALL SRCHAR (TEXT,CURLEN,OLD,OLDLEN,BEGIN,FOUND,POSOLD)
      IF (FOUND) THEN
C        CHECK REVISED LENGTH BEFORE REPLACEMENT
         REVLEN = CURLEN + NEWLEN - OLDLEN
         IF (REVLEN .GT. MAXLEN) THEN
            PRINT, 'REVISED TEXT TOO LONG. REPLACEMENT IGNORED'
         ELSE
C           REPLACE OLD AND TAIL WITH NEW AND TAIL
            COPY = NEW(1:NEWLEN)//TEXT(POSOLD+OLDLEN:CURLEN)
            TEXT(POSOLD : ) = COPY
            CURLEN = REVLEN
            PRINT, 'NEW VERSION OF TEXT'
         ENDIF
      ELSE
         PRINT, OLD, ' NOT FOUND, REPLACEMENT IGNORED'
      ENDIF
      RETURN
      END
```

Fig. A.7 The REPLAC subroutine.

characters to be replaced, we can cut down on the amount of searching that needs to be done. We may also be able to reduce the amount of *contextual information* required in order to have the correct replacement done.

For example, if BEGIN is the fifth argument in REPLAC, then

```
CALL REPLAC ('E', 1, 'A', 1, 5)
```

could be used instead of

```
CALL REPLAC ('MEN', 3, 'MAN', 3)
```

to correct the spelling of Friedman. The original contextual information 'M' and 'N' was needed to prevent the 'E' in 'THE' from being replaced by 'A'.

For each of the editing operations listed below, write two call statements to REPLAC. Write the first call statement using four arguments and the second call using five arguments, with BEGIN as the fifth.

a) Replace 'FRAC' with 'STRUC'

b) Replace the 'I' in 'IN' with an 'O'

c) Replace 'BOOK' by 'TEXT'

d) Insert an extra 'M' into 'PROGRAMING'

e) Delete an 'R' from 'GRREAT'

EXERCISE A.12 From Exercise A.11 (parts (d) and (e)) it is clear that REPLAC can be used to perform both insertions into and deletions from TEXT simply by providing enough contextual information in the arguments representing the new and the old strings. Nevertheless, we might wish to write subroutines DELETE and INSERT to handle all deletions and insertions.

a) Using the REPLAC subroutine as a guide, write a subroutine DELETE (OLD, OLDLEN, BEGIN) to delete the first occurrence of a string OLD of length OLDLEN from TEXT. The search for OLD in TEXT will start at BEGIN.

b) We can write a subroutine INSERT to insert a character string NEW of length NEWLEN into TEXT. In addition to NEW and NEWLEN, this subroutine will need a third input argument, BEGIN, which in this case marks the exact position in TEXT in which the insertion is to be performed. For example, the statements

```
CALL INSERT ('ELLIOT ', 7, 26)
CALL INSERT ('FRANK ', 6, 13)
```

would insert the strings 'FRANK' and 'ELLIOT' in front of 'FRIEDMEN' and 'KOFFMAN', respectively, in the original version of TEXT. Again using REPLAC as a guide, write the subroutine INSERT (NEW, NEWLEN, BEGIN)

A.8. COMMON PROGRAMMING ERRORS

Now that we know how to manipulate different types of data, we must be especially careful not to misuse these data types in expressions. Only logical constants and variables can appear as operands of logical operators (.AND., .OR., .NOT.). Character strings can be operands of the character operator (concatenation, //) and relational operators (.GT., .LE., etc.). Remember that character strings and character constants can be manipulated only with other character variables.

Misspelling the name of a logical or character variable (or neglecting to declare it) may result in compiler detection of syntax errors. This is because the type declaration intended for that variable will not be recognized if the variable name is spelled incorrectly. Consequently, the compiler will follow the implied type convention and assume that the variable is type integer or real. Since arithmetic variables cannot be operands of logical or character operators, diagnostic messages may be generated.

In specifying substrings, it is possible to reference a character whose position is outside of the string. For example, if the substring name were

$$PRES(IX/2:IX)$$

and the value of IX exceeded the declared length of PRES, a diagnostic message would be printed. This is analogous to an array range error and may be caused by a loop that does not terminate properly or simply an incorrect substring expression. If in doubt, print out the values of suspect substring expressions.

An additional source of error in character-assignment statements has been mentioned earlier. That involves referencing the same character position on both sides of the assignment operator ('=' sign). The statement

$$PRES(1:5) = PRES(4:9)$$

is illegal, because positions 4 and 5 are both defined and referenced in this statement.

PROGRAMMING PROBLEMS

Problems 9.7 through 9.19 are appropriate programming problems to test your skill at character manipulation. In these problems, use character variables for storage of character strings instead of arrays. For problems 9.9 and 9.19, supply your own function GETLEN.

GLOSSARY
OF FORTRAN STATEMENTS
AND STRUCTURES

Type of Statement	Sample Statements	Primary Page† References	Notes
1. Declarations			
Type declaration	INTEGER K,NMBR,COUNTR,LIST(50),N	14, 114ff	
	REAL GROSS,NET,X(25,25)		
	LOGICAL FLAG,FOUND,SWITCH		
	CHARACTER*26 ALFBET		W
Common declaration	COMMON BETA(25,50), A	266	
	COMMON /TXTBLK/ TEXT(240)		
Data declaration	DATA K,GROSS /5,−2.5/,FLAG/.TRUE./	18, 117	
	DATA X /625*0/		
	DATA (LIST(I),I=1,3)/10,20,30/	176	W

† Only the first page of a consecutive sequence is given.
P indicates that the feature is supported by most structured FORTRAN preprocessors.
W indicates that the feature is compatible with WATFIV-S.
The absence of a note means that the feature is part of standard FORTRAN.

Type of Statement	Sample Statements	Primary Page† References	Notes
2. Data Manipulation			
Arithmetic assignment	NMBR = LIST(I)+6 GROSS = (X*5.0)**2	16, 138	
Logical assignment	FLAG = .TRUE. SWITCH = K .LT. NMBR .AND. FOUND	124, 326	
Character assignment	ALFBET = 'ABCDEFGHIJKLMNOPQRSTUVWXYZ'	123	W
3. Execution Control			
Unconditional transfer	GO TO 193 (label between 1 and 9999)	24	
Exit	EXIT	221	P
Next	NEXT	222	P
Execution stop	STOP	20	
Remote block call	EXECUTE name	225	P, W
Conditional execution	IF(GROSS*.14 .LT. 100.0) TAX = 0.0 IF(FOUND) RETURN	78	
Logical IF	IF(K .GE. NMBR .AND. (.NOT. FOUND)) X GROSS = NET	183	
4. Input and Output			
Input	READ,K,NMBR	18,119,306	W
	READ 26,X	289	
26	FORMAT (8F10.3/)	293, 307	
	READ(5,32)N,(LIST(K),K=1,N)	175, 306ff	
32	FORMAT(I3/(10I8/))		

Type of Statement	Sample Statements	Primary Page† References	Notes
Output	`PRINT,'NMBR=',NMBR`	20, 63, 290	W
	`PRINT 401,ALFBET`		
	`401   FORMAT(' ALPHABET IS'/A27)`	288	W
	`WRITE(6,402) COUNTR`		
	`402   FORMAT ('1',70X,'PAGE',1X,I4)`		

5. Control Structures

Decision structure

Single-alternative

```
IF (condition) THEN

   ─────┐
   ─────│ executed if
   ─────┤ condition true
   ─────│
   ─────┘

ENDIF
```
74   P, W

Double-alternative

```
IF (condition) THEN

   ─────┐
   ─────│ executed if
   ─────┤ condition true
   ─────│
   ─────┘

ELSE

   ─────┐
   ─────│ executed if
   ─────┤ condition false
   ─────│
   ─────┘

ENDIF
```
73   P, W

Multiple-alternative

```
IF (condition₁) THEN

   ─────┐
   ─────│ executed if
   ─────┤ condition₁ true
   ─────│
   ─────┘
```
197   P

Type of Statement	Sample Statements	Primary Page† References	Notes
	ELSE IF (condition₂) THEN		

$$\text{ELSE IF (condition}_2) \text{ THEN}$$

```
_____ ⎫
_____ ⎬ executed if
_____ ⎪ condition₂ true
_____ ⎭

         .
         .
         .
```

ELSE IF (condition$_k$) THEN

```
_____ ⎫
_____ ⎬ executed if
_____ ⎪ condition$_k$ true
_____ ⎭
```

ELSE

```
_____ ⎫
_____ ⎬ executed if
_____ ⎪ all conditions
_____ ⎭ false (optional)
```

ENDIF

Loop structures

| Condi-tional loop | WHILE (condition) DO | 85 | P, W |

```
_____ ⎫
_____ ⎬ executed while
_____ ⎪ condition true
_____ ⎪
_____ ⎭
```

ENDWHILE

| Indexed loop | DO sn lcv = iv, fv, sv | 131ff | |

```
_____ ⎫ (lcv – integer
_____ ⎪ variable; loop
_____ ⎬ parameters – integer
_____ ⎪ variables or con-
_____ ⎭ stants)
```

sn CONTINUE

Type of Statement	Sample Statements	Primary Page† References	Notes

Indexed loop (structured version)	FOR (lcv = iexp, fexp, sexp) DO
	
	——⎤
	——⎟ (lcv – integer
	——⎟ variable; loop
	——⎬ parameters – integer
	——⎟ expressions)
	——⎟
	——⎦
	
	ENDFOR
		208	P

Remote block	REMOTE BLOCK name ——⎤ ——⎟ ——⎬ ——⎟ ——⎦ END BLOCK	225	P, W

6. Subprogram Features

Subprogram definition	SUBROUTINE SRCHAR	253	
	SUBROUTINE EXCH (NMBR,COUNTR)		
	LOGICAL FUNCTION SAME (A,B,C)	242	
	INTEGER FUNCTION SEEK (LIST)	242	
Subprogram exit	RETURN	243	
Subprogram call	CALL SRCHAR	254	
	CALL EXCH (LIST(I), LIST(J))		
	Y = SQRT (X)	145, 241	
Subprogram end	END	243	

ANSWERS TO SELECTED EXERCISES

Chapter 1

1.2   Legal: ARK, ZIP12, ITCH, GROSS
       Illegal: MICHAEL   contains 7 letters
              12ZIP   begins with a number
              P3$ $ illegal character in a variable name
              X123459   too many characters
              NINE + T   + illegal character in a variable name

1.3   The order of the pairs of statements

              READ, HOURS   READ, RATE
              PRINT, HOURS   PRINT, RATE

       can be interchanged provided the corresponding cards in the data section
       are also interchanged.

       The statements

              PRINT, NET
              PRINT, GROSS

       can be interchanged.

       The following statements cannot be moved:

       REAL   Declaration; must appear before executable statements and before
              DATA
       DATA   Must follow REAL; precede executable statements

       Read statements: Used to store data in RATE and HOURS; this must be
           done before RATE and HOURS are used to compute GROSS

GROSS   Must be computed before NET, because the computation of NET depends upon the value of GROSS

STOP   Will be the last statement executed

END   Must be the last statement in the program.

1.6   *Printed output:*

```
40.00
16.25
533.00
```

1.7
```
GROSS = HOURS * RATE
NET = GROSS
IF (GROSS .GT. MIN) NET = NET - TAX
```

1.9 c)

```
REAL A, B, C, X
REAL FOUR, TEMP1, TEMP2
DATA FOUR /4.0/
READ, A
READ, B
READ, C
TEMP1 = B * B
TEMP2 = A * C
TEMP2 = FOUR * TEMP2
X = TEMP1 - TEMP2
PRINT, X
STOP
END
```

1.11   Value of X cannot be determined, since the contents of COUNTR are unknown.

1.12   *Card   Error(s)*

1   No commas separating variable names.

2   No decimal after 3.

3   No decimal after 3.500 (comma not allowed either).

4   No comma after READ.

5   Incorrect assignment statement. Only one variable name should be to the left of the = sign.

6   Label 20 should be in label field (columns 1–5).

7   = is not a legal relational operator; IF (X .EQ. Y) is correct form.

8   Start of FORTRAN statement PRINT should not be to the left of column 7.

9   Transfer statement has illegal label (label must be a string of from 1 to 5 decimal digits).

10   Missing right parenthesis after ZERO.

11   Column 6 should be blank. READ, RATE or PRINT, RATE should begin in column 7.

12   No error.

Chapter 2

2.2   a)

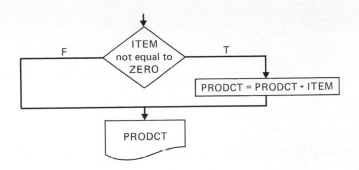

2.3   *Algorithm step*

	SUM	COUNTR	ITEM
	0.0	0	Unknown
21			−12.50
22	−12.50		
23		1	
21			8.25
22	−4.25		
23		2	
21			0.0
22	−4.25		
23		3	
21			−16.5
22	−20.75		
23		4	
21			.25
22	−20.50		
23		5	

2.4

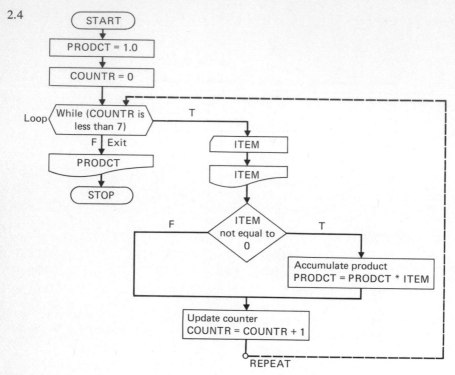

Chapter 3

3.1   Statement group ① : Initialize.

Statement group ② : Read in and print each item, accumulate sum, and update the loop-control variable.

Statement group ③ : Print the final sum; and stop.

Statement group ④ : Compute and print the sum of a collection of data items.

3.2 c)

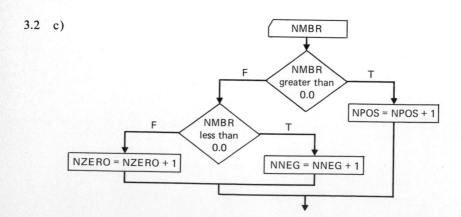

3.4   i)

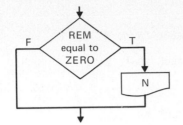

IF (REM .EQ. ZERO) PRINT, N

ii)

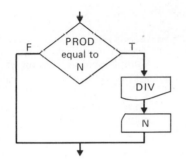

IF (PROD .EQ. N) THEN
    PRINT, 'DIV = ', DIV
    READ, N
ENDIF

iii)

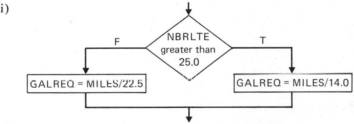

IF (NBRLTE .GT. 25.0) THEN
    GALREQ = MILES/14.0
ELSE
    GALREQ = MILES/22.5
ENDIF

3.5

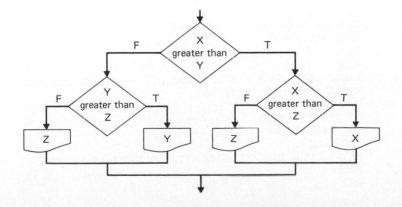

```
IF (X .GT. Y) THEN
   IF (X .GT. Z) THEN
      PRINT, 'THE LARGEST VALUE IS ', X
   ELSE
      PRINT, 'THE LARGEST VALUE IS ', Z
   ENDIF
ELSE
   IF (Y .GT. Z) THEN
      PRINT, 'THE LARGEST VALUE IS ', Y
   ELSE
      PRINT, 'THE LARGEST VALUE IS ', Z
   ENDIF
ENDIF
```

3.6

Condition in FORTRAN	Complement in FORTRAN
X .LT. Y	X .GE. Y
A .GT. ZERO	A .LE. ZERO
ITEM .NE. SNTVAL	ITEM .EQ. SNTVAL
COUNT .LT. NRITMS	COUNT .GE. NRITMS

3.7   *Refined flow diagram:*

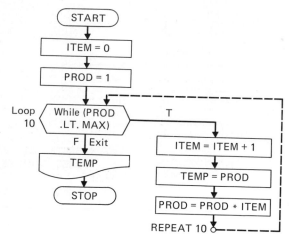

```
      INTEGER ITEM, PROD, TEMP, MAX
      DATA MAX /10000/
      ITEM = 0
      PROD = 1
C INCREMENT ITEM, SAVE PREVIOUS PRODUCT + COMPUTE NEW PRODUCT
      WHILE (PROD .LT. MAX) DO
            ITEM = ITEM + 1
            TEMP = PROD
            PROD = PROD * ITEM
      ENDWHILE
      PRINT, 'THE LARGEST CUMULATIVE PRODUCT IS ', TEMP
      STOP
      END
```

3.8   No execution of the loop body would occur. Printed output of the value of LARGE would be −1.0.

3.9   *Add to the data table:*

Output variables
NRSCRS: Contains a count of the number of scores read in and processed

Change the flow diagram as follows:

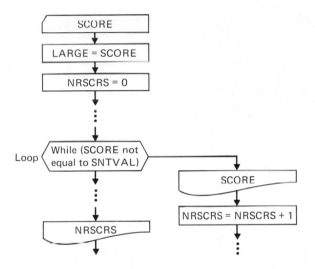

Changes to the FORTRAN program would be

```
REAL SCORE, LARGE, SNTVAL
INTEGER NRSCRS
        .
        .
        .
READ, SCORE
LARGE = SCORE
NRSCRS = 0
        .
        .
        .
WHILE (SCORE .NE. SNTVAL) DO
    PRINT, SCORE
    NRSCRS = NRSCRS + 1
        .
        .
        .
ENDWHILE
PRINT, 'LARGE =  ', LARGE
PRINT, 'NRSCRS =  ', NRSCRS
```

3.10   Initializing LARGE to 0.0 would not work if all of the data items were negative.

3.12   *Refined flow diagram:*

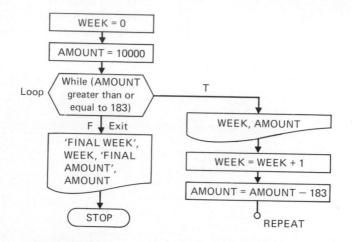

```
        INTEGER WEEK, AMOUNT
C INITIALIZE PROGRAM VARIABLES
        WEEK = 0
        AMOUNT = 10000
        PRINT, 'WEEK    AMOUNT'
C DEDUCT USAGE FOR A WEEK IF ENOUGH WATER IS LEFT
        WHILE (AMOUNT .GE. 183) DO
            PRINT, WEEK, AMOUNT
            WEEK = WEEK + 1
            AMOUNT = AMOUNT - 183
        ENDWHILE
        PRINT, 'FINAL WEEK ', WEEK, ', FINAL AMOUNT = ', AMOUNT
    STOP
    END
```

3.13   It is possible for an order to be filled even if the one before it was not.

	OLDINV	NEWINV	NOTFLD	ORDER	ADREQ
READ, OLDINV	75.0				
NEWINV=OLDINV		75.0			
NOTFLD=0.0			0.0		
READ, ORDER				20.0	
NEWINV=NEWINV−ORDER		55.0			
READ, ORDER				50.0	
NEWINV=NEWINV−ORDER		5.0			
READ, ORDER				100.0	
NOTFLD=NOTFLD+ORDER			100.0		
READ, ORDER				3.0	
NEWINV=NEWINV−ORDER		2.0			

(Unknown arrow spanning OLDINV through ADREQ for the READ, OLDINV row)

```
        READ, ORDER                                      15.0
        NOTFLD=NOTFLD+ORDER                    115.0
        READ, ORDER                                       2.0
        NEWINV=NEWINV−ORDER          0.0
        READ, ORDER                                       0.0
        ADREQ=NOTFLD−NEWINV                                      115.0
```

Chapter 4

4.1 a) Type real

b) Illegal (could be type character, but apostrophes are missing)

c) Illegal (only .TRUE. or .FALSE. may be delimited with periods as logical constants)

d) Type character

e) Type integer

f) Type real

g) Illegal (needs an E in front of + to be real)

h) Illegal (could be type character except for the extra (or missing) apostrophe in the middle)

i) Illegal (could be type real without the $)

j) Illegal (could be type character but the apostrophes are missing)

4.5
```
        INTEGER IDNMBR, CRHOUR, COUNT
        CHARACTER * 4 NAME, CLASS, COURSE        [or INTEGER NAME, . . .]
        CHARACTER * 1 GRADE                      [or INTEGER GRADE]
        READ, IDNMBR, NAME, CLASS
        COUNT = 0
        WHILE (COUNT .LT. 3) DO
            READ, COURSE, CRHOUR, GRADE
            COUNT = COUNT + 1
        ENDWHILE
              .
              .
              .
```

4.6

0	'Z'	0.00	'ZZZZ' 0
ID number	code	amount	Day of transaction

There must be four data items in the card: integer ID, a character code, a real amount, and a date consisting of the number of the day of the month (an integer). Only one of these items need be used as the actual sentinel value, and it really doesn't matter which one is chosen. The sentinel value must have the property that it cannot appear as a valid data item. The choice of the other items in the card is irrelevant, as long as their data type is correct.

4.7
```
PROD = 1                  PROD = 2
DO 40 I = 2, N            DO 40 I = 4, N, 2
    PROD = PROD * I            PROD = PROD * I
40 CONTINUE               40 CONTINUE
```

4.8   *Possible revisions (for each N):*

First check if N is 3. If so, N is prime. Next test to see if 2 divides N. If so, N is not prime. If not, compute

```
HALFN = N / 2
LIM = HALFN + 1
```

and rewrite loop 20 header:

```
DO 20 DIV = 3, LIM, 2
```

A smaller maximum test value is the square root of N, but we do not yet know enough FORTRAN to be able to use this in the program.

4.9   The correct evaluations are:

```
T1 = B * C        T1 = X / Y
X  = A + T1       A  = T1 * Z
```

4.10   One possible FORTRAN equivalent is:

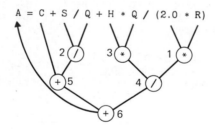

4.11 a) `X = 4.0 * A * C`
   d) `K = 3 * (I + J)`
   f) `I = J * 3`

4.13
```
LOGICAL BADAIM                                          ⇐ (Add)
    .
    .
    .
RADIAN = THETA * (PI / 180.0)
BADAIM = .TRUE.                                         ⇐ (Add)
WHILE (BADAIM) DO                                       ⇐ (Add)
    T = X / (V * COS(RADIAN))
    H = V * T * SIN(RADIAN) - G/2.0 * T ** 2
```

```
        IF (H .LT. 100.0) THEN
            PRINT, 'ARROW TOO LOW'
            IF (H .LT. 0.0) PRINT, 'ARROW DID NOT REACH TOWER'
            V = V + 10.0                                        ⇐ (Add)
        ELSE
            IF (H .GT. 110.0) THEN
                PRINT, 'ARROW TOO HIGH'
                V = V - 8.0                                     ⇐ (Add)
            ELSE
                PRINT, 'GOOD SHOT PRINCE'
                BADAIM = .FALSE.                                ⇐ (Add)
            ENDIF
        ENDIF
    ENDWHILE
    STOP
    END
```

4.14

	Y	*YNEW*
`Y = START`	3.0	
`YNEW = (Y+X/Y) /2.0`		3.1667
`Y = YNEW`	3.1667	
`YNEW = (Y+X/Y) /2.0`		3.1623
`Y = YNEW`	3.1623	
`YNEW = (Y+X/Y) /2.0`		3.1623

4.15   `ROUNDX = FLOAT (IFIX (X * 100.0 + 0.5)) / 100.0`
        `ROUNDX = FLOAT (IFIX (X * 10.0 ** N + 0.5)) / 10.0 ** N`

4.16 a)   1.666 ... (floating point) FLOAT (COLOR)

  b)   .666 ... (floating point) FLOAT (COLOR)

  c)   0   (fixed point)

  d)   −3.0   (floating point) FLOAT (COLOR + STRAW)

  e)   11   (fixed point)   FLOAT (RED), apply IFIX to entire expression

  f)   1   (fixed point)   FLOAT (STRAW) and FLOAT (COLOR), apply IFIX to entire expression

Chapter 5

5.1   X(ISUB) refers to the 4th element of array X.
       X(4) refers to the 4th element of array X.
       X(2*ISUB) refers to the 8th element of array X.
       X(5*ISUB−6) refers to the 14th element of array X.
       (This subscript is out of the legal range of subscript values of 1 through 10) for the array X.)

5.2 a)   X(I) refers to the 6th element.   (within bounds)

  b)   X(3*I−20) refers to the −2nd element.   (out of bounds)

  c)   X(4+I) refers to the 10th element.   (within bounds)

  d)   X(I*3−12) refers to the 6th element.   (within bounds)

e) X(4*I−12) refers to the 12th element.   (out of bounds)

f) X(I−2*I) refers to the −6th element.   (out of bounds)

g) X(30) refers to the 30th element.   (out of bounds)

h) X(I*I−1) refers to the 35th element.   (out of bounds)

References (c), (d), (f) and (h) do not conform to the standard (but are allowed by many compilers).

5.3 a) 12.0

b) 8.2

c) .FALSE.; .TRUE.

d) .TRUE.

e)

G(1)	G(2)	G(3)	G(4)	G(5)	G(6)	G(7)	G(8)	G(9)	G(10)
2.0	4.0	6.0	8.0	10.0	12.0	14.0	16.0	18.0	20.0

f)

G(1)	G(2)	G(3)	G(4)
12.0	18.0	22.0	−9.3

5.4

FACTOR(1)	FACTOR(2)	FACTOR(3)	FACTOR(4)	FACTOR(5)	FACTOR(6)	FACTOR(7)
1	2	6	12	20	30	42

5.5

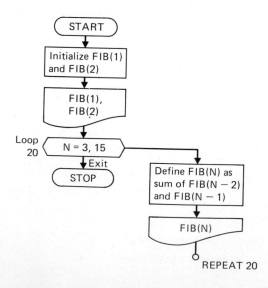

```
        INTEGER FIB(15), N
        FIB(1) = 1
        FIB(2) = 1
        PRINT,   FIB(1)
        PRINT,   FIB(2)
        DO  20   N = 3,  15
           FIB(N) = FIB(N-2) + FIB(N-1)
           PRINT,   FIB(N)
     20 CONTINUE
        STOP
        END
```

5.6 a) CHARACTER * 1 ALFBET (26) [or INTEGER ALFBET (26)]

   DATA ALFBET / 'A', 'B', 'C', 'D', 'E', 'F', 'G', 'H',
   Z   'I', 'J', 'K', 'L', 'M', 'N', 'O', 'P', 'Q', 'R', 'S',
   Z   'T', 'U', 'V', 'W', 'X', 'Y', 'Z'/

   b) INTEGER PRIME (10)

   READ, PRIME

```
  /‾‾‾‾‾‾‾‾‾‾‾‾‾‾‾‾‾‾‾‾‾‾‾‾‾‾‾‾‾‾
 /   1  2  3  5  7  11  13  17  19  23
 |
```

5.7
```
        PRINT, '    N              N(PRIME)'
        DO  20  N = 1, 10
           PRINT,  N, PRIME(N)
     20 CONTINUE
```

5.8
```
        IF    (COUNT .LT. 1) THEN
           PRINT,   'NEGATIVE VALUE FOR COUNT.  EXECUTION TERMINATED'
           STOP
        ENDIF
        IF  (COUNT .GT. 70) THEN
           PRINT,   'VALUE OF COUNT EXCEEDS 70.  EXECUTION TERMINATED'
           STOP
        ENDIF
```
   COUNT serves as the end value of an Indexed–DO loop whose loop-control variable is used as the subscript for the array SCORES. Therefore, the value of COUNT must be within the range of SCORES so as to ensure that the loop-control variable will represent legal subscript values. The value of COUNT must also be compatible with the rules for indexed–DO loop structures; i.e., be greater than or equal to the initial value 1.

5.9
```
        INTEGER SCORES(70), MAXKNT, SNTVAL, NEXT, COUNT
        DATA MAXKNT, SNTVAL /70, -99/
        COUNT = 1
        READ, NEXT
        WHILE (NEXT .NE. SNTVAL) DO
           SCORES(COUNT) = NEXT
```

```
        COUNT = COUNT + 1
        IF (COUNT .GT. MAXKNT) THEN
            PRINT, 'NUMBER OF SCORES EXCEEDS 70. EXECUTION STOPPED'
            STOP
        ENDIF
        READ, NEXT
    ENDWHILE
    IF (COUNT .EQ. 1) THEN
        PRINT, 'NO SCORES PROCESSED'
        STOP
    ENDIF
        .
        .
        .
```

5.10   The fact that TARGET was not present in any of the array elements can
be ascertained only *after all array elements* have been checked. As shown,
the message **'TARGET NOT FOUND'** would be printed with *each* non-
occurrence of TARGET as the array is scanned.

5.12

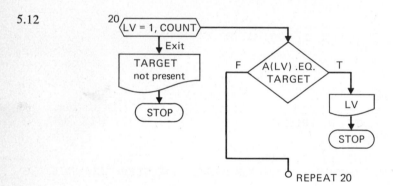

The program flag is no longer needed.

5.14   The easiest change to make is to increase the size of FREQ to 6, and
use FREQ (6) to store the error count. The only change required in the
flow diagram is the insertion of the box

INDEX = 6

directly under the box

'INVALID GRADE',
GRADE

The program changes are shown next.

```
         .
         .
         .
    INTEGER FREQ(6)
         .
         .
         .
    DATA FREQ(6*0)
         .
         .
         .
    IF  (CURGRD .LT. 0 .OR. CURGRD .GT. 100) THEN
        PRINT, 'GRADE ILLEGAL AND IS IGNORED'
        INDEX = 6
    ELSE
        INDEX = 10 - CURGRD / 10
        IF (INDEX .EQ. 0) INDEX = 1
        IF (INDEX .GT. 5) INDEX = 5
    ENDIF
C   UPDATE FREQUENCY CLASS COUNT
    FREQ(INDEX) = FREQ(INDEX) + 1
         .
         .
         .
    PRINT, (FREQ(LV), LV = 1, 5)
    PRINT, 'THE NUMBER OF ILLEGAL GRADES IS', FREQ(6)
    STOP
    END
```

Chapter 6

6.1

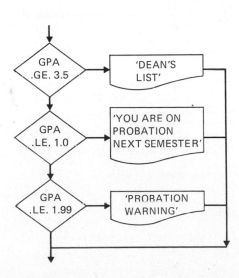

```
IF     (GPA .GE. 3.5) THEN
    PRINT,  'DEAN''S LIST'
ELSE IF (GPA .LE. 1.0) THEN
    PRINT, 'YOU ARE ON PROBATION NEXT SEMESTER'
ELSE IF (GPA .LE. 1.99) THEN
    PRINT,  'PROBATION WARNING'
ENDIF
```

6.2   *Problem 4.1*

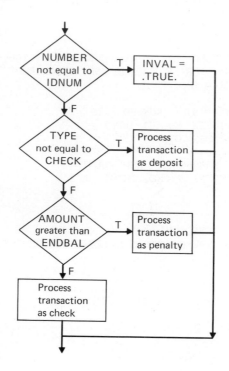

Example 4.16:

```
IF (H .LT. 0.0) THEN
    PRINT,  'ARROW DID NOT REACH THE TOWER'
ELSE IF (H .LT. 100.0) THEN
    PRINT,  'ARROW TOO LOW'
ELSE IF (H .GT. 110.0) THEN
    PRINT,  'ARROW TOO HIGH'
ELSE
    PRINT,  'GOOD SHOT PRINCE'
ENDIF
```

6.4   a)   READ, NDROP
```
         IX = 1
         WHILE    (NDROP .NE. CLIST(IX)) DO
            IX = IX + 1
```

```
              IF (IX .GT. N) THEN
                  PRINT, 'ID TO BE DELETED, ', NDROP, ' NOT FOUND.'
                  STOP
              ENDIF
          ENDWHILE
          WHERE = IX
   b)     READ, NADD
          IX = 1
          WHILE    (CLIST(IX) .LE. NADD) DO
            IX = IX + 1
            IF (IX .GT. N) GO TO 20
          ENDWHILE
       20 WHERE = IX
```

6.5 a) *Using the FOR loop*

```
       INTEGER FDEGR, RCDEGR
       REAL CDEGR
       PRINT, 'FAHRENHEIT     CENTIGRADE'
       FOR (FDEGR = 210, −30, −10) DO
           CDEGR = FLOAT (FDEGR − 32) / 1.8
           RCDEGR = IFIX(CDEGR + 0.5)
           PRINT, FDEGR, RCDEGR
       ENDFOR
       STOP
       END
```

6.5 b) *Without the FOR loop*

```
       INTEGER FDEGR, RCDEGR
       REAL CDEGR
       PRINT, 'FAHRENHEIT     CENTIGRADE'
       FDEGR = 210
       WHILE (FDEGR .GE. −30) DO
           CDEGR = FLOAT (FDEGR − 32) / 1.8
           RCDEGR = IFIX(CDEGR + 0.5)
           PRINT, FDEGR, RCDEGR
           FDEGR = FDEGR − 10
       ENDWHILE
       STOP
       END
```

6.8
```
       OUTER     1
       INNER J 1    1
       INNER J 1    3
       INNER K 1    2
       INNER K 1    4
       OUTER     2
       INNER J 2    1
       INNER J 2    3
       INNER K 2    2
       INNER K 2    4
```

6.11

```
          .
          .
          .
     INTEGER MEDIAN, MEDIX
          .
          .
          .
     PRINT,  (M(I), I=1, COUNT)
     IF (MOD(COUNT, 2) .EQ. 0) THEN
         MEDIX = COUNT / 2 + 1
         MEDIAN = (M(MEDIX)+M(MEDIX−1)) / 2
     ELSE
         MEDIX = COUNT / 2 + 1
         MEDIAN = M(MEDIX)
     ENDIF
     PRINT,      'MEDIAN = ', MEDIAN
     STOP
```

Inserted statements for computing median

6.12   *Example 6.9:*

```
        IX = 1
        WHILE (M(IX) .LE. 1000.0 .AND. IX .LE. 125) DO
            IF (M(IX) .GT. 0.0) THEN
C               PROCESS POSITIVE ELEMENTS
                ─
                ─
                ─
                ─
            ENDIF
            IX = IX + 1
        ENDWHILE
```

Chapter 7

7.1   a) 8   b) 5   c) 3   d) 1

7.2

Input variables	Program variables	Output variables
TABLE(100): Array containing data (real)	IX: Loop-control variable for real loop (integer)	RANGE (real) MEAN (real) MEDIAN (real)
N: Number of data items in TABLE (integer)		

Subprograms referenced:

LARGE (real function):   Finds the largest item in a collection of real data items

SMALL (real function):   Finds the smallest item in a collection of real data items

AVERAG (real function): Computes the average of a collection of real data items

FNDMED (real function):   Finds the median of a collection of real data
items

7.3 a) READ, XCOUNT
READ, (X(IX), IX = 1, XCOUNT)
RANGE = LARGE(X, XCOUNT) − SMALL(X, XCOUNT)
MEAN = AVERAG(X, XCOUNT)
MEDIAN = FNDMED(X, XCOUNT)

b) No changes would be required.

7.5
```
        REAL FUNCTION AVERAG(ARRAY, NRITMS)
C
C FIND THE AVERAGE OF A COLLECTION OF REAL DATA ITEMS
C ARGUMENT DEFINITIONS —
C   INPUT ARGUMENT
C       ARRAY — ARRAY CONTAINING DATA
C       NRITMS — NUMBER OF ITEMS IN THE ARRAY
C
        INTEGER NRITMS
        REAL ARRAY(NRITMS)
C
C LOCAL DECLARATIONS
        REAL SUM
        INTEGER I
C
C ACCUMULATE SUM AND COMPUTE AVERAGES
        SUM = 0.0
        DO  100 I = 1, NRITMS
          SUM = SUM + ARRAY(I)
   100 CONTINUE
C
        AVERAG = SUM / FLOAT(NRITMS)
        RETURN
        END
```

7.8
```
        SUBROUTINE TWOSUM (ARRAY1, ARRAY2, ARRAY3, ASIZE)
C
C COMPUTE SUM OF CORRESPONDING PAIRS OF ITEMS IN ARRAY1 AND
C         ARRAY 2
C STORE RESULT IN APPROPRIATE ELEMENT OF ARRAY3
C
C ARGUMENT DEFINITIONS —
C   INPUT ARGUMENTS
C     ARRAY1 — CONTAINS DATA TO BE SUMMED
C     ARRAY2 — CONTAINS DATA TO BE SUMMED
C     ASIZE — SIZE OF THREE ARRAYS
C   OUTPUT ARGUMENTS
C     ARRAY3 — CONTAINS RESULTS OF PAIR-WISE ADDITION
C
        INTEGER ASIZE
        INTEGER ARRAY1(ASIZE), ARRAY2(ASIZE), ARRAY3(ASIZE)
C
C LOCAL VARIABLES
```

```
            INTEGER IX
      C
      C MAIN LOOP
            DO  100 IX = 1, ASIZE
            ARRAY3(IX) = ARRAY1(IX) + ARRAY2(IX)
      100   CONTINUE
            RETURN
            END
```

7.9
```
            SUBROUTINE COUNT (ARRAY, SIZE, ITEM, TALLY)
      C
      C COUNTS NUMBER OF OCCURRENCES OF A REAL DATA ITEM IN AN ARRAY
      C
      C ARGUMENTS DEFINITIONS
      C   INPUT ARGUMENTS
      C     ARRAY - ARRAY TO BE SEARCHED
      C     SIZE - SIZE OF ARRAY TO BE SEARCHED
      C     ITEM - DATA ITEM SOUGHT IN ARRAY
      C   OUTPUT ARGUMENTS
      C     TALLY - THE NUMBER OF OCCURRENCES OF ITEM
      C
            INTEGER SIZE, TALLY
            REAL ARRAY(SIZE), ITEM
      C
      C LOCAL VARIABLE
            INTEGER I
            TALLY = 0
      C
      C INITIATE SEARCH. INCREMENT TALLY AS OCCURRENCES OF ITEM ARE
      C        FOUND
      C
            DO 100 I = 1, SIZE
               IF (ARRAY(I) .EQ. ITEM) TALLY = TALLY + 1
      100   CONTINUE
            RETURN
            END
```

7.10   **Data Table**

Input arguments

A: Represents the array of items to be searched (real)

SIZE: The number of elements of A to be searched (integer)

TARGET: Item being searched for (integer)

Output arguments

NOTFND: Program flag; set to false if TARGET found; otherwise set to true (logical)

Local variables

LV: Loop-control variable and subscript (also printed as output each time TARGET is found in A)

```
        SUBROUTINE SEARCH (A, SIZE, TARGET, NOTFND)
C
C SEARCH A REAL ARRAY FOR A REAL ITEM
C PRINT VALUE OF ARRAY SUBSCRIPT FOR EACH ELEMENT CONTAINING
C        ITEM
C
C ARGUMENT DEFINITIONS —
C   INPUT ARGUMENTS
C     A — ARRAY TO BE SEARCHED
C     SIZE — NUMBER OF ITEMS TO BE SEARCHED
C     TARGET — ITEM BEING SOUGHT
C   OUTPUT ARGUMENTS
C     NOTFND — FALSE IF ITEM FOUND ONCE OR MORE.  ELSE TRUE
C
      INTEGER SIZE
      REAL A(SIZE), TARGET
      LOGICAL NOTFND
C
C LOCAL VARIABLES
      INTEGER LV
C
C ASSUME TARGET NOT PRESENT.  IF TARGET FOUND, PRINT LOCATION
      NOTFND = .TRUE.
      DO 20 LV = 1, SIZE
         IF (A(LV) .EQ. TARGET) THEN
            NOTFND = .FALSE.
            PRINT, TARGET, 'FOUND IN ELEMENT', LV, ' OF A.'
         ENDIF
20    CONTINUE
      RETURN
      END
```

7.11 a) Y = 16.0

   b) A = −2.0

   c) X(3) = 1.0

   d) X(5) = 10.2

7.12 a) 1.0   2.0   4.0

   b) 7, 5, 3, 1, 9

   There is no relationship. Because the array NEXT is an argument in the call to DEFINE.

Chapter 8

8.1 a) Correct

   b) Incorrect; ⑩ FORMAT (1X, Ⓘ4 , 2X, F12.1)

   c) Incorrect; 16 FORMAT (F16.3Ⓒ5X)

   d) Correct

   e) Incorrect; 127 FORMAT (A2, FⒺ.3, X6, I2) [No room for decimal]

    f) Incorrect; 128 FORMAT (A3, 'X = Ⓘ, 13)

    g) Incorrect; 129 FORMAT (1X, A3, 'X = Ⓘ F3.1)

8.2 a) 1234555.4567

    b) (Line skipped)

       1234

       (3 lines skipped)

         555.4567

    c) K =   1234

       ALPHA = 555.46

    d) (Skip to top of next page)

       K =   1234   ALPHA =   555.457

    e)   K IS   1234 ALPHA IS   555.4567

8.3   *Variable*   *Maximum value*

Variable	Maximum value
AMOUNT	99999.99
MONTHS	999
RATE	99.99
MPAYMT	999.99
TPAYMT	999999.99

8.4

```
INTEGER SSNO1, SSNO2, SSNO3
REAL  HOURS, RATE, PAY
CHARACTER * 4 LAST, FIRST    [or INTEGER LAST, FIRST]
PRINT 10, SSNO1, SSNO2, SSNO3
10 FORMAT ('1SOCIAL SECURITY NUMBER', I4, '—', I2, '—', I4)
PRINT 20, LAST, FIRST
20 FORMAT ('0', A3, ',', A3)
PRINT 30
30 FORMAT ('0 HOURS    RATE    PAY')
PRINT 40, HOURS, RATE, PAY
40 FORMAT (' ', F5.2, 3X, F4.2, 3X, F6.2)
```

8.5

```
10 FORMAT ('1',50X,'SOCIAL SECURITY NUMBER',I4, '—',I2, '—', I4)
20 FORMAT ('0',62X,A3,', ', A3)
30 FORMAT ('0',57X, 'HOURS    RATE    PAY')
40 FORMAT (57X, F5.2, 3X, F4.2, 3X, F6.2)
```

8.6

```
INTEGER AGE, YEAR, OCCODE
CHARACTER * 11  SSNO        [or INTEGER SSNO(3)]
CHARACTER * 1 INIT          [or INTEGER INIT]
CHARACTER * 13 FIRST        [or INTEGER FIRST(4)]
CHARACTER * 20 LAST         [or INTEGER LAST(5)]
READ 10, SSNO, LAST, FIRST, INIT, AGE, YEAR, OCCODE
10 FORMAT(A11,A20,A13,A1,3X,I2,4X,I5,4X,I3)
 [or 10 FORMAT(I3,1X,I2,1X,I4,5A4,3A4,A1,A1,3X,I2,4X,I5,4X,I3)]
```

552–63–0179 BROWN   JERRY   L   38   23   12

1 2 3 4 5 6 7 8 9 10 11 12 13 14 15 16   •••   32   •••   45 46 47 48 49 50   •••   58 59 60 61 62 63 64 65 66   •••

8.10

```
/16312DAWN–321      49
|  1 2 3 4 5 6 7 8 9 10 11 12 13 14 15 16 17 18 19
```

8.13 a)   PRINT 10, X
          10 FORMAT (5(1X, 4F8.2/)) or FORMAT (1X,4F8.2)

   b)   PRINT 20, N, (X(I), I = 1, N))
          20 FORMAT (1X, 'N = ', I2/20(1X, 4F8.2/))

   c)   PRINT 30, QUEUE
          30 FORMAT (170(1X, 6E15.6/)) or FORMAT (1X, 6E15.6)

   d)   DO 40 I = 1, 120
              PRINT 50, ROOM(I), TEMP(I)
          40 CONTINUE
          50 FORMAT (1X, I3, 5X, F6.1)

Chapter 9

9.1 a) Logical operator .AND. must have logical expressions as operands.

   (I .LT. 1) .AND. (I .LT. 2) .AND. (I .LT. 3)

   b) Real variable (Z) cannot be used as operand of logical operator .OR.

   (X .EQ. Y) .OR. (X .EQ. Z)

   c) Real variable (X) cannot be used as operand of logical operator .OR.

   (X .LT. Z) .OR. (Y .LT. Z)

   d) Logical expressions (FLAG2, .TRUE.) cannot be used as operands of relational operator .EQ.

   FLAG1 .OR. FLAG2

   e) Logical expressions (FLAG1, FLAG2) cannot be used as operands of relational operator .EQ.

   ((FLAG1 .AND. FLAG2) .OR. (.NOT. FLAG1 .AND.
   (.NOT. FLAG2))) .OR. (X .EQ. Y)

9.2   True; false

9.3

   (1)

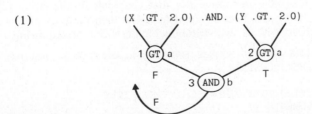

(4)

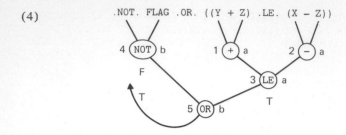

9.4   START must be added to the argument list, the argument definition list
(input) and the argument declarations (integer). A check should be made
to ensure that START lies between 1 and SIZE. The statement

NEXT = 1

should be changed to read

NEXT = START

9.6

```
        CHARACTER * 1 STRING (80)        [or INTEGER STRING (TO)]
        INTEGER N, LENGTH, GETLEN, SIZE
        DATA SIZE /80/
C READ IN N (NUMBER OF CARDS)
        READ, N
C LOOP 80 READ IN CARDS
        DO 20 IX = 1, N
        READ 10, STRING
10      FORMAT (80A1)
        LENGTH = GETLEN (STRING, SIZE)
        PRINT 15, STRING
15      FORMAT (1X, 80A1)
        PRINT, 'LENGTH OF STRING = ', LENGTH
20      CONTINUE
        STOP
        END
```

The declaration of STRING must be consistent with its declaration in
GETLEN.

9.8   If NEWS (END) is the last element of the string to be moved, NEWS
(FIRST) is the element to receive the first character of the string to be
moved, and FIRST is less than or equal to END, then the back end of the
string being moved will be overwritten with the front of the string.

```
        SUBROUTINE REVCOP(SOURCE,SRFRST,SRLAST,TARGET,TRGMAX,
        Z    TRFRST,COUNT)
C
C COPY ONE STRING TO ANOTHER, SHIFTING RIGHT
C    INPUT ARGUMENTS
C       SOURCE — ARRAY CONTAINING STRING TO BE COPIED
```

```
C      SRFRST — SUBSCRIPT OF FIRST ELEMENT TO BE COPIED
C      SRLAST — SUBSCRIPT OF LAST ELEMENT TO BE COPIED
C      TRGMAX — MAX NO. OF ITEMS THAT CAN BE PUT IN TARGET
C      TRFRST — SUBSCRIPT OF TARGET ELEMENT TO GET FIRST SOURCE
C           ELEMENT
C    OUTPUT ARGUMENTS
C      TARGET — ARRAY TO WHICH STRING IS COPIED
C      COUNT — NUMBER OF CHARACTERS COPIED
C
          INTEGER SRLAST, TRGMAX, SRFRST, TRFRST, COUNT, LCV
          CHARACTER * 1 SOURCE(SRLAST), TARGET(TRGMAX)
                                        [or INTEGER . . .]
C
C
C VALIDATE INPUT ARGUMENTS, COUNT, AND TARGET UPPER BOUND
C        AS IN SUBROUTINE COPY
                   .
                   .
                   .

C PERFORM COPY. START WITH RIGHTMOST POSITION IN SOURCE
          LCV = COUNT
          WHILE (LCV .GT. 0) DO
              TARGET (TRFRST+LCV−1) = SOURCE(SRFRST+LCV−1)
              LCV = LCV − 1
          ENDWHILE
          RETURN
          END
```

9.12   Introduce a new integer variable, ENDOLD, which marks the end of OLD (in TEXT) if OLD is found.

```
          REVLEN = CURLEN + NEWLEN − OLDLEN
          ENDOLD = POSOLD + OLDLEN − 1
          IF (REVLEN .GT. MAXLEN) THEN
              PRINT, 'REVISED TEXT TOO LONG. REPLACEMENT IGNORED.'
          ELSE IF (NEWLEN .EQ. OLDLEN .OR. ENDOLD .EQ. CURLEN) THEN
              CALL COPY (NEW, 1, NEWLEN, TEXT, MAXLEN, POSOLD, NEWLEN)
              CURLEN = REVLEN
          ELSE
              (FORM NEW VERSION OF TEXT BY MOVING TAIL AND COPYING NEW)
                   .
                   .
                   .
          ENDIF
```

9.16 a)

```
          SUBROUTINE DELETE (OLD, OLDLEN, BEGIN)
C
C DELETE STRING OLD FROM TEXT
C
C ARGUMENT DEFINITIONS
C   INPUT ARGUMENTS
C     OLD STRING TO BE DELETED FROM TEXT
C     OLDLEN — LENGTH OF OLD
```

```
      C        BEGIN — POSITION IN TEXT WHERE SEARCH FOR OLD STARTS
               INTEGER OLDLEN, BEGIN
               CHARACTER * 1 OLD (OLDLEN) [or INTEGER OLD (OLDLEN)]
      C
      C    COMMON BLOCKS
               COMMON /TXTBLK /TEXT(1000)
               COMMON /LENBLK/ CURLEN, MAXLEN
               CHARACTER * 1 TEXT                        [or INTEGER TEXT]
               INTEGER CURLEN, MAXLEN
      C
      C    LOCAL VARIABLES
               INTEGER BEGIN, COUNT
               LOGICAL FOUND
      C
      C SEE IF OLD IS IN TEXT.. IF SO, DELETE, IF NOT, IGNORE REQUEST
               BEGIN = 1
               CALL FNDSTR (TEXT,CURLEN,OLD,OLDLEN,BEGIN,FOUND,POSOLD)
               IF (.NOT. FOUND) THEN
                 PRINT, 'STRING NOT FOUND. NO DELETION PERFORMED'
                 RETURN
               ENDIF
      C PERFORM DELETION BY SHIFTING TEXT TO LEFT
               CALL COPY (TEXT,POSOLD+OLDLEN,CURLEN,TEXT,MAXLEN,POSOLD,
             Z      COUNT)
      C REDEFINE CURLEN
               CURLEN = CURLEN — OLDLEN
               RETURN
               END
b)             SUBROUTINE INSERT (NEW, NEWLEN, BEGIN)
      C
      C INSERTS STRING INTO TEXT
      C
      C ARGUMENT DEFINITIONS
      C   INPUT ARGUMENTS
      C   NEW — STRING TO BE INSERTED
      C   NEWLEN — LENGTH OF NEW
      C   BEGIN — POSITION IN TEXT WHERE INSERTION STARTS
      C
               CHARACTER * 1 NEW (NEWLEN)  [or INTEGER NEW (NEWLEN)]
               INTEGER NEWLEN, BEGIN
      C
      C COMMON BLOCKS
               COMMON /TXTBLK/ TEXT(1000)
               COMMON /LENBLK/ CURLEN, MAXLEN
               CHARACTER * 1 TEXT                        [or INTEGER TEXT]
               INTEGER CURLEN, MAXLEN
      C
      C LOCAL VARIABLES
               CHARACTER * 1 TAIL (1000)       [or INTEGER TAIL(1000)]
      C
      C CHECK REVISED LENGTH BEFORE INSERTION
               REVLEN = CURLEN + NEWLEN
```

```
        IF (REVLEN .GT. MAXLEN) THEN
            PRINT, 'REVISED TEXT TOO LONG. INSERTION IGNORED'
        ELSE
C FORM NEW VERSION OF TEXT
C     SAVE TAIL OF TEXT
            CALL COPY (TEXT,BEGIN,CURLEN,TAIL,MAXLEN, 1,TAILEN)
C MAKE INSERTION AT BEGIN
            CALL COPY (NEW,1,NEWLEN,TEXT,MAXLEN,BEGIN,NEWLEN)
C COPY TAIL BACK INTO TEXT AFTER INSERT
            CALL COPY (TAIL,1,TAILEN,TEXT,MAXLEN,BEGIN+NEWLEN,
     Z        TAILEN)
            CURLEN = REVLEN
        ENDIF
        RETURN
        END
```

9.10

```
        LOGICAL FUNCTION MATCH (ARRAY, SIZE, NEXT, SUBSTR,
     Z    SUBLEN)
C MATCHES STRING OF LENGTH SUBLEN WITH STRING IN ARRAY
C     STARTING IN POSITION NEXT
C INPUT ARGUMENTS
C   ARRAY - ARRAY TO BE SEARCHED
C   SIZE - NUMBER OF CHARACTERS IN ARRAY
C   NEXT - STARTING POSITION IN ARRAY
C   SUBSTR - ARRAY TO BE MATCHED
C   SUBLEN - LENGTH OF SUBSTR
        INTEGER NEXT, SIZE, SUBLEN
        CHARACTER * 1 ARRAY(SIZE), SUBSTR(SUBLEN)
            [or INTEGER . . .]
C LOCAL DECLARATIONS
        INTEGER J
C ASSUME NO MATCH
        MATCH = .FALSE.
C
C IS SUBSTRING TOO LONG ?
        IF (NEXT+SUBLEN-1 .GT. SIZE) THEN
            PRINT, 'NO MATCH, SUBSTRING TO BE MATCHED EXTENDS',
     Z        ' BEYOND ARRAY.'
            RETURN
        ENDIF
C MAIN LOOP
        DO 10 J = 1, SUBLEN
            IF (SUBSTR(J) .NE. ARRAY(NEXT-1+J)) RETURN
    10 CONTINUE
        MATCH = .TRUE.
        RETURN
        END
```

Chapter 10

10.1 a)
```
        JSUM = 0
        DO 10  I = 1, 50
             JSUM = JSUM + ENRANK (I, 3, 3)
     10 CONTINUE
```

b)
```
        SSUM = 0
        DO 10  J = 1, 5
             SSUM = SSUM + ENRANK (25, J, 2)
     10 CONTINUE
```

c)
```
        CLTOT = 0
        DO 10  I = 1, 50
           CRSSUM = 0
           DO 20 K = 1, 4
                CRSSUM = CRSSUM + ENRANK (I, 1, K)
        20    CONTINUE
           PRINT, 'NO. OF STUDENTS IN COURSE',I,'AT CAMPUS 1 = ',
        Z       CRSSUM
           CLTOT = CLTOT + CRSSUM
     10 CONTINUE
        PRINT, 'TOTAL NUMBER OF STUDENTS AT CAMPUS 1 = ', CLTOT
```

d)
```
        TOTSUM = 0
        DO 10 J = 1, 5
           CAMSUM = 0
           DO 20 I = 1, 50
              DO 30 K = 3, 4
                 CAMSUM = CAMSUM + ENRANK (I, J, K)
        30     CONTINUE
        20    CONTINUE
           PRINT 'NO. OF UPPER-CLASS PERSONS AT CAMPUS',J,'=',
        Z       CAMSUM
           TOTSUM = TOTSUM + CAMSUM
     10 CONTINUE
        PRINT, 'TOTAL NO. OF UPPER-CLASSPERSONS AT ALL CAMPUSES',
        Z      ' = ', TOTSUM
```

10.2
```
        LOGICAL FUNCTION SAME (VAR1, VAR2, VAR3)
        CHARACTER * 1 VAR1, VAR3, BLANK, VAR2      [or INTEGER . . .]
        DATA BLANK /' '/
        SAME = .FALSE.
        IF (VAR1 .EQ. VAR2 .AND. VAR2 .EQ. VAR3 .AND. VAR3 .NE. BLANK)
        Z    SAME = .TRUE.
        RETURN
        END
```

10.3 a) Prints only elements on the diagonal starting with TABLE(1,1).

b) Row number determines the number of row elements printed; e.g., from row 1 only element TABLE(1,1) is printed; for row 2 only elements TABLE(2,1) and TABLE(2,2) are printed; for row M all elements are printed... TABLE(M,1), TABLE(M,2), ..., TABLE(M,M).

c)

Row	1	All elements
Row	2	TABLE(2,2), ..., TABLE(2,M)
Row	3	TABLE(3,3), ..., TABLE(3,M)

  .   .
  .   .
  .   .

Row M   TABLE(M,M)

10.5 **Data Table for PRTCAP:**

Input arguments   *Output arguments*
ARRAY(3,5): Array to be   (None)
  printed (integer)
FLOORS: Number of rows
  in the array (integer)
ROOMS: Number of columns
  in the array (integer)

Local variables
I: Loop variable for implicit DO
  loop to print room-number heading
ROW: Outer loop-control variable
COL: Inner loop-control variable

```
      SUBROUTINE PRTCAP (ARRAY, FLOORS, ROOMS)
C
C PRINT TWO-DIMENSIONAL ARRAY, ROW BY ROW
C
C ARGUMENT DEFINITIONS (ALL ARE INPUT)
C     ARRAY - ARRAY TO BE PRINTED
C     FLOORS   ROOMS - DIMENSIONS OF ARRAY
      INTEGER FLOORS, ROOMS
      INTEGER ARRAY(FLOORS, ROOMS)
C LOCAL VARIABLES
      INTEGER I, ROW, COL
C PRINT HEADING, ROOM NUMBERS
      PRINT 10
   10 FORMAT ('1FLOOR          ROOM NUMBER')
      PRINT 25,  (I, I = 1, ROOMS)
   25 FORMAT (4X, ' II ', 5(I4, ' I '))
      PRINT 20
      PRINT 20
   20 FORMAT (1X, 127('-'))
C
C PRINT CONTENTS OF ARRAY, ROW BY ROW
      DO 100 ROW = 1, FLOORS
         PRINT 30, ROW, (ARRAY(ROW, COL), COL=1, ROOMS)
   30    FORMAT (1X, I3, ' II ', 5(I4, ' I '))
         PRINT 20
```

```
100 CONTINUE
    RETURN
    END
```

10.8   Keypunch a $ after each string. In the main program, use GETLEN to determine the value of LENGTH after STRING is read.

To draw: Add a third argument, LENGTH, used to indicate the length of XLIST. In the main program, call DRAW with

```
CALL DRAW(BLOCK, XLIST, LENGTH)
```

Change the declaration of XLIST to: `INTEGER XLIST(LENGTH)`

Change PRINT 29 to

```
PRINT 29, (BLOCK(VERT,XLIST(HORIZ)), HORIZ = 1, LENGTH)
```

10.9

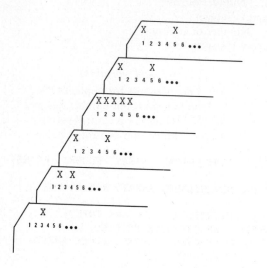

For a computer with C = 4:

```
      PRINT 29, (BLOCK(1,VERT,XLIST(HORIZ)),
   Z      BLOCK (2,VERT,XLIST(HORIZ)),HORIZ = 1,17)
29 FORMAT (1X, 17 (A4,A1,2X))
```

For a computer with C = 2:

```
   PRINT  29, ((BLOCK(I,VERT,XLIST(HORIZ)),I=1,3),HORIZ=1,17)
29 FORMAT (1X,17(A2,A2,A1,2X))
```

INDEX

absolute value (ABS) (*See* Function)
accumulating a sum, 52–53
address, 2
algorithm, 40–67, 224, 238
alphabet, 390
.AND., 183, 322
argument, actual, 244, 259
  arrays, 376–377
  dummy, 244, 259
  function, 145
  input, 252
  list, 244, 254, 258, 276–277
  output, 252
  structure, 246
argument address list, 274
argument list correspondence, 246, 260, 274
arithmetic expressions, 137
  evaluation of, 140
arithmetic-logic unit, 2, 4
arrays, base address, 177, 376
  data initialization, 177, 372, 375
  declaration, 162–163, 365
  element address, 180
  elements, 163
  errors in usage, 186

failure to declare, 185
implied indexed-DO loop, 174, 372
index, 166, 180–185
indexed-DO loops, 174, 372
linear, 187
loop-control variable as subscript, 173
multidimensional, 365–399
reading and printing , 171, 174, 301–305
search, 177, 179, 327
selection of elements, 180
size, 365
subprogram arguments, 376–377
subscript range, 185
subscripted variable, 163
subscripts, 163, 164, 365
assembler, 11–12
assembler language, 10–12
assignment statements, 15–17, 33, 35, 123, 137
average, 40–44, 187, 235, 238

bar graph, 213
base address (*See* Arrays)
basic FORTRAN statements, 14–28, 35, 80, 85, A27

best-fit algorithm, 384
binary number system, 151
binary operation, 140
blank common block, 266
block letters, 387–399
boundary conditions, 228, 333
bowling problem, 200
Bubble Sort, 216–218, 226

calling a function, 145, 185
CALL statement, 254
card reader, 5
CDC 6000 computer, 113
Centigrade-to-Fahrenheit conversion, 149, 205
central processor unit, 4, 10
character assignment statement, 123, A4
character capacity, 114, 118, 389, 398
character code, 114, 124
character data, 113, 387, 398, A1, A9
character declaration, 114, 330, 387
character expression, A6
character manipulation, 329, A12
character string, 110–124, 389
character-string comparison, 124, A9
character-string constants, 62–63, 123, 155
character-string length, 332, A2
character-string reading and printing, 330
character-string replacement, A20
character-string storage convention, 115
character substrings (See Substring)
character type declaration, 114
checking account, 67, 105–106, 125, 188
COBOL, 13
collating sequence, A9
columns of an array, 365, 372
column headers, 62–63
comment cards, 26, 28, 44
common block, 261, 347, 350, A19
COMMON statement, 261, 277
compiler, 12–13, 14, 21, 70, 110, 130
compiler role, in arithmetic expression evaluation, 140
    in array references, 176
    in decision structures, 79–80
    in format-free input/output, 122
    in indexed-DO loop, 130
    in multidimensional arrays, 376
    in multiple-alternative decisions, 198–199
    in subprograms, 277–278
    in WHILE loops, 85
complement of condition, 60, 80–81, 85–86
computer art, 387, 388
computer components, 2, 7
computer operations, 15
concatenation, 114, 348, A5
condition, 24–25, 47, 60, 72–73, 78, 79, 81, 82, 84
conditional statement, 24–26, 35, 71, 74, 78, 80–81
conditional transfer instruction, 25–26, 80–81, 85–86
constant, 18, 22–23, 117, 153
    in-line use, 59
    list, 117, 153
contextual information, 351, A23
continuation card, 28
CONTINUE statement, 80–81, 85–86, 131, 223
control card, 31
controlling loop repetition (See Loop control)
control operations, 15
control structures, 70–104
control transfer (See Transfer of control)
control unit, 2–4, 9
COPY statement, 17, 123
copying strings, 334
correspondence (See Argument-list correspondence)
counter, 55–57, 59, 82–84, 100, 130, 208, 229
COUNT function, 247
counting, 59, 130, 132
cumulative product, 84

data base, 262
data cards, 18–19, 31
data converter, 122–123
data definition, 40–42
data descriptors (See Format descriptors)

DATA initialization statement, 18, 21–
22, 33, 35, 60–62, 117–118, 155,
171–173, 375, 392
data-manipulation phase of algorithms,
53–54, 66
data-storage rule, 115
data structure, 186
data table, 41–42, 58, 64
data types, 109–137
'' external representation, 110–112, 122
internal representation, 112–114, 122,
130
debugging, 58, 64–65, 103, 277
decision steps, 47–49, 61, 66–67, 71–74,
103
decision structures, 72–81, 101–104,
A27
declaration statement, 14, 21, 35, 114–
119, 163–164, 365
definition of data (See Data table)
deletion from a list, 209, 231
dependent statement, 24
descriptors (See Format descriptors)
dictionary sequence, 124
division by zero, 76, 154
documenting programs, 26, 44, 271
double-alternative decision, 47–48, 66,
72–75, 80–81, 102, 194, 229
double spacing, 298
dummy block letters, 396–398
dummy argument list, 242

echo print, 21
END, 21, 35, 243, 249, 253
ENDIF, 73–74, 102, 197
ENDWHILE, 84, 102
error, argument list, 276, 400
    arithmetic overflow or underflow, 154
    character assignment, A19–A20
    control card and deck arrangement, 32
    data statement, 155
    diagnostic, 32–33, 65
    division by zero, 76, 154
    duplicate label, 32
    embedded blanks, 312
    end of file, 153
    execution time, 101, 153
    fatal, 34

flag, 264
imprecise representation, 130
incorrect use of character or logical
    data, 154, A19–A20
indexed-DO and FOR loop, 228
insufficient data, 101, 154
invalid substring name, A19–A20
mismatched parentheses, 154
missing commas, 153
missing label, 32
missing operator, 154
multiple-alternative decisions, 228
nonterminating loops, 100–101
numerical, 151
read past data-deck terminator, 101
remote block, 229
side effects, 65
spelling, 33, 153
structure nesting, 100, 227
subscript range, 186, 400
syntax, 31–32, 64, 100
unrecognizable statement, 32
evaluating arithmetic expressions, 140,
326
evaluating logical expressions, 324–326
exchanging two values, 76
EXECUTE statement, 224
EXIT statement, 220
exponentiation, 143
expression (See Logical expression, Arith-
    metic expression)
expression evaluation rules, 140
external representation (See Data types)

factorial, 67, 168
Fibonacci series, 151
fields, 27–29, 291
field width, 295–296, 303
fixed-point numbers, 113, 149–150
flag (See Program flag, Error flag)
floating-point numbers, 113, 149–150
flow diagram, 45–51, 53–55, 66, 70, 100,
212
flow-diagram refinement (See Refinement)
flow of control, 224
flow of information, 9–10
FNDMED function, 225–256
FOR loop, 204–209, 228

format analyzer, 122, 288
format descriptors, A-descriptor, 295, 302, 308
  data descriptor, 290, 295, 308
  E format descriptor, 309
  F-descriptor, 295, 302, 308
  I-descriptor, 295, 302, 308
  repetition, 308–308
  slash, 297
  space descriptor, 290, 295, 308
  X-descriptor, 297, 302
format-free input and output, 70, 119, 288
format statement, 215, 289
formatted input, 70, 289
formatted output, 70, 215, 289
formatted read/print, 289, 290
formula, 141–148
frequency distribution, 180–182, 231
frequency plot, 214
function, ABS, 145, 240
  ALOG, 145, 240
  ALOG10, 147
  AMAX, 147
  AMIN, 147
  arguments, 145
  call, 145, 185, 240
  COS, 147, 240
  definition, 145–154, 240
  EXP, 147
  FLOAT, 147, 240
  header, 240
  IABS, 145–147, 240
  IFIX, 147, 240
  library, 145, 240
  MAX, 145
  MIN, 145
  MOD, 145
  nested calls, 145
  reference, 145, 240
  result, 145
  SIN, 145, 240
  SQRT, 145, 240
  TAN, 145
  trigonometric, 145–147, 240
  type, 145, 242
  use in arithmetic expressions, 145–154, 79

games, 403–404
generalizing a solution, 61–62
GOTO statement, 23–25, 35, 47, 71, 79–81, 85–86, 101
graphics, 6, 8

head of a string, 348, A21
headed statement, decision structures, 74
  indexed-DO loop, 129–132
  WHILE loop, 84
heading for output columns, 62, 90, 292
hierarchy of operators, 140
higher-level languages, 12–13, 70

IABS (*See* Function)
IF-THEN (*See* Single-alternative decision)
IF-THEN-ELSE (*See* Double-alternative decision)
implicit type convention (*See* Type convention)
implied indexed-DO loop, 174–175, 372
imprecise representation of real numbers, 130
incremental distance, 87
incrementing a counter, 55–56
indentation, 74–75
index, 104, 180–185, 204
indexed-DO header, 130
indexed-DO loop, 82, 130–131, 155, 174–175, 187, 204, 372
indexed-DO rules of usage, 122
initialization phase of algorithms, 53–54, 66
initial value list, 117
in-line constants, 59, 123
inner loop, 212
input data, 19, 46, 62, 64–65
input device, 2, 4–5
input/output operations, 15, 35
insertion into a list, 207, 230
insufficient data (*See* Errors)
integer division, 133, 154
INTEGER statement, 14, 35, 113
integers, use in loop control, 59, 129–130, 154
interest computation, 156–158
internal representation (*See* Data types)

inventory control, 96–99
iteration (*See* Loop control)

job input deck, 18–19, 31

keypunch, 5–6
keypunching, 27–29

label, 23–24, 60–61, 80–81, 85, 103, 131
label field, 28–29
larger of two numbers, 76
largest-value problem, 91–94, 105, 245
LEN, A2, A11
length of a character string (*See* Character-string length)
level one (*See* Top-level)
lexicographic ordering, 124
library functions, 145–149, 240, 271–272
light pen, 8
line control, 292
linear array, 187
linear sequence of algorithm steps, 103
line-printer, 5
list, 187
loader, 9, 11, 13, 18, 22–23
loading data, 18, 22–23
loading programs, 22–23
local variables, 243
logarithm (*See* Function)
logical assignment statement, 124
logical constant, 112, 126, 134, 155, 322
logical data, 111, 113
logical expression, 183, 322–323, A9–A10
logical operators, 183, 322
logical organization of program, 72
logical variable, 124
loop, 50–57, 60–61, 71, 90, 129, 130, 131, 132, 155
  flow-diagram pattern, 54–55, 66–67, 82–83
  (*See* FOR loop, Indexed-DO loop, WHILE loop)
loop control, 54–57, 82–84, 86–87, 90–91, 93–94, 130, 155, 229
loop-control parameters, 84, 131, 208, 229
loop counting, 55–57, 83–84, 132, 208

loop exit, 56, 60, 83–84, 90–91, 221
loop, nonterminating, 100–101
loop range, 83–84, 131

machine language, 10–12, 70, 79–80
magnetic tapes, disks, and drums, 8
main program, 248
MATCH, 344
matrix, 365, 377
mean (*See* Average)
median, 221, 255
memory, 2, 22
memory after loading, 22–23
memory cell, 2–3, 14, 22
memory-cell contents, 3
MERGE subroutine, 261–263, 279–280
mixed-mode expression, 149–151
mixed-type assignment, 149–151
mnemonic code, 11
MOD (*See* Function)
modular programming, 103
module (*See* Program module)
monthly loan payment, 158
mortgage interest, 233
multidimensional arrays (*See* Arrays)
multiple-alternative decision structure, 199, 228, A27

named common block, 266
name independence, 258–261, 277
negation, 17, 143
nested control structures, 98, 100, 208, 227
nested double-alternative decisions, 197–199
nested function cells, 145
nested loops, 12, 368, 400
nested parentheses, 138
nested statement groups, 98, 221
NEXT statement, 221–230
nonexecutable statements, 21
nonterminating loop, 100–101
numerical error (*See* Errors)
numeric code (*See* Character code)

offset, 376
operating system, 29, 31
operators, 139–140

.OR., 183, 322
out-of-range subscripts, 186
outer loop, 212
output data, 46, 64
output device, 2, 4–5
output format program, 122–123
output identifiers, 62–63
output lists, 64
output phase of algorithm, 53–54, 66
overlapping structures, 100, 212

paper-tape reader, 5
parameters (*See* Loop-control parameters)
parentheses in expressions, 138–143
pass, 216, 220
payroll program, 20–27, 104, 283
PDP-11 computer, 11
plot a function, 317
plotter, 5
portable programs, 12, 70
prime number, 133, 278
print positions, 123
PRINT statement, 19–21, 34–35, 122, 171
problem analysis, 40–42, 64–66
program execution, 8–9, 22–23
program flag, 126, 135, 327
program loading, 22–23
program module, 238, 249
program system chart, 238–239, 262, 271
programming languages, 8–9
program output, 20, 46
punch cards, 5

quadratic equation, 234
quoted character strings, 291–299, 308

range of loop (*See* Loops)
range of numbers, 113, 255
range of subscripts (*See* Subscript)
READ statement, 18–19, 33–35, 119–122, 171–173, 179
readability of programs, 103
real numbers, 14, 113, 154
REAL statement, 14, 21, 34

referencing a function, 145
refinement, 43–47, 65, 70, 102–103, 135, 212, 224, 238
relational operators, 25, 60, 124, 322
remainder, 133
remote block, 224–229, 258–261
removing computations from loop body, 89–90
repeat condition (*See* Loop control)
repeat count, 307
repetition of descriptors, 308
repetition factor, 117
RETURN statement, 242, 253, 273–276
rounding a number, 150–151, 281
rows of an array, 365, 372

sales tax table, 68
scanning a character string, 330, A12
schedule and space problem, 378–386
scientific notation, 113
searching an array, 177, 281, 327–329, 342, 396
searching a string, A12–A16
selection of array elements, 177
sentinel card (value), 90, 96, 100, 129
shifting array elements, 207–209
side effects of errors, 65
simulation of bicycle race, 87–90
simulation of flow diagrams, 58–59, 64–65
single-alternative decision, 47–49, 66, 72, 74–81, 102, 229
SITGO, 114
SNOBOL, 13
sorting an array, 216, 255, 259–260, 261–267
sort/merge, 261–263, 279
SORT subroutine, 258, 267
space descriptors (*See* Format descriptors)
square root (SQRT) (*See* Function)
standard deviation, 187
standard FORTRAN, 70–71
standard FORTRAN implementation of WHILE loop, 89–90, 94, 99
statement field, 28
statement group, 71–72, 98, 103

statistics problem, 187, 235, 238, 249–251
stepwise refinement, 103
STOP, 20–21, 35
storage unit, 115
stored program, 9
string (*See* Character string)
structure entry, 221
structure nesting, 210
Structured FORTRAN, 71, 100, 220, 225, 230
subdividing a problem, 270
subproblem, 47, 224, 238
subprograms, 238–282
subprogram generality, 269
subprogram linking, 272
subprogram TABLE, 271
subroutine, 252–254
  arguments, 252
  call, 252
  definition, 252
subscript expression, 164–165
subscripted variable, 163
subscripts, loop-control variables as, 173, 368
  range, 185
  range error, 186
  value (index), 164
substring, 342, A2–A3
substring expression, A3
substring name, A3
subtasks, 71
symbolic names, 13
syntax rules, 8, 70, 100, 143, 322

tabular output form, 90

tail of a string, 348, A21
tax computation, 188
terminals, 5, 6, 8
terminator statement, in decision structures, 74, 78, 101
  in indexed-DO loop, 130–133
  in WHILE loops, 84, 101
text editing, 346, A18–A19
THEN statement, 74
tic-tac-toe, 368–371, 400–401
top-down programming, 224, 248–249
top level, 224, 225
tracing an algorithm, 58–59, 64–65, 76
transfer of control, 24–26, 61, 79–81, 85, 103, 221–224, 230, 274, 275
translation (*See* Compiler role)
transpose of a matrix, 377
trigonometric function (*See* Function)
truncation, 133
type convention, 114–115, 155
type conversion, 149
type declaration, 36–38, 114–116, 155

unary operation, 141
updating lists, 205

variable list, 117, 153
variable names, 13–14

WATFIV-S, 71, 114, 199, 223, 268
WHILE loop structure, 82–104, 132, 221, 223, 229
Widget problem (*See* Inventory control)
width specification, 295–296
WRITE, 289